ENLIGHTENED BEINGS

ENLIGHTENED BEINGS

Life Stories
from the
Ganden Oral Tradition

by

JANICE D. WILLIS

WISDOM PUBLICATIONS • BOSTON

Wisdom Publications
361 Newbury Street
Boston, Massachusetts 02115
USA

First published in 1995

ISBN 0-86171-068-1

Library of Congress Cataloging-in-Publication Data

Willis, Janice Dean.
Enlightened beings : life stories from the Ganden oral tradition / by Janice D. Willis.
p. cm.
Includes bibliographical references and index.
ISBN 0-86171-068-1 :
1. Lamas—China—Tibet—Biography. I. Title.
BQ7630.W55 1994
294.3'923'0922—dc20
[B] 94–29662

00 99 98 97 96

6 5 4 3 2

Typeset at Wisdom Publications in Diacritical Garamond and Mona Lisa Recut

*Cover Illustration:*a composite of two paintings derivative of the *Famous Sixteen Arhats,*18c., courtesy of Tibet House, New Delhi

Frontispiece: photograph of Lama Tsongkapa thangka courtesy of the artist, Åge Delbanco

Designed by: L·J·Sawlit

Wisdom Publications' books are printed on acid-free paper and meet the guidelines for permanence and durability of the Committee on Production Guidelines for Book Longevity of the Council on Library Resources.

Printed at Northeast Impressions, Fairfield, NJ USA.

I have had many teachers,
but only one root guru.
In memory of his great kindness,
I dedicate this work to

Lama Thubten Yeshe.
(1935–1984)

The human body, at peace with itself,
Is more precious than the rarest gem.
Cherish your body; it is yours this one time only.

The human form is won with difficulty.
It is easy to lose.
All worldly things are brief, like lightning in the sky.
Life you must know as the tiny splash of a raindrop:
A thing of beauty that disappears even as it comes into being.

Therefore, set your goal.
Make use of every day and night to achieve it.

Je Tsongkapa

The Great Je Rinpoche, Tsongkapa

Publisher's Acknowledgment

The publisher gratefully acknowledges the kind help of the Hershey Family Foundation in sponsoring the production of this book.

Contents

Illustrations

Frontispiece *Je Rinpoche, Tsongkapa,* the fourteenth-century founder of the Gelukpa order. In the foreground are his two famed disciples, Gyeltsab Je and Kedrub Je. The central figure of Tsongkapa is surrounded by the Three Chief Deities of the Ganden Oral Tradition: Guhyasamāja (top left), Cakrasaṃvara (top right), and Vajrabhairava (bottom center).

Page *vii* *Tsongkapa,* in teaching mudrā, seated upon the Lion Throne. On the lotuses above his shoulders are the sword of wisdom and the *Prajñāpāramitā* text, symbolic of Lord Mañjuśrī.

Page 32 *The Lord of Accomplishment, Jampel Gyatso.* Upholder of the practice lineage of the Ganden Oral Tradition, Jampel Gyatso is depicted without adorning features or implements. Beneath his outer monastic robes, however, he wears the meditation strap, worn only by strictly practicing, advanced yogis.

Page 42 *Baso Chökyi Gyeltsen.* Renowned as a teacher and tantric practitioner, Chökyi Gyeltsen is revered in the Ganden Oral Tradition for producing three accomplished disciples, each of whom attained the ultimate siddhi of Mahāmudrā realization.

Page 48 *The Great Siddha, Chökyi Dorje.* A consummate practitioner of the Ganden Oral Tradition, Chökyi Dorje attained the body of a "deathless vidyādhara." His devotion to his guru Baso Je, and the kindness he later showed to his own spiritual son Ensapa, have set the standard for such practice. His chief distinguishing physical attributes are the white beard and mustache he sported.

Page 56 *Gyelwa Ensapa.* Revered for having completely abandoned the eight mundane concerns, Ensapa is regarded as a Buddha in his own right and as being identical with both the Buddha Śākyamuni and Tsongkapa himself. He is therefore shown holding in his left hand the Wheel of the Dharma, and, in his right, a lotus

bearing the sword and *Prajñāpāramitā* text symbolic of Lord Mañjuśrī (and, by extension, Tsongkapa).

Page 72 *The Scholar-Siddha, Sanggye Yeshe.* Described in the Gelukpa Mahāmudrā Lineage Prayer as "the great scholar-siddha," Sanggye Yeshe earned the illustrious monastic degree of Rabjampa before undertaking his Oral Tradition Mahāmudrā studies. A suggestion of his vast learning is represented by the religious texts that flank him to the right.

Page 84 *The First Panchen, Losang Chökyi Gyeltsen.* Holding the dorje and bell of an accomplished tantric master, he is shown flanked on his right by religious texts and on his left by the begging bowl and staff of a mendicant monk. His staff has affixed to its top a small caitya and rings that dangle from it. The hat depicted here was designed by the First Panchen himself, following the shape of the hill upon which the Ensapa monastery was built. Since his time, it has been worn by the Panchens and by the chief abbots of Tashilünpo when presiding over the school's monastic debates.

Page 131 *Damchen Chökyi Gyelpo.* Chief protector of the Ganden Oral Tradition, this deity is also referred to as Kālarūpa. He appears in wrathful aspect, with a boar's head and erect penis, standing atop a bull. In his right hand he brandishes a club, and, in his left hand, a snare. His consort holds aloft a trident and offers him a skull cup filled with amrita. It is said that the *Great Miraculous Volume* containing the methods for practicing the Ganden Oral Tradition was entrusted to this deity for safekeeping.

Preface

According to the Buddhist tradition, until we reach enlightenment we are ordinary beings living within the diverse realms of suffering known as *saṃsāra.* Indeed, a late *Mahāyāna* scripture, the *Ārya-tathāgatagarbha-sūtra,* describes our current situation like this:

> Until you reach the path, you wander in the world
> With the precious form of the *Sugata*
> Completely wrapped, as in a bundle of rags,
> By things degrading and dirty.

Then, shortly afterwards, the same sūtra tantalizingly extends to us the following offer:

> Here it is. You have this precious *Tathāgata*
> Wrapped in rags. Unwrap it, quickly![1]

If we have any feeling at all that the earlier description might be accurate, this offer strikes us as a wondrous possibility, indeed as a priceless and jeweled opportunity: the rare chance to abandon completely—in this lifetime—countless lifetimes, past and future, of mundane miseries, and to unwrap, reveal, and make manifest the supreme enlightened being, the Buddha, resting in the very palms of our hands. If we are successful in this, we will ourselves become enlightened beings. This challenge is the promise that fuels and infuses the vehicle of Buddhist practice called the *Vajrayāna.*

"Buddha" is not a proper name. It is, rather, a generic term that is given, as a title, to one who has attained enlightenment [*bodhi*]. The term "Buddha" is actually derived from the Sanskrit root *budh* ["to awaken," "to wake up," "to realize," "to understand"]. What is understood is the true nature of reality, how things exist, and both the causes and the cessation of suffering. What flows out of such understanding is selfless compassion—offered fully, universally, and spontaneously—for all beings still bound in suffering. Thus, while we most often associate the term "Buddha" with the sixth-century B.C. historical figure Siddhārtha Gautama, the great Indian teacher who founded the tradition, there are, have been, and will continue to be countless Buddhas whenever and wherever beings awaken to the truth. This fact is made especially clear in the literature of the Mahāyāna, with its proliferation of enlightened beings, in which the Buddha himself assures us that he has no corner on the market.

Though there are, have been, and will be countless enlightened beings, there is no doubt that the life of Siddhārtha provides us with the chief model for a Buddha's career. Coming down to us after centuries of oral and literary accretions, the Buddha's various biographies have taken on all the qualities of legendary hagiography, replete with miracles, prescience, and other displays of supernatural power. Yet for all their diverse embellishments, these biographies agree on the fundamental importance of two "events" or "acts," two activities by virtue of which a Buddha *is* a Buddha in truth. First, such a one has, often through practicing the most rigorous ascetic austerities, won through to consummate understanding and insight, and, second, flowing naturally out of such understanding, that accomplished being illumines the way for others through compassionate and well-suited teaching. While the various Buddhist traditions offer numerous definitions of a Buddha—"Embodiment of all-goodness," "Vanquisher of the foes (of hatred, greed, and ignorance)," "Transcender of all negative qualities of mind," "Treasury of compassion and wisdom," "Truth-finder," and "Way-shower," etc.—the fact remains that what a Buddha *does,* through his or her efforts in meditation and teaching, most directly defines the term's central meaning.

These two chief activities of meditation and teaching are the same ones associated with the persons known to us as *siddhas*; and in whatever lifetime an ordinary being becomes an enlightened being, that one properly earns the title of siddha as well. This is borne out even by the name ascribed to the historical founder of the tradition; for while his family name was Gautama, all accounts agree that his given name was Siddhārtha—that is, one whose aims (*artha*) have been accomplished or perfected (*siddha*).

The translations that follow chronicle the lives of six renowned Tibetan Gelukpa (dGe-lugs-pa) siddhas who, armed with loving compassion and the insight that cognizes the truth of voidness, took up the challenge of becoming enlightened beings for our sakes and were successful. These six practitioners, men who lived between the mid-fourteenth and mid-seventeenth centuries in Tibet, were accomplished followers of the Ganden Oral Tradition—variously referred to in Tibetan as the Ganden Nyen Gyü (dGa' ldan sñan brgyud) or Genden Kagyü (dGe ldan bka' brgyud)—a system of *tantric* practice first conceived and taught by the great Je Rinpoche, Tsongkapa [1357–1419]. This tradition is also known, more fully, as the Ganden Oral Tradition of *Mahāmudrā* or, concisely, as the Gelukpa Mahāmudrā. According to the Gelukpa tradition, the Ganden Oral Tradition teachings are uniquely fashioned to bring about the swift attainment of enlightenment. The Ganden

Oral Tradition relies heavily upon two components in particular: first, a specialized form of *guru yoga*, and, second, a unique combination of advanced practices based upon the so-called Three Chief Deities: Guhyasamāja, Cakrasaṃvara, and Vajrabhairava. Indeed, it is said that "this tradition teaches that one can achieve Buddhahood within a period of only twelve years by holding guru yoga as the most vital element of the path and practicing the paths of the three tutelary deities Guhya Samaja, Cakra Samvara, and Vajra Bhairava all at once."[2] It is further declared that for some of the six adepts upon whom the present translations focus, the practice of the Ganden Oral Tradition made possible the attainment of enlightenment within the even shorter time-span of only three years.

Again, this study focuses on the lives of the first six Gelukpa practitioners of the Ganden Oral Tradition, the earliest siddhas to immediately succeed Tsongkapa in this lineage. The six are:

1. Tokden Jampel Gyatso (rTogs-ldan 'Jam-dpal-rgya-mtsho) [1356–1428]
2. Baso Je Chökyi Gyeltsen (Ba-so-rje Chos-kyi-rgyal-mtshan) [1402–1473]
3. Drubchen Chökyi Dorje (Grub-chen Chos-kyi-rdo-rje) [?]
4. Gyelwa Ensapa (rGyal-ba dbEn-sa-pa) [1505–1566]
5. Kedrub Sanggye Yeshe (mKhas-grub Sangs-rgyas-ye-śes) [1525–1591]
6. Jetsün Losang Chökyi Gyeltsen (rJe-btsun bLo-bzaṅ-chos-kyi-rgyal-mtshan) [1570–1662].

As can be seen from their dates, these six contiguous lives span some three hundred years of Tibetan religious history, covering in particular that most crucial period of the rise to power of the so-called Yellow Hat school, the Gelukpa. But these six life stories do much more than this. Considered within the Tibetan tradition as *namtar* (rnam-thar), that is, "liberation life stories," these accounts inform their readers on many different levels—historical, inspirational, and instructional—in ways geared to make manifest Buddhist liberation and enlightenment by describing its multilayered process.

Those readers familiar with the tantric traditions may think of siddhas only in connection with the group of wild, *yogi*-iconoclasts known as the Eighty-Four *Mahāsiddhas* of India. In the context of Tibetan practice, moreover, because of the fame of such great yogis as Milarepa, it might be assumed that siddhas are to be found only within the lineages of the Kagyüpa (bKa' brgyud pa) school of Tibetan Buddhism. Some years ago I, too, made such erroneous assumptions, and a brief note about how I initially came to undertake this project may prove instructive here. It was my own precious root guru, Lama Thubten Yeshe, who in 1979 first suggested that I translate the lives of some of the earliest Gelukpa siddhas. I was en route to Nepal to conduct some oral history research and had stopped in Zurich, where Lama Yeshe was spending a few days, to confer with him about it. After showing general approval of my proposed work, he said with a rather emphatic tone, "First, I want you to translate some of the early Geluk siddha life stories. Western readers should know that there were Gelukpa siddhas too!" At the time, I must have looked somewhat baffled. The thought went through my mind, 'But weren't all the siddhas Kagyüpas?' At that instant, Lama Yeshe looked at me piercingly and, with a brief look of disgust, turned abruptly and left the room. It was a wonderfully enlightening teaching! It took me only a few seconds to realize that a siddha is any accomplished being who wins enlightenment in one lifetime, using tantric means; that neither those means, nor the persons employing them, are limited to any one particular school or sect; and that of course there were Gelukpa siddhas—just as there have been and continue to be accomplished tantric adepts in all the orders and wherever and whenever beings win through to enlightenment. Though embarrassed by my lack of sensitivity and insight, the next time I saw Lama Yeshe I told him that I'd be glad to do the translations he'd requested.

Still, I was not alone in my misconception. The siddha tradition is generally thought to be associated only with the Kagyüpa order, and this assumption is especially evidenced in most Western accounts of that system. However, as the present translations will attest, this tradition was also always present in the Gelukpa. Indeed, according to Gelukpa tradition, the great Tsongkapa, who founded the order, synthesized three great Indian lineages: the "profound," or wisdom lineage of Mañjuśrī and Nāgārjuna; the "vast," or method lineage of Maitreya and Asaṅga; and the "practice" lineage of the Eighty-Four Mahāsiddhas, tantric adepts such as Saraha, Tilopa, Nāropa, and Luipa. This fact notwithstanding, the Geluk order, especially in the West, continues to be regarded predominantly as a scholastic tradition that produced few accomplished tantric practitioners. It is my hope that the present translations will help to reverse this misconception.

As sources for the complete written accounts of the lives of these six Ganden Oral Tradition siddhas, I had access to two Tibetan editions of the great compendium of Kadam (bKa' gdams) and Gelukpa biographies compiled in the late eighteenth century [circa 1787] by the great Yongdzin Yeshe Gyeltsen (Yongs 'dzin Ye-śes-rgyal-mtshan) [1713–1792] called *Byaṅ chub lam gyi rim pa'i bla ma brgyud pa'i rnam par thar pa rgyal bstan mdzes pa'i rgyan mchog phul byung nor bu'i phreṅ ba* (*Biographies of the Eminent Gurus in the Transmission Lineages of the Graded Path Teachings, called The Jeweled Rosary*). One edition was the woodblock-printed version kept in the library of the Nepalese Mahayana Centre Gompa (dGon-pa) of Lama Yeshe in Kopan, Nepal. The other was the edited, and often much abbreviated, version found in Volume V of Ketsün Sangpo's *Biographical Dictionary of Tibet and Tibetan Buddhism* [Dharamsala: Library of Tibetan Works and Archives, 1973]. Ketsün Sangpo's versions of the biographies abbreviate—either by summarizing or by omitting certain sections—the lengthier standard namtar. This abbreviation is particularly noticeable in Sangpo's treatment of the Baso Chökyi Gyeltsen account and in his presentation of the biography of the First Panchen, Losang Chökyi Gyeltsen.

Taken together, the six namtar translated here comprise some 286 folio sides of the *Jeweled Rosary* collection, with the First Panchen's life alone running to 155 folio sides. [The First Panchen himself wrote an autobiography that runs to some 447 folios!] In order to give more balance to the presentation of the lives here, I have not translated the account of his life in full. While I read both versions of the namtar, in producing the translations I have been guided more by the length of the biographies as treated in Sangpo. However, where it seemed to me that Sangpo had omitted material that was pertinent to a fuller appreciation of a given biography, I have incorporated material from the lengthier Tibetan versions. In addition to the two editions of Gelukpa namtar referred to above, I also read and have included as Appendix II the short Gelukpa liturgical text called *dGa' ldan bka' srol phyag rgya chen po'i 'khrid kyi bla brgyud gsol 'debs kha skoṅ bcas bźugs* (*Prayer, with Supplement, to the Lineage Lamas of the Ganden Oral Tradition of Mahāmudrā*.) The prayer's colophon declares that it too was composed by Yongdzin Yeshe Gyeltsen and that additions were made by the first Pabongka Rinpoche, Dechen Nyingpo (Pha-bong-kha Rin-po-che, bDe-chen-snying-po) [1878–1941].

What I have tried to present in the following pages is as full and helpful a picture of these six Gelukpa siddhas' lives as possible. Primarily, I have attempted to do two things: to present accurate and readable translations of the life stories themselves and to provide enough critical apparatus to give Western readers of these accounts an appreciation of the ambiance and richness of this particular genre of religious writing. It is my hope that the material in the *Introduction* will help to accomplish this latter aim.

Translating these life stories presented several difficulties. Before doing them, I had been accustomed primarily to working with philosophical texts, and, while my former work with Tibetan meditation cycles proved helpful, I soon came to realize that the translation of namtar offered unique problems.

To translate them accurately and well requires knowledge of a variety of subjects and areas not frequently met with in other types of Buddhist literature. For example, in addition to being familiar with colloquial forms of the Tibetan language, including some archaic forms, one needs to know about such diverse things as geography, monastic calendars and curricula, and even the names of certain monastic apparel. Often, a term that has one meaning in other types of literature has another in these contexts. As examples, one could note that the term *damcha* (dam bca'), which is normally rendered "vow" or "oath," in these namtar usually refers to the debates conducted by the different monastic colleges, and that in the account of the First Panchen's life, *zimkang-pa* (gzim khang pa) does not mean "room" or "house," but refers instead to a certain monastic official chosen by the government. In an interesting twist, some terminology that has a mundane and concrete meaning in other literature seems to take on a "mystic" sense in these stories. This is so for the term *zamatok* (za ma tog), for example. Generally, the term means "receptacle," "vessel," or even "the human physique," but in the namtar of Chökyi Dorje it takes on the additional meaning of "a magically assumed and mystically supported appearance of a physical body" taken on as a means, or vehicle, in order to communicate with disciples.

Since these namtar are biographies of tantric adepts, it should not be surprising that the language in them is sometimes employed in a tantric, or "veiled," way. However, it sometimes happens that the translator of namtar may be tempted to read into a given text mystical occurrences where none are present. This was made clear to me in dramatic fashion when I attempted to translate a particular passage in the namtar of Sanggye Yeshe. The passage clearly was a description of one of Sanggye Yeshe's meditative experiences. As part of the account, the text said that once it had happened that Sanggye Yeshe had awakened from sleep because of feeling very cold. He had then envisioned his guru, Ensapa, perched above the door to his meditation cell. Ensapa then covered him with his *kubem* (sku bem). Sanggye Yeshe at once felt a suffusion of warmth and bliss, and this event ushered in an experiential breakthrough for him.

Now, the term that presented the difficulty was, of course, kubem. *Ku* alone is a common honorific term for "body." *Bem* is a bit more unusual and is hardly ever, to my knowledge, used in isolation. Given the context of the term's appearance, I read into the description all sorts of mystical connotations. I *knew* that kubem must refer to some ineffably pure and wholly intangible offering, some indescribable direct transmission. The reader can perhaps imagine, then, my stunned surprise when later, as I was talking one day with some monk-teachers at Kopan, they asked, "Oh! Haven't you seen Lama

Yeshe's kubem yet? Surely he will show it to you if you ask." My knees were trembling as I made my way across the courtyard, determined to ask him, even if it meant my life! When I finally got the question out to him, Lama Yeshe jumped up from the table and left quickly, promising to return with it. My wait seemed interminably long. Then Lama Yeshe reappeared, holding up a heavy winter robe. It was battered and beaten, faded red, and lined inside with wool. "This is my kubem," he said. So, kubem is the name for a lama's winter meditation robe. It *is* special, in the sense that it is part of the apparel allowed only to lamas of the tantric colleges, but it is *not* an indescribable mystic entity. For reasons like these, then, one has to be careful when translating this type of literature.

Equally important, I feel, is the issue of proper transcription and transliteration. Over the course of many years of Tibetan scholarship, inconsistencies and confusion have resulted from the various attempts to deal with the difficulties of Tibetan spellings. Because Tibetan has an abundance of homophones, phonetic spellings often create more problems than they solve. For example, though the terms *bka' bcu* and *dka' bcu* sound exactly alike, the first refers to a novice monk who observes the ten (*bcu*) precepts (*bka'*) while the second is used only in reference to an accomplished teacher who, having completed the difficult (*dka'*) higher studies, can explain the meaning of a text from ten different points of view! In this case, even though both terms apply to monks, in terms of meaning they are quite distinct, and to render them only as "ka chu," for example, completely obscures this important distinction. Thus, phonetic spellings may sometimes do considerably more harm than good. I should like it if everyone interested in Tibetan studies learned to spell Tibetan properly.

However, there is the issue of readability. Especially in a work like the following—replete with Tibetan names for persons, places, deities, and texts—had we correctly transliterated each name at every appearance we would have produced an unwieldy book. To avoid this situation, the editors and I have agreed to use phoneticized forms. Each first appearance of phoneticized terms will appear in italics, followed immediately in parentheses by the appropriate transliteration. The names of deities, people, and places will not be italicized. In this way, we hope to enable interested readers to distinguish and to spell correctly the actual Tibetan terms.

It will quickly be observed that my notes are extensive, as they provide information that is intended to help round out the picture of each siddha's world as he might have experienced it. Though stylized in form, namtar are the life stories of actual people, historical figures who lived and breathed, who read and wrote books, who traveled to various places, and who meditated and taught unceasingly. I hope that my notes will help foster an appreciation of these siddhas' humanity.

In countless respects, this work belongs to Lama Yeshe. It was his idea that I undertake it and his guidance that oversaw it and nudged it along when it lagged. I hope that he knows it's done, and I hope that it pleases him.

Acknowledgments

If it is true that human beings are happiest when they help others, then I have been the cause of making many beings happy, for I have received abundant help over the course of this long project. The initial draft translations of these namtar were completed in Nepal during the first four months of 1980. They were prepared at that time with the help of Mr. Ugen Gombo, who was then a doctoral candidate in Anthropology at SUNY, Stony Brook. I wish here to offer him my sincerest thanks. Given the date of those early drafts, it would certainly seem that publication of these materials is long overdue; indeed, many friends and students of the Dharma have inquired about them. I believe, however, that the research and retranslation efforts of the intervening years have strengthened the work overall. At least, that is my hope.

In annotating this work, some previously published sources proved to be of inestimable value. Turrell Wylie's translation of *The Geography of Tibet*, for example, proved to be indispensable. Similarly focused studies by Tucci and Ferrari also were extremely useful, as was the work of Nebesky-Wojkowitz.

During my 1980 stay in Nepal, two Gelukpa monk-scholars at the Nepalese Mahayana Centre Gompa—Geshe Jampa Gyatso and Lama Lündrub Riksel—answered some of my numerous queries regarding these stories and others, and I greatly appreciate their cheerful willingness to help. In August of 1981, Lama Zopa Rinpoche and I jointly taught a month-long course in California on the Geluk Mahāmudrā tradition. At that time, as he had done previously in Nepal, Lama Zopa graciously answered many more of my questions. I thank him most sincerely, even as I pray that he will remain to teach us for a very long time.

During the academic year of 1984–85, while I held a visiting appointment at the University of Virginia, I made good use of that library's fine resources and personnel. It was also while I was in Charlottesville that I had a number of informative discussions about this material with Geshe Jampel Tardö. He is a most generous teacher, and I sincerely thank him as well.

I also wish to thank Andy Weber for preparing so well the line drawings that appear here, and my old and wonderful friend Åge Delbanco, first for painting, and then for allowing me to use, his masterfully executed *tangka* (thang ka) of Tsongkapa as a frontispiece. For her constant support and friendship throughout this long endeavor and many others, I offer thanks immeasurable to my good friend Professor Vera Schwarcz.

As this manuscript was finally being readied for publication, three other individuals stepped in who greatly enhanced the presentation of the book you have before you. The first was a student of mine at Wesleyan, David Gray, who, as a senior religion major accomplished in Tibetan, read through my translations and offered suggestions. The second was Connie Miller, Editorial Project Manager at Wisdom Publications, who stepped in at just the right time—not only to assure the book's publication but to orchestrate in detail its production—with energy, wisdom, and good cheer. Thanks, Connie! Lastly, I wish to thank Rick Finney, who served as chief copyeditor for this work. It was Rick who took on the task of systematically phoneticizing all the Tibetan used here and who helped in other important ways to make the text much more readable.

For time to travel, write, and conduct research for this book, I am grateful for having received a National Endowment for the Humanities Fellowship (for 1980–81) and for two subsequent sabbaticals from Wesleyan University.

Part I

Introduction

Namtar as Literature and Liturgy

A General Definition

In the Tibetan Buddhist tradition, written accounts of the lives of accomplished practitioners form a distinct genre of literature. That genre is referred to as namtar, an abbreviation of *nampar tarpa* (rnam par thar pa), which literally means "complete liberation." Such liberation life stories are meticulously recorded, narrated, and studied, not simply as the biographies of highly regarded persons, but as accounts serving to make manifest that liberation by describing its process. Thus, namtar serve as both inspirational and instructional models for practitioners of the Buddhist path. Because they center upon beings who are revered as having accomplished enlightenment by using tantric means—"in one lifetime, in one body, even in these degenerate times," as the traditional phrase goes—the subjects of these biographies are called siddhas: "accomplished" or "perfected ones." Namtar, then, as the lives of Buddhist siddhas, present the lives of enlightened beings, and thus they may be characterized as sacred biography.

The very definition of namtar highlights an important distinction between Western and Buddhist notions concerning the biographies of holy persons. In the West, the term "sacred biography" is generally reserved only for the life of the *founder* of a particular religion, while the term "hagiography" is used in reference to the biographies of all the succeeding saints in that tradition.[3] In Buddhism, however, and especially in its Mahāyāna and Vajrayāna forms, the belief is that anyone can become a Buddha. In fact, these forms of Buddhism assert that it is not only possible, but incumbent upon the adept, to attain Buddhahood. There are thus countless enlightened beings, and for Tibetan Buddhists the written lives of all of them are considered to be sacred biography.

It is important to note that Buddhism traveled from India into Tibet primarily in its tantric or Vajrayāna form.[4] Thus, while figures like Śāntirakṣita[5] and Kamalaśīla[6] were instrumental in propagating the rules of monastic discipline and the nontantric philosophy and practice of both the Theravāda and Mahāyāna branches of Buddhism, it was tantric Buddhism that successfully captured the minds of Tibetans, and thus it was the tantric adepts, the siddhas, who succeeded in effectively advancing the new religious tradition of Buddhism in Tibet.

The pre-Buddhist world of Tibetan folk religion was populated by multifarious spirit beings, many of them malevolent. Even after the various strains of the broader-based shamanism of the area and the more localized folk traditions were finally brought together and systematized as the religion of *Bön*, this basic psychospiritual worldview continued to hold sway.[7] For Buddhism to gain acceptance in such an environment it would have to prove itself on that environment's own terms. Thus almost all accounts agree that Padmasambhava, the figure usually credited with establishing Buddhism in Tibet,[8] was able to do this precisely because he was a siddha possessed of a siddha's wonder-working powers. By subjugating Tibet's malevolent spirits, Padmasambhava effectively demonstrated the power and efficacy of the Buddhist religion, and it was owing to this superior display of power that, together with Śāntirakṣita, he was able to found the first Tibetan lineage of Buddhism, called the Nyingmapa (rÑiṅ-ma-pa).

Over the next seven centuries, several other schools were founded in Tibet as the Buddhist Dharma made continued inroads there. And as each new order came into its own, more and more namtar were produced glorifying the persons most influential to a given school's creation and development.

Generally speaking, though the style and content of siddha biographies may differ from one historical period and setting to another [as between Indian and Tibetan examples of the genre],[9] and from one Tibetan order to another,[10] all share some of the same ingredients. It is to these shared ingredients, and to a method of interpreting them, that I now turn.

First, all siddhas are said to have attained *siddhis*, or magical powers of various sorts. Indeed, the terms siddha and siddhi go hand in hand, each term being part of the definition of the other. In written accounts, siddhas are said to speak at birth, to fly through the air, to read other's thoughts, and to pass through walls unhindered. Additionally, miracles are said to have accompanied their births, and they are said to have had exceptional childhoods. [It is interesting to note that many of the early Christian "confessor" hagiographies include similar descriptions.][11]

It is largely in reaction to the prominent place of siddhis in siddhas' life stories that some Western Buddhist scholars have judged namtar to be the products of popular spirituality and, therefore, to be of little scholarly or historical value.[12] Using this "peculiar hermeneutical device,"[13] such scholars belittle the genre and close themselves off to the wealth of information and inspiration that it contains.

The six Gelukpa namtar presented here reveal quite another picture of this literature's value and richness, for they provide us not only with a wealth of valid historical information but with an entrée into the world of tantric practice itself by setting forth, even if only in veiled language,[14] descriptions and instructions regarding tantric meditations. It is particularly with respect to this latter feature that, I believe, Tibetan namtar go beyond Western hagiography in creating a religious literature of richness and depth.

We can begin to appreciate this by considering two important points. First, a namtar, by presenting the significant experiences of a tantric adept in his or her quest for enlightenment, is first and foremost a piece of tantric literature. To put it another way, siddha biographies, in terms of their content and function, are comparable to and complement the tantras and their commentaries.[15] One of their main functions is thus the imparting of esoteric and exoteric practice descriptions and instructions. Viewed in this way, namtar are indeed vehicles for providing inspirational models; but they are, in addition, vehicles for providing detailed instructions to persons seeking to put the teachings of a particular siddha into practice.

Second, it should be borne in mind that all Tibetan namtar contain elements of what are actually three distinct levels or kinds of life story:[16] (1) *chi namtar* (phyi'i rnam thar), the so-called "outer biography," which most resembles Western notions of biography, presenting details about birth, schooling, specific teachers, texts consulted, etc.; (2) *nanggi namtar* (naṅ gi rnam thar), or "inner biography," which chronicles the specific meditation cycles, initiations, etc., imparted to the future siddha; and (3) *sangwai namtar* (gsaṅ ba'i rnam thar), or "secret biography." This last level or kind of narrative describes the meditative accomplishments, mystic visions, and other spiritual realizations and experiences of the accomplished one.[17] The first two levels of namtar as described here do not seem to present problems for the scholars who work with this literature. It is from the third, the so-called "secret biography" that most have usually shied away, calling it magical or fantastic, folkloric or obscure. My own suggestion, as I have already stated, is to view this third level as providing inspiration and encouragement, along with descriptions of esoteric practices and instructions for their accomplishment.

This traditional threefold structured model of namtar can be usefully employed to introduce Western readers of these life stories to their multifaceted richness and ambiance. I suggest that we take it to represent respectively what, for purposes of organization, I term: (1) the "historical," (2) the "inspirational," and (3) the "instructional" levels of the stories. Furthermore, I suggest that levels 1 and 3 may be fruitfully discussed under the broader rubric of "literature" [where the first level speaks to us directly, though the third level requires further elaboration][18] and that level 2 naturally lends itself to consideration under the heading of "liturgy" and, in fact, often functions that way within the tradition. Moreover, as might be expected, the "inspirational" and the "instructional" levels of namtar overlap in many respects.

Applying this three-tiered model to the six biographies presented here, one could say that the outer or "historical" level of these accounts introduces us in a direct way to the lived world of mid-fourteenth to mid-seventeenth century Gelukpa practitioners. Figures previously known only because their names appear in lineage enumerations or religious chronicles become living, breathing human beings. We witness their childhoods and education, their practice hardships and triumphs. In addition to learning more about them as individuals, we see the world, with all its historical and political vicissitudes, in which they moved: the cultural, social, and political contexts in which they practiced the Dharma. Moreover, we learn about the world experienced by these siddhas' disciples and by the general populace of Tibet during this time.

Next, by "inspirational" I refer to the data within these stories that serve to inspire Buddhist practitioners themselves, the *nangpa* (naṅ pa) or "insiders,"[19] those who already profess the faith and wish to emulate its exemplary figures. Here we witness the utter devotion and commitment to practice demonstrated by these siddhas, how each pleased his guru, the dynamics of the guru-disciple relationship, and how, for each of these "realized ones," study and compassionate teaching—both verbal and through written compositions—were continued unbroken. All of this combines to uplift, encourage, inspire, and empower those seeking to practice.

Lastly, by "instructional" I mean those elements in the stories that serve advanced practitioners seeking to learn more about how and when to put into practice the diverse skillful methods of the Vajrayāna. Even today, the most erudite Tibetan teachers continually refer to ancient namtar. Within namtar themselves, a future siddha is often shown searching out a particular namtar or requesting permission to study it. Moreover, the authors and the readers of such biographies have often been the most venerated teachers, the elite of the tantric tradition, precisely because namtar *are* instructional. Thus, in addition to shedding much light on what the world of the traditional Tibetan tantric practitioner was like, the particular accounts translated here tell us how these Gelukpas practiced Mahāmudrā and inform us about the specific contours of the Ganden Oral Tradition. They are not just fantastic tales. Nor are they "merely inspirational," if by that one means products of and for popular spirituality. Rather, they are spiritual biographies brimming with information on many levels.

In what follows I briefly attempt to indicate how the threefold model I have suggested and the two rubrics of literature and liturgy can help reveal the depth and richness of this genre. Because each translation is accompanied by abundant annotation, I will address only a few points by way of example here.

CHI, THE HISTORICAL

In his monumental work *Tibetan Painted Scrolls*, published in 1949, the great Tibetologist Giuseppe Tucci compared namtar with Christian hagiography and suggested that "history" was never the intended purview of the genre. He wrote:

> *rNam t'ar* much resemble the lives of saints widely circulated during our Middle Ages; they must be considered neither histories nor chronicles. The events they relate with a particular satisfaction are spiritual conquests, visions and ecstasies; they follow the long apprenticeship through which man becomes divine, they give lists of the texts upon which saints trained and disciplined their minds, for each lama they record the masters who opened up his spirit to serene visions, or caused the ambrosia of supreme revelations to rain down upon him. Human events have nothing to do with these works, and how could they, being a vain flow of appearances in the motionless gleam of that void, never to be grasped, into which the experience of truth dissolves and annuls us?... All the rest is shadows.[20]

For all its poetry, it must be admitted that Tucci's description of namtar does not do much to inform us about the actual nature or function of the genre. To be sure, the siddha's spiritual biography [the inner and secret levels] takes precedence over the outer biography in such literature. Still, for the six Gelukpa examples translated here, Tucci's assessment would be quite inappropriate. For in these six, human events do figure in. Names, places, and verifiable dates are mentioned, and human beings are historical as well as religious actors in the central drama which unfolds the path to enlightenment.

To begin, the six siddhas and their respective dates should be considered. They are:

1. Tokden Jampel Gyatso [1356–1428]
2. Baso Chökyi Gyeltsen [1402–1473]
3. Drubchen Chökyi Dorje [?]
4. Gyelwa Ensapa [1505–1566]
5. Kedrub Sanggye Yeshe [1525–1591] and
6. Jetsün Losang Chökyi Gyeltsen [1570–1662].

Again, as can be seen from their dates, these six lives span some three hundred years of Tibetan religious history, particularly that period covering the rise to power of the Yellow Hat,[21] or Gelukpa, order. Because the lives are contiguous, through them we are able not only to witness a continuous lineage of Gelukpa Mahāmudrā practitioners but to view continuously unfolding historical developments—both as they impacted upon and were influenced by these six. Through them, one learns who knew whom, what places were frequented, and where certain monasteries were founded and why. Moreover, through this particular set of lives, we can observe directly the intricate interweaving of politics and religion in Tibet during this period.

It is of interest, for example, to learn that four of these six siddhas, who succeeded Tsongkapa [1357–1419] in the Geluk Mahāmudrā lineage, were personally connected with the first five Dalai Lamas. Baso Chökyi Gyeltsen became abbot of Ganden (dGa'-ldan) monastery on the order of the First Dalai Lama, Gendündrub (dGe-'dun-grub) [1391–1475]. One of Baso's Mahāmudrā disciples, Pelden Dorje (dPal-ldan-rdo-rje), studied with and taught the Second Dalai Lama, Gendün Gyatso (dGe-'dun-rgya-mtsho) [1476–1542]. Later, Gyelwa Ensapa was ordained by the Second Dalai Lama and studied under him. Following the death of Ensapa, Sanggye Yeshe accompanied and served the Third Dalai Lama, Sönam Gyatso (bSod-nams-rgya-mtsho) [1543–1588], until the latter went to Mongolia. Lastly, the First Panchen Lama, Losang Chökyi Gyeltsen, was the chief tutor of both the Fourth Dalai Lama, Yönten Gyatso (Yon-tan-rgya-mtsho) [1589–1616], and the Great Fifth Dalai Lama, Ngawang Losang Gyatso (Ṅag-dbaṅ-blo-bzaṅ-rgya-mtsho) [1617–1682].

Tsongkapa had not been seeking to found a new order of Buddhism in Tibet. Yet, owing to his vast intelligence, the great assiduity he evidenced towards his studies, the purity of his moral and monastic discipline, and his tireless energy for teaching, that new order gradually came into being. Two other factors, however, contributed to its development: an ever-growing number of devoted disciples and a conducive political climate in and around the environs of Lhasa. Speaking to this latter point, Snellgrove has observed:

> In and around Lhasa Tsong-kha-pa found ready support from the local nobility and people. This was a sort of border zone between the old religious rivals, 'Bri-khung and Sa-skya, and had more recently come under the influence of the Phag-mo-gru and gDan-sa-mthil who gave a friendly welcome to the teachings of Tsong-kha-pa and his disciples. The example of a religious school which was as yet taking no part in the political rivalries of the day and insisted on the observance of strict monastic discipline, may well have appealed to many who were critical of the apparent worldliness of the older established orders.[22]

While it would be impossible in the space of an introduction such as this to go into any detail regarding the numerous vicissitudes of Tibetan history, one general comment can be posited: one would be hard-pressed to distinguish Tibet's religious history from its political history. Owing to the pervasive power exerted by religion throughout Tibet, whatever rival factions existed—whether indigenous royal houses or foreign hegemonies—all found it necessary to ally themselves with sectors of the religious community. Similarly, a religious order often waxed or waned depending upon the stabilities of its secular alliances.[23]

If the political climate during Tsongkapa's own lifetime greatly served his new order, the situation immediately following his death took a turn for the worse. Prior to his death, not only had Tsongkapa founded—with the aid of his disciples Je Darma Rinchen (rJe Dar-ma-rin-chen) and Je Dülwa Dzin (rJe 'Dul-ba-'dzin)—his own monastery, called Ganden [erected in 1409], but two others of his disciples, Jamyang Chöje Tashi Pelden ('Jam-dbyaṅs-chos-rje bKra-śis-dpal-ldan) and Jamchen Chöje Shakya Yeshe (Byams-chen-chos-rje Shākya-ye-śes),[24] had founded the great monastic establishments of Drepung ('Bras-spuṅs) [in 1416] and Sera (Se-ra) [in 1419], respectively. These monasteries are famed as the Three Great Seats of the Gelukpa.[25] All were constructed very near to Lhasa during Tsongkapa's lifetime.

Now the namtar of Baso Chökyi Gyeltsen translated here provides us with a brief but interesting comment on the Gelukpa tradition's development just after Tsongkapa had passed away. One of Tsongkapa's youngest and most energetic disciples was Gendündrub.[26] He was twenty-five years old when, in 1415, he joined Tsongkapa in Lhasa and became one of his most devoted followers. Tsongkapa was already advanced in age. Later, in 1445, Gendündrub founded what became the fourth most important Gelukpa monastic establishment, the famed Tashilünpo (bKra-śis-lhun-po).[27] Even more importantly, he built this monastery not in Lhasa but far to the west of it, near the town of Shigatse (gŹi-ka-rtse) in Tsang (gTsaṅ).[28] This action was of great importance and is usually interpreted as the chief activity that signaled the active expansion of the new order and its ever-growing prestige. However, this expansion was not, by Gendündrub's time, viewed with the acceptance and warmth that Tsongkapa had experienced some thirty-five years before.

As previously noted, Baso Chökyi Gyeltsen became abbot of Ganden on the order of Gendündrub. From Baso Je's namtar we get an insider's view of the reasons behind this decision, for here we find the dramatic words of Gendündrub himself. The relevant passage reads:

> At that time, the All-knowing Gendündrub Pelsangpo was residing at Tashilünpo, carrying out numerous virtuous activities... Then the precious throne-holder of Ganden and many other illustrious lamas of that institution prayed to the Venerable Gendündrub, urging him to become the next Regent of the Second Buddha [Tsongkapa]. But Gendündrub replied saying: "I myself must hold the Dharma reins of Je Rinpoche right here [at Tashilünpo] since it is necessary to build a fortified mansion [here] in the midst of an enemy camp."[29]

After offering appropriate praise to Baso Je, Gendündrub then advised the monks of Ganden to name Baso Je to the position, which they did.

Within the few years between Tsongkapa's passing and the founding of Tashilünpo, many changes had occurred, and these would continue as the growing prestige and power of the new order began to arouse the hostility of the older orders and their lay patrons. Without going into this quite complicated history here, suffice it to say that the above remarks by Gendündrub are of *historical* importance and that they appear within a namtar.

A survey of the next five namtar in this set shows that while all of these siddhas continued to journey to and study at one or another of the Gelukpa monasteries in Lhasa, for the most part the main seats of their religious activity remained in the province of Tsang. Monasteries like Gangchen Chöpel (Gaṅs-can-chos-'phel), Rong Jamchen (Roṅ-byams-chen), Neynying (gNas-rñiṅ), and especially Ensa, and hermitages like Riwo Dechen (Ri-bo-bde-chen) and Garmo Chö Dzong (mGar-mo-chos-rdzoṅ)—all located in Tsang—were the primary centers for this group. And for all of them, the great Tashilünpo shone like a dazzling beacon, signaling the Gelukpa's expanding influence throughout the region. Thus, through the lives of these six, we witness the Wheel of Dharma of the Gelukpa advancing into and establishing itself in new territory.

This particular set of six namtar concludes with a figure of great importance to Tibet's religious and political history: the First Panchen, Losang Chökyi Gyeltsen.[30] In his namtar we can observe the various ebbs and flows of seventeenth-century Tibet, when not only the various orders and royal families vied for authority, but foreign powers as well. The First Panchen is renowned not only because he served as chief tutor to two Dalai Lamas [one, the greatly powerful Fifth Dalai Lama] but also because on numerous occasions he himself sued for peace among various rival factions.[31] The First Panchen was extremely important to the Gelukpa Mahāmudrā lineage and to other practice lineages for his compositions explicating them. Like those of the great Ensapa, the First Panchen's writings extended and clarified Gelukpa meditative practice, ritual, and liturgy.[32] His namtar reveals him to be a humble though greatly influential figure, incredibly learned, and an accomplished yogi, astute diplomat, prolific writer, and thoroughly compassionate teacher of the Buddha's doctrine.

An important issue relating both to Tibetan religious and political history is the concept of reincarnation. In Tibet, the older Buddhist notions of transmigration and rebirth were transformed and refined in such a way as to become a tool for ensuring the stability of religious authority, prestige, and wealth. Thus the concept of the *tulku* (sprul sku), or incarnate lama, evolved.[33] Prior to the general acceptance of this new concept, "the previous pattern in Tibetan society had been one of a religious aristocracy passing both religious and secular power from father to son or from paternal uncle to nephew."[34] The Sakya (Sa-skya) order, for example, made use of the latter "inheritance" channel. However, in time, the incarnate lama lineages took priority over familial claims in the transmission and safeguarding of religious authority.

While the Gelukpa did not invent this practice in Tibet, reincarnation did become a most important means of ensuring the stability of the new order's ever-growing authority, given the fact that it enjoined strict celibacy on its monks. Within the six namtar presented here, we see accounts of early instances of the use of reincarnation within the Gelukpa tradition.

For example, the First Panchen was recognized as being the reincarnation of Gyelwa Ensapa. The fact that Ensapa had chosen to reincarnate is recorded both in the namtar of Sanggye Yeshe and of the First Panchen. In the latter's namtar, we are told that Ensapa had informed his chief spiritual son, Sanggye Yeshe, regarding the details of his next incarnation, and we learn how Sanggye Yeshe went about having his teacher's rebirth verified.

The concept of reincarnation is mentioned as well with regard to other teachers referred to in the six stories. For example, Ensapa is instructed by the ḍākinī Vajrayoginī to entrust his teachings to one Künkyen Lekpa Döndrub (Kun-mkhyen Legs-pa-don-grub), who is further described as being "the reincarnation of the great siddha Peldre Dorje (dPal-'bras-rdo-rje)." Likewise, Langmikpa (gLaṅ-mig-pa), one of the chief tutors of Sanggye Yeshe, and the lama who confirmed the First Panchen as being Ensapa's reincarnation, is himself described as "the reincarnation of Jamyang Lekpai Lodrö ('Jam-dbyaṅs-legs-pai-blo-gros)."

In other passages, the subjects of these stories are given additional prestige by being born in places where other revered masters had been born, taught, or served as abbots. Thus, Ensapa's birth is said to have occurred "in a place that had itself been blessed by the presence of many holy ones of the past, all of princely lineage, like Sönam Choklang (bSod-nams-phyogs-glaṅ) and others...." Now, this Sönam Choklang is none other than the lama who retroactively became recognized as the second in the lineage of Panchens, in which Ensapa himself was later recognized as the third.[35]

Not all of the "outer" information in these namtar concerns religious or political issues. For example, we are told twice about a widespread epidemic of smallpox. Ensapa first meets his Mahāmudrā guru, Chökyi Dorje, when he [Ensapa] is continuing his meditations in spite of having contracted the disease. The relevant passage reads:

> When the great Ensapa was seventeen years old, there was a widespread epidemic of smallpox, and he also contracted the disease. One day, while reciting verses regarding Dependent Origination near his door, he heard a voice. The moment he heard the sound of this voice, the hairs of his skin stood on end, and [immediately] he went outside. There he saw a monk with a white mustache and goatee, wearing religious robes of the finest cloth, whose bearing and purity were striking. Instantly realizing that this person must certainly be a great siddha, Ensapa invited him inside and there paid him the appropriate respect.

Because the passage mentions Ensapa's age at the time of his meeting his chief guru, we know that Tibetans, at least in the regions of Tsang, experienced an epidemic sometime in 1521. Another epidemic is mentioned in the namtar of the First Panchen. Reference is also made to it in Sanggye Yeshe's story. We are told that this second epidemic occurred when the First Panchen was nineteen years old, making the year 1588. Since the time of each epidemic is remembered and recorded, it can be assumed that the disease had a widespread and perhaps even devastating impact on Tibetan society. One other bit of information is of interest in this connection. It is the fact that, of these six Geluk siddhas, the two who are remembered as having contracted the disease are the same two who are said to be bound directly to each other through the process of reincarnation. Gyelwa Ensapa contracted the disease, and, some sixty-seven years later during another epidemic, his reincarnation, the First Panchen, also contracted it.

But these stories inform us about more than just the various external factors affecting these six practitioners; they also provide an inside look at the dynamics of Gelukpa monastic life, describing in detail such things as monastic organization, college curricula and examinations, and ordination ceremonies. Most of the subjects of these six stories were at some time affiliated with one or more of the Three Great Seats of Gelukpa learning near Lhasa, though Sanggye Yeshe and the First Panchen were more closely tied to Tashilünpo in Tsang. We hear of all these institutions and of their respective colleges. We also hear of important colleges or institutions which by the seventeenth century were no longer thriving, like Sangpu (gSaṅ-phu),[36] the famed college of logic where Jampel Gyatso had studied.

From these accounts, we get a clear sense of what Tibetan monastic education involved. The Gelukpa order has emphasized that training in logic be coupled with proper meditation on the Buddha's teaching, and we see that approach come to life in these stories. Siddhas are usually viewed as wild yogis who shun book-learning in preference for yogic meditation. These stories, though, show the Gelukpa's style of joining the two. Jampel Gyatso's namtar gives a good example of this through its descriptions of his early encounters and subsequent meditation retreats with Tsongkapa.

Further, all of these siddhas, being followers of the Gelukpa, became at some point in their lives fully ordained monks and, therefore, holders of the three sets of vows. Here, we are allowed to view the ordination ceremonies for each, and all relevant data regarding their ordinations are described in detail.

None of these six enlightened beings founded great monastic institutions. One could say that that is to be expected of siddhas. While each was affiliated with one or more of the famed Geluk monasteries [the First Panchen at one time served as abbot of five such institutions simultaneously!], each spent considerable time meditating in isolated retreat. Some, like Chökyi Dorje, became primarily associated with specific retreat sites,[37] rather than with any monastery. Gyelwa Ensapa's small monastery[38] is probably the most venerated of those places today. Still, Baso Je, Sanggye Yeshe, and the First Panchen are remembered for the generous financial and other donations each made to the monasteries with which they were connected. Each was a true patron of the arts and did much to enrich the Dharma through art.

Another fact becomes apparent as one reads these six accounts: that each siddha studied not only the major treatises that formed the standard curricula for Gelukpa institutions but also a wide variety of other texts and meditative systems, including many that are usually associated only with the other Tibetan orders. Thus, these siddhas are shown studying the manuals of *Lamdre* (Lam-'bras) and *Taknyi* (brTag-gñis),[39] two systems associated mainly with the Sakya tradition. The First Panchen not only observed for a time the Kagyü practice of wearing only a cotton covering but, on another occasion, made the practice of "taking only essences"[40] his main meditative endeavor. All six siddhas received instructions on the oral tradition of *Chöd* (gCod), and, because they were Mahāmudrā siddhas, they of course received full instruction in Nāropa's Six Yogas.[41] Thus, like the great Tsongkapa, these are examples of the unbiased and true nonsectarian character and spirit with which the lamas of old approached the Buddha's teachings.

Lastly, each of these six contributed to the Gelukpa lineage in direct and lasting ways. Jampel Gyatso upheld the purity of the Ganden Oral Tradition of Mahāmudrā through his strenuous efforts in meditating just as his guru had instructed him. He thus maintained the practice lineage for future disciples. Baso Je successfully trained three disciples in the Oral Tradition. Chökyi Dorje won the siddhi of immortality, becoming a *vidyādhara*,[42] and passed on the living practice tradition to the great Gyelwa Ensapa. Ensapa not only successfully completed the tantric path but composed numerous treatises on its practice, as well as texts that clarified, refined, and advanced Gelukpa ritual and liturgy in general. Sanggye Yeshe upheld the teachings of Ensapa even as he generously provided for the spiritual and material well-being of his followers. And the First Panchen—owing as much to his peacemaking activities as to his tireless efforts in study, meditation, and teaching—placed the Gelukpa order on sound footing to continue its spiritual work.

Many other observations regarding Tibet's religious, political, and social history could be cited, drawn solely from the information provided by the "outer" level of the six namtar translated here. It is my hope that the notes accompanying each translation will help the reader to draw out more of these, and I move on now to what I have called the "inspirational" level of these accounts.

Nang, the Inspirational

It is easy to see how such exemplary figures as these six siddhas would inspire those coming after them. The accounts of their selfless deeds, often performed under the most difficult circumstances, have remained as trusted guides for later practitioners.

The names of these six are found enumerated—along with those of thirty other Geluk Mahāmudrā lineage-holders—in the short liturgical text called the *Prayer, with Supplement, to the Lineage Lamas of the Ganden Oral Tradition of Mahāmudrā*.[43] This prayer, written in verse, is chanted daily in convocations of monks and nuns engaged in tantric practice and by individuals practicing in isolated retreats. It is usually intoned very slowly and with great sincerity, solemnity, and devotion.

After offering homage to the Mahāmudrā meditative system, the prayer proceeds in thirty-six verses, each composed of two eight-syllable lines that briefly describe the life and merits of each lineage-holder, with a third line bearing that one's name. These are then followed by refrains of four eight-syllable lines. For example, after naming Vajradhara, the first member of the lineage, the refrain is recited as follows:

> By generating a mind of compassion and loving kindness,
> And by completely severing the continuum that clings
> to holding a "self,"
> May I be blessed to quickly attain the highest state
> Of Mahāmudrā, [through] the path of total integration.[44]

As this prayer is solemnly intoned, attention is focused on the verse summations of each lineage holder's liberation life story: upon his struggles, efforts, and accomplishments. Supplication is made to each lineage-holder in turn, and the practitioner prays to be blessed by each of them so as to attain the ultimate realization of Mahāmudrā[45] in his or her own lifetime.

At the prayer's conclusion, a fervent wish is posited, a wish characteristic of tantric practice in general and of this system of guru yoga in particular: that one be enabled to receive the direct transmission of insight from one's own root guru, which alone can usher in consummate realization. The prayer's concluding verses state:

> Having developed strong revulsion for dwelling in saṃsāra
> And taking full responsibility for liberating all sentient beings
> [without exception],
> And seeing my Blessed Guru as Lord Buddha himself,
> May I be blessed to quickly attain the state of Mahāmudrā,
> That most exquisite state of total integration.
>
> Your body, Father, and my own body;
> Your speech, Father, and my own speech;
> Your mind, Father, and my own mind:
> May I be blessed to realize quickly
> Their true inseparability![46]

Chanting this prayer helps to bring to mind the continuous *living* lineage of those who have, in following the Buddhist path, successfully reached its goal. Moreover, because it causes one to contemplate the good qualities of each siddha of the lineage, it trains the mind to appreciate goodness and virtue and to dwell on such qualities as a direct and practical means of generating them in oneself. The solemn request for inspiring strength from those who are identical with the Buddha himself is continuously made. Whenever there is a break in the daily routine of practice, the fuller namtar themselves are read and contemplated if they are available.[47] Throughout all these activities, there is an air of heartfelt devotion; the accomplishments of the siddhas are inspiring. And they are *empowering.*

"What concrete benefits do people derive from reading namtar?" "How do they function within the lived world of Tibetan Buddhist thought and practice?" I asked these questions of many lamas. A remarkably concise and candid response was given me by the Gelukpa Geshe, Jampel Tardö, who said:

> Well, some people use them in their teaching or to write books! Lamas, too, use them to teach and write books. But they are much more useful and interesting when associated with one's practice. For example, if one is practicing the *Guhyasamāja Tantra,* first one reads the prayer to the lineage lamas. Second, for understanding in detail the qualities of each lama in the lineage—in order to obtain that lama's *power*—one reads the namtar of that lama.[48]

In point of fact, lamas often use namtar in their teaching activities. No lama would, for example, introduce a new teaching or begin a series of initiations without first narrating one or more namtar of the teachers in the lineage who practiced that teaching or meditation successfully. This makes for very practical instruction. The recitation of namtar sets the stage for practice by giving authority and credence to the lineage of teachings, by prefiguring the conditions conducive to practice, and by subtly sowing the seeds for similar liberation.[49]

Such preparations are all the more necessary when the imminent undertaking is tantric practice. Deciding to commit oneself fully to the tantric path—with its strict discipline, rigorous yogic practices, and numerous pitfalls—is by no means a small matter. Thus it is only natural that it is inspirational, even joyously uplifting, to contemplate real persons who have traveled that path successfully. Namtar provide examples of human beings not very different from ourselves, who, owing to the guidance of a kind teacher and through their own efforts in practice, were able to transform themselves for the better. Were namtar solely tales of miraculous births and fantastic feats, their capacity to inspire would be lacking, as they would seem to place success out of the reach of ordinary human beings. In truth, only those examples that are capable of being replicated are also capable of inspiring.

Central to all of this—to the success of the siddhas of the past and to our own future success—is the guru. One could say, in fact, that devotion to the guru is the central thread running through all namtar. In the Tibetan tradition, the *lama* (bla-ma), or "superior teacher," is the *sine qua non* of all practice. The title of "lama" is not applied, as is sometimes wrongly assumed, to just any

Tibetan monk but rather is strictly reserved for a teacher who is capable of leading disciples to a direct and genuine experience of the Buddha's teachings. Anyone may teach the words of a particular doctrine, but only a lama is able to give those words life, to reveal to a disciple their ultimate meaning and true spirit. Thus, a lama is one who can confer both instruction and power, the living spirit of the teachings. We see this central theme of guru devotion echoed in the concluding verses of the Geluk Mahāmudrā Lineage Prayer and throughout these six accounts. It is what lies behind the statement in Sanggye Yeshe's namtar that "Ensapa gave him instructions for *tasting* [the Teachings]."

Indeed, the lama is so essential for preserving and ensuring the continued vitality and purity of the teachings that he or she is placed first in the traditional Tibetan Buddhist Refuge formula.[50] Tibetans hold that "Without the lama, there is no Buddha," and it is said that Sanggye Yeshe always advised his followers that "Before there is the guru, there is not even the name of the Buddha!" Ensapa's main practice was always "to train the mind to see the guru as the Buddha," and he is quoted as having said: "The size of one's realizations is completely dependent upon the size of one's guru devotion."

It is the lama who introduces us to the teachings, and it is he or she who assists us all along the way. It is from the lama that we derive the benefit of the Buddha's actual presence as a teacher. The Buddha Śākyamuni passed away more than 2,500 years ago. We cannot see or communicate directly with that historical being, but we can do these things with our guru of this life. Since the guru embodies all good qualities, he or she is identical in essence with the absolute nature of the Buddha.

Commenting on the importance of guru devotion, His Holiness the Fourteenth Dalai Lama has said:

> In order to safely traverse the paths and stages that untie the knots of emotional and karmic bondage, one must correctly apply an effective method. The most certain way to ensure this correct application is to rely upon a fully qualified spiritual friend, someone who has personally realized the fruits of spiritual training and who has gained the ability to communicate his or her experiences to trainees... In general, the more powerful the method being applied, the more qualified must the teacher be. For instance, one must rely upon a guru who is a fully enlightened Buddha in order to engage successfully in the final yogas of Highest Tantra....[51]

Another account says: "Without the guru, there would be no teachings and no path. Therefore devotion makes possible the transmission of sacred outlook, enlightened mind, from guru to disciple. Devotion to one's guru is thus the ground, path, and fruition of vajrayāna…."[52]

This is especially true with regard to tantric practices such as the Mahāmudrā. In fact, it is held that the ultimate realization of the supreme siddhi, Mahāmudrā itself, is attainable *only* through the guru's blessing.[53] This realization is not something that can be learned from books. In order to experience it, one must learn directly from a teacher who has such realization. Then one must follow that teacher's instructions. The practices of guru devotion and guru yoga are, therefore, the ones that immediately precede Mahāmudrā practice itself.[54]

After carefully choosing a guru—and there are numerous texts on how one ought to go about investigating before doing so[55]—the disciple should observe three general types of behavior toward him or her. These behaviors are known as the "three ways to delight a guru" or the "three joys":[56] to make material offerings to the guru, always to show respectful behavior towards the guru, and always to follow the guru's instructions. In this context, the special bonds between lama and disciple are unique, and owing to their closeness, the two are often referred to as "father and son."

In these six namtar we see the dynamics of these guru-disciple relationships played out, and we witness in them the continuous transmission of the living lineage of Buddhist realization. The Buddha's teachings have come down to us without interruption through a continuous stream of realized ones, all of whom, it may be said, now stand before us in the form of the guru.[57] This is the central meaning of "lineage" in Tibetan Buddhism.

Jampel Gyatso's utter commitment to practice, for example, not only pleased his root guru, Tsongkapa, but also greatly inspired the other members of the famed Wölka ('Ol-kha) retreat. When Chökyi Dorje first approached his Mahāmudrā guru, Baso Je, his namtar tells us that he did so "as if he were approaching his own father; and arriving at his feet, with much reverence and single-pointed devotion, he no longer thought of anything of this world, not even of his actual mother and father of this life." The great Ensapa had two gurus whom he counted as his root gurus, and through his strenuous efforts he delighted them both. Sanggye Yeshe was incredibly intelligent, but it was only after surrendering himself to Ensapa that he became "truly learned, both from the side of thought and of practice." The first meeting of a future siddha with the lama destined to become his guide to the ultimate siddhi is a momentous event. Often the disciple has had many illustrious teachers prior to this all-important meeting and has trained with zeal in numerous studies as well as in practice. Ensapa's story is an excellent example of this; Chökyi Dorje has a dramatic impact on him! Jampel Gyatso is completely turned around when he finally comes face to face with Tsongkapa. Each disciple knows when the real lama comes along. And for each future siddha, once the bond is made, there is the complete giving over of full commitment to the lama. Knowing that the lama's instruction is the vital link to highest attainment, nothing is held back.

These six life stories are inspirational not only for Buddhist practitioners today. They show us that not only were these six practitioners inspired by their own gurus and by siddhas previous to them, they themselves were inspiring to their own contemporaries. Thus, there are numerous layerings of inspiration woven throughout these stories that continually become manifest to the reader.

For example, having won the ultimate fruit of practice, these siddhas go on to exhort and to inspire those around them. Thus Ensapa, famed for having completely abandoned the eight mundane concerns,[58] and who was, it is said, "completely without guile," exhorted practitioners of the Dharma with these simple words of advice:

> If the Dharma is listened to, pondered, and practiced merely for the sake of attaining honor and reputation in this life—even if one really desires to learn the path to enlightenment—these actions, being connected with saṃsāra, become tainted, like turning *amṛta* into poison, and serve only to render this precious human rebirth completely empty.[59] Instead, when hearing, pondering, and practicing the Dharma, one's aim should be first of all to subdue one's own mind. Then one should carefully investigate the path, continuously using stainless reasoning as the antidote for the defiling emotions. Moreover, anyone who claims to study the Dharma without thoroughly investigating all the traditions of the Mahāyāna, and who likes to bicker over the slightest points of language—saying "You say this, but I say this"—completely misses the point!

Even though Jampel Gyatso desired only to meditate in isolated retreat, news of his unique intimacy with Lord Mañjuśrī brought people of every sort to him seeking counsel. As already mentioned, the First Panchen was admired so much that at one time he was requested to assume the abbacy of five Gelukpa monasteries simultaneously. In Baso Je's namtar he is praised by the distinguished *Shabdrung* (Źabs-druṅ) of Neynying, Künga Delek (Kun-dga'-bde-legs), with the following words:

> I do not take pride in having been born into an ancient lineage,
> but I do take pride in being a student of Baso Chöje.

One of the students of the First Panchen, known as Shungkang Rabjampa (gŹun-khaṅ Rab-'byams-pa), was himself a famous teacher from the Gomang (sGo-maṅ) college at Drepung. Still, referring to the First Panchen, he said:

> Even though I have received many Dharma teachings from many lamas in Central Tibet and Tsang, including even Ganden's throneholder himself; and even though I am myself extremely hardheaded, all of your teachings have so helped my mind that a supreme reverence for you has been born in me that formerly was not possible for any others.

Finally, through these accounts we witness the reverence with which each of these six regarded the great siddhas who lived and practiced before them, like the tantric master Nāropa. The First Panchen wished to imitate the great siddhas Milarepa and Śabaripa. His namtar mentions Chökyi Dorje and Saraha in the same sentence. Like others of the six, he also went on pilgrimage to visit the places where the famed Wölka retreat had taken place and where Jampel Gyatso had later practiced and where his relics were enshrined. Naturally, they all revered Tsongkapa, that living example of the "model of virtue" and of accomplished practice; we see each of them reflecting continuously upon the life of Tsongkapa as inspiration for their own practice.

The Tibetan tradition holds that in addition to a lama's ability to confer instruction and initiation, he or she should also possess three other "perfect virtues." These are the abilities to explain the Doctrine; to debate, skillfully refuting an antagonist's position; and to compose, committing one's own system of explanation to writing.[60] As their respective namtar attest, these six Gelukpa siddhas were masters in all these areas, and their tradition greatly reveres them for this.

Sang, the Instructional

I have already suggested that one of the major ways in which namtar surpass Western hagiography is in their role as vehicles for specific instruction. This is because, being the biographies of tantric practitioners, they operate in ways similar to other tantric literature. One of the things we know about tantric literature in general is that, in it, things are not always as they seem. Intricate systems of symbolic correspondences are used, and ordinary language is called upon to function in an extraordinary way to suggest the richness, the taste, of a reality that is ultimately ineffable.

The "secret biography" of a siddha is said to describe that siddha's meditative accomplishments, mystical visions, and other spiritual experiences. For many who work with this material, this amounts to saying that a secret biography simply presents descriptions of siddhis. In the judgment of some Western scholars, it is the inclusion of this kind of material that makes namtar "popular" compositions of dubious value. I would only suggest again that these assessments betray a narrow and elitist perspective that prevents such scholars from seeing that these texts can be, at the same time, both popular *and* profound.

Now it seems to me only natural that the biographies of siddhas should include some mention of siddhis, or magical powers, since the latter go hand-in-hand with the very definition of the former. Moreover, the inclusion of descriptions of siddhis not only testifies to the truth of the title "siddha" but enhances the siddha's capacity to inspire. The importance attached to Padmasambhava's ability to display such powers has already been noted. These six Geluk siddhas also, owing to their success in practice, are shown to have had these attainments.

Jampel Gyatso's namtar tells us that he came to possess "fierce siddhis" to cure illness, subjugate evil spirits, make predictions, and even prolong life. He is even credited with extending Tsongkapa's life through his prayers to Mañjuśrī.[61] Chökyi Dorje is famed for having won the siddhi of immortality. The great Ensapa, as a result of his training with Chökyi Dorje, was able to pass through walls unhindered, count the individual particles of a mountain, and speak foreign languages without prior study.

Ensapa's life was also tremendously rich in visionary experiences. At a very early age, as he was practicing meditation in a cave, he was visited by the Buddha and Tsongkapa, both of whom blessed him. At the age of eight, he envisioned that he flew upwards one night and seated himself upon the moon, holding in his hands a *dorje* (rdo rje) and bell with which he proclaimed the spread of the Buddhist Dharma. Numerous miraculous displays are said to have accompanied Ensapa's birth. It is said that upon being born he uttered the six-syllable *mantra* of Avalokiteśvara[62] and that the gods, in response, rained down flowers throughout the region.

Having successfully mastered the propitiation of the wrathful Lord of Wisdom, Vajrabhairava, Sanggye Yeshe overpowered frightening apparitions with the force of his *samādhi*. The First Panchen Chökyi Gyeltsen also enjoyed a visionary life. He was visited and blessed by goddesses and *yoginīs* and by Tsongkapa himself. Using his "subtle body" in the dream state, he is said to have memorized by heart all the root commentaries of the Mahāyāna. These are but a few examples.

Because they do figure so prominently within namtar, the question of siddhis must be tackled head on. Magic plays no part in a siddha's meditative discipline, nor is it viewed as a means to his or her ultimate realization. Indeed, the term "magic" is itself so negatively charged in the West as to be almost completely inappropriate in such contexts. Still, so-called "magical" or "miraculous" displays do have a prominent place in almost all namtar. Because of this, siddhas are often referred to in Western translations as "magicians" and even as "sorcerers"! All such characterizations, however, miss the mark of accurately describing a siddha, who is, viewed properly, "an accomplished one, possessed of *power.*"

Now, the Buddhist tantric practitioner's main goal is not to gain such powers but rather to win ultimate realization in this very life. This is the highest, the superior, siddhi or success. All other siddhis are subordinate; however, the lesser siddhis are said to come by the way as one advances along the path. Buddhist texts are very careful to distinguish between "mundane" or "worldly powers," attainable by yogis of any ascetic tradition, and the highest, supramundane siddhi, enlightenment, which alone is to be sought by the true Buddhist adept. In the six namtar translated here, this highest siddhi is called the "siddhi of Mahāmudrā" because it was by using this particular tantric method that these six practitioners attained enlightenment.

The crux of the problem regarding siddhis seems to have to do not so much with "magic" as with "power." Siddhas are said to possess powers, mainly powers to control natural phenomena. Still, and in spite of the fact that quantum mechanics has discredited much of Newtonian physics, as one modern scholar puts it: "Contemporary science continues, despite its relativistic tendencies, to expect a certain stability and uniformity in nature, and to be suspicious still of alleged events which seem to disturb its expected order...."[63] Within the Buddhist tradition, though, siddhis are viewed as quite natural phenomena: the results that accrue to those who, through rigorous meditation, have gained an increased awareness regarding the true nature of reality. Owing to such increased awareness, reality itself becomes malleable in a siddha's hands. It is then said that such a one has gained extraordinary powers: the ability to control or to alter certain natural and psychic forces.

It should be noted that while much is made of the possession and displays of siddhis in tantric literature, this same sense of power appears under the name *ṛddhi* in some of the earliest strata of Buddhist literature. For example, perhaps the best known enumeration of the mundane siddhis is that found in *Dīgha-Nikāya,* I. 78. There, when the Buddha enumerates for King Ajātasattu the fruits of the life of a monk, he mentions the attainment of various ṛddhi and describes them as follows:

> Being one he becomes many, or having become many, he becomes one again; he becomes visible or invisible; without obstruction he passes through walls, through fences, through mountains, as if they were but air; he penetrates up and down through solid earth, as if it were but water; he walks on water without parting it, as if it were solid ground; cross-legged he travels through the air, as a bird on the wing; he touches and handles the moon and the sun, though they be so potent and mighty; even in this body of his, he scales the heights of the world up to the heaven of Brahma; just as a clever potter could succeed in making out of clay any shape of vessel he wanted to have.[64]

In the context of this sūtra, the Buddha describes thirteen progressively higher fruits of asceticism and the monastic life. His description of the attainment of such magical powers immediately precedes the final fruit for the Theravādin monk: "realization of the Four Noble Truths, the destruction of the defiling emotions, and the full attainment of Arhatship." Even while such ṛddhi are subordinate to complete liberation, they are ranked high in terms of the aspirant's progressive meditational development and accomplishment.

Indeed, accounts of the Buddha's own life—especially the later, more embellished ones—record numerous instances when he himself demonstrated such powers. The Sanskrit *Lalitavistara*[65] as well as the earlier *Mahāvastu*[66] offer good examples of this. And it is well known, even in the early Theravādin literature, that the Buddha had two greatly renowned disciples: Śāriputra, famed for his wisdom and insight, and Mahā-Maudgalyayāna, renowned for his mastery of ṛddhi.

As mentioned above, all siddhis, except the supreme siddhi of complete enlightenment, are regarded as only mundane and worldly powers—even if they appear extraordinary to us! Nonetheless, such siddhis are a feature of namtar. Their presence highlights the esteem accorded to a given siddha; they are signs of his or her holiness and success along the path. Moreover, such powers are said to be employed by tantric adepts as a means to aid, teach, and inspire others. For a true Buddhist practitioner, who has abandoned the false idea of "self" and who, with developed compassion for all beings, treads the path toward complete enlightenment, siddhis are never sought after or used as ends in themselves. A Buddhist tantric adept must already have had some genuine realization of the Bodhisattva's vow of compassion before even embarking upon the tantric path. Thus, the tradition holds that all powers are manifested and employed only to "help a bodhisattva in the attainment of all his aims for his own good and for the good of others."[67]

Having noted all of this, I wish here to make an additional observation that bears directly upon the special nature—and what I suggest is the *dual sense*—of the term "secret" in the context of namtar. Within the genre of Buddhist sacred biography as a whole there are various kinds of narrative, which bear different titles. For example, there are the namtar, or "complete liberation" life stories; there are other narratives termed *dzepa* (mdzad pa) that focus primarily on the specific deeds and spiritual activities of the accomplished one; and there are still others that bear the name *tokjö* (rtogs brjod). This latter group is of particular interest here, since this title literally means an "utterance" or "declaration" [jöpa] of the siddha's own spiritual realization [tok].

Above, I have given a general definition of the "secret" level of siddha biographies. Here, I present what an eminent Tibetan lama had to say on the subject. Geshe Lobsang Jampa[68] described for me what "secret" means in the context of a secret biography:

> A true yogi does not wish to become famous in the world. That would be to mix up Dharma practice with worldly concerns. The great yogis, therefore, would keep their innermost realizations and meditative accomplishments secret. They might sometimes, however, have told their very closest disciples about such experiences in order to spur the disciples' faith, and sometimes these disciples later wrote down these experiences.

While such an explication of "secret" may be surprising to those intrigued solely by the esoteric features of Tantric Buddhism, Geshe Jampa's remarks are surely reliable and are borne out by many examples. One need only recall, for example, a text that forms an essential part of every Gelukpa monk's recitations: the *Secret Biography of Tsongkapa*,[69] written by Jamyang Chökyi Tashi Pelden [1379–1449], one of Tsongkapa's direct disciples. After some initial verses of praise, the text consists almost entirely of an enumeration of Tsongkapa's meditative and mystic experiences and realizations:[70]

> At the age of seven you directly perceived
> Dipaṃkara Atiśa, the great Path Clearer,
> And Vajrapāṇi, Lord of the Secret.
> The exhortations of both the sūtras
> and tantras dawned upon you;
>
> O illustrious lama, at your feet I pay homage...

You directly perceived Mañjuśrī...
Seated in a radiant aura as blue
as the color of perfect sapphire...
From this time onward, O High One,
Whenever you desired you could invoke
Mañjuśrī... and listen to the teachings...
When practicing the seven-limbed ritual
Of the Thirty-five Purification Buddhas,
Continually and clearly you beheld them
And all their forms, *mudrās* and symbols...
All the mahāsiddhas of India and Tibet...
Appeared to, then constantly cared for, you...
Having touched your heart
To the wisdom sword of Mañjuśrī,
A stream of undefiled ambrosia
Flowed into the depths of your being
Spontaneously arousing the propitious
Absorption of highest joy...
Your mind absorbed in the mystic circle of Heruka...
Myriads of ḍākinīs of the outer, inner, and secret places
Made you offerings of vajra songs,
Transporting you in ecstasy;
O illustrious lama, at your feet I pay homage.

Clearly, the meditative realizations and achievements being described above are Tsongkapa's own, visions and mystical events that could have been experienced and known only by him. They were later told to Tashi Pelden, who recorded them. According to tradition, such personal disclosures qualify as secret biography.

Countless other examples of this level of biography can be found throughout the vast corpus of Tibetan sacred literature. When we read, for example, in the namtar of Jampel Gyatso that he "experienced a continuous, steady, and clear appearance of the body and speech of Jetsün Mañjuśrī," we are reading secret biography. We are also reading secret biography when, in a passage describing the performance of the Completion Stage practice of Guhyasamāja, Jampel Gyatso says that "During that time, I held to the practice [of not allowing the *bodhicitta*—here, semen—to slip away] for twenty-six full days."

But is a secret biography merely an enumeration of the siddha's magical/mystical accomplishments? Is it only a listing of siddhis? I think not. The enumeration of such realizations and powers is what defines and validates a siddha, and in a sense there would *be* no siddha biography without the incorporation of at least some of these descriptions and accounts. Yet, while such a listing may certainly be viewed as a basis for faith, inspiration itself is not the sole aim of the secret level of these stories. This is why I suggest that they also often contain the siddha's own personal advice and pith instructions on practice for future practitioners, and this is why I believe that this instructional character is the second meaning of "secret" in these contexts. On the one hand, "secret" refers to those innermost meditative achievements experienced by the siddha. On the other, it refers to the tantric text's use of veiled or hidden analogical and symbolic language to prevent the uninitiated reader's ready access to practice instructions that might be too advanced. The meanings of these passages are thus hidden or secret until one is prepared and able to interpret the symbolic language with the proper understanding. Thus, what is "instructional" to advanced practitioners is "secret" to unskilled, ordinary beings.

The following passage from the namtar of the Gelukpa siddha Chökyi Dorje [there are no dates given for him since he is said to have gained the siddhi of immortality], best demonstrates the convergence of these two meanings of the term "secret":

> In accordance with the words of advice of Chökyi Gyeltsen, he wandered to many solitary places—to lonely forests and ravines as well as to snow-covered mountains. Then, at one time during this period, as he meditated near the sacred water of Pema Chan (Padma-can), all the surrounding areas were suddenly transformed, becoming in an instant like the actual twenty-four places [in India], while the earth surrounding the water itself turned into *sindhura.* Thereupon at that famous spot, he performed the contemplations on guru yoga related to the Completion Stage, and he beheld the countenance of the King of Dharma, the great Tsongkapa. It was then that Je Rinpoche himself gave to this holy one the complete instructions of the ordinary and extraordinary Oral Tradition. In particular, Je Rinpoche taught him the extraordinary practice of the three-tiered mental exercise of guru yoga wherein he visualized his own outward form as that of an Indian pandit and his inner aggregates and sense organs as a host of deities. In his heart, the Buddha Shakyatubpa was clearly manifest, and in that one's heart resided Vajradhara.[71]

It is clear that this passage describes events that could have been experienced directly and known only by Chökyi Dorje himself. We are given a description of his meditative visions: his surroundings are "transformed," and Tsongkapa appears and instructs him. We, too, are "told" these instructions. Even so, there is yet another level to this particular account, and several of its features are intriguing. To begin with, the name of the supposed "place"[72] where this event occurred is of interest because Pema Chan—literally, "having a lotus"—is often a veiled reference to a woman. ["Lotus" in this context may mean the vagina.][73] Moreover, Pema Chan sometimes refers to a female sexual partner in certain advanced tantric practices, particularly those of the *mahānuttara yoga* category. The Pema Chan of the Chökyi Dorje account may or may not be a tantric consort, but I do think that there is at least the suggestion that the place-name Pema Chan may indicate the Completion Stage practice of using sexual union, whether actual or imaginary, as a means to higher insight.

Now, with regard to the "twenty-four places" mentioned in the passage, there can be little doubt that these refer simultaneously to the so-called "outer" pilgrimage places, called *pīṭhas*, said to be the dwelling places for various groups of yoginīs or ḍākinīs, and also to the "inner" places, yogically generated and located throughout an adept's body. The body-*maṇḍala* of the long Heruka Sādhana mentions these twenty-four places,[74] and the theory of the twenty-four places is also found in the *Hevajra Tantra*.

Shin 'ichi Tsuda has given a detailed analysis based on the *Hevajra Tantra* of the various correspondences among these external and internal pīṭhas in his *A Critical Tantrism*.[75] As with tantric literature and practices in general, the whole of ultimate reality, external and internal, is made manifest through an intricate and delicately balanced ordering of correspondences. These correspondences are expressed symbolically. As there are external pīṭhas, so there are internal pīṭhas. The external pīṭhas have corresponding points on the "vajra body" once this is successfully generated by a tantric adept, such that the twenty-four sacred external places are matched with corresponding places on the body: head, fingernails, teeth, ears, backbone, liver, shoulders, eyes, nose, penis, thighs, thumbs, knees, etc. Successfully generating the vajra body adorned with these twenty-four spots, the tantric practitioner is said to be able to compel the ḍākinīs of the external pīṭhas to approach and enter the corresponding spots on his or her body. This again is symbolic, or intentional, language. To quote from Tsuda:

> Internal *pīṭhas*' are abodes of veins (*nāḍīsthāna*) as 'external *pīṭhas*' are abodes of *ḍākinīs*. There are twenty-four parts of a body, such as the head corresponding to the external *pīṭha*

> *Pullīramalya,* etc. There are twenty-four veins (*nāḍī*) which rely on these internal pīṭhas such as (a vein) flowing through fingernails and teeth (*nakhadantavahā*), etc. These veins (*nāḍī*) are regarded as deities (*devatā*), that is, *ḍākinīs*. A *nāḍī* is nothing other than a *ḍākinī*... A human body is composed of these twenty-four 'internal *pīṭhas*' such as the head, etc., as the world, that is, the *Jambudvīpa* in this case, is composed of twenty-four 'external *pīṭhas*,' i.e., twenty-four countries such as *Pullīramalya*, etc. An 'internal *pīṭha*' is existent as long as it is an abode for a vein. A vein in turn is existent as long as it conveys a humour in it or it flows in an internal organ. Therefore, if one makes (the) twenty-four veins of one's own body *active*, through (the) yogic practice of making each of the humours flow through the corresponding veins or each of (the) veins flow through the corresponding internal organs, he transforms his body into an aggregate of internal *pīṭhas* or an aggregate of *ḍākinīs*, a homologous miniaturization of the world as an aggregate of external *pīṭhas* or an aggregate of *ḍākinīs* (*ḍākinījāla*). Thus he can unite himself with the ultimate reality on the basis of the Tantric logic of symbolism.[76]

One other element of this passage from Chökyi Dorje's namtar deserves mention here: the "sacred water" itself. Tibetan tradition says that there is a certain type of water found in sacred caves in Tibet that is a kind of holy nectar. Padmasambhava is said to have given long-life initiations to his disciples using this holy nectar.[77] However, there is room for further elaboration with respect to this. In tantric literature, water is often a symbol for the female or, more specifically, for menstrual blood.[78] The fact that the earth surrounding the water mentioned here is said to have turned into sindhura would seem to have specific reference to the supreme ḍākinī-consort, the Goddess Vajrayoginī, chief consort to Lord Cakrasaṃvara, since marking the disciple's "three doors"[79] with a sindhura powder is a special feature of the initiation into the higher tantric practice using this particular deity. In fact, it would seem that this episode narrates—using the veiled language of the tantras—the unfolding and acting out in Chökyi Dorje's own body of the yoga of the Completion Stage techniques involved, in this case, with the practice based upon the cycle of Cakrasaṃvara. If this is so, then this passage, in addition to providing us with a list of siddhis or mystical visions, also employs the symbolic language of the tantras to describe and to impart information about the advanced practice associated with Cakrasaṃvara.

The above is an analysis of a brief and isolated event in a single namtar, but similar events appear in other life stories as well. Studying these texts has strongly suggested to me that an approach to this literature like the one I have indicated above may indeed prove helpful. Treating a given namtar as a piece of tantric literature that is intended to provide instructions and inspiration to practitioners can help us to glean valuable information about the Vajrayāna in general and about specific practices in particular. In this way, Tibetan sacred biographies become less obscure and certainly less folkloric and are shown to be capable of providing us with valuable insights into the lived world of Tibetan Tantric Buddhism.

Before concluding this Introduction, one specific and unique feature of these six namtar should be mentioned: the so-called *Miraculous Volume* of the Gelukpa. It is said that the text is of "mystical origins" and that it is "accessible only to the most holy of the lineage gurus."[80] As will be seen, the *Miraculous Volume* figures prominently in these namtar, where it is said to be entrusted to each succeeding disciple once that one has accomplished the highest goal of practice. It thus functions in these stories as a type of seal of accomplishment. It should be noted that many Gelukpa lamas claim that, from the time of the First Panchen, the *Volume* has been entrusted to the deity Kālarūpa for safekeeping. One can find more information about the *Miraculous Volume* in the notes to the various translations here.

Regardless of our individual approaches, I believe that there is much in these namtar to inspire us. These six figures contributed greatly to ensuring the purity and vitality of the Gelukpa tradition in particular and of Buddhism in Tibet in general. For their selfless efforts in mastering and spreading the Dharma, they have fully earned the title "siddha" and "enlightened being." Such exemplary figures have continued to inspire those within the Tibetan tradition to this very day. May that inspiration, like ambrosia, spill across cultural boundaries to inspire us as well.

Until you reach the path, you wander in the world
With the precious form of the Sugata
Completely wrapped, as in a bundle of rags,
By things degrading and dirty.

Here it is. You have this precious Tathāgata
Wrapped in rags. Unwrap it, quickly!

From the *Ārya-tathāgatagarbha-sūtra*

Part II

The Translations

The Lord of Accomplishment, Jampel Gyatso

The Lord of Accomplishment, Jampel Gyatso

Jampel Gyatso was born in the region of Tsongka (Tsoṅ-kha) in lower Amdo in the Fire Male Monkey year of the sixth sexagenary cycle [1356]. Owing to the ripening of previous positive [karmic] imprints, during the time of his youth he sought only the Holy Dharma. He learned by heart many sūtras and commentaries such as the *Candrapradīpa*[81] and others. In particular, he continually recited the *Candrapradīpa*. Then, owing to the force of contemplating the path for a long time [according to this sūtra], he developed in heart and mind fierce revulsion toward this life.[82] And so, without the urging of others, he became ordained into the teaching of Lord Buddha, and he guarded his ordination in the same way that we would protect our own eyes. Then, his heart being guided solely by the Holy Dharma, in his eighteenth year he journeyed to Central Tibet.

[Here he visited all the famous monasteries]. However, thinking to himself that if he took up residence in any one of these monastic colleges much of his time would be frittered away[83]—owing both to the various duties that might be required and to the individual demands of the other residents—he determined not to enter a monastic college. Instead, reflecting on the rarity of obtaining precious human rebirth as well as the uncertainty of the time of death,[84] he decided to continually seek out the Dharma by paying respect to a great many revered teachers [*kalyāṇamitras*][85] and requesting from them oral recitation blessings for studying various scriptures and detailed instructions for practicing both the sūtra and tantra [traditions]. He hoped in particular to pay his respects to the great master Tsongkapa and to receive from him some detailed practice instructions which he would then continually attempt to perfect before the end of his life.

Shortly after his arrival in Central Tibet, Je Rinpoche gave lectures on the *Gyü Lama* (*rGyud-bla-ma*)[86] at Dewachen (bDe-ba-can)[87] monastery, and Jampel Gyatso went to listen. Having listened to Tsongkapa's discourses, "good understanding"[88] arose in him. After that, Je Rinpoche advised him thus: "In order to realize the essence of Dharma practice, it is necessary to obtain understanding in the complete path; and in order for that to happen, one has to study, using stainless reasoning, the [two] traditions of the

Mahāyāna.[89] Only in this way can one properly differentiate the true path from the nonpath. Therefore, you must study all the traditional subjects, beginning with logic and so forth."

When he had been thus favored by the advice of Je Rinpoche, Jampel Gyatso plunged into the study of the various traditions, at many monastic colleges like Sangpu[90] and others, and he became well acquainted with these subjects. He listened especially to the teachings on the traditions from Je Rinpoche himself, and he achieved the proper usage of the path of logic. Thus, having become thoroughly learned in the great traditions, he thought that he should now meditate on these single-pointedly. Thereafter, he approached many teachers, and, after receiving from them numerous explanatory commentaries on meditation, he experienced those teachings through practice.

Then, at Kyormolung (sKyor-mo-luṅ),[91] Lama Umapa (bLa-ma dbU-ma-pa) and Je Rinpoche gave instructions for the practice of Demchok (bDe-mchog) from the cycle of teachings on Mañjuśrī. Because of meditating in accordance with these instructions, Jampel Gyatso visited in his dreams many holy places, such as Riwo Tse Nga (Ri-bo rTse-lṅa)[92] and others.

After that, during the time when he stayed at Lama Yönsangwa's (bLa-ma Yon-bzaṅ-ba's)[93] place, he thought: "From now on I shall never again mix with men or with worldly things. Instead I shall seek out a hermitage that is like a *gandola* (gan-dho-la)[94] in the part of Kashmir called Semodo[95] so that I may practice for the rest of my life." [Having informed Tsongkapa of this idea], he traveled with Je Rinpoche towards the outskirts of Tsang to consult with Lama Umapa regarding it. After [jointly] counseling with Lord Mañjuśrī[96] himself, they decided to abide by that which had been pronounced by the ascetic.[97] Je Rinpoche then left Tsang. Afterwards, Lama Umapa thought in his heart: "If Je Rinpoche becomes a hermit, I too must do likewise." But further considering that he could not at that time journey to other places, Lama Umapa went to see Tsongkapa and explained his situation. Tsongkapa then said: "I'll go and practice meditation. You finish your work with the remaining branches of Lamdre[98] and then come [to join us afterwards]. So he said, and this is what Lama Umapa did.

Je Rinpoche then asked the Lord [Mañjuśrī] how many other disciples he should take with him into retreat, and the Jetsün (rJe-btsun) replied:

(1) This lama, Jampel Gyatso,
(2) Lama Jamkarwa (bLa-ma 'Jam-dkar-ba),
(3) Lama Sherabdrak (bLa-ma Śes-rab-grags),
(4) Lama Ringyelwa (bLa-ma Rin-rgyal-ba),

(5) Lobpön Sangkyong (sLob-dpon bZaṅ-skyoṅ),
(6) Lama Jangshengwa (bLa-ma Byaṅ-śeṅ-ba),
(7) Lama Jampel Tashi (bLa-ma 'Jam-dpal-bkra-śis), and
(8) Pönpo Pelkyong (dPon-po dPal-skyoṅ).[99]

[Having assembled], this party of learned ones traveled from Tölung (Stod-luṅ) [southeastward] towards Dakpo (Dvags-po). They followed the main channels of the rivers, came to Kartak (mKhar-ltag) and up to Kok (lKog) and thereafter arrived at Wölka.[100] There the district chief of Wölka, as well as all the other townspeople, showed them much reverence and respect and asked them to remain for the year. [The party agreed, and established a retreat camp at Chölung (Chos-luṅ)]. At Chölung,[101] Je Rinpoche lived in a hut made of grass. Each of the others also established himself in a single hut.

During that time their chief mental training centered on the ordinary path[102] such as the general meditative exercises of the Kadampa. Then, by degrees, having performed the ordinary practices as the basis of the discipline [necessary] for individual liberation, they entered the tantric practices. It was thought that to enter into the tantric practices from the beginning, without having first built up the necessary foundation by degrees, was to appear like a *Nyime Sengge* (gÑis-med seṅ-ge)[103] [i.e., to outwardly appear mighty and strong like a lion but, inside, to be worth nothing]. Therefore, Jampel Gyatso had not taken any manuals of tantra with him into retreat, nor even a single painting of any deity. Nevertheless, when he requested teachings on Lamdre, it is said that, owing to his continual veneration of Jetsün Mañjuśrī, a small painting and an exposition on Lamdre were [miraculously] manifested. Noting this, Lama Umapa said from the first that the entire cycle of meditative practices associated with Mañjuśrī ought to be granted to this lama. Thereafter, Je Rinpoche did bestow the complete cycle of practices of Jetsün Jamyang (Je-btsun 'Jam-dbyaṅs) [Mañjuśrī] in detail to this lama. And having performed the practices single-pointedly, exactly as given, Jampel Gyatso experienced a continuous, steady, and clear appearance of the body and speech of Jetsün Mañjuśrī.

Later, after the group had moved to a cave in Gar (mGar),[104] these teachings were also given to the others, and it is said that on account of their practicing them, blessed signs occurred. During this time, each of the retreatants served Je Rinpoche in turns of seven days. One day, this attendant lama, advised by Umapa, asked if a few of the teachings that he had been given could be given also to the others in the group. The others also asked. Subsequently, they decided to extend their retreat. The offerings were arranged, and prayers were recited.

Even though all of them—with one mind—pleaded with the two lamas, Je Rinpoche and Lama Jamkarwa,[105] not to perform such strict privations, they themselves decided to practice the juniper-berry austerity,[106] and from the beginning, Jampel Gyatso set the example. Out of respect for their religious vows, they [ate no meat but rather] fashioned tiny pill-like substances from juniper kernels and mud and washed these down without [the customary] *chang* (chaṅ).[107] [While the two lamas ate some meager food], the rest of the retreatants consumed eighty such pills per day. But Jampel Gyatso required only thirty pills each day. Because of this, the food requirements for the extended retreat were sufficient. It is said that during that time they were so pitifully poor that their outward physical [karmic] bodies did not in any way compare with their inner mental condition [of supreme well-being]. Nevertheless, for three years, without resort to begging, they were maintained solely on the nourishment of juniper berries. Owing to his conscientiousness during this circumstance, Jampel Gyatso earned the nickname "Juniper Berry."[108]

In such a way this Great Person[109] pleased Je Rinpoche by his strong offering of [commitment to] meditative practice. Thus, for a long time, he received teachings from Je Rinpoche: the oral commentaries and detailed practice instructions for the *Stages of the Path to Enlightenment* and the detailed practice instructions for all the 84,000 Dharma teachings of Lord Buddha abridged into a single essential meaning, together with the necessary vows for avoiding hindrances to their practice; the oral advice, explanatory commentaries, and detailed practice instructions[110] for the Generation and Completion Stages of tantric practice[111] for the Three: Guhyasamāja, Cakrasaṃvara, and Bhairava,[112] together with the vows for avoiding hindrances; the cycle of teachings on the profound path of Chöd[113] together with the branch commentaries for it; and in particular, the complete precepts, commentaries explaining the view, and the accompanying commentaries for the Ganden Oral Tradition. And Jampel Gyatso completely severed all webs of doubt.

Now, the *Great Miraculous Volume*,[114] containing the complete detailed practice instructions of the Oral Tradition that quintessentially abridges the pith teachings of the path of both the sūtras and the tantras, was given directly by the Venerable Lord Mañjuśrī only to Je Rinpoche, to this lama, and to a few of the gods of Ganden. It was at this time that this very wondrous *Miraculous Volume* was delivered into the hands of Jampel Gyatso.

When all these virtuous activities had been performed by Je Rinpoche for his disciple, it was as if he [Jampel Gyatso] had experienced a [spiritual] earthquake.[115] Owing to this, from the depths of his heart, Jampel Gyatso determined to single-pointedly practice meditation from then on. Thinking,

"Now I must search for an isolated spot in which to meditate," he [first] stayed for some time at Meldro Gyelteng (Mal-gro-rgyal-steṅ).[116] Afterwards, at the invitation of the abbot of Pangsa (sPaṅ-sa),[117] he stayed a while in a dwelling on top of a mountain. Next he was offered a cell at the Ravine of Roses hermitage[118] near Pangsa, and he stayed there. It was primarily while at this hermitage that he gave many Dharma lectures on the *Stages of the Path to Enlightenment* to numerous fortunate ones.

Then he thought, "Teaching the Dharma before one has attained the stage of an Ārya provides only a little benefit to others and is itself a hindrance to the accomplishment of Buddhahood." Thinking this, he sealed up with mud the door to his meditation room, and in such isolation he passed his time. Meditating in this way, he equalized gold and excrement, enemies and friends, and the very source of the eight mundane concerns.[119] Thus, casting far away all evil desires and all concerns for fame or reputation, he passed his time by turning the wheel of total concentration.

During this time, however, owing to his practice of generating the appearance of the body, speech, and mind of Jetsün Mañjuśrī, his fame spread, and from every direction men came to seek his advice. Good, bad, and middling scholars came. Ordinary folk sought him out, as well as people of prominence. But even those who gained an audience with him from the very beginning were prevented from seeing the face of his *yidam* (yid dam). As for their questions, however, he allowed them to ask whatever ones they had [directly] to Jetsün Mañjuśrī.[120]

Now this one himself, due to the excellence of his knowledge, was able to accomplish fierce activities,[121] such as the curing of diseases caused by evil spirits and the subjugation of other malevolent forces. He was able to cause an increase of fortune for some and even to prolong life itself. Owing to such accomplishments as these, Je Rinpoche, Chöje Dülwa (Chos-rje 'Dul-ba),[122] and others, performed *pujas* for Jampel Gyatso's long life and for a lessening of obstacles, such as sickness, for him. And this precious lama advised numerous lamas and discussed with teachers of every sort the ways of benefiting the Teaching and of giving instruction in it.[123] If a problem of great importance arose, he also counseled various types of householders.

Due to the force of his moral and religious discipline, he guarded his three vows[124] without the slightest transgression, like one would protect the very essence of sight. At all times, without forgetfulness and with exceptional watchfulness, he concentrated upon each and every activity of his three doors,[125] and he cast far away all the causes of mental wavering and the bustle of worldly affairs, along with the causes of fatigue. Especially at midmonth he confessed all nonmeritorious deeds of his three doors, vowing that in the future he would not repeat such activities, even if his life depended upon it. When he observed the *Poṣadha*[126] vow of fasting, he never broke it short, nor was he ever slothful with respect to what was to be taken up and what abandoned. Thus, with regard to the three vows, having blocked all the causes for any manifestation of the *kleśas*,[127] and having made himself completely free of any fault that might cause shame,[128] he became a supreme example of discipline and a veritable field of peace.

Thereafter, at Wölka Samten Ling ('Ol-kha bSam-gtan-gliṅ),[129] Je Rinpoche gave teachings on the Generation and Completion Stages of *Guhyasamāja*, and all his principal disciples assembled there. Having performed the meditation, all had clear visualizations. Next they requested a very profound pith instruction on those two stages, and, offering a golden maṇḍala, they held a *gaṇacakra*.[130] Now for successfully practicing the Generation and Completion Stages of tantra, all attachment to any form of evil and all manifestations of vulgarity must be completely opposed. Later this lama said, "During that time, I held to the practice for twenty-six full days." Continuously throughout the day and night he did not allow his bodhicitta to slip away.[131] Holding firm to his practice, many excellent qualities began to become apparent: his body became youthful as if he were just entering upon the stage of youth, and his complexion turned rosy. And, steadily, he gained dominion over the samādhi of Bliss-Void.[132]

Even when he reached the age of seventy, it was said of him:

> The lotus of your mouth
> Is like the lotus opened by the sun;
> If seen by bees, no doubt
> It would become their perch.

His face was white like amound of cotton; his complexion looked as if color had been applied to the surface of his cheeks. In coming, going, and sitting, his body was extremely agile, and it was straight like an arrow, completely free from any signs of crookedness.

When one attains to these exceptional qualities as a result of perfecting the samādhi of Bliss-Void, then, like the moon's reflection in water, one can naturally see with one's own eyes numerous Buddhas and Bodhisattvas. Such is said of this precious lama's experience. But since in many previous births he had amassed the causes for being an inseparable follower of the Venerable Lord Mañjuśrī, in this life also he continued to have [special] faith in him. Thus, whenever he experienced the appearances or speech of various other Buddhas and Bodhisattvas coming and going, all these became as if dream-like phantoms, and he was unable to steady his mind upon them. However, due to the pith instructions he had obtained for accomplishing the unwavering samādhi of single-pointed concentration upon the form of Mañjuśrī, he was able to meet with that Lord whenever he wished and to thereby sever completely whatever doubts arose in his mind. Regarding the experiences of this lama, Je Rinpoche himself performed much careful examination. In particular, whenever Jampel Gyatso asked of Lord Mañjuśrī questions regarding the most profound pith instructions regarding the Dharma, these were answered completely without error, and all his doubtful questions were vanquished in an instant.

Now once when Je Rinpoche was recovering from an illness, Lord Mañjuśrī appeared before him and said, "From now on if you exert yourself in the yoga of the Generation and Completion Stages, superior realizations will arise for you. Also, in seven of your fortunate disciples superior understanding will be born." Je Rinpoche then thought that he ought to inquire about [and verify] this experience from a realized one[133] [here, Jampel Gyatso]. Jampel Gyatso responded to Je Rinpoche, saying, "It is not necessary to ask Mañjuśrī again. The unique knowledge of Bliss-Void born in your mind from long ago is the immediate cause of the birth of that path now planted in your heart. The secondary causes for the future practice of that path will now quickly come to fruition also, like the inevitable maturation of what has been sown in a field." Having thus heard Lord Mañjuśrī's reply to his question, Je Rinpoche's heart was satisfied.[134]

Again, according to this lama, a beautiful woman used to visit Je Rinpoche regularly, wearing fine clothes and a flat red hat. But though she did not appear to be a deity, she was not a human receptacle. That she appeared so [to some] was due to a fault in their own practice of the secret teachings of tantra. Indeed, after Tsongkapa had composed the famed commentary on the tantric method of [the siddha] Luipa, called the *Döjo* ('Dod-'jo),[135] a superior friend came to visit him in the appearance of Dorje Neljorma (rDo-rje rNal-'byor-ma).[136] Moreover, during the construction of the *tsuklakang* (tsug lag khaṅ)[137] of Ganden, offering songs such as the *Tingdzin Pir Lekma* (Tiṅ-'dzin-spir-legs-ma),[138] together with accompanying tunes, were performed by many ḍākinīs.[139] It is said that these goddesses were actually seen by ordinary beings as well.

Jampel Gyatso asked Lord Mañjuśrī to give him the liberation life story of Je Rinpoche. [His wish having been granted], he then learned by heart all the very profound teachings comprising the main parts of this extremely excellent and inconceivable life story of the Lord. That is, he learned by heart—and with powerful and genuine understanding—all the three bases [principles] of the path,[140] together with their fruits. Moreover, Jampel

Gyatso attained numerous powers from many previous births, such as the super-knowledges, the powers of magical transformation and so on;[141] the ability to remain in samādhi, and self-reliance [and skill] in mantras. In the presence of the most reverend enlightened Buddhas he prayed and vowed to spread all the Dharma teachings, including those of the Vajrayāna. And so he was blessed in return by all the Buddhas of the ten directions, and he was perpetually held dear by Lord Mañjuśrī himself.

Thus having well laid the foundation for Buddhahood by accomplishing in one lifetime the taming of all that was to be tamed, he became [fully united with] Buddha Sengge Ngaro (Seṅ-ge-ṅa-ro)[142] [Mañjuśrī]. Now, if one meditates likewise and diligently prays to be reborn in that [Lord's] realm, after being reborn in that Pure Land, one will most certainly accomplish enlightenment. So [the great Lord Mañjuśrī] has said. And as it was said by Lord Mañjuśrī, just so Jampel Gyatso did. First, he created with his mind the bodily appearance of Buddha Sengge Ngaro, and then, with great reverence and faith, he engaged in single-pointed meditation. Following great effort, he experienced for eleven days very clear visions of Buddha Sengge Ngaro. Thus, he said that the signs of success for which he had prayed did in fact occur.

As for his chief spiritual sons, he commissioned[143] Baso Chökyi Gyeltsen to become chief holder of the Oral Tradition, giving over to him the complete and extensive detailed practice instructions for it together with the *Miraculous Volume*. Then, having widely disseminated all the detailed practice instructions for both the sūtras and tantras to many learned masters of the Dharma such as his closest heart-disciple,[144] Chennga Lodrö Gyeltsen (sPyan-sṅa bLo-gros-rgyal-mtshan)[145] and others, he felt that he had accomplished the majority of the tasks of this life. And, like the heroic warrior victorious in battle or the businessman having made much profit, he realized the essential reason for birth[146] in this support of leisure [human body].[147] Thus, all the purposes that should be fulfilled in this life were accomplished by him completely.

Then, wishing to "cross over"[148] in the Dharma Palace of Ganden, the very place where the Je Lama [Je Rinpoche] resides, he journeyed to that illustrious institution, and on the first day of the first month he asked that a special offering ceremony be performed—even though this ceremony was usually performed on either the fifth or sixth day of the second month. On that very same day, at the age of seventy-three, in the Earth Male Monkey year [1428], he passed into happiness.[149] At that time many wondrous signs occurred.

As for his bodily remains, the inhabitants of Pangsa in Rilpo fashioned a golden *caitya*[150] and placed the remains inside that support of their prayers.

Baso Chökyi Gyeltsen

BASO CHÖKYI GYELTSEN

[BASO] CHÖKYI GYELTSEN was born in the northern region of Latö (La-stod) to a father of the lineage of noble lords of the area, Tashi Pelsang (bKra-śis-dpal-bzaṅ), and a mother called Budren Gyelmo (Bu-'dren-rgyal-mo) in the Water Male Horse year [1402]. From an early age, he showed no fondness for domestic life, and being completely unattached to worldly affairs he very soon entered the door of the precious teachings of the Buddha.

After being ordained and paying respect to Je Rinpoche and his spiritual sons, he listened to many holy teachings.[151] Wishing then to master the complete teachings of Lord Buddha as collected in the Three Baskets[152] and the Four Classes of Tantra,[153] he especially entreated Yongdzin Kedrub (Yoṅs-'dzin mKhas-grub) Rinpoche[154] to instruct him. And by studying under his guidance, he quickly became a great scholar.

Thereafter, wishing to perform the essential practices associated with the numerous traditions he had studied, he listened to the detailed practice instructions aimed at engendering liberation according to the precepts of those traditions, together with the complete and extensive corpus of literature of the paths of both sūtra and tantra. Thus, from the All-knowing[155] Kedrub he heard a commentary on the *Stages of the Path to Enlightenment*, followed by various explanations and commentaries on the Two Stages together with the empowering initiations for the Incomparable Three [Deities]: Guhyasamāja, Cakrasaṃvara, and Bhairava, as well as numerous others.

Then, owing to the great compassion of all the Bodhisattvas and to the power of having been held in their heart lineages, and in accordance with the prophecy of the Venerable Mañjuśrī,[156] he came into contact with the great siddha[157] Jampel Gyatso. From him he listened to further commentaries on the *Stages of the Path to Enlightenment* and received directly the detailed practice instructions of the Oral Tradition.[158] Moreover, he received commentaries on the Three: Guhyasamāja, Cakrasaṃvara, and Bhairava,[159] together with direct oral practice instructions, and commentaries on the profound path of Chöd,[160] together with direct detailed practice instructions.

In addition, this all-knowing master instructed him in the complete and extensive corpus of literature associated with the detailed practice instructions for the Oral Tradition that had been given by the Protector Mañjuśrī,[161] as well as in the complete and extensive secrets of the so-called "secret" practices[162] of the incomparable method for accomplishing total integration[163] "in one's own body and in only one lifetime, even during degenerate times" according to the method of the profound path of guru yoga.[164] Then, as advised by the Venerable Mañjuśrī, the great siddha Jampel Gyatso, having granted Baso the complete detailed practice instructions of the Ganden Oral Tradition, finally gave over to him also the *Great Miraculous Volume* and sealed it [i.e., the transmission] with a mystic oath, swearing him into this singular lineage.

Thereafter, this great learned one [Baso Chökyi Gyeltsen] taught a few secret texts. But finally, contemplating what might occur in the future, he traveled to a ravine in Tsang.[165] Thereafter remaining single-pointedly fixed on his chief meditative practice, he came to take hold of the great self-originated happiness at Baso.[166] Subsequently, owing to his sweet delivery and to the skill with which he administered the nectar of the Dharma to the fortunate ones dwelling in that region, his fame spread far and wide, and he became celebrated as the Dharma Master[167] of Baso.

Thereafter, he practiced the essence of meditation in many other isolated retreat places, and with skill and kindness he taught the Holy Dharma to many fortunate ones. Then he established a hermitage called Riwo Dechen at a place near to Sengge Tse (Seṅ-ge-rtse) in Shab Tö (Śab-stod),[168] and he made that place the seat of his chief religious activities. And to many fortunate persons of that region he bestowed the nectar of the Dharma as was fitting and appropriate to each.

Then, after contemplating the fact of his having attained a precious human body—so difficult to find even if searched for in all the realms of the Buddhas—and reflecting upon the extreme rarity of having encountered in his lifetime the practice instructions for actually experiencing the essential meaning of the sūtras and tantras as set forth in detail by the Oral Tradition of the Je Lama [Tsongkapa], fierce renunciation was born in his mental continuum, and he decided to abandon worldly activities altogether.[169] He therefore determined to go to an isolated retreat place where no other being would be seen or heard—like Pelgyi Ri (dPal-gyi-ri)[170] to the south, or Senmodo,[171] an appendage to the country of Kashmir—and there to practice thoroughly like the Venerable [siddha] Śawari.[172] While he was making preparations to do this, Je Rinpoche appeared to him in a dream and ordered him to assume the throne of Ganden. Vajrayoginī[173] also advised him, saying that even while he held the throne at Ganden, he would come to master the detailed practice instructions of the Oral Tradition.[174]

Now at that time, Chöje Lodrö Chökyong (Chos-rje bLo-gros-chos-skyoṅ)[175] who sat on the throne of Ganden, wished to be released from further activities as soon as a worthy replacement could be found. At that time, the All-knowing Gendündrub Pelsangpo (dGe-'dun-grub-dpal-bzaṅ-po)[176] was residing at Tashilünpo and carrying out numerous virtuous activities there, like [the swelling of] a lake in summer.[177] Then the precious throne-holder of Ganden and many other illustrious lamas of that institution prayed to the Venerable Gendündrub, urging him to become the next Regent[178] of the Second Buddha[179] [Tsongkapa]. But Gendündrub replied, "I myself must hold the Dharma reins of Je Rinpoche right here [at Tashilünpo] since it is necessary to build a fortified mansion here in the midst of an enemy camp.[180] Now, the younger brother of Kedrubje Rinpoche, Baso Chöje, is unequaled by any other with respect to the excellence of his understanding of the scriptures. My advice, therefore, is that you invite this one to assume the throne of Ganden." And just as was advised by the All-knowing Gendündrub, so Chöje Lodrö Chökyong and the others did. And so, after offering praises, they invited Baso Chöje. [On his way to Ganden], Baso Je journeyed to Tashilünpo. Upon their meeting, the All-knowing Gendündrub declared, "Since you are now going to assume the throne of the Venerable and Great Tsongkapa, I prostrate before you. Please do not prostrate to me in return." Then the Venerable, All-knowing Gendündrub, together with all his entourage, prostrated before Baso Je. Thereafter, proceeding in stages, Baso Je continued his journey.

Then, in accordance with the advice of the Venerable Gendündrub, in the Water Female Sheep year of the seventh *rabjung* (rab-byuṅ)[181] [1463] he arrived at Ganden Nampar Gyelwai Ling (dGa'-ldan-rnam-par-rgyal-ba'i-gliṅ)[182] and was installed as Regent. Thereafter, taking hold of the Dharma reins of the Jamgön Lama ('Jam-mgon bLa-ma)[183] he gave innumerable empowering initiations, oral recitation blessings, and detailed practice instructions to the ordained monks dwelling there, as well as to countless other fortunate ones. In particular, he set in motion the Wheel of the Dharma regarding the *Stages of the Path to Enlightenment*, and he gave the detailed practice instructions for the "overflow heart-essence"[184] of the tradition of the Jamgön Lama. In short, he taught the path of the two (Wings) of the Mahāyāna,[185] which constitute the one path tread by all the Buddhas of the Three Times. And owing to this he became widely celebrated throughout the world as the Greatly Learned One, King of the Dharma, Panchen,[186] and Chökyi Gyelpo (Chos-kyi-rgyal-po). Now this Baso Chöje had attained an exceptionally excellent understanding of the scriptures, and additionally he was blessed—unlike others[187]—to fully comprehend the Oral Tradition of Je

Rinpoche. Because of this, the Shabdrung[188] of Neynying,[189] Künga Delek,[190] said with regard to him:

> I do not take pride in having been born into an ancient lineage;
> but I do take pride in being a student of Baso Chöje.

Such was his declaration. If one analyzes this, it would seem that anyone who saw, heard, or came into contact with Baso Chöje would immediately become his disciple. Such was the power of this great treasury of blessings.[191]

Later, Baso Je transformed the principal chapel of Ganden into a great tsuklakang, and it became even more marvelous and wondrous than the precious body of Gyelwa Sengge Ngaro [himself]. Many images and statues of previous abbots were also fashioned and installed there.[192] Thus, from both the spiritual and material points of view, he [Baso Chöje] was responsible for much progress and great improvement at Ganden, the joyous place of victory for the Gelukpa.

Moreover, as had been foretold by the Venerable Mañjuśrī, three disciples of this Precious One, owing to their practice of the secret teachings and detailed instructions associated with the Oral Tradition, became the three students who accomplished total integration. They were the great siddha Chö Dorje (Chos-rdo-rje); Pelden Dorje (dPal-ldan rDo-rje) of Tölung, and Dorje Pelwa (rDo-rje dPal-ba) of Kham. These three became famed as the Three Dorje Brothers[193] who all accomplished the Rainbow Body[194] in one body and in one lifetime by virtue of mastering the teachings of the Jamgön Lama. [In fact], anyone who wishes to follow the teachings of the Jamgön Lama and who possesses the self-discipline to practice them should become firmly established in the certainty that, by this method, supreme success will result. All who enter upon this practice of the Venerable Tsongkapa should be convinced of this fact.

Now as to those Three Dorje Brothers who accomplished total integration: regarding Dorje Pelwa of Kham, not much is known regarding his origins or whereabouts prior to his meeting with the others of the Three Dorjes or regarding his subsequent stay at Gepel (dGe-'phel),[195] during which time he received the detailed practice instructions of the Oral Tradition from Panchen Chökyi Gyelpo (Paṇ-chen Chos-kyi-rgyal-po). It is not known whether he formerly lived amidst ordinary people or in extraordinary dwelling places amidst *ḍākas*.[196] Neither is it known how he happened to arrive at this particular region of purity [rather than another], nor how he came to be blessed to greatly experience the kindness of the Dharma in this region.

As for Pelden Dorje of Tölung,[197] after he obtained the kind blessings of the Dharma from Baso Je, this heroic one[198] accomplished total integration.

He then gave teachings on the nectar of the Oral Tradition together with detailed practice instructions to one or two fortunate ones. He also exchanged teachings with Gyelwa Gendün Gyatso,[199] and the meeting of these two—with regard both to what was said and heard—appears to have been exactly on a par.

And regarding the great siddha Chö Dorje, as had been prophesied by the Venerable Mañjuśrī and by Vajrayoginī: he became the lord to eventually possess the *Miraculous Volume* [composed of] the complete and extensive practice instructions of the Oral Tradition. As for this great siddha, his most marvelous liberation life story will now be explained.[200]

Then, as Panchen [Baso] Chökyi Gyeltsen's life was coming to an end, he requested—having seen adverse signs—the Dharma Master Lodrö Tenpa (bLo-gros-brtan-pa)[201] to take over the abbot's seat. Then, in order to benefit future practitioners, this reverend Baso Je set down in writing a number of works: *Instructions on the Generation and Completion Stages of Kālachakra*, *The Great Exposition on the View of the Middle Way*, *Instructions on the Generation and Completion Stages of Vajrabhairava*, and *Instructions on the Three Essential Meanings*.[202] Thereafter, casting away everything and remaining single-pointedly fixed upon his tutelary deity, he passed away at the age of seventy-two at the end of the Water Female Snake year [1473]. His ashes were installed in the Ganden Dharma Palace,[203] and from there he journeyed to the feet of Lords Maitreya and Mañjuśrī.[204]

The Great Siddha, Chökyi Dorje

The Great Siddha, Chökyi Dorje

Chökyi Dorje was conceived when two wandering ascetics,[205] a woman called Peldzom (dPal-'dzoms) and a man called Künga Gyelpo (Kun-dga'-rgyal-po)—who came from the eastern region of the country where Je Rinpoche was born[206]—came on pilgrimage to Ü-Tsang (dbUs-Tsaṅ).[207] When the two arrived at Tanak Dorje (rTa-nag rDo-rje) monastery[208] in the Year of the Ox,[209] the babe destined to become lord of the Oral Tradition teachings of Je Rinpoche was born, accompanied by wondrous signs. Owing to a tender upbringing by his parents, the boy grew well, like a lotus in water, and when he reached eleven years of age his parents took him with them as they visited various holy places. They stopped wherever learned ones had been born, wherever they had practiced meditation, wherever they had attained siddhis, and wherever they had turned the Wheel of the Dharma.[210] Then, having wandered from place to place among many such holy regions—due to the great kindness of all the Buddhas and Bodhisattvas of the ten directions and to the blessings of the Jamgön Lama, and as urged by the power of all the protectors of the teachings of the Jamgön Lama and of the holy Dharmarājas[211]—they arrived at the place of victory, Ganden.

The night before this great young son was to arrive at Ganden, Vajrayoginī prophesied[212] to Baso Chökyi Gyeltsen: "Tomorrow there will arrive at this place a fortunate one who is able to grasp the Oral Tradition of Je Rinpoche. You should therefore reveal to him the complete practice instructions of that Oral Tradition." On the following day, as Baso Chökyi Gyeltsen waited, he reflected in his heart about what kind of fortunate being would be able to hold the teachings of the Oral Tradition of the Jamgön Lama. At just that moment, the wandering ascetic-parents and their son crossed in front of his line of vision, and Baso Chökyi Gyeltsen thought, "This young boy must certainly be that great being prophesied by the wisdom ḍākinī." And coming to know this with certainty, he presented to those two parents much food and drink and abundant quantities of gold and silver and all other worldly necessities. And after offering immeasurable gifts to them, he said: "Give this son of yours to me!"[213] And as soon as they were asked, those two parents gave over the young child willingly and with reverence. And instantly this young Bodhisattva went near to Baso Chökyi Gyeltsen as if he were approaching his own father, and arriving at his feet with much reverence and single-pointed devotion, he no longer thought of anything of this world, not even of his actual mother and father of this life.

Thereafter, Chökyi Gyeltsen [ritually] bathed that young son and cast far away all his householder habits. He cut his hair, dressed him in religious robes, and made him a novice monk,[214] naming him Chökyi Dorje.[215]

Then even though that young Bodhisattva already possessed the powers [and abilities] of training in the path from long before [in many previous lives], he assumed the role of a gifted beginner able to learn the complete path quickly and without difficulty. Thus he first mastered the sciences of orthography, spelling, and so forth.[216] Then, Baso Chökyi Gyeltsen gave that young Bodhisattva an explanatory commentary on the *Stages of the Path to Enlightenment* as well as detailed practice instructions regarding the great path traversed by all the Buddhas and Bodhisattvas which were like the very heart-nectar of the King of Dharma, Tsongkapa, and which are the essence of the eighty-four thousand collections of Dharma. Chökyi Dorje galloped [like a steed] through all of these with unreserved agility.

[Next], according to the methods prescribed by his kalyāṇamitra, this Bodhisattva-Mahāsattva[217] achieved [the stages of] calm abiding[218] and higher vision,[219] and [owing to this, an understanding of] the stages of the paths of the three types of beings[220] was born in his mental continuum. Then he was given detailed instructions for meditating on the stages of the path to enlightenment, together with the appropriate prayers for ridding obstacles to his practice. Thereafter, owing to the forceful urging of his innate thought of enlightenment,[221] this great being felt compelled to enter upon the short-cut path of the Vajrayāna.[222] He then received numerous oral recitation blessings and detailed practice instructions on the Four Classes of Tantra and empowering initiations for practicing Guhyasamāja, Cakrasaṃvara-Heruka, and Vajrabhairava, as well as empowering initiations for Kālacakra,[223] and others. And of particular importance, he received the extraordinary Oral Tradition given by the great Protector Mañjuśrī to Gyelwa Tsongkapa, together with complete practice instructions for the performance of guru yoga according to the profound path that encompasses the complete corpus of the paths of both the sūtras and tantras. Lastly, the *Great Miraculous Volume* itself was delivered into his hands.

Now, this Oral Tradition of Je Rinpoche is revealed to only a very few fortunate disciples who have been predestined to receive it by the ḍākinīs.[224] One is even bound by oath not to speak to others of its existence. Because of this required secrecy, for five years Chökyi Dorje was Chökyi Gyeltsen's only chief spiritual son, and he alone received the complete instructions. And when later the time came for this great one's departure, Baso Chökyi Gyeltsen counseled him in detail about how afterwards to best teach the Dharma to other fortunate beings at opportune times and about how, at the close of his life, he should conduct his own practice in isolated places. And this great Bodhisattva, taking Baso Chökyi Gyeltsen's words of counsel to heart, touched his head to that one's feet and prayed.

With regard to all this, the great Gyelwa Ensapa himself [later] composed the following [verses] in praise of the manner in which the great siddha Chökyi Dorje came to possess the detailed practice instructions of the Oral Tradition:

> Then, as prophesied by the wisdom beings,[225]
> The lord of meditative accomplishment, Chökyi Gyeltsen,
> bedecked you with religious robes
> and named you Chökyi Dorje.
> To you of incomparable success, I bow most respectfully.
> Having been taught by you so graciously
> for a long time, O Great Protector, [I have come to see how]
> The amṛta of the Profound Path
> Flows continuously as nectar from your heart.
> Bowing to you, O Great Refuge,
> who give [the teachings] so completely,
> May I become chief among your spiritual sons.[226]

Thereafter [taking leave of his teacher], the great Bodhisattva Chökyi Dorje journeyed to Drepung[227] in order to study logic in accordance with the stainless path of logical reasoning associated with the traditions of the Mahāyāna and to join this with the detailed practice instructions of the Oral Tradition of Je Rinpoche. At Drepung, in the presence of the lord of learned ones, Delek Tobden (bDe-legs-stobs-ldan), he perfected his training in the traditions of the Mahāyāna chiefly by undertaking the study of the *Prajñāpāramitā* and the *Mādhyamika*. Then, having become perfected in these traditions, and in order to be in accordance with the liberation life stories of Je Rinpoche and his [two chief spiritual] sons, he received the vows of a *gelong* (dge sloṅ)[228] at that institution [Drepung], asking Jepön Losang Nyima (Je-dpon bLo-bzaṅ-ñi-ma) to serve as abbot and Dharma Master Delek Tobden to serve as senior instructor. Thereafter, minutely and carefully guarding each and every rule like the very sense organs of life, he became [known as] a great keeper of *Vinaya*.

Thereafter, he journeyed to Tsang and requested many teachings on the sūtras and tantras from Jamyang Mönlam Pelwa ('Jam-byaṅs sMon-lam-dpal-ba). Also, from the Vinaya-holder Lodrö Bepa (bLo-gros sBas-pa), he received many other teachings, including the practice permissions of Hlamo Maksorma (Lha-mo dMag-zor-ma)[229] and Mahākāla,[230] an explanatory commentary on the *Five Stages*,[231] an explanatory commentary on the *Stages of the Path*, and an explanatory commentary on Guhyasamāja called *The Pith-essence in a Small Volume Which Brings Fruitful Experience*.[232] In this way, making many holy and learned masters his guides, he heard teachings so extensive as to transcend the oceans.

Moreover, in spite of having been thoroughly trained in the path from long before, and in spite of the fact that [in this life] he had once received from Baso Chökyi Gyeltsen the quintessential meanings of the paths of both the sūtras and the tantras and had practiced those in great depth until he attained confidence with respect to them, nevertheless—for the sake of showing future disciples how to properly practice the path that is pleasing to all the Buddhas—this great being demonstrated that it is not enough just to receive a single short explanatory commentary from a single lama or just to recite a single oral recitation blessing. Moreover, he showed that in order to obtain the quintessential meaning of the path with regard to any practice, one ought to make use of the stainless reasoning derived from the [two] traditions of the Mahāyāna and to arrive at definite certainty with regard to those. Thus, in order to exhort those future ones, he demonstrated the proper behavior for searching out and listening to the many teachings, for contemplating them, and for putting them into practice.[233]

Then, in all the isolated places that had been especially praised by the Buddhas, he performed the essential meditative practices associated with the complete corpus of the path, moving from one lonely place to another without attachment. And his virtuous activities increased greatly, like the moon during the early part of the month.

Once, while remembering the great kindness of Baso Chökyi Gyeltsen, Chö Dorje spontaneously sang the following verses:

> At the feet of Chö Gyel[tsen]
> Universally famed as the one from Baso,
> To you, Reverend One, I bow,
> Who are the very essence of the Four Kāyas[234]
> and Gyelwa Dorje Chang (rGyal-ba rDo-rje-'chaṅ),
> Chief of the Mystic Lineage.[235]
> Thinking of you single-pointedly as my father,
> I prostrate.
> The ocean of saṃsāra is immeasurably deep.
> In it, the ignorant mind is turned to ice.

May my experience of Bliss and Voidness
Set ablaze the wisdom that is [identical with]
the profound meaning of Je Rinpoche.
In these degenerate times, O Reverend One,
I think of you as a magically created treasure.
O Lord of Dharma, protector of all transmigratory beings,
With great force of mind and body
I pray to you most fervently,
May you be the ornament that decorates the crown of my head.

In accordance with the words of advice of Chökyi Gyeltsen, he wandered to many solitary places—to lonely forest and ravines and to snow-covered mountains. At one time during this period, near the sacred water of Pema Chan,[236] the surrounding areas were suddenly transformed, becoming in an instant like the actual twenty-four places [in India], while the earth surrounding the water itself turned into [red] sindhura. Thereupon, at that famous spot, he performed contemplations on the guru yoga relating to the Completion Stage, and he beheld the countenance of the King of Dharma, the great Tsongkapa. It was then that Je Rinpoche himself gave to this holy one the complete instructions of the ordinary and extraordinary Oral Tradition. In particular, Je Rinpoche taught him the extraordinary practice of the three-tiered mental exercise[237] of guru yoga wherein he visualized his own outward form as that of an Indian paṇḍit and his inner aggregates and sense organs as a host of deities. In his own heart the Buddha Shakya Tubpa (Śākya Thub-pa) was clearly manifest, and in that one's heart resided Dorje Chang.

Yet in spite of having successfully accomplished all these practices, for a while longer the great siddha Chökyi Dorje chose not to cast away his coarse karmic body. Rather, for the sake of giving the nectar of the Dharma to countless fortunate ones, he remained in a mystic support body[238] [which served as but a prop] for his supremely pure Body of Total Integration. Thus, while he awaited the arrival of the great Ensapa, future holder of the teachings as prophesied by Mañjuśrī, he showed the good path of the Vajrayāna to numerous fortunate human beings and to countless numbers of ḍākas and ḍākinīs of the three chief realms,[239] dwelling in that mystic body until he passed [well beyond] the age of a hundred years.

Thereafter, the great Gyelwa Ensapa was born into this world. When he reached the age of seventeen, he was stricken with smallpox[240] and remained at Ensa. It was then that the great siddha Chökyi Dorje went near to the door of Ensapa's dwelling and sang:

When one sees or hears
An incomparable learned one, a teacher,
There arises in association with that
A basis of faith in the Buddha.
In the presence of such a vision and exhortation,
One [properly] bows.

When he had thus composed these well-explicated verses praising the Buddha, there immediately arose [for Ensapa] from the door of Chökyi Dorje's speech that same profound basis [mentioned in his verses]. And as soon as Gyelwa Ensapa heard the sound of his voice, the hairs of his body stood on end and he experienced a complete change of feeling.[241] Thinking, "This must certainly be a great being," he rushed to his door to investigate. Then, coming to know with certainty that he was indeed beholding a great siddha, a holder of the Oral Tradition of Je Rinpoche, he prayed to him to hold him dear. Chökyi Dorje then told him to come at such and such a time to Garmo Chö Dzong[242] at the upper point of the valley of Tashi Dzongga (bKra-śis-rdzoṅ-dga). Thereafter, as soon as Gyelwa Ensapa recovered from his illness, he went straightaway to the Garmo Chö Dzong hermitage without veering from the time that had been specified by the great siddha-lama. And that great siddha Chökyi Dorje was pleased with him. When Ensapa, bowing respectfully, prayed to be given the complete detailed practice instructions of the Oral Tradition of Gyelwa Tsongkapa, the greatly accomplished one, Chökyi Dorje, gladly agreed.

First, [skillfully] abridging the essential meaning of the sūtras and tantras, he gave him an incisive explanation of all the religious discourses, with special reference to how individuals should practice from the beginning stages up to the stage of Buddhahood. Next, he imparted the pith instructions on the methods associated with the doctrine of the the Path and Fruit.[243] This was followed by complete teachings, together with the appropriate explanatory commentaries and detailed practice instructions, for the *Stages of the Path to Enlightenment*, together with the empowering initiations of the incomparable Guhyasamāja, Cakrasaṃvara-Heruka, and Vajrabhairava, and the complete detailed instructions for the Two Stages. In this way the great Gyelwa Ensapa became chief holder of the detailed practice instructions for the Oral Tradition of the Jamgön Lama, [Tsongkapa] in their entirety.

Thereafter, the great siddha Chökyi Dorje and Gyelwa Ensapa—as guru and disciple traveling together—returned once again to the province of Ü-Tsang, and there they ministered to many fortunate disciples. Then, taking advantage of the unique opportunity afforded by living in proximity to each other and the unique happiness and benefit that derived from being able to meditate together, they journeyed together to many places possessing abundant auspicious signs and to many isolated districts and regions among the snowy mountain ranges.

Finally going to Pema Chan, that most excellent place for meditating, they remained for a long time in the uppermost realms of meditative absorption. And afterwards, Chökyi Dorje gave Ensapa the *Great Miraculous Volume*, sealing the transmission with an oath. Then for some time, in numerous isolated places, Ensapa undertook the essence of practice, and when a complete understanding of the ordinary path as well as of the two stages of the extraordinary path was born in his mental continuum, he obtained confidence regarding both his experiences and his abilities. Chökyi Dorje then gave him specific advice about how to purely preserve and spread the teachings of Je Rinpoche's Oral Tradition. In this way Gyelwa Ensapa was blessed to become the chief holder of the Oral Tradition teachings.

After that, the great siddha Chökyi Dorje, having well accomplished all the purposes for remaining in his coarse karmic body, dissolved [even this mystic support-body] into the Clear Light and entered into what may be likened to a Diamond-Rainbow Body.[244] From this, he continually manifests for all transmigratory beings in numbers and forms encompassing the sky, in accordance with the degree [of development] of their faculties and inclinations and their mental and bodily forms, for the purpose of supplying the various needs of each. And he accomplishes this without [the least trace of] discursive thought,[245] like a wish-fulfilling jewel and like the wishing tree.[246] Wherever any disciple offers prayer, there he manifests in conformity with that one's powers [and abilities]. Here too in this snowy region, by fortunate ones leading a pure and virtuous life, he has been seen in various configurations of form too numerous to measure.

Gyelwa Ensapa

Gyelwa Ensapa

From a time in the past so far away that one cannot imagine it, there was one who had produced the thought of supreme enlightenment. And even though he had himself passed completely beyond the ocean of misery, yet, for the sake of spreading the sūtras and tantras taught by Lord Buddha for this suffering world, he took on the role of a Bodhisattva. That one assumed many incarnations and spread the teachings of the Jina[247] in numerous lands in Nepal, in Kashmir, and in India. Here also in this snowy region of the north [Tibet], he assumed various forms and established well the light of the Buddha's Dharma. In places where it had not been spread before, he spread it; in places where it had spread but a little and later declined, he rejuvenated it; and in the places where only a little had remained, he increased it. Such were the activities carried on by him continuously and without interruption. Now, during our time, he came intent on furthering the propagation of the Oral Tradition teachings of the Jamgön Lama [Tsongkapa]. Consequently, in a part of the country called Hlakü (Lha-khud)[248]—near to where the prayer hall of Gegyel Jema (dGe-rgyal-bye-ma)[249] was situated on the [northern] bank of the river Tsang—in a place that had itself been blessed by the presence of many holy ones of the past, all of princely lineage like Sönam Choklang[250] and others, Ensapa took birth.

He was born into a distinguished lineage, where the mother's lineage too was not a lowly one. His father was Sönam Dorje (bSod-nams-rdo-rje). That one's complexion was ever-radiant, his behavior well-mannered, and his speech always flawless and eloquent. His mother was known as Pel Dzomkyi (dPal-'dzoms-skyid). She was perfectly endowed in bodily appearance. Determining to be born to exactly such parents as these,[251] on the tenth day of the first month of the Wood Female Ox year, called Trowo (khro-bo) of the eighth sexagenary cycle [1505], he [Ensapa] took birth, accompanied by wondrous signs.

Owing to his great compassion for all sentient beings cultivated from beginningless time, immediately after being born he uttered the six sacred syllables OṂ MA ṆI PAD ME HŪṂ,[252] and these reverberated throughout the universe. Owing to their tumultuous sound, the chiefs of the gods and the four great [guardian] kings, together with all the gods and goddesses protecting the white side[253] marveled; and greatly rejoicing, they said:

Now the Lord of the World has come.
May the waning Dharma be rejuvenated,
May the forces of evil decline, and
May the gods of the white side be victorious!

Their jubilant cries resounded up to the Okmin ('Og-min) heaven,[254] where all the Buddhas and Bodhisattvas of the ten directions, after being gladdened, prayed: "May the purpose of this great Bodhisattva be realized!" Then they threw flowers into the air.

From the time that the great Gyelwa Ensapa issued from his mother's womb, it was the natural disposition of this brave Bodhisattva to teach with clarity. With regard to his great roar of compassion, his chief spiritual son, Kedrub Sanggye Yeshe, later composed this praise:

Immediately upon issuing from the womb
of his fortunate mother,
Ensapa, taking hold of the supreme wish for success,
Roared his great cry of compassion for the sake of all beings.
At the feet of that [holy one] Losang Döndrub (bLo-bzaṅ-don-grub),
I respectfully bow down.

At the precise moment of being born from his mother's womb at Ensa in upper Shang (Śaṅs), this same great Bodhisattva was perceived by the understanding of Kenpo Je Lekpa (mKhan-po Je-legs-pa)[255] of Riwo Gepel (Ri-bo dGe-'phel) [monastery]. That abbot envisioned the young Döndrub as issuing from the womb of the mother, Mahāmāyā,[256] and as immediately being ritually bathed by all the gods. [So, going to that place] while [envisioning] all the protectors and guardians of the world along with scores of other friendly assistants sprinkling the babe, this illustrious abbot did likewise, and gave him the name Gönpo Kyab (mGon-po-skyabs). This was the nature of this great one's birth.

As to his physical appearance, the shape of his head was like a great canopy, and his forehead was broad, with tufts for eyebrows. He had a sublime nose and long, hanging ears. His primary and secondary limbs were complete, lacking nothing. His sense organs were perfect, and the complexion of his skin was as white as a water-lily. Owing to such splendid features, unlike those of any other human, he was like ambrosia for the eyes.[257]

Now, [also] at that time, Je Kyabchok Pelsang (rJe-skyabs-mchog-dpal-bzaṅ)[258] discerned the prophecies of the lamas as well as his own extraordinary tutelary deities that there would soon be born a holy one who would come to hold the teaching of the Oral Tradition of the Jamgön Tsongkapa and that a teacher to instruct that one in all the main points of the path of the sūtras and tantras would soon be needed at Ensa. He therefore proceeded toward the lower Ensa Gönpa and took up residence at the monastery where the All-knowing Sönam Choklang had been abbot. There, to a select group, he offered the opportunity to study the Dharma. [Now as to this great one, Pelsangpo], after completely putting an end to the play of the eight mundane concerns,[259] he had meditated single-pointedly on all the paths—which are very extensive and profound—and had attained immeasurably clear comprehension regarding them.

Now, when Je Kyabchok went to the lower monastery of Ensa, the great Gyelwa Ensapa himself had just recently been born and was still very young. But long before, it had been predestined that these two would meet. Thus, owing to the power of all the protectors of the Jamgön's doctrine, this young Bodhisattva Ensapa, just on hearing the name Je Kyabchok Pelwa, felt overwhelming respect and reverence for him. And Je Kyabchok Pelwa also, simply at the sight of Gyelwa Ensapa, was greatly gladdened, and he rejoiced and held it as a precious trust. It was as if father and son had met after a long separation.

In the eyes of ordinary people, it seemed at that time that Je Kyabchok Pelwa simply felt kindly towards that young Bodhisattva born in Ensa. But in reality, this heroic Je Kyabchok had perfected total integration in its true sense; and Ensapa, too, had but taken on this magical appearance as a young Bodhisattva for the sake of beings. Therefore, the two in fact came together as equals and discussed in detail what was needed for the sake of the Dharma and for sentient beings and—looking into the three times—how they should carry out their future activities.

Moreover, owing to the immensity of his training in the activities of a Bodhisattva from long before, this young Ensapa passed completely beyond the ordinary behavior of other children. From the very moment of his birth and even while he suckled his mother's breasts, without being taught by others he felt revulsion toward everything he saw of the [mundane] world. And seeing any sentient being, he felt only great compassion and thought to himself, "How shall I rescue this poor being from the prison of saṃsāra?"

In particular, he prayed to the great Tsongkapa, King of Dharma, determining that when he could himself perfectly hold the essence of Tsongkapa's teaching, he would then be able to spread it in the future. Thinking solely of this and keeping it always in his heart, he used to go to live in a cave in the eastern part of that region that was difficult for others to find. He would remain there for five or six days at a time and had to be searched for again and again.[260] Once while he was in the wilderness, he prayed to Lord Buddha and to Gyelwa Tsongkapa day and night, and after this, he had a vision that both the Buddha and Losang Drakpa (bLo-bzaṅ-grags-pa) [Tsongkapa] appeared and blessed him. In this way, he passed his early days.

Then, when he turned eight years old, when the moon rose full one night and shone through the peaks of the Sek (Seg) mountains, he [dreamed that he] bedecked himself in precious ornaments and fine materials and, taking a dorje and bell in his hands, seated himself upon that moon and said, "Let the sounds of the ringing of this bell spread to all the realms of the universe." That [event] occurred in anticipation of his spreading far and wide, and without interruption, Tsongkapa's teachings of the sūtras and tantras.

Because Gyelwa Ensapa entered the practice of guru yoga immediately upon being born, and because he was personally blessed by the Buddha and the Jamgön Lama [Tsongkapa], and owing to other such extraordinary occurrences, that Bodhisattva's chief disciple, Kedrub Sanggye Yeshe, later praised him in this way:

> Having been seen to be the supreme refuge of beings,
> Ensapa was blessed from the time of his childhood
> By supernal deities[261] and the highest lamas.
> To that holy Losang Döndrub, I respectfully bow.

Then, when all these significant omens had occurred, and owing to the force of the good imprints of his previous activities performed repeatedly in various lives in the past, Ensapa saw the entirety of saṃsāra as a limitless fire blazing without end. And day and night, feeling much aversion, with great force he thought only of how to become ordained.

Then, just as he had prayed, at eleven years of age, on the tenth day of the first month of the Hog year,[262] at the monastery of Chökor Üding (Chos-'khor dbUs-sdiṅs),[263] with Drakpa Döndrub (Grags-pa-don-grub) of Hlari Tse (Lha-ri-rtse) serving as abbot and Tsültrim Rinchenpa (Tshul-khrims-rin-chen-pa) serving as senior instructor, he took the vows of ordination. In the midst of many faithful monks such as Rabjampa Lekpa (Rab-'byams-pa Legs-pa) and Chökyi Gyeltsen (Chos-kyi-rgyal-mtshan) of Neyten (gNas-brtan), he went forth from the life of one having a home to the homeless state.[264] And he became known thereafter as Losang Döndrub.

Just as formerly the Buddha was named Dön Tamche Drubpa (Don-thams-cad grub-pa) [Accomplisher of his Goals][265] by King Ze Tsangma (Zas-tsaṅ-ma)[266] as soon as he was born from Mahāmāyā, so too this great Bodhisattva, immediately after entering the door of the teachings of the Buddha and being blessed by his two teachers and by all the Buddhas and Bodhisattvas of the ten directions, was named Losang Döndrub on account of having been judged by all of them to be the one who would, from that very moment, definitely accomplish all his goals of spreading the complete teachings of the Oral Tradition of the sūtras and tantras of the great Losang Tubwang Dorje Chang (bLo-bzaṅ-thub-dbaṅ-rdo-rje-'chaṅ).[267]

Thus, this Bodhisattva-Mahāsattva became known in all the holy places in every realm of the world as a second Buddha.[268] Then those two teachers, along with the other members of the *saṅgha*, threw flowers and prayed for his good fortune [and the success of his goals]. That event was later described by the great Ensapa himself:

> On the tenth day of the Horse month in the Hog year,[269]
> I donned the victorious yellow robes;
> And accepting the vows of deliverance,[270]
> I entered into the Buddha's teaching.

Now even though Ensapa himself already had, from long before, perfect education vast as an ocean in the activity of a Bodhisattva, yet for the sake of demonstrating to all future disciples the three proper trainings with respect to hearing, contemplating, and meditating upon the Dharma, after entering into the Buddha's Dharma, he acted as follows. First, from his main lama Je Kyabchok, he heard teachings on the Gyelchen (rGyal-chen).[271] Next, he was informed about the precepts of all the various religious traditions. Finally, having contemplated all these with excellent motivation, and for the purpose of developing those teachings, he put them into practice day and night. Then, greatly desiring to hear the teaching more extensively and to investigate it so that he might, as he said, "truly follow in the footsteps of his father,"[272] he entered the rains retreat [summer session] at Gepel [monastery].[273]

Just at that time, Lobpön (sLob-dpon) Tsültrim Rinchen was leaving Tsültrim Gang (Tshul-khrims-sgaṅ) monastery and journeying to Drepung. He was joined by the precious abbot, Drakpa Döndrub (Grags-pa-don-grub), and Ensapa accompanied them both. He then remained at Drepung for the summer and fall [terms] and took to heart various sorts of religious activity. From the Venerable Je Hlaripa (Lha-ri-pa)[274] he requested many religious discourses and instructions on such subjects as the *Stages of the Path to Enlightenment*, the *Rinpung* (Rin-spuṅs) *Book of Dharma*,[275] the empowering initiation for Kālacakra, and the complete instructions on the four empowering initiations of Vajrabhairava. It was this Je Hlaripa who was so incredibly kind as to be the first to open to him the door of the Vajrayāna. Then, at the end of ten months, he returned to Ensa.

Later, once again at Riwo Gepel, at the feet of Chökyi Je Lodrö Gyeltsen (Chos-kyi-rje bLo-gros-rgyal-mtshan), he received the complete instructions together with the *lung* (luṅ) and *jenang* (rjes gnaṅ)[276] for the *Set of the One Hundred Rites of Nartang* (sNar-thaṅ),[277] the lung and jenang of Bhaiṣajyaguru,[278] the lung for various *dharanis* and mantras; the jenang and empowering initiation of Vajra-Akṣobhya, and the lung for the root tantras, together with the four empowering initiations of Guhyasamāja and Akṣobhya.

Then, after having deeply entered the teaching of the Buddha, Gyelwa Ensapa exhorted all those wishing to master the path, saying:

> If the Dharma is listened to, pondered, and practiced merely for the sake of attaining honor and reputation in this life—even if one really desires to learn the path to enlightenment—these actions, being connected with saṃsāra, become tainted, like turning amṛta into poison, and serve only to render this precious human rebirth completely empty. Instead, when hearing, pondering, and practicing the Dharma, one's aim should be first of all to subdue one's own mind. Then one should carefully investigate the path, using stainless reasoning as the antidote for the defiling emotions. Moreover, anyone who claims to study the Dharma without thoroughly investigating all the traditions of the Mahāyāna, and who likes to bicker over the slightest points of language, saying 'You say this, but I say this,' completely misses the point.

Still, having seen the great need to actually demonstrate the proper behavior for advancing to the elevated stages of accomplishment, this great one went during the next winter to Tashilünpo. There at the Tösam Ling (Thos-bsam-gliṅ) college,[279] studying under the kalyāṇamitra Jampelyang Losang ('Jam-dpal-dbyaṅs-blo-bzaṅ), he first received instruction in *düdra* (bsdus-gra) [precise definitions][280] and then in astrological calculation. This was then followed by the oral recitation blessings for numerous verses of Dharma and for the various traditions.

Again, at Gepel, from the Venerable Lodrö Gyeltsen, he learned the Vinaya according to the explanation composed by the All-knowing Tobbar Öser (sTobs-'bar 'Od-zer),[281] and received many oral recitation blessings for such discourses as the Venerable Tsongkapa's life story.

Also while at that place, under the tutelage of the Dharma Master Tubten Namgyelwa (Thub-bstan-rnam-rgyal-ba), he received many practice permissions and oral recitation blessings, together with detailed practice instructions, for accomplishing the eleven-headed form of Avalokiteśvara, the four-armed form of Avalokiteśvara, the father-mother form of the Red Dzamla,[282] and the famed *Thirteen Great Pronouncements of the Protector*.[283] Additionally, he received many other instructions, such as the outer, inner, and secret Chögyel (Chos-rgyal),[284] the detailed instructions on the Five Fierce Garudas,[285] the empowering initiations for the Five Sisters of Long Life,[286] and the empowering initiations for Chöd together with an explanatory *ṭika* on the tradition of the Chöd rites associated with Jamyang Gönpo ('Jam-dbyaṅs mGon-po).

Likewise, from that venerable lama [Tubten Namgyel], he received an explanatory commentary on the Six Dharmas of Nāro,[287] a branch explanatory commentary and practice permission for the Five Stages of Guhyasamāja, the instructions of Panchen Chögyen (Paṇ-chen Chos-rgyan),[288] and many smaller treatises such as the precepts of the *Chakgya Soktsöl* (Phyag-rgya Srog-rtsol), and the *Potri Chenmo* ('Pho-khrid Chen-mo).[289] Further, he heard the explanatory commentary on the Six Doctrines of Negu[290] and the sādhanas of Hlamo Shamani (Lha-mo Śa-ma-ṇi), Seng Dongchen (Seṅ-gdoṅ-can), Pelden Maksor Gyelmo (dPal-ldan dMag-zor-rgyal-mo) Four-armed Vaiśravana, and all the Bektse spirits,[291] together with their essential permissions and oral recitation blessings.

Thereafter, he returned to Chökor Üding and there received teaching once more at the feet of his heroic guru, he who had accomplished total integration, the Venerable Kyabchok Pelsangpo. These teachings included the complete empowering initiations of the Three: Guhyasamāja, Cakrasaṃvara, and Bhairava; the Protector Chögyel;[292] Eleven-headed Avalokiteśvara, Dönshak (Don-źags);[293] and the oral recitation blessings and permissions for the Five Fierce Garudas.

Finally, when he received the complete religious treatises of the sūtras and tantras as well as extensive life-preserving empowerments for perfecting the tradition of the Jina, Gyelwa Ensapa, while viewing the actual maṇḍala of knowledge,[294] experienced the inseparability of the lama and the yidam.[295] Some time later, when Je Kyabchok Pelwa had reached sixty-three years of age, while performing an offering ritual to Śrī Vajrabhairava, Ensapa actually beheld with his own eyes the maṇḍala of the Five Red and Black Executioners,[296] together with the whole of the maṇḍala of Śrī Vajrabhairava himself. It was during that time that, owing to his having received the empowering initiation of that yidam, Gyelwa Ensapa's body caught fire and the earth trembled if his legs struck it. And he witnessed many other miraculous signs, such as his maṇḍala being encircled by five different colors of fire.

Then at dawn, on the eighth day of the fifth month of the Monkey year,[297] while observing the maṇḍala of Bhagavān Akṣobhya, he experienced the meditative stages called isolation of body and isolation of speech.[298] Thereafter, owing to his taking the empowering initiation of Guhyasamāja, while bringing forth the [mind of] knowledge, he saw in the five colors of the maṇḍala the body rays of his guru, Je Kyabchok Pelwa, who was walking back and forth on it without doing harm to the colored powders of which it was made. These and others were some of the many wondrous signs that occurred.

By the time Je Kyabchok Pelwa turned seventy-eight years of age,[299] he had given the complete teachings of the Dharma to the great Gyelwa Ensapa. Accordingly, he felt fulfilled, like a merchant returning to his own country after obtaining the wish-fulfilling gem. He therefore determined to traverse the stages of the path, step by step, firmly based upon the detailed instructions of Gyelwa Tsongkapa. And so, after first attaining the confidence of nonreturning, even to the limits of space and time itself, he cast away his coarse karmic body and merged with the Buddha-Body of Total Integration.[300] Then, as even this Total Integration Body dissolved, the surrounding regions—especially those regions where the Jamgön Lama [Tsongkapa] himself had lived—were pervaded by profound mystic knowledge, as if by a continuous shower of fine rainbow rays.[301]

When the great Ensapa was seventeen years old, there was a widespread epidemic of smallpox, and he also contracted the disease. During his illness one day, while reciting verses regarding Dependent Origination near his door, he heard a voice. The moment he heard the sound of this voice, the hairs of his skin stood on end, and [immediately] he went outside. There he saw a monk with a white mustache and goatee,[302] wearing religious robes of the finest cloth, whose bearing and purity were striking. Instantly realizing that this person must certainly be a great siddha, Ensapa invited him inside and there paid him the appropriate respect.

Kedrub Sanggye Yeshe later eulogized the occasion of that first meeting between Ensapa and the great siddha Chö Dorje, calling it a "most auspicious confluence."[303] At the moment of their meeting, Ensapa knew in his heart that this siddha was definitely one who had attained the supreme fruition. Therefore, without hesitation he asked him to hold him dear thereafter. The great siddha Chö Dorje accepted this request with a joyful countenance and told him to come, at a specified time, to join him at [the hermitage called] Garmo Chö Dzong in the upper region of Tashi Dzong (bKra-śis-rdzoṅ).

Thereafter, as soon as Gyelwa Ensapa's smallpox abated—it not being beyond the specified time—he proceeded, just as his siddha-guru had instructed him, to the hermitage of Garmo Chö Dzong. And after he had delighted the great siddha Chö Dorje with the three types of delight,[304] that great siddha gladly gave him the complete and extensive instructions he had requested, starting with the *Stages of the Path to Enlightenment* up to the complete detailed practice instructions for the Oral Tradition of Tsongkapa. And the manner of communication between the two of them was like the pouring of water from one vessel into another.[305]

After this, Ensapa went to Pema Chan, one of the best places for attaining [siddhi]; and after practicing for a long time, he was able to remain completely absorbed within the circle of samādhi. It was then that the great siddha Chö Dorje entrusted to him the *Miraculous Volume* and gave him other secret precepts. Ensapa then felt that he must leave that retreat place so that he might practice in earnest in deserted foothills and in isolated ravines and hollows. Finally, having reached perfection in the complete instructions of the path of the sūtras and tantras, he obtained increasing confidence in himself and in his ability to explain to others, who were fortunate enough to receive them, the precise and detailed practice instructions associated with the Oral Tradition.

First however, in accordance with the directions of the great siddha Chö Dorje and the precepts given him formerly by Kyabchok Pelsang, Ensapa completely cast away the eight mundane concerns.[306] Then, in numerous solitary places, thinking continuously of nothing but yogic practice, he performed the heart of the profound path. He smeared his body with ashes of dung,[307] and, wearing no other adornments, he seated himself in the diamond posture and with great effort concentrated on his tutelary deity. He thought neither about how long it might take nor about the great effort that would be required, and finally he accomplished the ability to remain settled in samādhi at all times, day and night.

On account of this, he was able to subdue whatever manifestations of the afflictive emotions,[308] such as desire, might arise; and by degrees, even the tendency to count himself afraid or unable to follow the meritorious path was cast far away. He was able to settle his mind upon meritorious meditative objects of any nature, and all harmful habits relating to the places [and methods] of breathing were completely countered, so that whenever he applied his body-mind to any activity a unique bliss was born in him. [Describing this period of his life], he said that at that time, if he looked at a mountain, he could count even the most minute constituent particles of it, and that once it had happened that while he was living at Gepel, he had left his room at dawn and walked through the walls of many adjoining rooms without obstruction, and all there had been amazed.

After that, at just over the age of twenty, because he practiced Guhyasamāja at the hermitage of Gyelwa Gyung (rGyal-ba-gyuṅ) in the Diamond Palace of Drakgya Wo ('Brag-rgya-bo),[309] he attained unique insights of a marvelous nature such as being able to recite by heart and without the slightest hindrance all the traditions of the great scholars and siddhas of both India and Tibet as well as the exceptionally wise sayings of Lord

Buddha himself. He also became well-versed in the many different kinds of languages of the Land of the Āryas [India] in both their colloquial and classical forms. He also said that at one time, as he journeyed to Shang (Śaṅs), just after crossing the Gyelpo (rGyal-po) river in Takbü (Thag-bud), he had joined and traveled along with some yogis and conversed with them using their Atsaryī [Bengali] language.[310] There were many traders present who, on hearing them, were amazed.

Then, knowing this venerable one to be his chief [spiritual] son, the great siddha Chökyi Dorje gave over to him a [special] volume of the Oral Tradition as well as the *Miraculous Volume*. And by a great host of gods and lamas Ensapa was then empowered, becoming their Regent.

In this way, the great siddha Chökyi Dorje gave to Gyelwa Ensapa the complete detailed instructions on the Oral Tradition of the sūtras and tantras of the Jamgön Lama [Tsongkapa], and finally, after he delivered even the *Miraculous Volume* into Ensapa's hands, Ensapa became the chief holder of the Oral Tradition teachings. Thereafter, at the most excellent hermitage of Pema Chan, also known as Pema Ö (Padma-'Od),[311] the great Gyelwa Ensapa gave his first teachings of the Dharma to a congregation of religious persons gathered there. During this time also, wherever he traveled, he accomplished the virtuous activity of completely subduing all the evil spirits of those places.

The great Gyelwa Ensapa then stayed for a while at Riwo Gepel. During that time, he occupied himself performing austerities and behaving in such a way as to cause [the experience of] Bliss-Void to arise continuously in his consciousness. Then the wisdom ḍākinī advised him: "Tomorrow you will meet a paṇḍita who is the reincarnation of the great siddha Peldre Dorje. To that one you should impart all the detailed practice instructions without reservation." Ensapa went the next day to Tashilünpo and there met the All-knowing Lekpa Döndrub.[312] Because of their mutual excellence in understanding the scriptures, they took to each other immediately, becoming close. Then, at the urging of the great All-knowing one, they jointly composed a branch commentary dealing with Bhairava and Guhyasamāja, and in order to extend even more their combined virtuous activity, Ensapa dictated to the All-knowing one *The Treasury*.[313] At that time it was generally believed that this work had been composed by the All-knowing one [alone], but in reality it was done [primarily] by Ensapa. Nowadays, this is well-known, and it is listed [properly] in the *Collected Works of Ensapa*.[314]

Moreover, at that time, the great Gyelwa Ensapa was directed by the wisdom ḍākinī to entrust the whole of the Oral Tradition's extraordinary practice instructions—which had been given by Lord Mañjuśrī to Je Rinpoche—as well as some of the relevant portions from the *Great Miraculous Volume* to the

All-knowing Lekpa Döndrub. Also a section of the *Mirror of Secret Prophecy*[315] which nowadays forms a part of Ensapa's *Collected Works*, was taught to the All-knowing Lekpa Döndrub. These teachings were the same ones that, in expanded versions, were later taught to Kedrub Sanggye Yeshe.

Then on the eighth day of the winter month called Rawa (Ra-ba), at the age of thirty-three, Ensapa journeyed once again to the great monastic university, the illustrious Drepung, birthplace of the famed heirarch Dromtön ('Brom-ston).][316] And there, amidst innumerable faithful ones of the saṅgha, with the All-knowing Gendün Gyatso[317] acting as abbot, and Hlawang Rinchen (Lha-dbaṅ Rin-chen) as master of discipline, and Drepung Yangdren Chenmo ('Bras-spuṅs bYaṅ-'dren-chen-mo) as confidant, he received the vows of ordination. And from that time forward, he discarded his former appearance and took on the deportment and activities that were in accordance with the Dharma and the Vinaya as prescribed [by the Buddha]. And for as long as he lived, he guarded those vows, never sullying even a single one with the dirt of evil speech or [bodily] moral downfall.

Thereafter, he went to Lhasa and prayed in front of the Jo-Śāka[318] for the spread of the Dharma and for the happiness and welfare of all beings. Then, having taken out from a pillar the text called *Kachem Kakölma* (bKa'-chems bKa'-khol-ma),[319] just as he was preparing to look at it, he declined, saying it was not necessary to do so.

Later, in a dream one night, a yogi of dark purple color wearing a bear-skin undergarment and named Vinaya-holder Śākya Kalyāṇamitra, gave him a book called *The Three Flowers of Mañjuśrī, Which Clarify* and then admonished him, saying, "When all your good deeds have been accomplished here, [only] then return to Tsang." He then disappeared. On the following day, owing to all his exertions in preparation for going to visit Ganden, Radreng (Rva-sgreṅ), and the other famed institutions nearby, he became violently ill in the middle of the road. Remembering his dream of the previous night and taking note of this occurrence, he decided that it would not yet be good to leave. And as soon as he began to return [to his lodging in Lhasa] his body became well again by itself.

Thereafter, he went to Sera Tekchen Ling (Se-ra Theg-chen-gliṅ)[320] monastery and at the feet of the All-knowing Gendün Gyatso, he received an explanatory commentary on the *Drubgyel Lukkyi Tse* (Grub-rgyal lugs-kyi-tshe), a long-life empowering initiation, commentaries on the *Sūtra of Liberation*,[321] the *Chödrak* (Chos-sgrags) *Sūtra*,[322] and the *Collected Works* of the All-knowing one [Gendün Gyatso] himself, as well as numerous oral recitation blessings for assorted smaller texts.

He then returned to Tsang. There again, from the abbot of Gepel, Lekpai

Lodrö (Legs-pa'i-blo-gros), he received an oral recitation blessing for the ritual ceremony of fasting,[323] a practice permission for joining together certain mantras of his yidam, a permission for the practice of developing the knowledge of the inseparability of guru and protector, and an oral recitation blessing for the Medicine Buddha, Bhaiṣajyaguru.

Next, from Panchen Jangchub Lodrö (Byaṅ-chub-blo-gros), he heard the root tantra of Śrī Guhyasamāja and the branch commentary called *The Clear Light*.[324] Then, from Ngari Lochen Namgyel (mṄa'-ris Lo-chen-rnam-rgyal) he listened to the precepts of the *Four Secrets* and innumerable other profound teachings based on the Mother Tantras, such as the *Four Positions of Cakrasaṃvara*.[325] Thus, after considering his unique opportunity for studying the Dharma and taking advantage of it by listening to all the vast and profound precepts from a great many teachers, all of them [meditatively] accomplished and wise, he truly became a master of the entirety of the teachings of the scriptures.

In this way, the great Gyelwa Ensapa became master of the complete teachings in general and, in particular, chief lord of the complete practice instructions for the Oral Tradition given by Mañjuśrī to Gyelwa Tsongkapa. As Ensapa himself said:

> Of the Oral Tradition, essence of the speech
> of that lama known as Losang Drakpa,
> most excellent chief of the spiritual sons of Mañjuśrī,
> I alone am the holder.

Now, to summarize, from the age of seventeen until the age of forty-two he not only studied widely but performed extensive retreats in numerous hermitages: the Diamond Palace at Drakkya (Brag-skya); the Red Hermitage, where great beasts, tigers, and leopards roamed; at Kodrak (Ko-brag); and in particular on the snowy mountain of Jomo Hlari (Jo-mo Lha-ri) at Panam (Pa-snam). Thereafter, for the duration of his life, he sought out even lonelier retreat places far away from settlements, where people could not be heard or seen, and in those places he meditated unceasingly.

At one such place, on a brilliant dawn, as he meditated on his tutelary deity with complete evenness of mind, there suddenly arose a violent wind and a great trembling. Then, from the painted image of his Protector [Mahākāla] hanging behind him, a thunderous voice came, saying:

> Chief of the twenty-four ḍākas,
> the great Terrifying One resides at this place.
> Like the white lotus sprung forth from the water,

May it be blessed in a secret way.[326]

So Ensapa said, describing the event. Now with regard to this blessed painting of the Protector, it is housed nowadays in the temple of the wrathful deities at Ensa monastery. Thus, owing to the blessings and prophecies of lamas and gods, the monastery of Ensa was established atop Üri (dbUs-ri) mountain. And there Ensapa turned the wheel of the vast and profound Dharma for the great congregation of fortunate disciples who assembled there from Central Tibet and Tsang and from Ngari (mṄa'-ris), Amdo, and Kham.

To list, from among their inconceivable number, even but a few of the principal disciples holding Ensapa's lineage, they included such ones as the All-knowing Lekpa Döndrub; Mawai Wangpo (sMra-ba'i dBaṅ-po) of Jangtön (Byaṅ-ston); the great meditator Öser ('Od-zer); the Dharma Master Lodrö Namgyelwa (bLo-gros-rnam-rgyal-ba) from the monastery in Amdo that was the seat of the All-knowing Sherab Pelwa (Śes-rab-dpal-ba); the Dharma Master Gelek Namgyel (dGe-legs-rnam-rgyal); Sanggye Gyeltsen (Saṅs-rgyas-rgyal-mtshan); the Dharma Master Ngawang Drakpa (Ṅag-dbaṅ-grags-pa), a kinsman [of Ensapa]; the Dharma Master Jamyang Gyelpo ('Jam-byaṅs-rgyal-po) from Kongtön (Koṅ-ston); Tashi Gyeltsen (Kra-śis-rgyal-mtshan) from near Tönpa (Thon-pa); the Bhutanese Dharma Master Lodrö Namgyel (bLo-gros-rNam-rgyal); the great meditator Jepön Lektsok Lündrub (Je-dpon Legs-tsogs-lhun-grub), and the wise and accomplished Norsang Gyatso (Nor-bzaṅ-rgya-mtsho).

In short, whether to masters of the Three Baskets from Central Tibet and Tsang, or to gatherings of simple monks and laymen, he spread the vast and profound Holy Dharma with extreme kindness and impartiality. Of all these, the one blessed to become his chief spiritual son and to be consecrated as his heir and bearer of the Oral Tradition was the greatly wise and accomplished Sanggye Yeshe.

Moreover, for the sake of future disciples, the great Gyelwa Ensapa also wrote extensively, composing *The Wish-fulfilling Explanatory Commentary on the Stages of the Path to Enlightenment, The Wish-fulfilling Treatise on How to Apply the Basis of Chöd as the Essential Meaning of the Perfection of Wisdom,* and a work on the history of *Terdung* (gTer-duṅ)[327] along with many other venerated texts.[328]

Thereafter, having perfectly accomplished the fulfillment of his physical activities—like a warrior returning victorious from battle or a merchant returning to his own country after obtaining precious gems—on the twenty-third day of the Month of Miracles[329] during the ninth rabjung of the Fire Tiger year [1566], the great Gyelwa Ensapa dissolved his coarse bodily form into the Dharmadhātu. And during his funeral ceremonies, many remarkable events occurred that struck the minds of everyone with great wonder, such as the appearance of numerous rainbow canopies and a continuous rain of flowers that fell from the sky as if showered down by gods. His bodily remains were then placed in the chapel called Palace of the Dharma at Ensa monastery.

The Scholar-Siddha, Sanggye Yeshe

The Scholar-Siddha, Sanggye Yeshe

In the Wood Female Bird year of the ninth rabjung called Sakyong (Sa-skyoṅ) [1525] in the town of Drukgya (Drug-brgya)[330] in Yül-hlen (Yul-lhan) of the Tsang valley, Sanggye Yeshe was born. His father was the vajra-holding *upasāka* known as Lama Rinchen, and his mother was called Chöten (Chos-bstan). She was free of conceit, of few defilements, and by nature earnest, conscientious, and friendly to all beings. The birth was accompanied by wondrous signs. As soon as he was born his parents bathed him and made offerings to all the gods of the white side.[331] They then paid reverence to the community of monks, and these benevolent gurus in turn gathered together and celebrated the birth according to custom.

Now his parents had four sons, this great one being the youngest. Accordingly, this young Bodhisattva was cherished like a sprout of medicine by his parents and elder brothers alike, and he grew well, like a lotus in a pond.

During that time the greatly revered master of accomplishment, the great Ensapa, beheld that young one.[332] And just as when a world monarch, producing a son, is pleased and gladdened by that young one who in the future will become his heir, and wishes him to be well cared for, just so the great Gyelwa Ensapa, knowing this young Bodhisattva to be the future heir of his own doctrines, showed much delight in him and urged his parents to take good care of him.

When the child neared ten years of age, at the feet of that one who was like a treasury of precepts of the sūtras and tantras, the kalyāṇamitra Yönten Sangpo (Yon-tan-bzaṅ-po),[333] [Sanggye Yeshe] received the vows of an upasāka[334] and was given the name Chökyab Dorje (Chos-skyabs-rdo-rje). Thereafter, as soon as he entered the monastic school of that place, he mastered by heart and with no difficulty whatever the grammatical sciences of orthography and semantics as well as the more advanced levels of writing and reading, in addition to the preliminary practices of Dharma.

Then, beseeching the perfected guide Yönten Sangpo to serve as his teacher, at Baso Hlündrub Dechen (Ba-so Lhun-grub-bde-chen) monastery,[335] he received the restraining vows of a novice monk.[336] Then, discarding his former appearance, this young Bodhisattva donned the saffron religious robes with a view to quickly attaining enlightenment. Accordingly, he was named Sanggye Yeshe. And taking in hand the alms bowl of a *muni*, he became as a Second Buddha,[337] a holy abode of offerings for all transmigratory beings, up to and including even the gods.

Next, under the tutelage of Lama Yönten Sangpo, Sanggye Yeshe received complete instructions on the four empowering initiations of Śrī Vajrabhairava, Guhyasamāja, and Akṣobhya; a long-life empowering initiation; the practice permission and empowering initiation of the Protector [Mahākāla]; and many other practice permissions and empowering initiations associated with other armed deities.[338] In addition, he received numerous other holy teachings, such as the oral recitation blessings for the sacred books of the Kadam [school].

Afterwards, Sanggye Yeshe reflected on all these in his heart until he gained certainty with respect to them. He [later] said:

> When the darkness of all-encompassing confusion
> Is unillumined by the torch of much learning,
> One cannot discern the path
> To that foremost city of Liberation.
>
> In order to enter upon just that path,
> I studied the works of Mipam (Mi-pham) [Maitreya],[339]
> The Six Ornaments of Jambudvīpa,[340]
> And those renowned as The Two Most Excellent Ones.[341]
>
> Furthermore, not being satisfied with only a rough summary
> Or a one-sided presentation of the views,
> I studied them all, in detail.

Then, desiring to study the traditions of the Mahāyāna in the company of a congregation of many learned ones, in his fifteenth year he journeyed to the great monastic institution of Tashilünpo and entered at the time of the winter session. There, under the guidance of the master of logic at the college of Tösam Ling, the Venerable Tsöndru Gyeltsen (brTson-'grus-rgyal-mtshan), he studied metaphysics and various lists of vocabulary together with a little instruction in astrological calculations and other religious discourses.

Then, in the spring of the next year, Kedrub Sanggye Yeshe, along with three or four friends, discussed the possibility of going to Sera monastery to study under the foremost scholar, the Venerable Dampa Chökyi Gyeltsen (Dam-pa-chos-kyi-rgyal-mtshan). One friend then said: "We ought really to go to study with the one called the Venerable Gendün Losang (dGe-'dun-blo-bzaṅ)[342] of Tanak (rTa-nag) monastery who now resides at Lekdrub Dratsang (Legs-grub grva-tshaṅ).[343] He is the true disciple of Jetsün Chökyi Gyeltsen himself and is unrivaled with respect to his mastery of the three religious activities."[344] At that very moment, owing to the force of karmic connections in many previous rebirths between our learned lama and Jamyang Gendün Losang, as soon as Sanggye Yeshe heard the name Jamyang Gendün Losang, his hair stood on end and tears sprang to his eyes. And he immediately agreed to go to study at Lekdrub Dratsang.

The time of his arrival at Nyangtö (Myaṅ-stod)[345] coincided with the arrival of all the other students entering Lekdrub Dratsang for the spring Dharma session. Then, when he had taken the feet of Jampelyang Gendün Losang on his head,[346] he began his studies, starting at the very beginning with the rudimentary exercises dealing with noun lists and definitions, followed by a detailed study of the six particles and word formation, the various traditions of connecting words, and the sciences of mathematics and reasoning.

Finally, during the winter Dharma session, he received from Jamyang Gendün Losang an explanatory commentary on the general meaning of the *Pramāṇavārttika*[347] and received further instructions and directions, upon which he reflected perfectly.

At that point, Jampelyang Losang drew together—according to the path of stainless reasoning—all the pith instructions of the paths of the three vehicles, explained systematically and in detail in the *Pramāṇavārttika.* Finally, he drew into the discussion the root texts themselves. Afterwards, he revealed the general essence of the texts' internal meaning and then the manner of attaining valid knowledge with respect to all the various branches of the path and to disentangling the various arguments regarding the respective explanations of a given tradition from the essential meanings of those traditions. Sanggye Yeshe recited all three from the beginning [having learned them all by heart] and impressed them thoroughly upon his mind. Later, all this material was again put back into written form, and it now comprises that treatise that is found at Tösam Ling known as Jamyang Gendün's *Manual of Explanatory Notes,*[348] which sets forth a definitive treatment with regard to the general purport of the *Pramāṇavārttika* and which is incomparable in all the regions of Tibet. Indeed, after seeing the power and persuasiveness of this explanation, the great siddha Jampa Püntsok (Byams-pa-phun-tshogs) praised Jamyang Gendün Losang in this way:

> Having abridged into one [volume] the wisdom of all the
>   Buddhas
> In the guise of a kalyāṇamitra clad in religious robes,
> Even the superior ones, well beyond taking up and abandoning,
> Come to touch their heads to the dust of your feet
> And to receive your blessings.

Thereafter, Sanggye Yeshe returned to Tashilünpo for the winter Dharma session. Entering various classes and doing extremely well in all of them, his sublime mastery of both scripture and logical reasoning was such that he quickly attracted the attention of the most learned instructors, and their minds were captivated by him.[349] Then, during most winters and most springs, until he was eighteen years old, he concentrated on the study of the Mādhyamika and became well-versed in all areas of Mādhyamika and in dialectical reasoning in general.

Then, in order to listen to a certain discourse at Tösam Ling, the Venerable Gendün Losang himself came to stay there. That lama, too, witnessed this superior one's great mastery of both the scriptures and logical reasoning. Thus, when asked by the superintendent of the Mādhyamika section who was best in the class, the great scholar Gendün Losang proclaimed Sanggye Yeshe to be perfect in scriptural recitation, even though he was only eighteen. Thereafter, for two winter sessions, in the midst of the assembly of monks at Tösam Ling, he sat for debate[350] on the traditions of Mādhyamika.

Then, in the first month of his nineteenth year, in the great courtyard of Tashilünpo, in the midst of a gathering of all the monks and abbots, he sat for debate. When he debated with a renowned scholar-teacher from [Ganden's] Sharste (Śar-rtse)[351] [college] he proclaimed far and wide the lion's roar of his erudition in scriptural recitation and logical reasoning, without fear, panic, or timidity, and completely overwhelmed his opponents. He thereby won the fame of victory from all sides.[352]

Thereafter, he took up the study of the later texts, such as the *Pāramitās* and the *Vinaya.* And here, also, he developed unhindered intellectual acumen. After learning by heart the literal meanings of all of the commentaries that analyze [according to] both the indirect [or interpretive] meaning and the final [or definitive] meaning,[353] he satisfied his teachers with the nectar of his own explication. Following these accomplishments, when he had reached the age of twenty-five, at the great religious institution Pelkor Dechen (Pal-'khor-bde-chen),[354] in the midst of a sea of learned masters, he sat for the school rounds in the Four Difficulties.[355] And here again he sounded his roar of good explication so that all those learned ones gathered there from various places were satisfied by the sounds of his "summer-born" explication[356] and understanding. It is said that, owing solely to the excellence of this great scholar's pronouncements, the time flew by, and none was left for discussion by others.

Then, when he turned twenty-six, he was charged by Jamyang Gendün Losang to assume the duties of head disciplinarian at Tashilünpo. Consequent to that, light rays of his Dharma discipline were emanated, and henceforth he spent his time challenging others in debate and making all the Kunda groves of that religious institution blaze forth in glory. Also, due to his abundant material patronage,[357] all the monks were well satisfied.

At the conclusion of his term as head disciplinarian, Sanggye Yeshe journeyed to the great monastic institution of Gangchen Chöpel (Gaṅs-can-chos-'phel)[358] in order to study with Panchen Rinpoche Dönyö Gyeltsen (Don-yod-rgyal-mtshan), who, as [former] abbot of Tashilünpo, had mastered many Dharma teachings of the sūtras and tantras. Staying there from the spring session until the autumn session, Sanggye Yeshe requested [of this Rinpoche] many Dharma teachings. In particular, he requested a practice explanation for the *Dön Dünma* (Don-bdun-ma)[359] as well as various other explanations and oral recitation blessings for other *lojong* (blo-sbyoṅ) teachings.

Then he determined to enter the glorious garden of the greatly profound Vajrayāna, as Je Rinpoche had said, "to reach complete enlightenment in this very life." In his heart he contemplated in this way: "This singular opportunity to meet with the supreme Vajrayāna is more rare even than the Buddhas. I would therefore be completely wasting my leisure were I not to attempt to study the Vajrayāna path and to arrive at its essence." Therefore he journeyed to the glorious Lower Tantric College,[360] the place holding the secret treasury of the tantric doctrines of the Jamgön Lama [Tsongkapa]. There, at the feet of the Dharma Master Gendün Losang, he prostrated.

Now, on his way down [traveling from west to east], he had stopped at Ensa monastery, and bowing at the feet of that revered lama [Ensapa himself], he had asked to be taken under his protection so that obstacles to his practice might not arise. He had also asked permission to return to Ensa at a later time. Then, having accomplished this, he had turned his feet in the direction of the aforementioned itinerary and proceeded towards Central Tibet.

[In Central Tibet], on his way up [traveling from east to west], after making pilgrimages to Sera, Drepung, and other monasteries in the environs of Lhasa, he went to Riwo Genden (Ri-bo dGe-ldan), the place of victory. There, having very respectfully paid reverence to the headmaster of the Lower Tantric College, Dorje Chang Namke Drak (rDo-rje-'Chaṅ Nam-mkhas-grags), he entered and took up residence there. After only a short while, owing to his unabated display of assiduity towards his studies, he arrived at the true essence hidden beneath the literal meaning of the *King Tantra* [the Guhyasamāja tantra].[361]

Then, having resided in the Tantra College for slightly less than a year, he developed an illness in his legs due to having come into contact with some very cold water, and for a while it was his main task to look after this medical problem. However, not very long afterwards, his body became well again, like the moon when released from an eclipse. Then, continuing his studies, he became thoroughly proficient in the three arts of ritual dance, maṇḍala drawing, and ritual music,[362] as well as in all the various rites associated with fire offerings and maṇḍala preparation[363] and in the methods of propitiating the Three—Guhyasamāja, Cakrasaṃvara, and Vajrabhairava—according to the practices and traditions of the Lower Tantric College. When he had thoroughly impressed all these upon his mind, he headed once again in the direction of Tsang.

At first he went to Tösam Ling, and bowing to the Dharma Master Gendün Losang, he began his practice. Now, in the meantime, it had occurred that an inner voice spoke to his future teacher, Gyelwa Ensapa, saying, "It is good that my *Rabjampa* (Rab-'byams-pa)[364] has not wandered too far away. I must ask [the goddess] Pelden Hlamo (dPal-ldan Lha-mo)[365] to bring my brilliant one back to me, since his remaining in Central Tibet could be harmful [to him]." This explains why, when Sanggye Yeshe had developed the illness in his legs while in Lhasa, he had strongly determined at that time to return to Tsang as soon as his illness left him. Moreover, it had also happened that one night in a dream a young girl had said to Sanggye Yeshe, "Now you have accomplished your aims here. Let's go back to Tsang." Those events occurred owing to Ensapa's feelings of concern [for his heart-disciple].

Then, [owing to the force of their karmic connection], Sanggye Yeshe went to practice at Ensa monastery; and studying under the great lord of accomplishment, Ensapa himself, Sanggye Yeshe became truly learned both from the side of thought and of practice. Ensapa gave him instructions for "tasting" the stages of the path to enlightenment as set forth by the Second Buddha, the great Tsongkapa, as well as for experiencing the path upheld by the glorious Atīśa and by both Nāgārjuna and Asaṅga, that singular path of the Mahāyāna tread by all the Buddhas. This was followed by detailed practice instructions for actualizing the great Oral Tradition, together with the necessary pledges for removing obstacles to its practice. And at the feet of the great Gyelwa Ensapa, without concern for food or shelter and holding no attachment whatsoever for this life, Sanggye Yeshe exerted himself greatly. And for a long time he meditated, so that Ensapa was greatly pleased, as a father is gladdened by the birth of a son.

After some time, practicing in this way, a feeling of fierce revulsion towards the various sorts of worldly phenomena arose naturally in his mental continuum, and he asked Gyelwa Ensapa to allow him to take the vows of full ordination so that he might train extensively in the treasury of discipline set forth by the Buddha's teaching. Then, just as was advised by the great Ensapa himself, so it occurred that at Riwo Gepel monastery in Shangdo (Śaṅs-mdo)—with the great lord of accomplishment, Chokle Nampar Gyelwa (Phyogs-las-rnam-par-rgyal-ba) serving as abbot, the Dharma Master Gelekpa (dGe-legs-pa) of Deyang (bDe-yaṅs)[366] [monastic college] acting as senior instructor, and the Dharma Master Shakya Pelsangpo (Śākya-dpal-bzaṅ-po) of Nordeng (Nor-gdeṅs) as confidant—he was duly ordained in the midst of innumerable faithful members of the saṅgha.

At the feet of that same abbot, Sanggye Yeshe received many holy Dharma teachings: the oral recitation blessings and practice permissions for the set of the one hundred [meditative practices] of Nartang (sNar-thaṅ) and the practice permissions for the four deities of the Kadam [school].[367] Then he once again returned to Ensa monastery and continued his assiduous practice of single-pointed meditation.

In particular, he requested from the great Ensapa the details of the devotional services associated with attaining the protection of his tutelary deity. Then, in a lower chamber of Ensa monastery, he performed these devotions to the resplendent Vajrabhairava, and after only a short while he perfected the stages of practice associated with that tutelary deity. Then, one night as he lay in his bed, just at midnight, a fierce coldness overtook his entire body. He then experienced the strong sensation that he saw, perched atop the edge of the door to his quarters, Gyelwa Ensapa himself. That one then approached him and, with his own hands, covered Sanggye Yeshe with his winter meditation robe.[368] Sanggye Yeshe then experienced a very clear sensation of limitless bliss and warmth. Just then, a scorpion with horns the size of a hand appeared menacingly in front of him, but he felt no fear or timidity whatsoever, and, seeing the scorpion twirling its horns and even exuding fire, he kept his mind in equipoise. Finally, he vigorously laughed aloud, and immediately the scorpion disappeared.[369] In addition, a host of other apparitions appeared, but all were overpowered by [the strength of] his samādhi. After that, at the feet of Gyelwa Ensapa, he received the practice permissions of the Thirteen Pronouncements of the great Mahākāla, the complete cycle of teachings on Chöd, and the extensive cycle of meditations and practice permissions for numerous personal deities, gods, tutelary deities, and Protectors of the Dharma.

Some time after that, on an auspicious day as rainbows appeared overhead, Sanggye Yeshe mounted the Dharma throne of Shangdo's Riwo Gepel monastery, the [former] seat of the great All-knowing Sherab Pelsang (Śes-rab-dpal-bzaṅ).[370] And from there this great one [Sanggye Yeshe] sent forth good explanations of the Dharma that purely attended to the various needs of his students.

In the meantime, the great master Ensapa had passed beyond misery. For the sake of perfecting his sacred memory, after erecting a new main chapel and a chapel for the wrathful protectors, as well as a new lama's residence,

Sanggye Yeshe had the precious relics [of Ensapa] installed in the main chapel. Moreover, he commissioned a finely wrought and blessed likeness of the Jetsün [Ensapa] that blazed brilliantly and was like ambrosia for the eyes of all who saw it. Further, in addition to the images of Kālacakra, Hevajra, and the Three—Guhyasamāja, Cakrasaṃvara, and Vajrabhairava—he also commissioned the fine likenesses of each and every lama of their lineage with the images of the various protectors engraved underneath.[371] There then occurred the fortunate confluence of circumstance that the All-knowing Sönam Gyatso,[372] traveling on horseback in the direction of Tsang, was invited to Ensa monastery, and a great profusion of flowers was made to shower down upon this most excellent seat of the Dharma. Thereafter, Kedrub Sanggye Yeshe, that king of master teachers, accompanied the All-knowing Gyelwa Sönam Gyatso to Tashilünpo, acting as his servant. And there he received many Dharma teachings, such as the practice permissions for the twenty-one forms of Tārā.[373]

Further, just prior to their journey to Mongolia, Sanggye Yeshe requested many teachings from the precious master Langmikpa,[374] the reincarnation of Jamyang Lekpai Lodrö, and from the great tantric master Rikpai Sengge (Rig-pa'i-seṅ-ge),[375] as well as from the All-knowing Sönam Gyatso himself. Likewise from countless other geshes—such as Hlatsün Sönam Pelsangpo (Lha-btsun bSod-nams-dpal-bzaṅ-po)—as well as other virtuous gurus and disciples who turned the powerful wheel of the Dharma, he listened to teachings, and he reached perfection in contemplating these. He also prostrated before many other kalyāṇamitras.

Then, when this Great Person reached the age of fifty-eight, in the winter of the Water Male Horse year called Natsok (sNa-tshogs), owing to the fervent request of Samdrub Tse (bSam-grub-rtse),[376] he once again ascended the throne at Gepel monastery. And there he turned the wheel of the Holy Dharma for another five years. Thereafter, he made his chief aim the care and protection of the Dharma Palace of Ensa. When Sanggye Yeshe relinquished the abbot's seat of Gepel, the Venerable Jampelyang from Neynying, the place blessed by many beings who were heirs to the holy lineage of Ārya Jigten Wangchuk ('Jig-rten-dbaṅ-phyug),[377] ascended the Gepel Dharma throne. After returning to Ensa, Sanggye Yeshe taught extensively, giving Dharma discourses on the profound and extensive sūtras and tantras to all those established in the natural state.[378]

Then the great Gyelwa Ensapa, thinking to further propagate the Oral Tradition of the Jamgön [Tsongkapa], once again took human form. Knowing this, Sanggye Yeshe invited to Ensa monastery the Venerable Losang Chökyi Gyeltsen.[379] Sanggye Yeshe then gave him the upasāka and novice vows, followed by a complete and extensive set of initiations, oral recitation blessings, and detailed practice instructions. Following additional initiations, Losang Chökyi Gyeltsen was installed on the fearless Lion Throne of the Dharma Palace at Ensa. Moreover, at that time, he was empowered to become the chief holder of the teachings of the Oral Tradition. Thereafter, he returned to the care of Tashilünpo.

When, at the age of nineteen, Losang Chökyi Gyeltsen was about to perform his college rounds at Tashilünpo and be tested in the Four Difficulties, he became ill with smallpox. Kedrub Sanggye Yeshe went there immediately, blessed him with numerous initiations, and helped him to study all the great traditions. At that time, he also gave him many mirror-like secret admonitions and concise, perfect, and complete advice—his final testament to him of this life[380]. Three days later, Sanggye Yeshe returned to Ensa monastery.

Then, in order to ensure that the detailed practice instructions of the Oral Tradition would not decline, Sanggye Yeshe himself composed many works: a prayer to and biography of the Venerable Losang Döndrub [Ensapa]; a method for practicing the guru yoga of the Profound Path; the outer, inner, and secret methods of guru yoga according to what was established by Je Rinpoche; a prayer praising the *Stages of the Path to Enlightenment* together with the appropriate guru yoga for it; numerous guru yoga methods established for many supernal deities; meditative cycles on the *Stages of the Path to Enlightenment* for persons of lesser ability; and a set of texts on Chöd.[381]

Finally, when he had accomplished all these goals for his disciples of this life, at the age of sixty-seven, on the twenty-fifth day of the tenth month[382] of the Iron Female Hare year called Bongbu (Boṅ-bu), he traveled to Rong Jamchen [monastery][383] thinking of other tasks remaining to be done. And there, whatever there was to be done, he did. Finally, on the fourteenth day of the eleventh month of the Iron Hare year of the tenth sexagenary cycle [1591], accompanied by many wondrous signs, he showed the manner of passing beyond suffering.

Thereafter, for a full seven days, the gods rained down flowers, which remained cool and fresh without diminishing. Then, as commanded by the Venerable Losang Chökyi Gyeltsen, Sanggye Yeshe's relics were returned to Ensa monastery, where they have remained until the present day.

Until the forty-ninth day [following his death][384] a special ceremony was conducted with a maṇḍala of Śrī Vajrabhairava by an assemblage of monks. The rites of offering to the lama[385] were performed continuously till late into the night. To the students at the colleges of Tashilünpo and Gepel monastery, abundant offerings were made by various sorts of patrons of those monasteries. Even a woman wine-seller, owing to her great faith, made offerings.[386]

Thus, Losang Chökyi Gyeltsen was completely satisfied.

Afterwards, when the place of cremation was opened up, many precious *ringsel* (riṅ-bsrel)[387] were found: one large one the size of a pea was found in the central core of ashes, and surrounding that were many others. Two clumps formed the shape of a heart, while others formed a tongue, eyes, and the central vein filled with the white and red *jangsem* (byaṅ-sems).[388] There was also a mound of ringsel resembling a brain. Numerous other very minute ones also appeared.

The First Panchen, Losang Chökyi Gyeltsen

The First Panchen, Losang Chökyi Gyeltsen

As for the First Panchen Lama, Losang Chökyi Gyeltsen, he was born in the town of Drukgya (Drug-brgya) in the region called Hlen (Lhan) of Tsangrong (gTsaṅ-roṅ). There, many greatly learned ones—such as Ba Yeshe Wangpo ('Ba' Ye-śes-dbaṅ-po)[389] and the incomparable Yakde Panchen (gYag-sde Paṇ-chen)[390]—had previously taken birth. Likewise, into a [family] lineage of many holy ones, in the Iron Male Horse year [1570],[391] to a father called Künga Öser (Kun-dga'-'od-zer)[392] and a mother called Tsogyel (mTsho-rgyal), he was born accompanied by numerous incomprehensibly wondrous signs. As was advised by lamas and gods, he was given the name Chögyel Pelden Sangpo (Chos-rgyal dPal-ldan-bzaṅ-po).

From early childhood, he learned by heart and without effort various prayers and recitations such as the *Heart Sūtra*[393] and the *Mañjuśrī-nāma-saṅgiti*,[394] simply by hearing them once.

Now, moreover, the great Gyelwa Ensapa himself had formerly admonished his Rabjampa [Sanggye Yeshe] not to worry too much since, in order to further propagate the Dharma, he would soon come again to that place. Kedrub Sanggye Yeshe knew also, owing to a dream, when Gyelwa Ensapa had reincarnated at Drukgya. Even so, in order to be absolutely certain, the Venerable Langmikpa Chökyi Gyeltsen,[395] who possessed the supernormal faculty of "seeing arisings and passings away," was asked [by Sanggye Yeshe] to investigate whether this newborn prince of Drukgya was in fact the true incarnation of the great Gyelwa Ensapa. The Venerable Langmikpa responded: "Even though this son of Drukgya had to advance one lifetime, he is without doubt Ensapa's reincarnation. Further, there ought to be a match between his name and mine, so he should be named Chökyi Gyeltsen." In this way, the great Gyelwa Ensapa's reincarnation was verified. As was advised by the Venerable Langmikpa, the boy was named Chökyi Gyeltsen when he was ordained, and, beyond that, Losang was also added.

At five years of age, he memorized the ritual texts of the Seven Sūgatas and performed his pujas daily, never missing any important occasion. During this time, the learned Sanggye Yeshe stayed at Drukgya during most autumns, giving instruction [to this young one]. In addition, he conferred many initiations upon him: a long-life initiation; the complete discourses on the Six-armed Mahākāla; many practice permissions for the stages of practicing Hayagrīva;[396] an oral recitation blessing for Tapö (rTa-pod) and for the three lineage protectors,[397] the goddesses Tārā,[398] Vijaya,[399] and Namjom (rNam-'joms); practice permissions for many other Dharma protectors; and numerous other oral recitation blessings and empowering initiations.

[The young incarnation] also received oral recitation blessings for many sūtras, such as the hundred-thousand verse *Prajñāpāramitā-sūtra*[400] and others, from countless other kalyāṇamitras. His grandfather and his elder brother also instructed him, especially in those teachings associated with the protectors of the tantric lineages of the noble Hayagrīva, as well as the precepts of the lineage of the Great Righteous One, Rahula.[401] In addition, they gave him extensive oral recitation blessings for other precepts and a cycle of meditative practices and practice permissions for properly propitiating Shanglön (Źaṅ-blon).[402] Occasionally he also received oral recitation blessings and empowering initiations associated with the corpus of texts on medicine, such as the oral recitation blessing for the *Four Tantras* [of medical science].[403]

When he was seven years old, two new molars[404] grew in his mouth. According to a popular saying, "When a wisdom tooth is grown, one has passed half one's life." Having heard that saying, and thinking these two new teeth to be "wisdom teeth," Chökyi Gyeltsen became convinced that if this were truly the case, he would doubtless die very soon. He thereby, without instigation from outside, became conscious regarding [the meaning of] death. Likewise, the meaning of impermanence was born in his mental continuum.[405]

Thereafter, when he reached the age of thirteen, in the Water Male Horse year [1582], on the tenth day of the Month of Miracles,[406] he left his home and journeyed to the Dharma Palace at Ensa monastery; and on the thirteenth day of that month, at the feet of Sanggye Yeshe, he was ordained and given the name Losang Chökyi Gyeltsen. During the summer session, Sanggye Yeshe instructed him in a number of explanatory commentaries on the *Stages of the Path*. Then, during the autumn session, he gave him the complete oral recitation blessings for all the root commentaries of the Supreme [Mahāyāna] Path, the *Collected Works* of Gyeysey (rGyas-sras),[407] the *Stages of the Path* according to Sharawa (Śa-ra-ba),[408] and the extensive and abridged versions of the *Lamyik* of Jowo [Atīśa],[409] as well as for the books of the Kadampa [school][410] together with their branch commentaries.

In the Water Female Sheep year, when he was fourteen years old, while propitiating the goddess Sarasvati,[411] he successfully generated a vision of the White-faced Sarasvati. From the very heart of that Sarasvati there then came forth a [second] two-armed blue Sarasvati holding in her hand a ripe new fruit, which appeared to be the most precious of wish-granting objects. Seeing it, Losang Chökyi Gyeltsen offered absolutely everything to that most sublime goddess. Thereupon, from that fruit itself, which was held in the goddess's left hand, there arose a red Brahmanī. This red one took the fruit along with the tray [on which it rested] and offered these to this venerable one. He greatly enjoyed that offering, and from that time he showed the signs of having opened the door to the treasury of intelligence, vast as the sky.

From the age of fourteen to eighteen—except for those times when he was required to go to various places to perform ritual observances—he remained in the presence of Sanggye Yeshe and received countless teachings: oral recitation blessings for the inconceivably great religious discourses of the All-knowing Butön (Bu-ston),[412] oral recitation blessings for many works on mental development techniques,[413] a root commentary on the great *Rinpung Volume*,[414] and the root commentary for the collection of texts known as the *Blue Books*.[415] Furthermore, he received all the oral recitation blessings for the *Great Stages of the Path* and for most of the famed extensive religious treatises composed by that great master's [Tsongkapa's] chief spiritual sons, the Venerable Gendündrub, Baso Chöje, and others, as well as for a few of the famous so-called *Four Combined Commentarial Texts* on Guhyasamāja.[416] And he gained confidence with respect to all that he heard and all the instructions he had received, whether explanatory commentaries on the *Stages of the Path* or the two tantric stages of Generation and Completion. Then, in the autumn, he received the practice permissions for the set of the several hundred meditative practices of Nartang, the practice permissions for the twenty-one forms of Tārā, the practice permissions for the four [chief] deities of the Kadam,[417] the complete and extensive oral recitation blessings and empowering initiations associated with the *Vajramālā*[418] and the *Mitra Gyatsa* (Mi-tra brGya-rtsa),[419] as well as oral recitation blessings for various other sacred texts.

Thereafter, on the thirteenth day of the first half of the eleventh month, he journeyed to the great monastic university Tashilünpo and there entered the college of Tösam Ling. Seeing his manner and his gracious and generous offerings, all the ācāryas and teachers of Tashilünpo were greatly pleased with him and responded with extreme gratitude. And immediately a great desire to hear and reflect upon the Dharma according to the manner of this particular college arose in this venerable one's heart.

He began his studies under the ācārya Peljor Gyatso (dPal-'byor-rgya-mtsho), taking up first the science of astrological calculation. Many exceptional occurrences were associated with his arrival at Tösam Ling. For example, once it happened that in his sleeping quarters a yoginī appeared and held up before him a skull-cup filled with milk. Smiling, Chökyi Gyeltsen expressed the desire to practice the cycle of left-handed practices of the Mother Tantras.[420] Holding up the vessel in front of this venerable one's body, she offered its contents to him and moved a little closer. Having seen this with his other eye,[421] he began to think about what kind of yoginī this was, whereupon she disappeared.

Thereafter, having made a start with the common and general subjects such as calculations and so forth, he returned once again to Ensa monastery, his summer residence. There, Sanggye Yeshe taught him the Six Dharmas of Vajrapāṇi and gave him oral recitation blessings for the *Collected Works* of the Lord of Dharma Barawa ('Ba'-ra-ba)[422] as well as for the famed eight great explanatory commentaries of the extraordinary Oral Tradition of Je Tsongkapa, together with numerous practice permissions and empowering initiations. And showing extremely quick intelligence, Chökyi Gyeltsen learned them all. That autumn, after receiving instruction and oral recitation blessings for the *Songs* of the Venerable Mila,[423] he returned to Tashilünpo. There he took part in the arrangements for the great logic debates involving all the most prestigious Dharma colleges of both scripture and logic. In all the colleges [of Tashilünpo] great enthusiasm and effort was expended on these logical disputations, and from every corner the sound of weighty clapping, as palms met palms, could be heard. And it seemed that from between the fingers of those clapping hands Utpala[424] flowers sprang.

Following that, in the Earth Female Ox year at the beginning of the time of the great [fourth] month,[425] returning to Ensa monastery, Sanggye Yeshe kindly gave him the initiation into Cakrasaṃvara using a colored sand maṇḍala. Later, leaving [once again his primary guru], Chökyi Gyeltsen returned to Tashilünpo.

At that time a smallpox epidemic swept throughout the country, and Chökyi Gyeltsen also contracted the disease. He then performed breathing exercises[426] continuously. When Sanggye Yeshe heard that Chökyi Gyeltsen had fallen ill, he went immediately to Tashilünpo. Staying there for three days, he blessed Chökyi Gyeltsen and then, after giving him some final words of advice, returned to Ensa monastery on the third day.

Then, as it was the strong tradition at Tösam Ling that this precious lama [Chökyi Gyeltsen] should sit for examination on the *Pramāṇavārttika*, he agreed to do so. And so, in the midst of a sea of learned ones, he sat for the examination on the *Pramāṇavārttika*, and the thunderous sounds of his flawless logic made it seem as if the resplendent Dharmakīrti[427] himself had come again. In this way, he completely captivated the mind of every scholar there.

Then, after hearing of the "passing over" of Sanggye Yeshe, he went to Ensa and oversaw the funeral. [For the monastery], he commissioned a new *chöten* (mchod-brten)[428] for outside and had statues made for the inside. In this way he accomplished extensive services for his guru's funeral.

Thereafter he returned to Tashilünpo and took up the study of the traditions of Mādhyamika; and here again his unhindered intelligence with regard to both scriptural recitation and logic completely overwhelmed and subdued all dispute. And it was as if the great ācārya Candrakīrti[429] had appeared again in this region of snowy mountains.

Then, in the Iron Hare year called *Drozün* (Gro-zun), on the third "white" day of the month, in view of the Banner of Victory of his residence, in the presence of Panchen Damchö Yarpelwa (Pan-chen Dam-chos-yar-'phel-ba)[430] as abbot, with Rinchen Peljor Gyatso (Rin-chen dPal-'byor-rgya-mtsho) as senior instructor, and Panchen Hlawang Lodrö (Pan-chen Lha-dbaṅ-blo-gros) as confidant, he knelt in the midst of a countless number of faithful members of the saṅgha and received the full ordination of a gelong. Then it was as if the Teacher, Lord Buddha[431] himself, had come again to this snowy region.

At the end of the autumn of that same year, he traveled towards Central Tibet. There, in the presence of such sacred statues as the two of Jo,[432] with true sincerity of body and mind, he offered very pure prayers for the spread of the Dharma. As a result, many unique and blessed signs occurred. Thereafter, he journeyed to Riwo Genden.[433] There, at the request of such holy ones as the precious throneholder of Ganden and others of that district, in the midst of a gathering of many thousands of monks and laypersons, he sat for examinations in the Four Great Difficulties. And the force of this great one's intelligence could not be equaled by anyone. Thus he became victorious over all sides, his fame covering every corner of the world.

While at that place, from the Venerable Namkai Tsenchen (Nam-mkha'i-mtshan-can), he received inconceivable teachings such as explanatory commentaries, oral recitation blessings, and empowering initiations for the secret tantras associated with the "armed" deities. He also received from this lama abridged teachings on some initiations and on the *Drelchen* ('Grel-chen),[434] as well as the abridged and extensive empowering initiations for the principal Kālacakra. Next, from the vajra-holding ācārya, Gendün Gyeltsen (dGe-'dun-rgyal-mtshan),[435] he received a commentary and oral recitation blessing for *Düpai Drelpa Shidrak* (Dus-pa'i 'Grel-pa Źi-sbrags). In addition, he received empowering initiations, as well as many other oral recitation blessings, for miscellaneous sections of the *Collected Works* of the Venerable Gendün Gyatso.

From the precious ācārya Namgyel Pelsang (rNam-rgyal-dpal-bzaṅ) he listened to many teachings, receiving the oral recitation blessing for a commentary called the *Clear Light of the Five Stages of Lord Sahaja* and other tantric instructions. And from the great Bodhisattva, the throneholder Damchö Pelbar (Dam-chos-dpal-'bar),[436] he received the empowering initiation of Trönak (Khros-nag),[437] the empowering initiation into the practices of Chöd that "open the vault of the sky," and other extensive cycles on Chöd like the oral recitation blessing for the three cycles called *The River-crossing by Which the Fortunate Enter into the Traditions of Chöd.*[438] Thereafter, for all those who concerned themselves with Dharma, he fulfilled their desires by offering the nectar of the teachings extensively. After that he made a pilgrimage[439] to particular places at Yerpa (Yer-pa) and at Tsel Gungtang (Tshal Guṅ-thaṅ).[440] He then returned to Ensa monastery.

There, in the summer, many renowned kalyāṇamitras, lamas, ācāryas, and Kachu (dKa'-bcu) Rabjampas[441] attended his Dharma discourses and listened to his explanatory commentary on the *Abridged Stages of the Path,*[442] which he spoke to all assembled there as if truly from the heart. He offered extensive and profound commentary, ornamented by well-chosen quotations from numerous Indian sūtras and śastras. And on many he conferred the ranks of ācārya and Rabjampa.

One of his students during this time was an ācārya from Gomang college known by the title Shungkang Rabjampa. He said, referring to Chökyi Gyeltsen, "Even though I have received many Dharma teachings from many lamas in Central Tibet and Tsang, including even Ganden's throneholder himself; and even though I am myself extremely hardheaded, all of your teachings have so helped my mind that a supreme reverence for you has been born in me that formerly was not possible for any others."

Then, having constructed many new religious supports[443] at Ensa monastery, Chökyi Gyeltsen became troubled and fed up with the activities of this life. Discussing the matter with his personal attendant, Losang, he decided to enter immediately into complete retreat. During breaks in his meditation sessions, he read scriptures, and for about six or seven months he worked hard to accumulate merits. He felt that if he could continue [his retreat] he would no doubt reach the end of the path. An exceedingly great and sorrowful renunciation entered his heart during that time, and as this feeling continued it developed into a desire to equal in accomplishment, and in this life, the deeds of the Venerable Milarepa (Mi-la-ras-pa) and Shavaripa (Śa-ba-ri-pa).[444] Once, during this time, there appeared in the space in front of him [a vision of] the Venerable Tsongkapa, who said:

> In order to benefit oneself as well as others,
> Do not be satisfied by hearing [alone].

A mind that would attain the stages[445]
Is not satisfied by [merely] hearing.

Shortly afterwards, while liberated from the limits of his body through the path of sleep,[446] and after receiving infinite oral recitation blessings and empowering initiations, he saw in detail all the root commentaries of the *Abhisamayālaṃkāra, Uttaratantra, Prajñā-mūla (Madhyamakakārikā), Ratnāvalī, Yuktiṣaṣṭika, Suhṛllekha, Catuḥśataka, Madhyamakāvatāra, Śikṣā-samuccaya, Bodhicaryāvatāra*, the *Root Text of (the Mahāyāna Tradition of) Lojong* (*bLo-sbyoṅ*), the *Root Tantra of Guhyasamāja*, the *Root Tantra of Cakrasaṃvara*, the *Hevajra-tantra, Kālacakra-laghu-tantra*, the *Pañcakrama of Nāgārjuna*, and others.[447] He then recited and memorized each text in the series. In this way did Je Rinpoche bless him.

Later, at a gathering of some ten kalyāṇamitras, such as the famed abbot, Rin-gyampa (Rin-rgyam-pa),[448] he received many teachings, which finalized his studies. Then he received the empowering initiation for the practice of Cakrasaṃvara in the tradition of Luipa. Also, from Abbot Ringyampa of that great assembly, he received countless other profound instructions, such as the empowering initiation of Nāro Ḍākinī.

Then, in order to take on the conduct of a strict ascetic, he subjected himself to numerous forms of the very strict practice called "taking only essences,"[449] and he attained excellence in meditating on the artifice of the body and the activity of its various winds. Then, in order to enrich these practices even more, in the autumn of that year he journeyed to Drakgya hermitage and there expended great effort for several days, abandoning all adornments and adopting only the cotton covering prescribed by the Kagyü tradition.[450] Thereafter, his ability to perform virtuous activities for his disciples greatly increased. He returned to Ensa, and there, as well as at other places such as Gangchen (Gaṅs-can),[451] he caused a rain of the Holy Dharma to shower down upon them. In between teachings, he passed his time meditating in isolated retreats near Ensa and amidst the snow mountains.

Then, having been strongly requested to come to Je Gendündrub's see at Tashilünpo, in the Iron Mouse year on the third day of the twelfth month, at the age of thirty-one, he mounted the Fearless Lion Throne amidst an ocean of learned ones and was installed as reigning abbot.[452] He thereafter brought forth a continuous great shower of Dharma teachings.

During the fall, after journeying to Gangchen, he gave ordination to a great many persons gathered there and caused the great Wheel of Dharma to be set in motion. Next, going to the Prayer Festival at Tropu (Khro-phu), he planted the seeds of liberation in countless laypersons and performed many other extensive deeds for the sake of the Buddha's teachings.

From the third "white" day of the Horse month until the sixteenth day, he sponsored the Great Prayer Festival [for the first time in Tsang] at Tashilünpo.[453] For that occasion he commissioned many images, statues, and other incomparable religious and ritual objects. Following that, the All-knowing Yönten Gyatso[454] arrived from the north [from Mongolia]. For many inner and outer reasons, Losang Chökyi Gyeltsen directed every abbot, teacher, and student of Tashilünpo to meet Yönten Gyatso's party.[455] Thereafter, Chökyi Gyeltsen himself, from his own possessions and wealth, provided extensive offerings and entertainment for all who were gathered there. At Drepung also, he provided tea and entertainment for all the monks. At Tashilünpo, all the ācāryas were additionally offered monetary support.

For some time afterwards, Chökyi Gyeltsen remained in Central Tibet. Then the Victorious All-knowing Yönten Gyatso requested that he come to stay at Drepung[456] during the winter. Once there, Chökyi Gyeltsen brought about the general elevation of beings who were stationed at a lower level, instructing them in the principal basic subjects. To those who were more advanced, like the Kachu Rabjampas, he gave extensive oral recitation blessings for the root texts of the Four Great Difficulties. Moreover, to Gyelwa Yönten Gyatso and to those who served him as teachers, he gave profound explanatory commentaries, detailed practice instructions, practice permissions, and empowering initiations for such practices as the Two Traditions of the Red and Black. And the manner of his instruction was like pouring water from one vessel into another.

Then, going on pilgrimage, he traveled from Möndröl (sMon-grol) in the south to Radreng (Rva-sgreṅ)[457] in the north, and he gave profound teachings to whoever gathered along the way. Once again joining Yönten Gyatso, he traveled to Gyel Metok Tang (rGyal-me-tog-thaṅ).[458] As they traveled, Chökyi Gyeltsen made it his chief purpose to accomplish two goals: to give continuous detailed practice instructions, oral recitation blessings, and empowering initiations to Gyelwa Yönten Gyatso and to make offering prayers to all the sacred places of pilgrimage along the way. In particular, at the place where the great Jampel Gyatso, that chief nourisher of the Ganden practice lineage, had practiced, and at the Pangsa monastery at Meldro [where Jampel Gyatso's relics were enshrined], he made extensive offerings.[459] Likewise, at Wölka Chölung, where Je Rinpoche and his group of eight retreatants had meditated, he offered sincere prayers. At many places in Dakpo (Dvags-po) he prayed from his heart. At Gyel Metok Tang, when he had offered prayers to the goddess Pelden Hlamo, many wondrous signs occurred. At whatever place they stopped, there and then he gave to all the faithful gathered there the nectar of the Dharma according to each one's abilities, and he did his best to sow the seeds of liberation for all of them.

Then, returning once again to Tashilünpo, he again gave oral recitation blessings and empowering initiations to all those gathered there. Continuing to sponsor such miraculous events as the Great Prayer Festival, he then traveled again to Central Tibet. There, during the full-moon festival, in a dimly lit tiny chamber of the palace of Ganden, he constructed a colored-sand maṇḍala of Śrī Kālacakra, and there he gave the complete empowering initiation of Kālacakra, together with the necessary supporting instructions, to the All-knowing Yönten Gyatso.

Thereafter, for a while, he went on pilgrimage, accompanied by a group of ācāryas, to the southern regions of Hloka (Lho-kha). He then returned to Tashilünpo and carried on his teaching there. Sensing some obstruction, he went into strict retreat for twenty-one days. Then, traveling to Chenlung (gCen-luṅ) during mid-autumn, he, along with many hundreds of others, practiced fasting.[460] They also performed other "white" Dharma practices such as giving up the taking of life. Thereafter, he constructed and offered many supports for body, speech, and mind. He also gave whatever was needed by members of the saṅgha. Then, at Tashilünpo, he taught the lineage texts such as those associated with the great empowering initiation for Bhairava. After that, the All-knowing Yönten Gyatso was invited to Tashilünpo and traveled to Tsang. All the students and ācāryas of this great monastic institution went out to meet the great party [of Gyelwa Yönten Gyasto], consisting of hundreds of horses fantastically arrayed. That meeting [between Chökyi Gyeltsen and the Dalai Lama] was like the meeting of father and son. The gods took part also, showering down flowers continually and providing music as if with great drums. For just over two months, Chökyi Gyeltsen provided well for all those gathered there. Afterward, at Tashilünpo, he entered another strict retreat.

Following the retreat, with renewed energy, he once again undertook great construction projects. He had new stūpas built and completely refurbished the retreat dwellings surrounding Tashilünpo, making their appearance so excellent as to invite the actual coming again of such great meditators as the great yogi Chökyi Dorje and the great siddha Saraha.[461] Moreover, he established a tantric college at Tashilünpo. Such were the exceedingly pure and genuine offerings that this great one made.

In the Iron Female Pig year, after going to Lhasa for the Great Prayer Festival and giving abundant teachings there, he once again returned to Tashilünpo. Thereafter, Gyelwa Yönten Gyatso invited him to Drepung; and to the government monastic official Gong Tulku (Goṅ sPrul-sku),[462] to

Yönten Gyatso, and to many lamas from Sera and Drepung, when the valleys were encircled by sunbeams, he gave the complete empowering initiation of *Vajramālā.* Later, he also gave much instruction to other practitioners in that region before returning to Tashilünpo.

In the Water Male Mouse year, having been invited, on the nineteenth day of the eighth month he journeyed towards Hlomön (Lho-mon) [Bhutan].[463] After visiting Taklung (rTag-luṅ), Padro (sPa-gro), and Timpu (Tim-phu), he stopped at Darkar (Dar-dkar). Here he offered instruction and material offerings to countless numbers of lamas. In addition, he gave many profound explanatory commentaries and empowering initiations, such as those for Bhairava and Śrī Guhyasamāja, and he thereby greatly extended the base of the Dharma in all directions. Through these kinds of activities, he did much for the spread of the Dharma and for the benefit of sentient beings. Then he returned to Tibet.

At that time, there was much trouble in both Central Tibet and Tsang and much shifting between high and low. For some there was much real suffering, and for others this very suffering was a cause for happiness. Seeing this, Chökyi Gyeltsen felt great sadness and prayed: "Namo Guru Mañjughoṣa ya! Above all, may [those of] the spiritual lineages transcend this evil!"

Then, gradually, he moved on towards Tashilünpo, and there, once more, after providing extensive offerings to the congregation, he also taught extensively. Thereafter he was again requested by the All-knowing Yönten Gyatso to come to Lhasa and lead the Great Prayer Festival. From the Water Ox year to the Earth Horse year, he served as leader of the Festival. When the Prayer Festival of the Ox year ended, he gave ordination to about forty geshes such as Tulku Sönam Gelek Pelsangpo (sPrul-sku bSod-nams-dge-legs-dpal-bzaṅ-po)[464] and others from Sera, Drepung, and the Upper and Lower Tantric Colleges. Afterwards, to a great gathering at Drepung, he gave the complete instructions on Mahākāla, as well as oral recitation blessings for the common and uncommon *Be'u Bum* [books of the Kadampa]. Then he returned to Tashilünpo, and for all the Rabjampas gathered at the Tantric College there, he established a new lecture series on the *Explanatory Tantras* of Śrī Kālacakra.

Then, in the Wood Male Tiger year [1614], he journeyed to Lhasa to once again lead the Great Prayer Festival. There he continued the tradition of the Jamgön Lama [Tsongkapa] by giving a detailed explication of the *Jātakas.* At this time, with Chökyi Gyeltsen serving as abbot, the All-knowing Yönten Gyatso was ordained. Countless other prominent ones also took ordination at this time, such as the Tongkor Tulku Jamyang Gyatso (sToṅ-'khor sPrul-sku 'Jam-dbyaṅs-rgya-mtsho) and the Kyishö Shabdrung Tendzin Losang Gyatso (sKyid-śod Źabs-druṅ bsTan-'dzin-blo-bzaṅ-rgya-mtsho), as well as many other hundreds of lamas. Afterwards, Chökyi Gyeltsen returned to Tashilünpo and gave the complete empowering initiations for *Vajramālā* and *Mitra Gyatsa.* Later, the Dharma community at Hlüntse (Lhun-rtse) invited him there, and he gave the practice permissions and empowering initiations for many Protectors of the Dharma and for the deities Guhyasamāja, Cakrasaṃvara, and Vajrabhairava.

Then, in the twelfth month of the Fire Snake year [1617], the All-knowing master Yönten Gyatso entered into the Dharmadhātu[465] without warning. Chökyi Gyeltsen continued as leader of the Great Prayer Festival. As soon as it ended, he went to Radreng, and for a little over a month he went into strict retreat at its upper monastery. Thereafter, returning to Drepung, he assumed the Dharma reins of both Drepung and Sera.[466] [Translation hiatus][467]

During those times many troublesome changes were taking place, and, owing to these, many lamas and other great men were being deprecated. In the year of the Wood Hog [1635] things were particularly bad,[468] with numerous inner and outer signs of trouble. Most of Chökyi Gyeltsen's disciples and all the monks at Tashilünpo therefore asked him to perform a long-life ceremony for himself. Even though they requested him to do this and to perform a ritual for banishing evil forces, Chökyi Gyeltsen—just as in the biographies of the great siddhas of the past—refused. Instead, equalizing the eight mundane concerns, he told his followers not to worry. Whatever good or bad was to be his lot, he said, he would bear it without performing such rituals for his own welfare. To demonstrate his abandonment of the eight mundane concerns, he sang this verse:

> Homage to the Three Jewels!
> Holding on to that which leads to no temptation,
> The Three Jewels and the Venerable Lama
> Residing in the lotus of one's heart,
> May all sides and all beings
> Realize their wishes.

During this time in the Land of Snow, the Mongolians were fighting with [the Tibetan noble lords] the Tsangpas, the Dri ('Bris) were at war with the Pak (Phags),[469] and it was as though the world of human beings had been transformed into the realm of Shinje (gŚin-rje).[470] Things were that bad. There was much fighting and killing and impoverishment of all sorts, so much suffering, like the rupturing of a lake. People were unable to distinguish higher from lower or enemies from friends. In particular, the shameless ones of the time—especially those who had entered the door of Dharma in the guise of religious beings—were completely carried away by the evil forces of the five forms of degeneracy.[471] Witnessing this drama played at the edge of the fearful pit of a fiery hell and caused by those whose minds had become intoxicated with the drink of rivalry, deceit, and envy, Chökyi Gyeltsen sued many times for reconciliation with humble statements and humble songs.[472] [During this time there was much trouble for Tibet due to internal strife and threatening events in the neighboring countries of China and Mongolia. At one point, owing to an aggressive attack on Tibet by Mongolian troops, the Tibetan army drew up for battle on Chakpori (lCags-pho-ri) hill, but Chökyi Gyeltsen negotiated a settlement and, after paying a ransom, won peace].[473]

[Thereafter, the Fifth Dalai Lama arose as a strong ruler], and as if pouring water from one vessel into another, Chökyi Gyeltsen gave the teachings on all the stages of the paths of sūtra and tantra to [the Dalai Lama] Ngawang Losang Gyatso,[474] and he empowered him to be the holder of the complete teachings of Je Rinpoche. Chökyi Gyeltsen also added to his own followers, converting Chamdo Pakpa Hla (Chab-mdo 'Phags-pa-lha) and teaching the Dharma to many others. And it was as if Tsongkapa himself had come once again. For the sake of his disciples,[475] he also composed numerous treatises.[476] Such was this great one's incomparable and long-lasting kindness.

And at the end, at the age of ninety-three, during the eleventh rabjung, in the Water Male Tiger year [1662],[477] having completed the aims of his existence, he entered into the Dharmadhātu.

Part III

The Appendices

Appendix I

The Gelukpa Mahāmudrā Lineage

(According to the devotional text called *The Prayer, with Supplement, to the Lineage Lamas of the Ganden Oral Tradition of Mahāmudrā*)

1. Vajradhara Dorje Chang (rDo-rje-'chaṅ)
2. Mañjuśrī Pakpa Jampel ('Phags-pa 'Jam-dpal)
3. Jetsün Losang Drakpa (Tsongkapa) (rJe-btsun bLo-bzaṅ-grags-pa [Tsoṅ-kha-pa])

*4. Tokden Jampel Gyatso (rTogs-ldan 'Jam-dpal-rgya-mtsho)
*5. Baso Chökyi Gyeltsen (Ba-so Chos-kyi-rgyal-mtshan)
*6. Drubchen Chökyi Dorje (Grub-chen Chos-kyi-rdo-rje)
*7. Losang Dönyö Drubpa (Ensapa) (bLo-bzaṅ Don-yod-grub-pa [dbEn-sa-pa])
*8. Kedrub Sanggye Yeshe (mKhas-grub Saṅs-rgyas-ye-śes)
*9. Jetsün (Panchen) Losang Chögyen (Losang Chökyi Gyeltsen) (rJe-btsun [Panchen] bLo-bzaṅ-chos-rgyan [bLo-bzaṅ-chos-kyi-rgyal-mtshan])

10. Drubchen Gendün Gyeltsen (Grub-chen dGe-'dun-rgyal-mtshan)
11. Drubpai Gyeltsen Dzinpa (Grub-pa'i-rgyal-mtshan-'dzin-pa)
12. Gyüchen Könchok Gyeltsen (rGyud-chen dKon-mchog-rgyal-mtshan)
13. Jetsün (Panchen) Losang Yeshe (rJe-btsun [Panchen] bLo-bzaṅ-ye-śes)
14. Jetsün Losang Trinley (rJe-btsun bLo-bzaṅ-'phrin-las)
15. Drubchok Losang Namgyel (Grub-mchog bLo-bzaṅ-rnam-rgyal)
16. Drinchen Yeshe Tsenchen (Tsechok Ling Yongdzin Yeshe Gyeltsen) (Drin-can Ye-śes-mtshan-can [Tshe-mchog-gliṅ Yoṅs-'dzin Ye-śes-gryal-mtshan])
17. Jetsün Ngawang Jampa (rJe-btsun Ṅag-dbaṅ-byams-pa)
18. Panchen Pelden Yeshe (Pan-chen dPal-ldan-ye-śes)
19. Kedrub Ngawang Dorje (mKhas-grub Ṅag-dbaṅ-rdo-rje)

20. Jetsün Dharmabhadra (rJe-btsun Dharma Bha-dra)
21. Yangchen Drubpai Dorje (dbYaṅs-can Grub-pa'i-rdo-rje)
22. Kedrub Tendzin Tsöndrü (mKhas-grub bsTan-'dzin-brtson-'grus)
23. Losang Tsöndrü Gyeltsen (bLo-bzaṅ brTson-grus-rgyal-mtshan)
24. Losang Dönyö Drubpa (bLo-bzaṅ Don-yod-grub-pa)
25. Jetsün Gelek Gyatso (rJe-btsun dGe-legs-rgya-mtsho)
26. Drinchen Ngawang Jampa (Drin-can Ṅag-dbaṅ-byams-pa)
27. Kechok Jigme Wangpo (mKhas-mchog 'Jigs-med-dbaṅ-po)
28. Jetsün Tenpa Drönme (rJe-btsun bsTan-pa'-sgron-me)
29. Jetsün Könchok Gyeltsen (rJe-btsun dKon-mchog-rgyal-mtshan)
30. Drubchen Ngödrub Rabten (Grub-chen dṄos-grub-rab-brtan)
31. Yongdzin Gendün Gyatso (Yoṅs-'dzin dGe-'dun-rgya-mtsho)
32. Pelden Tenpai Nyima (dPal-ldan bsTan-pa'i-ñi-ma)
33. Jetsün Trinley Gyatso (rJe-btsun 'Phrin-las-rgya-mtsho) [Pabongka Rinpoche]
34. Drinchen Losang Yeshe (Drin-can bLo-bzaṅ-ye-śes) [H.H. Trijang Rinpoche]
35. Pelwai Trinley Da-me (sPel-ba'i 'Phrin-las-zla-med) [H.H. Ling Rinpoche]
36. Drinchen Tsawai Lama (Drin-can rTsa-ba'i-bla-ma) [one's own root guru]

* Life stories contained in this study

Appendix II

Praises and Supplication to the Gelukpa Mahāmudrā Lineage

Homage to the Great Seal!
You are the Primordial Buddha, chief of all Buddha lineages,
Dweller in the palatial mansion of the spontaneously created Three Bodies.
I bow at your precious feet, great Vajradhara, all-pervading lord.

Refrain:
By generating a mind of compassion and loving-kindness,
And by completely severing the continuum that clings to holding a "self,"
May I be blessed to quickly attain the highest state
Of Mahāmudrā, [through] the path of total integration.

You are the father of all the Conquerors of the Three Times,
A Holy Field of Wisdom covering the earth's ten directions.
I bow at your feet, all-wise Ārya Mañjuśrī.

Refrain…

Here in the snowy provinces of this northern country,
You are a second Buddha of the Buddha's Doctrine.
I bow at your feet, Reverend Losang Drakpa.

Refrain…

You are principal among those holding the teachings of the practice lineage
Of Tsongkapa, great son of Mañjugoṣa.
I bow at your feet, Tokden Jampel Gyatso.

Refrain…

After opening the treasury of counsel of the Oral Tradition,
You matured well the fortunate candidates.
I bow at your feet, Baso Chökyi Gyeltsen.

Refrain…

After reaching the end of praxis of the two [tantric] stages,
You attained the body of a deathless vidyadhāra.
I bow at your feet, Great Siddha Chökyi Dorje.

Refrain...

Having completely shed the bonds of the eight mundane concerns,
You held high the banner of victory of the teaching of Absolute Truth.
I bow at your feet, Losang Dönyö Drubpa.

Refrain...

Your dance of saffron robes guides all transmigratory beings
Into the delightful palace of the Three Bodies.
I bow at your feet, Scholar-Siddha Sanggye Yeshe.

Refrain...

Knowing everything with respect to the teachings of Gyelwa Je Losang,
You are indistinguishable from that very Refuge.
I bow at your feet, Reverend Losang Chögyen.

Refrain...

Having abridged into one essential meaning all the Buddha's speech in the sūtras, tantras, and commentaries,
You achieved perfection in putting these into practice.
I bow at your feet, Great Siddha Gendün Gyeltsen.

Refrain...

Owing to great exertion, you experienced unique enjoyment
And tasted the very essence of Je Rinpoche's teaching.
I bow at your feet, accomplished Gyeltsen Dzinpa.

Refrain...

As master expositor to the fortunate candidates,
You gave the richness of the nectar of the Dharma that is profound and vast.
I bow at your feet, Great Tantrika Könchok Gyeltsen.

Refrain...

For the welfare of beings as well as the Dharma,
You reincarnated again like the Venerable Losang Chökyi Gyeltsen himself.
I bow at your feet, Reverend Losang Yeshe.

Refrain...

You achieved mastery of the profound path of the Oral Tradition
And were blessed by Lord Buddha himself.
I bow at your feet Reverend Losang Trinley.

Refrain...

You reached the limits of putting into practice the essential meaning
of the Oral Tradition of Je Tsongkapa.
I bow at your feet, Great Siddha Losang Namgyel.

Refrain...

With great kindness, you correctly elucidated
All the essential precepts of Je Rinpoche's Oral Tradition.
I bow at your feet, kind Yeshe Tsenchen.

Refrain...

You propagated everywhere, in central and border lands alike,
The essence of the errorless teaching of the complete Path.
I bow at your feet, Reverend Ngawang Jampa.

Refrain...

You matured, by means of the Dharma, all of Tibet and China
While sporting the saffron robes of the Primordial Buddha.
I bow at your feet, Panchen Pelden Yeshe.

Refrain...

You arrived at the accomplishment of single-pointed concentration
On the complete and extensive good path of the sūtras and tantras.
I bow at your feet, wise yogi Ngawang Dorje.

Refrain...

O Protector, you clarified Lord Buddha's teaching
through verbal explanation and composition
With regard to steadfast knowledge, like a Second Buddha.
I bow at your feet, Reverend Dharma Bhadra.

Refrain...

Your superior knowledge of the profound and vast Dharma is like Mañjuśrī's,
And your eye of inconceivably great compassion is never closed.
I bow at your feet, Yangchen Drubpai Dorje.

Refrain...

After perfecting the yoga of bliss-voidness,
You arrived at the victorious stage of total integration.
I bow at your feet, Scholar-Siddha Tendzin Tsöndrü.

Refrain…

After attaining perfection in the understanding of the profound path,
You upheld the banner of victory of the teachings of commentary
and practice.
I bow at your feet, Losang Tsöndrü Gyeltsen.

Refrain…

As holder of the essence of the teachings of the three higher trainings,
You bear no trace whatever of the stains of moral faults.
I bow at your feet, Losang Dönyö Drubpa.

Refrain…

You reincarnated again, showing the dance of a saffron-robed monk
Like the Second Buddha himself, Je Losang Drakpa.
I bow at your feet, Reverend Gelek Gyatso.

Refrain…

You clarified for innumerable fortunate ones
The treasury of the extensive Dharma's vast and profound paths.
I bow at your feet, kind Ngawang Jampa.

Refrain…

You are skilled in clarifying the Noble Path, free of extremes,
By means of the loud laughter of your stainless logic.
I bow at your feet, supremely wise Jigme Wangpo.

Refrain…

You are unequaled in propagating through explanation and practice
The most excellent doctrine of the Protector, Tsongkapa.
I bow at your feet, Reverend Tenpai Drönme.

Refrain…

By tasting the nectar of the Oral Tradition of the Lord Jamgön,
You waxed forth in physical strength and experiential understanding.
I bow at your feet, Reverend Könchok Gyeltsen.

Refrain…

You upheld the banner of victory of the teaching of the practice lineage
While dwelling in one-pointed concentration on "no abode."
I bow at your feet, Great Siddha Ngödrub Rabten.

Refrain...

After going to the limits of excellence in what was to be abandoned and understood,
You showered down a Dharma-rain of good explanation.
I bow at your feet, Esteemed Tutor Gendün Gyatso.

Refrain...

You attained the rank of an accomplished one of the two stages
And so were crowned wisest of the wise.
I bow at your feet, glorious Tenpai Nyima.

Refrain...

Owing to the force of your loving-kindness for all sentient beings,
You upheld the banner of victory of the teachings of the sūtras and tantras.
I bow at your feet, Reverend Trinley Gyatso.

Refrain...

You are the good friend who extends to all the fortunate candidates
The heart-essence of the Second Buddha, Tsongkapa.
I bow at your feet, kind Losang Yeshe.

Refrain...

You understand the extensive scriptures of Śākyamuni's Holy Dharma
And increase them according to the Buddha's intentions.
I bow at your feet, exalted Trinley Da-me.

Refrain...

For the sake of faithful disciples, you manifest magnificently
On the Dharma-seat of all these Accomplished Ones.
I bow at your feet, most kind root guru.

Refrain...

Having developed strong revulsion toward dwelling in saṃsāra
And taking full responsibility for liberating all sentient beings without exception,

And seeing my blessed guru as Lord Buddha himself,
May I be blessed to quickly attain the state of
Mahāmudrā, that most exquisite state of total integration.

Your body, Father, and my own body;
Your speech, Father, and my own speech;
Your mind, Father, and my own mind;
May I be blessed to realize quickly their true inseparability.

COLOPHON:

The above prayer and offering service to the lamas was originally set down by Yongdzin Yeshe Gyeltsen, and additions were made by Pabongka Tulku. Owing to its being printed in this form, may the Holy Refuge Gurus and all sentient beings, human and nonhuman, manifest intelligent and insightful knowledge of the Supreme Vehicle; may the darkness of illusion and ignorance become completely purified; and may all, without exception, become Buddhas.

This prayer to the lineage of the Gelukpa Mahāmudrā siddhas, with the additions up to Trijang (Khri-byaṅ) Rinpoche, was set into print by the excellent Dampa Lodrö (Dam-pa-blo-gros) of Tsawarong (Tsha-ba-roṅ). It was published by the Hidden Treasury of Good Explanations Press. [A newer reprint of this prayer bears the addition: "Printed and published by the Mongolian Lama, Guru Deva, at the Pleasure of Elegant Sayings Printing Press, Tibetan Monastery, Sarnath, Varanasi U.P. India, 1965."]

Appendix III

Praises and Supplication to the Gelukpa Mahamudra Lineage

(Tibetan Text)

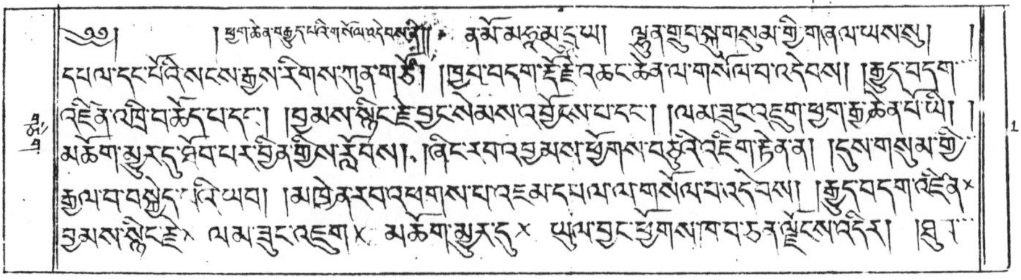

1

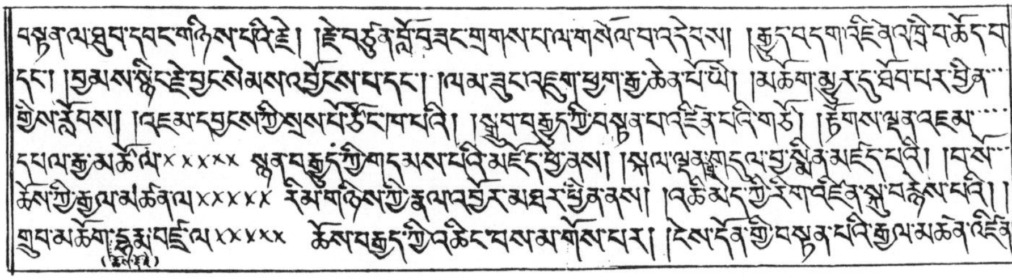

2

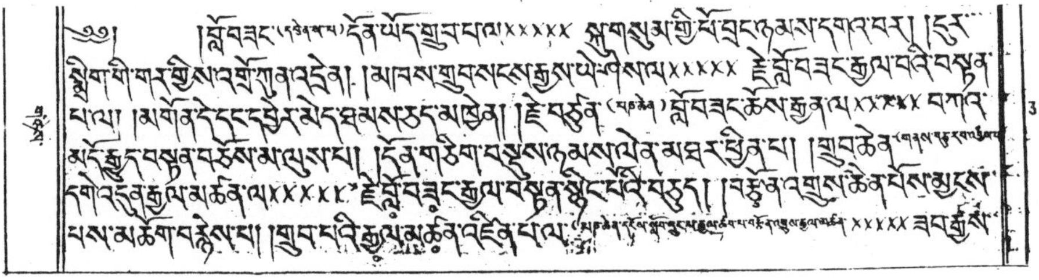

3

ཀྱི་དམ་ཚིག་བདུད་རྩིའི་བཅུད། །སྐལ་ལྡན་གྱི་གདུལ་བྱར་འདོམས་མཁས་པ། །རྒྱུད་ཆེན་དཀོན་མཆོག་རྒྱལ་མཚན་ལ་
XXXXX རྗེ་བློ་བཟང་ཆོས་ཀྱི་རྒྱལ་མཚན་ཉིད། །སླར་བསྟན་འགྲོའི་དཔལ་དུ་ལེགས་བྱོན་པ། །རྗེ་བཙུན་
བློ་བཟང་ཡེ་ཤེས་ལ་XXXXX རྗེ་སངས་རྒྱས་དངོས་ཀྱིས་བྱིན་བརླབས་ཤིང་། །ལམ་སྙན་བརྒྱུད་ཟབ་མོར་མངའ་བརྙེས་པ། །
རྗེ་བཙུན་ བློ་བཟང་འཕྲིན་ལས་ལ་XXXXX རྗེ་བློ་བཟང་རྒྱལ་བའི་སྙན་བརྒྱུད་ཀྱི། །དོན་སྙིང་པོའི་ཉམས་ལེན་ 4
མཐར་ཕྱིན་པ། །གྲུབ་མཆོག་ བློ་བཟང་རྣམ་རྒྱལ་ལ་XXXXX རྗེ་བླ་མའི་སྙན་བརྒྱུད་གདམས་པ་རྣམས། །དོན་མཐོར་
བརྩེ་བས་འདོམས་མཛད་པ། །དྲིན་ཅན་ ཡེ་ཤེས་མཚན་ཅན་ལ་XXXXX ལམ་ཚང་ལ་མ་ནོར་བསྟན་པའི་སྙིང་། །

༄༅། །ཡོངས་མཐར་དབུས་ཀུན་ཏུ་རྒྱས་མཛད་པ། །རྗེ་བཙུན་ ངག་དབང་བྱམས་པ་ལ་XXXXX དཔལ་
དང་པོའི་སངས་རྒྱས་དུར་སྒྲིག་གར། །ཡུལ་རྒྱ་བོད་ཀུན་ཆོས་ཀྱིས་སྨིན་མཛད་པ། །པཎ་ཆེན་དཔལ་ལྡན་ཡེ་ཤེས་
ལ་XXXXX མདོ་སྔགས་ཀྱི་ལམ་བཟང་ཡོངས་རྫོགས་ལ། །རྩེ་གཅིག་གིས་སྒྲུབ་པའི་མཐར་སོན་པ། །མཁས་གྲུབ་ 5
ངག་དབང་རྡོ་རྗེ་ལ་XXXXX བརྟན་མཁའ་ཁྱབ་ཀྱི་ཐུབ་དབང་གཉིས་པ་བཞིན། །འཆད་རྩོམ་གྱིས་རྒྱལ་བསྟན་གསལ་
མཛད་མགོན། །རྗེ་བཙུན་ [illegible] ལ་XXXXX དམིགས་མེད་ཀྱི་བརྩེ་ཆེན་མིག་མི་འཛུམ། །ཟབ་ཡངས་
ཀྱི་མཁྱེན་རབ་འཇམ་དཔལ་བཞིན། །དྲིན་ཅན་གྲུབ་པའི་རྡོ་རྗེ་ལ་XXXXX བདེ་སྟོང་གི་རྣལ་འབྱོར་མཐར་

ཕྱིན་ནས། །ཟུང་འཇུག་གི་རྒྱལ་སར་མངོན་གཤེགས་པ། །མཁས་གྲུབ་ བསྟན་འཛིན་བརྩོན་འགྲུས་ལ་XXXXX
ཟབ་ལམ་གྱི་རྟོགས་པ་མཐར་ཕྱིན་ནས། །བཤད་སྒྲུབ་ཀྱི་བསྟན་པའི་རྒྱལ་མཚན་འཛིན། །བློ་བཟང་ བརྩོན་
འགྲུས་རྒྱལ་མཚན་ལ་XXXXX ཉེས་ལྟུང་གི་དྲི་མས་མ་གོས་ཤིང་། །བསླབ་གསུམ་གྱི་བསྟན་པའི་སྙིང་པོ་འཛིན། །བློ་བཟང་
དོན་ཡོད་གྲུབ་པ་ལ་XXXX རྗེ་རྒྱལ་བ་གཉིས་པ་བློ་བཟང་གྲགས། །སླར་རྡུར་སྒྲིག་གར་གྱི་རྣམ་རོལ་པ། །རྗེ་ 6
བཙུན་ དགེ་ལེགས་རྒྱ་མཚོ་ལ་XXXXX ལམ་ཟབ་དང་རྒྱ་ཆེའི་ཆོས་ཀྱི་མཛད། །རྒྱུད་སྐལ་ལྡན་ཡོངས་ལ་གསལ་མཛད་
པ། །དྲིན་ཅན་ ངག་དབང་བྱམས་པ་ལ་XXXXX དྲི་མེད་ཀྱི་རིགས་པའི་གད་རྒྱང་གིས། །མཐར་གྲོལ་གྱི་ལམ་བཟང་

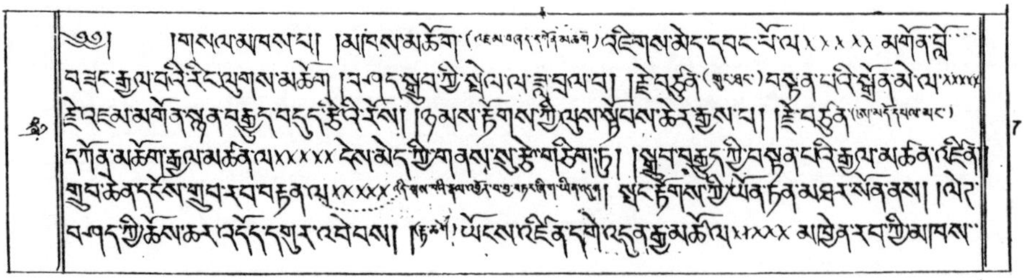

7

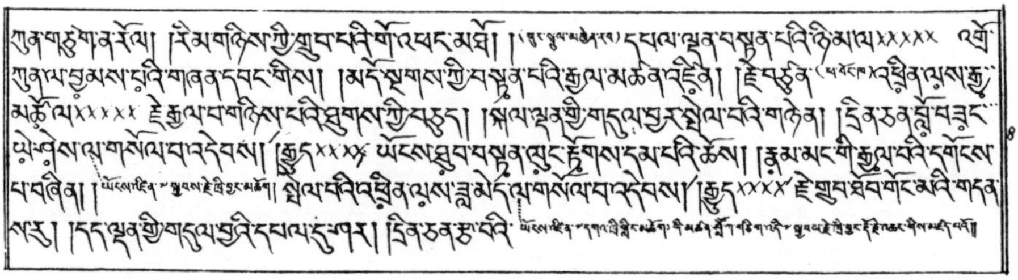

8

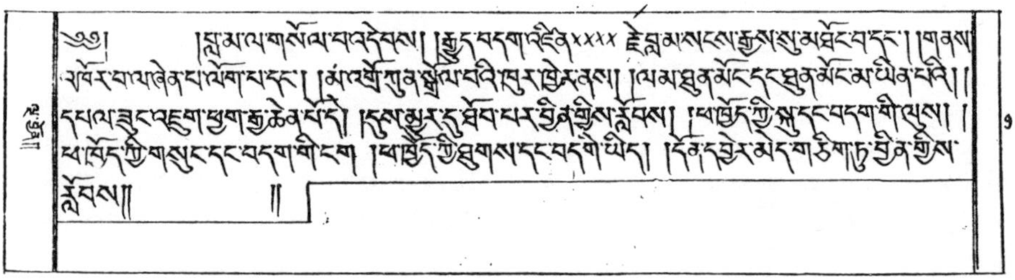

9

Appendix IV

The Meaning and Methods of Mahāmudrā

Mahāmudrā as Ground and Goal

There are various meanings in Buddhist treatises given to the term Mahāmudrā (Tib. *Chakgya Chenpo*/phyag rgya chen po)—depending upon whether one is speaking of the supreme *goal* of practice or of the meditative methods associated with the *path* for accomplishing that goal. Additionally, the term refers to the very *basis* or *ground* of all things, to that which makes such accomplishment possible, namely ultimate reality itself. With respect to this last aspect, the term bears close affinity with the meanings of *vajra* in tantric literature, where vajra connotes the diamond-hard indestructibility of ultimate reality, and of *jñāna-ḍākinī*, the feminine symbol that stands for the direct, unmediated experience of that reality.

Literally, the term Mahāmudrā may be translated as follows: Mahā (Tib. chenpo) means "great" and Mudrā (Tib. chakgya) means "gesture," "seal," or "symbol." Thus, Mahāmudrā may be rendered as Great Gesture, Great Seal, or Great Symbol. From the point of view of reality itself, such phraseology refers to the ultimate, basic, true nature of all things, whether mind or phenomena. From the point of view of the tantric practitioner, it refers to that naturalness of the innate mind, freed of all self-originated superimpositions onto the real, wherein distinctions of subject and object are completely dissolved and transcended and reality as a whole is experienced directly, as it really is. Such direct experience transcends intellection and conceptualization. It is hinted at by the description Great Gesture [or, as Keith Dowman has glossed it in *Masters of Mahāmudrā*, Magnificent Stance] of the mind, but in its factualness, it is beyond thought and expression. It is this last aspect of Mahāmudrā—its having reference to direct experience—that makes it such a difficult topic of discourse even for the siddhas themselves, who most often resorted to extemporaneous songs, or *dohās*, in their attempts to point to it.

In Buddhism, the primary doctrine to be mastered—through direct experience as opposed to mere intellectualization—is that of "voidness" [the voidness of independent, inherent existence, whether of things or of the so-called self], termed *śūnyatā* or *anātman*. The earliest Buddhist practitioners concentrated their efforts on coming to an understanding and realization of *ātman nairātmya*, "the nonself of a self in the so-called 'self'." With the advent of the Mahāyāna, śūnyatā and anātman became all-encompassing categories, and Mahāyāna practitioners made it their goal to fully comprehend both *ātman nairātmya* and *dharma nairātmya*, the nonself of inherent existence in any *thing* [here, dharma] whatsoever. The Vajrayāna sought to make the philosophical or intellectual understandings of both these principles living experiences for its practitioners and to thereby usher in their direct realization beyond words. Having developed meditational methods to engender this direct experience of supreme voidness, as opposed to a mere intellectual understanding of it, is what distinguishes the Vajrayāna and what has earned for it the characterization of being the "speedy path" to the ultimate realization of the Buddha's teachings.

The "two crown jewels" of Mahāyāna philosophy, Nāgārjuna and Asaṅga, had deftly articulated the doctrine of śūnyatā (Tib. *tongpanyi*, stoṅ pa ñid). Each had also continually warned against grasping this doctrine as merely another intellectual concept. Thus, Nāgārjuna advocated *śūnyatāśūnyatā* [the voidness of even voidness], and Asaṅga asserted that true insight into the ultimate meaning of śūnyatā was possible only through direct "knowledge of it that was completely freed of the distortions of discursive thought" (*nirvikalpa-jñāna*).

While a proper intellectual understanding of voidness is recognized as an essential first step in advancing towards the ultimate goal, such understanding must be brought to full fruition through meditative practice, which alone is capable of bringing one face-to-face with that reality. This is where the *methods* of Mahāmudrā are brought into play.

Gö Lotsawa's ('Gos lo-tsa-ba) famed *Blue Annals* discusses the dispensation of the Mahāmudrā lineage of doctrine and practice in Tibet. As translated by Roerich, Gö Lotsawa, in his introductory remarks on the system of Mahāmudrā, notes that even though one may use scriptures and philosophical reasoning in order to come to an understanding of voidness, such reasoning still represents discursive thought and, owing to this, is still—from the ultimate point of view—tied to ignorance. However, the inference of voidness cannot be logically rejected, since it represents a valid, ultimate, and true conception. The point then is that the only remedy that is able to move one beyond the logically valid *understanding* of voidness is direct intuition and realization. Roerich's translation of this section [p. 841] continues:

> Thus the antidote of this inference... which is not a mere theory, represents the knowledge of Mahāmudrā. This (knowledge) can

> be gained only through the blessing of a holy teacher (i.e. through initiation, and not through reasoning).

Roerich's own note on this subject is also worth noting here:

> (The author's conclusion is that one should at first grasp the notion of Relativity [here = voidness] in order to avoid moral defilement. Then in its turn the *notion* of Relativity should be abandoned, but as it represents an ultimate/true/conception it cannot be rejected with the help of reasoning and theories, and thus it can only be abandoned by intuiting the Mahāmudrā).

Thus, the Vajrayāna developed and set forth a variety of methods to bring the disciple to the direct intuition of this most central principle of Buddhism. With the direct experience of all-encompassing śūnyatā comes the utter shattering of the apparent duality of subject and object and the reconciliation of both those formerly held false perceptions in the unborn and undying indestructible nature of pure awareness itself. This is the "Great Gesture," the goal and the ground, as realized.

With respect to Mahāmudrā as the ground of practice—as the ultimate abiding nature of all things, as reality itself—not much more can be said. Mahāmudrā is the *fact* of reality, completely as it is, uncluttered by false superimpositions. In the words of Ludwig Wittgenstein, such reality is "all that is the case." Thus, Mahāmudrā encompasses all of reality—as does the mind, when realizing it— without veering from it.

A Buddha's all-pervasive knowledge is said to cover the entirety of reality without going beyond it into error at any point. Many texts describe this by saying that a Buddha lives within the "limits of reality" [*bhūta-koṭi*], where knowledge is pristine and perfect awareness, neither exaggerated nor underestimated, owing to being completely free of both the coarse obscurations caused by the afflictive emotions [*kleśa-avaraṇa*] and the subtle obscurations to the knowable [*jñeya-avaraṇa*]. A Buddha thus has, it is said, simultaneous and direct knowledge of all phenomena and their mode of being. It would seem that this sense of all-encompassing omniscience—perfect because it does not stray from perfection or lapse back into false, dualistic perceptions—is what was intended by the Mahāyāna term bhūta-koṭi. Moreover, this sense is in keeping with certain definitions advanced for mudrā in tantric contexts. For example, the following definitions were suggested by two famed Kagyüpa masters. Pema Karpo (Pad-ma-dkar-po) explained mudrā as follows:

The term mudrā has the double meaning of 'to seal' and of 'not to go beyond.'

And Milarepa sang:

Chak: the indivisibility of bliss and voidness.
Gya: not to go beyond it.

Many phrases are used to intimate or point to Mahāmudrā as the ground and the fruition of the path. It is called the "natural state of mind," the "effortless," "pure awareness," and "the diamond-hard voidness of the mind, beyond all words." Because of its absolute experiential nature it is impossible to express it in conventional language or in conventional forms. Thus, the siddhas resorted to unconventional behavior in their attempts to instruct their disciples and to aesthetic forms, usually poetry, to communicate its essence. In two verses sung by the Mahāsiddha Tilopa for his disciple Nāropa, the three aspects of Mahāmudrā as ground, path, and goal are indicated. Translated by Garma Chang in *Teachings of Tibetan Yoga*, p. 25, the verses go as follows:

The Void needs no reliance.
Mahāmudrā rests on nought.
Without making an effort,
But remaining loose and natural,
One can break the yoke,
Thus gaining Liberation.

If one sees nought when staring into space,
If with the mind one then observes the mind,
One destroys distinctions
And reaches Buddhahood.

TWO MEDITATIVE PATHS OF MAHĀMUDRĀ

Since Mahāmudrā practice offers the possibility of seeing the mind directly and of attaining a direct experience of the insight into reality that makes one a Buddha in this very life, it bears resemblance to other "sudden" or "speedy path" traditions such as the *Dzokchen* (rdzogs chen), or Great Encompassment, of the Nyingma order and the *satori*, or Sudden Illumination, of the Japanese Zen and Chinese Ch'an schools. Still, in spite of reference to the naturalness of the goal and to the speed with which it finally dawns upon the practitioner, the practice of Mahāmudrā is no small undertaking. Requiring rigorous and determined discipline and effort, often over many years, it is not a path that can be mastered by the lazy or fainthearted. Milarepa, after having reached the "stage beyond meditating," declared to one disciple that he had "forgotten how to meditate." But to another, he wisely counseled in one of his songs [translated by Lama Kunga Rinpoche and Brian Cutillo in *Drinking the Mountain Stream*, p. 23]:

> Because the natural state is the root,
> It looks so easy, but is very hard.
> But when awareness is focused on reality
> After analysis by learning and reflecting,
> This is the one realization that liberates totally;
> It looks so hard, but is very easy.

Tsongkapa's *lam rim* teachings stress, as did Lord Atīśa's before him, that the methods of the tantric path cannot be entered upon successfully by one who does not have proper training in the methods basic to the Theravāda and Mahāyāna paths. Milarepa's song above also points this out by alluding to the necessary prerequisites of insight gained from learning and reflecting. While perhaps appearing simple and easy to master, the Mahāmudrā path only begins after success has been attained in the higher levels of calming meditations. The analytic practice that aims at supreme transcendent insight must be grounded on complete mental stability, which is achieved in stages. Just as one cannot skip over the basics of Buddhist learning and reflecting, so one cannot skip over the basics of Buddhist meditation and its two wings: mental stability and tranquillity [*śamatha*] and analytic, or insight, meditation [*vipaśyanā*].

Though Mahāmudrā as path refers to a whole variety of meditative practices, all aimed at engendering the direct experience of voidness, all these may nevertheless be grouped under two basic headings or viewed as two basic approaches: (1) those techniques involving little bodily yoga, but which call for clear, attentive observation of one's own mind, and (2) those that demand rigorous yogic discipline coupled with awareness. These two are sometimes technically referred to as the Path of Liberation and the Path of Skillfulness, respectively. They are also called the Path Without Form and the Path With Form. The direct observation of the mind is also sometimes termed "mind yoga," while the Path of Skillfulness is referred to as "energy yoga." Lastly, these two approaches are also respectively termed Sūtra Mahāmudrā and Tantric Mahāmudrā. In each case, the latter method refers specifically to the deity yoga techniques of the highest, *anuttara yoga* tantric class.

To be sure, siddhas like Milarepa, Nāropa, Tsongkapa, and the six Gelukpa siddhas whose lives are translated here practiced both these Mahāmudrā methods. Though in most recent Western accounts, the tantric yogic exercises [especially Nāropa's Six Yogas] have received more attention, the so-called Sūtra Mahāmudrā methods are equally to be treasured. Both paths, together or apart, are capable of leading one to direct realization in this very life.

It should be mentioned, however, that a number of scholastic controversies have been spawned surrounding the issue of the value and validity of the Sūtra Mahāmudrā method versus the Tantric Mahāmudrā method. The controversy seems to have first surfaced in connection with the development of the Kagyü practice lineage, when the great master Gampopa (sGam-po-pa) was said to have led some of his disciples to Mahāmudrā realization using *only* the methods of Sūtra Mahāmudrā. Some scholars declared this an impossibility, claiming that true Mahāmudrā realization should be considered to correspond only to the results of the Completion Stage practices of the anuttara yoga class. These scholars argued that the latter approach was that used by Marpa and Milarepa, Gampopa's root guru. Moreover, these scholars claimed that the term Mahāmudrā is not found in any of the *Prajñāpāramitā sūtras* and that knowledge of Mahāmudrā is knowledge born only of tantric initiation. It would seem that scholars in the past who took up this controversy were strong adherents of one or the other approach, or path, to Mahāmudrā realization, and that while advocating the one, they disavowed the other.

Gelukpa scholars have not been immune from such controversy. Particularly as it relates to the Sūtra Mahāmudrā, some Gelukpas have leveled charges of there being mistakes in the formulation of the proper *view* of voidness, which serves as the basis and starting point for Mahāmudrā practice. For example, these Gelukpas have asserted that while Padmasambhava and his first twenty-five Tibetan disciples attained infallible realization of Dzokchen [here, an equivalent of Mahāmudrā], later meditators of the Nyingma school fell into wrong views regarding voidness and came to claim mistakenly that the mere clarity of the natural mind is the right view. These accusations have gone back and forth from one Tibetan order to another over the centuries. Sometimes one even finds that the realizations and the general practice of great saints are called into question. Thus, Chang, in his "Yogic Commentary" to Evans-Wentz's *Tibetan Yoga and Secret Doctrines*, p. xxxiii, could state: "Tsongkhapa was a great Bodhisattva and a great scholar, but there is some doubt among Tibetans as to whether or not he was an accomplished yogin." Fortunately, not all scholars—and hardly any true siddhas—have engaged in such divisiveness, and genuine practitioners seem to have found few actual contradictions in the various methods.

Those wishing to review detailed expositions of the Gelukpa view regarding voidness, as this relates to the basis of Mahāmudrā practice, should be advised to read [in addition to Tsongkapa's key works: the *Lam rim chen mo*, *sṄags rim chen mo*, *Rim pa lṅa rab tu gsal ba'i sgron me*, and *Zab lam nā ro'i chos drug gi sgo nas 'khrid pa'i rim pa*] three Gelukpa texts in particular. Two were written by the First Panchen, Losang Chökyi Gyeltsen: *rGyal ba'i gźuṅ lam* [a root-text verse exposition on Mahāmudrā translated into English as *The Great Seal of Voidness*] and *Yaṅ gsal sgron me* [*The Lamp of Re-illumination*, the First Panchen's autocommentary on the former text]. The third was authored by Yongdzin Yeshe Gyeltsen, our biographical anthologist and Geluk Mahāmudrā siddha in his own right. It is titled *sNyan rgyud lam bzaṅ gsal ba'i sgron me*, [*The Lamp of the Clear and Excellent Path of the Oral Tradition Lineage*] and is a commentary on the First Panchen's autocommentary. These texts clearly set forth the Ganden Oral Tradition of Mahāmudrā practice.

Summarizing once again, there are basically *two* different approaches to Mahāmudrā practice. Regarding these two, the First Panchen's *Great Seal of Voidness* [as translated by the Library of Tibetan Works and Archives, pp. 5–7] says the following:

> There are many different ways of approaching the actual teachings of Mahāmudrā. In general, these can be divided into two basic classifications—the Mahāmudrā teachings of the sūtras and those of the tantras.
>
> For the latter, you must concentrate on the energy-channels of your vajra body, and especially on the central energy-channel... From following such methods as this and others, you can come to experience the blissful realization of the Clear Light of Voidness on the finest level of consciousness.
>
> This explanation of Mahamudra as the blissful realization of Voidness attained by channeling your body's energy-winds into the central energy-channel is attested to by Saraha, Nagarjuna and Maitripa. It is taught specifically in 'The Seven Texts of the Mahasiddhas' and 'The Three Core Volumes' of Saraha. These Mahamudra teachings, thus, are the quintessence of the highest classification of tantra, anuttarayoga. This then, in brief is the explanation of Mahamudra according to the tantra system.
>
> As for the previous one, the Mahamudra teachings of the sutras, this refers to the ways of meditating on Voidness as taught in the three '*Prajnaparamita* Sutras' and in all three traditions of the Sravakas, Pratyekabuddhas and Bodhisattvas. Nagarjuna has said that except for these methods there is no other path to Liberation.

[In a commentarial note to these passages from the First Panchen's text, on p. 7, the following is added:

> There is no difference between Voidness understood by tantra methods and that by sutra ones. The difference lies in what understands Voidness. With the tantra methods, it is understood by the finest level of consciousness that has been channeled into the central energy-channel. With the sutra ones, it is understood by rougher levels of consciousness.]

In keeping with this basic two-fold approach to Mahāmudrā, it is customarily the case that the results associated with practicing one or the other are also distinguished. Thus, the result, or siddhi, of practicing according to the Sūtra Mahāmudrā methods is said to be the experience of the indivisibility of appearance [or apparent reality] and voidness, while the siddhi attained as a result of practicing the Tantric Mahāmudrā methods is described as the experience of the indivisibility of bliss and voidness.

A graphic summary may serve best to bring all of the above into sharper focus:

The Two Meditative Paths of Mahāmudrā

	Path of Liberation	Path of Skillfulness
Alternate Names	1. Path Without Form 2. Mind-yoga [owing to relying on direct observation of the innate mind not conjoined with visualization of a deity-form] 3. Sūtra Mahāmudrā [as set forth in the *Prajñāpāramitā-sūtras*]	1. Path With Form 2. Energy-yoga [owing to relying on yogic channeling of energies in conjunction with visualization of a deity-form] 3. Tantric Mahāmudrā [as set forth in the *Tantras* and in specific works of Indian and Tibetan Buddhist siddhas]
Results	Realization of the indivisibility of appearance and voidness	Realization of the indivisibility of bliss and voidness

The Practice of Seeing the Mind Directly, Called The Path of Liberation, Through Direct Observation of the Mind Itself

The path of "seeing the mind directly" [alternately called the Path of Liberation, mind yoga, or Sūtra Mahāmudrā] is so named because this approach stresses the observation of the innate mind in its pristine, natural state. Thus, the practice is based and grounded upon the *fact* of this pristine nature of mind—pure, clear, and radiant—which embraces and contains all things. In ordinary beings, however, and under ordinary nonmeditative circumstances, this mind remains clouded over and obscured by afflictive emotions and other obstructions. We see neither ourselves nor others in truth, as we really are [*yathābhūtam*], because we view all things through veils [*āvaraṇa*] created through ignorance.

The methods associated with Sūtra Mahāmudrā aim to help us cut through such veils and to peer directly at the innate abiding mind. In the words of Alexander Berzin [see the "Preface" to his translation of *The Mahāmudrā Eliminating the Darkness of Ignorance*, p. xiii]: "...you become aware of the nature of the mind without deliberately ceasing rougher levels of consciousness. Instead, you see right through them. But this abiding nature is not at all obvious to the uninitiated and can easily be mistaken for something else, in which case meditation on it would be disastrous."

Looking into one's mind may appear a simple process, but anyone who has attempted to observe with genuine attentiveness for just a few seconds the "natural" mind—apart from anger, lust, or fear; at rest, naturally luminous, and pure—can attest to the difficulties of sustaining this experience. The process cannot be performed haphazardly but requires a gradual buildup of alertness and awareness that ultimately remains undisturbed and undistracted by the visions, sounds, feelings, or emotions that may arise.

As with all Mahāmudrā practices, the guidance of a qualified guru is imperative. The guru alone is able to point to the nature of the mind, to impart to the disciple a key simile or hint regarding it, and to ensure that the disciple, once practicing, remains on track. In the beginning, the disciple performs the preliminary practices for purifying defilements and for increasing his or her store of merit. Then, when some measure of meditative tranquilization and stabilization has been achieved, the guru imparts pith instructions and directly indicates to the disciple the true nature of the mind. Then the time for "sitting" in earnest has arrived.

With regard to this approach to Mahāmudrā practice and realization, Tilopa advised Nāropa [as translated by Chang in *Teachings of Tibetan Yoga*, p. 26] as follows:

Do nought with the body but relax,
Shut firm the mouth and silent remain,
Empty your mind and think of nought.
Like a hollow bamboo
Rest at ease your body.
Giving not nor taking,
Put your mind at rest.
Mahāmudrā is like a mind that clings to nought.
Thus practicing, in time you will reach Buddhahood.

And again [p. 29]:

Whoever clings to mind sees not
The truth of what's Beyond the mind.
Whoever *strives* to practice Dharma
Finds *not* the truth of Beyond-practice.
To know what is Beyond both mind and practice,
One should cut cleanly through the root of mind
And stare naked. One should thus break away
From all distinctions and remain at ease.

In recent years, several texts that address the various methods associated with the practice of Sūtra Mahāmudrā have appeared in English translation. These include Evans-Wentz's *Tibetan Yoga and Secret Doctrines* [especially the text by Pema Karpo, titled *The Epitome of the Great Symbol*] and Stephen Beyer's translation of a similar work, also by Pema Karpo, in *The Buddhist Experience.* Of course, works that treat of the life and songs of Milarepa are of inestimable value for the clarity with which they describe this particular approach. Among these works are the translations of Milarepa's *Life* by Evans-Wentz and, more recently, by Lhalungpa, and Chang's *The Hundred Thousand Songs of Milarepa.* Selections from Milarepa's songs can also be found in *Drinking the Mountain Stream* and in *The Rain of Wisdom.* Recent works specifically describing the meditative practice of Sūtra Mahāmudrā include *The Mahāmudrā Eliminating the Darkness of Ignorance, Teachings of Tibetan Yoga, The Garland of Mahāmudrā Practices,* and *Mahāmudrā; the Quintessence of Mind and Meditation.* Such works provide useful guidance indeed.

The Path of Skillfulness, called "Energy-yoga," or Tantric Mahāmudrā

A basic operational principle underlying all of Tibetan tantrism is the interdependence of the mind and *prāṇa* [the "psycho-physical winds" or "energy-currents" of the body]. The simile is often suggested that one's mind *rides* upon the currents, or winds, as does a horseman upon a horse. Particular states of mind are always accompanied by certain types of prāṇa. In the rigorous yogic techniques of the Tantric Mahāmudrā Path of Skillfulness, this principle is of key importance, since the yogi who can master the one simultaneously masters the other. Thus, a practitioner of this yogic method seeks to gain mastery of the mind through gaining control of the prāṇas, engendering a loosening of the "knots" of the channels [called *nāḍīs*] through which they flow, and, by stages, winning the ability to cause them to enter into the central channel [*avadhūti*]. This forcing of the currents into the central channel is what is meant by the Tibetan term *zungjuk* (zuṅ 'jug), or "total integration," as it appears throughout these six Gelukpa namtar. It is the crowning yogic achievement for the tantric Mahāmudrā practitioner. When the subtlest energy-winds are thus guided into the central channel, and the yogi is able to remain focused upon voidness, he or she is said to experience the bliss of the Clear Light.

This type of yogic practice is aligned with the highest classification of tantra, the anuttara yoga. Accordingly, it is based upon the two pillars of this practice system, called the Generation or Arising Stage and the Completion or Perfection Stage, respectively. In the Generation Stage, the yogi masters the processes of visualization so that he or she is able to transform his of her own physical body into the body of the main meditational Buddha of a given tantric cycle, equipped with the "arcane" tantric anatomical arrangement of channels and energy centers [*cakras*]. This yogically created arcane body is often referred to as the Vajra- or Diamond-Body. In the Completion Stage, through a complex series of inner psychophysical maneuvers, the yogi directs the flow of the coarse and subtle energy-currents, finally forcing them to enter the central channel and there to dissolve at the heart center into the most subtle life-bearing wind. This accomplishment ushers in the experience called "the blissful realization of the Clear Light," wherein consciousness has reached its most subtle form. [Beings are said to have experiences approximating the Clear Light experience even under certain nonmeditative conditions: for example, during fainting or orgasm, just before and after sleeping, and sometimes when dreaming. Increasing subtlety is experienced during the various "dissolutions" of the death process, and, in a sense, the advanced tantric yogi is simulating in this life the features of dissolution associated with death.] The practitioner's aim then is to focus this most subtle and pristine consciousness upon a nonconceptual direct observation of voidness.

A more detailed description of this method is given in the First Panchen's

Great Seal of Voidness, p. 6:

> There are 72,000 energy-channels (tza, nadi) in the human body, eight of which are considered major. The vajra-body corresponds to your subtle physical body when used for tantric practice. The central energy-channel (tza-u-ma, avadhuti, or susumna) runs parallel to and slightly in front of your spine and is normally blocked by channel-knots. In the practice of the completion stage (dzog-rim, sampanna-krama) of anuttarayoga tantra, the various energy-winds (lung, vayu, prana) of the body are channeled into the central energy-channel for the purpose of realizing Voidness with the resulting blissful fine consciousness.
>
> From following such methods as this and others, you can come to experience the blissful realization of the Clear Light of Voidness on the finest level of consciousness.
>
> Once all the energy-winds of the body have been channeled into the central energy-channel, if the resulting blissful fine consciousness has an intellectual or conceptual understanding of Voidness, this understanding is known as the approximating Clear Light. The full non-conceptual direct understanding of Voidness by the finest level of consciousness is called the actual Clear Light.

The teachings on the Tantric Mahāmudrā yogic methods that lead to the experience of the unity of bliss and voidness were developed and expounded upon by many of the famed eighty-four Indian Buddhist siddhas and were then passed on and preserved, most notably by the Kagyü lineage in Tibet. One of the best known works on the subject was written by the Indian siddha Nāropa, root guru of the Tibetan translator Marpa, and is called *The Six Yogas of Nāropa.* The six are: (1) *tummo* (gtum mo) or "heat yoga," a yogic process that manifests physically in the raising of the body's temperature; (2) *gyülü* (sgyu lus), or "illusory body yoga"; (3) *milam* (rmi lam), or "dream yoga"; (4) *ösel* ('od gsal), or "clear light yoga"; (5) *powa* ('pho ba), or "transference yoga," involving the transference of consciousness at death into other forms of existence; and (6) *bardo* (bar do), the "intermediate state yoga."

These six yogas have been studied, practiced, and commented upon by tantric masters down through the ages and are specifically mentioned in three of the six Gelukpa namtar translated here. Tsongkapa himself wrote two treatises on Nāropa's Six Yogas, one of which in particular is acknowledged as an extremely important commentary on this system. Various works treating of this particular series of practices have recently appeared in English. Guenther's translation of *The Life and Teaching of Nāropa* and Geshe

Kelsang Gyatso's *Clear Light of Bliss; Mahāmudrā in Vajrayāna Buddhism* should especially be mentioned.

Again, as we have noted, the Gelukpa tradition recognizes both the Path of Liberation [Sūtra Mahāmudrā] and the Path of Skillfulness [Tantric Mahāmudrā], and its lineage of siddhas practiced both approaches. However, Tsongkapa's *Great Exposition of Secret Mantra* does clearly advise that the Tantric Mahāmudrā methods ought to be practiced by those seeking to become Buddhas in this very life. According to His Holiness the present Dalai Lama's remarks [translated by Hopkins in *Tantra in Tibet*, p. 22]: the "extremely subtle obstructions to omniscience are mentioned only in the teachings of Highest Yoga Tantra, the fourth and highest mantra path." Since only the Path of Skillfulness is aligned with this highest class of tantra, it alone can lead successfully to the complete purification of these extremely subtle obstructions.

Moreover, Tsongkapa counsels, only the Tantric Mahāmudrā methods—owing to their emphasis on deity yoga—can successfully lead one to the attainment of a Buddha's two Form Bodies, the *Saṃbhogakāya* or Enjoyment Body and the *Nirmāṇakāya* or Emanation Body, in addition to the Buddha's Formless Body, otherwise called the *Dharmakāya*, or Truth Body, which [according to Tsongkapa] can be achieved by meditating on voidness in accordance with Sūtra Mahāmudrā methods alone. Tsongkapa argues that the attainment of *all three* bodies, the complete *trikāya*, is necessary if one is actually to transform oneself into a Buddha in this life in order to aid all beings. Thus, it is essential to practice the Tantric Mahāmudrā methods.

The Gelukpa order is often characterized as a school of scholars as opposed to yogis, and, as I have mentioned, it has sometimes been alleged that Tsongkapa himself was not an accomplished tantric practitioner. Yet anyone who has read the various namtar of Tsongkapa or studied his voluminous written works on the tantras will realize immediately the falseness of such claims. In relation to the system of Tantric Mahāmudrā, Tsongkapa made a unique contribution. After studying under numerous masters of his day—many of them Kagyüpa, but many from the other orders as well—and after receiving instructions on the practice systems directly from his main tutelary deity, Lord Mañjuśrī himself, Tsongkapa fashioned a concise explication of the essentials of such practice, which has been passed since his time through the Gelukpa Mahāmudrā practice lineage known as the Ganden Oral Tradition. These pith instructions call for practices involving the three chief tantric deities: Cakrasaṃvara for the development of the clear light attainment, Guhyasamāja for accomplishing the illusory body, and Vajrabhairava to protect against hindrances to the practices overall. According to the Ganden

Oral Tradition, successful practice focusing on these three deities aligned with the highest classification of tantra will lead both to the ultimate siddhi of Mahāmudrā and to the consequent realization of the Three Bodies of a Buddha in this very life.

In the translations presented here, we see each of the six Gelukpa siddhas concentrating their efforts toward mastering the practices associated with these three deities as described by Tsongkapa. The fact that Tsongkapa could pass on this lineage to his disciple, Jampel Gyatso, means that he himself had completely accomplished its fruits.

Appendix V

The Life of Yongdzin Yeshe Gyeltsen

We would not have any of these Gelukpa life stories had it not been for the efforts of Yongdzin Yeshe Gyeltsen [1713–1793] to collect and print them in a great two-volume anthology of namtar finally produced in 1787. The anthology is entitled *Byaṅ chub lam gyi rim pa'i bla ma brgyud pa'i rnam par thar pa rgyal bstan mdzes pa'i rgyan mchog phul byuṅ nor bu'i phreṅ ba* [*Biographies of the Eminent Gurus in the Transmission Lineages of the Graded Path Teachings, called The Jeweled Rosary*]. The work's colophon tells us that it was completed at the Potala and that one of its chief sponsors was the Eighth Dalai Lama himself, Losang Jampel Gyatso (bLo-bzaṅ 'Jam-dpal-rgya-mtsho) [1759–1804].

The namtar of a given saint was normally written very shortly after that one's death and was usually authored by that teacher's closest disciple. We know, for example, that Drubchen Jampel Gyatso's namtar was written by his "heart-disciple" Lodrö Gyeltsen (bLo-gros-rgyal-mtshan) [1402–1471] and that Sanggye Yeshe wrote a work praising the accomplishments of his Mahāmudrā guru, Gyelwa Ensapa. The First Panchen, Losang Chökyi Gyeltsen, not only authored a lengthy autobiography but also wrote a small anthology of namtar chronicling the lives of three of his immediate predecessors: Je Kyabchok Pelsangpo, Ensapa, and Sanggye Yeshe. Still, these and numerous other accounts might have remained in limited editions, the treasured property of individual Gelukpa monasteries, had not Yongdzin Yeshe Gyeltsen undertaken the enormous task of bringing them all together and publishing them in his famed anthology.

But what do we know of the anthologist's own life? Here we come up against a great irony, for about the man who gave us such a wealth of information regarding many of the key figures of Tibetan religious history, Western scholarship seems to know very little. W. Rockhill's *The Dalai Lamas of Lhasa* and Luciano Petech's *The Dalai-Lamas and Regents of Tibet*, for example, never mention him. Ferrari's translation of the *Guide to the Holy Places of Central Tibet* mentions Tsechok Ling (Tshe-mchog-gliṅ) [Yeshe Gyeltsen's main see in Lhasa], but the *Guide* cannot furnish information about a "Ye-śes-rgya-*mtsho*" who was apparently connected with it. [The Eighth Dalai Lama himself comes off only slightly better in these works. Petech and Rockhill dismiss him as having been a weak and ineffectual ruler. Often it has been said that he was more interested in spiritual matters than in political ones—as though that were a valid criticism of a Dalai Lama!] Even Ketsün Sangpo's *Biographical Dictionary of Tibet and Tibetan Buddhism* does not record the life of this great master.

Luckily, however, within the Gelukpa religious tradition Yeshe Gyeltsen is remembered with a good deal of admiration and devotion. Indeed, he is regarded with awe. Here, the great compiler is usually referred to by the longer title, Tsechok Ling Yongdzin Yeshe Gyeltsen or, more simply, as Tsechok Ling Rinpoche. His dates are 1713–1793. Those familiar with Tibetan political history will recognize this as a time of instability in Tibet, during which there were at least two attempted invasions of the country by Gurkha armies from Nepal and ever-increasing incursions into local Tibetan governance by the Chinese. It was the time when the Manchu *ambans* assumed power in Lhasa and when the Chinese Emperor Ch'ien-lung sought to directly control the selection of the Panchen and Dalai Lamas.

Gelukpa history reveres Yeshe Gyeltsen as having been a remarkably gifted teacher, an incredibly prolific author of religious works, and a realized Mahāmudrā siddha in his own right. In the Geluk Mahāmudrā Lineage Prayer, he is referred to as "the kind" Yeshe Gyeltsen. He is also referred to as Kachen Yeshe Gyeltsen owing to his special affiliation with the famed Tashilünpo monastic institution from which, after demonstrating his mastery of the subjects studied under the heading of the [Four] Great Difficulties [Kachen], he earned its highest degree. But perhaps nothing outshines the fame he enjoys, at least in the minds of Gelukpa monks, by virtue of his having risen from lowly beginnings to become the Esteemed Spiritual Preceptor [Yongdzin] of the Eighth Dalai Lama. It was the Eighth Dalai Lama himself who composed the only full biography of Yeshe Gyeltsen that we possess.

His account is divided into seven chapters and runs to 415 folio sides, and it often includes quoted passages in which Yeshe Gyeltsen narrates episodes from his own life with considerable candor. The text's full title is *dPal ldan bla ma dam pa rigs daṅ dkyil khor rgya mthso'i mṅa' bdag bka' drin gsum ldan yoṅs 'dzin pandi ta chen po rje btsun ye śes rgyal mtshan dpal bzaṅ po'i sku gsuṅ thugs kyi rtogs pa brjod pa thub bstan padmo 'byed pa'i ñin byed.* It was completed by the Eighth Dalai Lama in 1794. [The only other account of Yeshe Gyeltsen's life is a brief four-folio summary, together with praises and a prayer for protection. It is no. 6053 in *The Complete Works of Yeshe Gyeltsen.*]

Thus, it is from the Eighth Dalai Lama's biography that we may learn in some detail of Yeshe Gyeltsen's remarkable career. His beginnings were lowly. He was born the son of an illegitimate and outcast father and a village woman of Tingkye (gTiṅ-skyes). The parents, we are told, were constantly engaged in bitter quarrels. Once, when only about six years old, Yeshe Gyeltsen apparently prevented his enraged father from killing his mother and her paramour. [These are not the typical elements of hagiographical accounts!] At age seven, Yeshe Gyeltsen was placed at the Rikü (Ri-khud) monastery, where he was cared for by a kindly nun named Tsewang (Tshe-dbaṅ). It was she who taught him how to read, and he remembered her always with great affection. In 1722, he entered Tashilünpo and received his first ordination from the Second Panchen Lama, Losang Yeshe (bLo-bzaṅ-ye-śes) [1663–1737]. He excelled in his studies there and came to have numerous illustrious teachers, among them the Panchen Lama himself, Kachen Yeshe Tokme (dKa'-chen Ye-śes-thogs-med), Purbuchok Ngawang Jampa (Phur-bu-lcog Ṅag-dbaṅ-byams-pa) [1682–1762], and the renowned tantric master, Drubwang Losang Namgyel (Grub-dbaṅ bLo-bzaṅ-rnam-rgyal) [1670–1741] of Kyirong Ganden Pukpoche (sKyid-groṅ dGa'-ldan Phug-po-che) monastery. It was this latter teacher who oversaw Yeshe Gyeltsen's Mahāmudrā practices.

By the time he had completed his studies, received final ordination, and spent many years practicing in isolated retreats, Yeshe Gyeltsen's fame had greatly increased. Everyone wanted him to come to their respective institutions to teach. He chose instead to journey in 1751 to the Nepalese border regions where his Mahāmudrā guru had taught; and later, in 1756, he established a monastery there called Kyirong Samten Ling (sKyid-groṅ bSam-gtan-gliṅ). [Today, this monastery continues to thrive in Bodhanath, Nepal.] Here he gave instruction to a number of eminent disciples, among them the famed Changkya Rölpai Dorje (lCang-skya Rol-pa'i-rdo-rje), and authored some works on philosophy. He remained primarily in Nepal from 1751 until 1782 when—owing to the death of the Third Panchen Lama, Pelden Yeshe (dPal-ldan-ye-śes) [1737–1780], so famed for his diplomatic dealings with the Chinese, and to the debilitating illness of the Sixtieth Ganden Tripa (dGa'-ldan Khri-pa), the Yongdzin Losang Tenpa (bLo-bzaṅ-bstan-pa)—he was personally requested by the Eighth Dalai Lama to become his tutor. In order to please his new tutor, and to ensure that he would comfortably remain in Lhasa, the Dalai Lama had a new monastery constructed in 1790 just across the Kyichu river, called Tsechok Samten Ling. Yeshe Gyeltsen accepted this post and served in the capacity of yongdzin for the next eleven years until his death in 1793. Following his death, the Tsechok Ling monastery joined Künde Ling (Kun-bde-gliṅ), Tengye Ling (bsTan-rgyasgliṅ) and Tsomön Ling (mTsho-smon-gliṅ) to make up the famed Four Lings, whose resident incarnations were eligible to become Regents during the minority of a Dalai Lama.

This much, and more, we can learn from the Dalai Lama's written account of Yeshe Gyeltsen's life. In the oral traditions of Gelukpa practitioners today, however, Yeshe Gyeltsen remains nothing short of a religious folk hero. Among the Tibetans, there is a saying: "If a youth is talented enough, even the throne of Ganden is open to him," and this is often quoted with reference to Yongdzin Yeshe Gyeltsen, since his life proves that regardless of one's background, through intellectual ability and spiritual attainment one can in fact rise to one of the loftiest posts within the Tibetan religious hierarchy. Yeshe Gyeltsen *was* in fact offered the throne of Ganden as well, but he declined it.

The Gelukpa Geshe, Jampel Tardö, once summarized for me how the tradition thinks of Yeshe Gyeltsen. It is a story worth repeating in full:

> Yeshe Gyeltsen's life is a famous story! It shows how far one can advance through hard work, and it also illustrates how the "tables can be turned." Yeshe Gyeltsen was a very fine student. He received the Kachen degree from Tashilünpo and studied with many famous teachers. He studied the tantras with the great Yongdzin Purbuchok. He retreated for many years in Kyirong and established the Samten Ling monastery there. The Eighth Dalai Lama invited him to Lhasa to stay in the Potala and teach him. Yeshe Gyeltsen wanted to go back to Kyirong, but His Holiness told him, "Please stay. We will build a Kyirong-like monastery right here!" That was Tsechok Ling. It was built just across the Kyichu river from the Potala and housed about thirty to forty monks. When Yeshe Gyeltsen died, his corpse was not buried. It was preserved by covering it, using a special process like that used for Tsongkapa and, more recently, for Kyabje (Kyabs-rje) Ling Rinpoche. He was a *very* famous teacher. He took three months to explain one verse! He had been very poor. His brothers were ashamed of him. His family had disowned him. But later, when he became famed as the tutor to His Holiness, they came to Lhasa to visit him, and he received them kindly. So the tables had turned!

The latter portions of the above account are often repeated as Gelukpa teachers recount the moral of the "tables being turned." Thus, one finds that more than seventy years ago, when the renowned teacher Pabongka Rinpoche counseled his listeners about the benefits of study, he illustrated his remarks by narrating this section of Yeshe Gyeltsen's life story. As recorded in *Liberation in the Palm of Your Hand*, p. 100, Pabongka Rinpoche said the following:

> Study is also a relative who will never forsake you in hard times. Ordinary relatives pretend to be your friends when you are well-off; when times are bad, they pretend not to recognize you. But study is the best of relatives, for it will be particularly helpful to you when times are bad and you undergo suffering, illness, death, etc.
>
> Before great Tsechogling Rinpoche became tutor to one of the Dalai Lamas, there was a time when he was poor. He met an uncle of his on the road, who was going off to do some trading. Tsechogling Rinpoche said something to him, but the uncle spoke as if he did not recognize Rinpoche. After Rinpoche became the Dalai Lama's tutor and occupied one of the highest positions of authority, the uncle went to see him and told Rinpoche that he was his uncle.

Concerning Yeshe Gyeltsen's Mahāmudrā studies and accomplishments [he appears as no. 16 in the Geluk Mahāmudrā Lineage Prayer], one must look to his esteemed tantric guru, the greatly respected Losang Namgyel. The latter's full title was Jadrel Drubpai Wangchuk (Bya-bral Grub-pa'i-dbaṅ-phyug). Losang Namgyel had studied, and later taught, at the Gyüto (rGyud-stod) Tantric College, but he preferred to spend most of his time doing long retreats or making pilgrimages throughout southwestern Tibet in the border regions of Nepal. There he established his main monastic seat, calling it Ganden Pukpoche.

Losang Namgyel was especially fond of the works of Atīśa, Tsongkapa, and the First Panchen, Losang Chökyi Gyeltsen, and he was often called upon to give discourses on these great scholar-yogis. He was famed mostly, however, for his masterful command of the tantric traditions—both from the side of study and of practice. His own life story is replete with descriptions of the retreats he performed and the siddhis he attained. Namgyel apparently exchanged teachings with such illustrious practitioners as the Shabdrung Lhasa Tulku Losang Trinley (Źabs-druṅ Lha-sa sPrul-sku bLo-bzaṅ-'phrin-las) [who appears as no. 14 in the Lineage Prayer and thus was Namgyel's direct Mahāmudrā guru] and the Second Panchen Lama, Losang Yeshe [who appears there as no. 13]. But it was to Yeshe Gyeltsen that Namgyel passed on the special Ganden Oral Tradition teachings on Mahāmudrā.

Yeshe Gyeltsen later wrote the namtar of his teacher. The text is entitled *rJe btsun bla ma grub pa'i dbaṅ phyug blo bzaṅ rnam rgyal dpal bzaṅ po'i rnam par thar pa, Thub bstan mdzes rgyan rin po che'i phreṅ ba.* It comprises some 84 folio sides and is found as no. 6073, Tome 129, of Yeshe Gyeltsen's *Collected Works.* Here one can directly see the great reverence and devotion Yeshe Gyeltsen has for his Mahāmudrā guru, for the namtar is replete with praise.

Yeshe Gyeltsen began his studies with Namgyel in 1735 when he was twenty-three. Immediately after taking final ordination, Namgyel having given him instruction on the Oral Tradition of Mahāmudrā, Yeshe Gyeltsen began constructing a solitary meditation cell. After successfully completing his first extensive retreat, Yeshe Gyeltsen sought further esoteric instruction, but his teachers were dying—the Second Panchen in 1737 and Losang Namgyel in 1741. Still, for ten more years Yeshe Gyeltsen continued to study with other teachers and to do long retreats. His efforts attracted the attention of many. Then, in 1751, he made his first visit to the Nepalese border regions.

In 1756 he founded the monastery of Kyirong Tashi Samten Ling, and in 1759 he supervised restorations at the monastic complex that had been founded by his guru, Namgyel. In 1767 he made further additions to Kyirong Samten Ling. Between 1770 and 1782 he made trips back and forth to Lhasa to give instruction to the youthful Eighth Dalai Lama, and, of course, he continued to care for his own disciples.

In the light of such demanding activities, one can only be amazed by Yeshe Gyeltsen's prodigious literary output. But write he did, voluminously and on a very wide range of subjects. He authored some 163 individual texts comprising over 14,000 folio sides on subjects ranging from specific meditative rituals to the making of "sacred pills," and from explanations of specific philosophical views to the Ganden Oral Tradition of Mahāmudrā and diverse methods for performing guru yoga.

In addition to his authoritative works on the Ganden Oral Tradition, Yeshe Gyeltsen's renown as an author stems from his voluminous compositions in the area of religious biography. For example, he wrote a detailed commentary of 758 folia on the *Jātakamālā,* which is regarded as one of the best books on the Buddha's life composed in Tibet. In 1783 he completed an important work on the *avadānas* of Śākyamuni and the cult of the Sixteen Arhats known as the *gNas brtan rtogs brjod rgyal bstan rinpoche'i mdzas rgyan phul byuṅ gser gyi phreṅ ba.* In 1787, while serving as yongdzin to the Eighth Dalai Lama, he worked in the Potala to complete the massive two-volume anthology of namtar setting forth the lives of the eminent teachers of the Kadam and Gelukpa traditions. For these impressive accomplishments, and for countless others, we remember him and offer him our thanks.

Damchen Chökyi Gyalpo

Abbreviations

BA	George Roerich's translation of *The Blue Annals.*
BDOT	Ketsün Sangpo's *Biographical Dictionary of Tibet and Tibetan Buddhism.*
BIT	Warren's translation, *Buddhism in Translations.*
Contributions	Das's *Contributions on the Religion and History of Tibet.*
Dictionary	Das's *A Tibetan-English Dictionary.*
EOB	*Encyclopaedia of Buddhism.*
GOT	Wylie's translation of *The Geography of Tibet According to the 'Dzam-gling-rgyas-bshad.*
Guide	Ferrari's translation of *mK'yen brtse's Guide to the Holy Places of Central Tibet.*
History	Sumpa Kenpo's *History of Tibet.*
JAAR	*Journal of the American Academy of Religion.*
LAB	Tucci's *To Lhasa and Beyond.*
LTWA	Library of Tibetan Works and Archives.
Materials	Lokesh Chandra's *Materials for a History of Tibetan Literature.*
ODT	Nebesky-Wojkowitz's *Oracles and Demons of Tibet.*
ROT	Tucci's *Religions of Tibet.*
TPH	Shakabpa's *Tibet: A Political History.*
TPS	Tucci's *Tibetan Painted Scrolls.*

NOTES

NOTES TO THE PREFACE

1. As translated by Geshe Wangyal in *The Door of Liberation*, p. 205.

2. See *Liberation in Our Hands* [trans. by Geshe Lobsang Tharchin, with Artemus B. Engle], Howell, New Jersey: Mahāyāna Sūtra and Tantra Press, 1990, p. 163.

NOTES TO THE INTRODUCTION

3. For example, see the "Introduction" to Reynolds and Capps' *The Biographical Process: Studies in the History and Psychology of Religion*, especially pp. 3–5, where this distinction is discussed in some detail.

4. Basically, there are only two major divisions or "vehicles" (*Skt. yāna*) of Buddhist doctrine and practice: (1) the Hīnayāna, or "Lesser Vehicle," which aims at individual liberation, and (2) the Mahāyāna, or "Great Vehicle," which aims at universal liberation. The Vajrayāna, variously referred to as the "Diamond Vehicle" and the "speedy path," is in actuality a subdivision of the Mahāyāna, being based firmly on those ideals. Because it makes use of the yogic techniques offered in the Tantras, the Vajrayāna is also referred to as the Tantrayāna.

   Meditation has always remained the heart of Buddhist practice. Still, as Buddhism developed over time, such practice came to be overshadowed by concerns with scholarly disputations and expositions of the doctrine. Two major movements within Buddhism sought to moderate the emphasis on such scholasticism. The first was the emergence of the Mahāyāna, which stressed the Bodhisattva ideal and the practice of compassion and which also placed these goals within the reach of the lay community. However, the Mahāyāna movement also produced its own resurgence of philosophical interests, owing most notably to its "two crown jewels," Nāgārjuna and Asaṅga. These two great sages, who were also master meditation practitioners, splendidly articulated Buddhism's quintessential doctrine, that of śūnyatā, the voidness of inherent existence in all things as well as in the so-called self. Thereafter, basing itself firmly upon the fruits of the Mahāyāna's explication of voidness, a second movement emerged, which, while not repudiating the value of such crystalline exposition, sought to re-emphasize the practice side of Buddhism as a balance to theoretical preoccupations. This supplementary movement within the Mahāyāna is known as the Vajrayāna, the "Diamond Vehicle," which posits the goal of complete liberation in one's own lifetime through rigorous practice aimed at bringing about direct realization of the teachings. Practitioners who enter upon this "speedy path" and who are successful in winning its fruits are called siddhas. It was primarily this latter form of Buddhism that was successful in winning over Tibetan converts.

5. Śāntirakṣita, a learned Indian Buddhist monk from the great Nālandā University, was invited to Tibet during the reign of King Trisong Detsen (Khri-sroṅ-lde-brtsan) [755–797(?)]. He was initially unsuccessful in his attempts to establish Buddhism there and advised that the tantric adept Padmasambhava be sent for. Later, these two worked together to introduce Buddhism. History records that it was actually Śāntirakṣita who presided over the architectural design and construction of the first Buddhist monastery in Tibet, called Samye (bSam-yas), and that it was he who served as its first abbot and who ordained the first seven indigenous Tibetan monks. For more on the life of Śāntirakṣita, see Chapter 25 of Alaka Chattopadhyaya's *Atīśa and Tibet* and my own summary of his life in *The Encyclopedia of Religion*, New York: The Free Press, Macmillan Publishing Co., 1986.

6. Kamalaśīla, on the counsel of the aged Śāntirakṣita, was later summoned from India. He is remembered in the annals of Tibetan religious history especially owing to the part he played in the famed Council of Lhasa debates convened to settle the issue of which form of Buddhism—the Indian or the Chinese—would predominate in Tibet. Kamalaśīla, representing the Indian side, defeated the Chinese representative, one Hua-shang Mahāyāna, and the Tibetans opted for Indian Buddhism. The debates, which took place at Samye, circa 792–94, were not without serious results, however, and it appears that Kamalaśīla was later murdered. For more on this famed debate and its aftermath, see Paul Demiéville's *Le Concile de Lhasa*; and on the life of Kamalaśīla see my summary in *The Encyclopedia of Religion*, *op. cit.*

7. Much still remains to be learned regarding Tibet's indigenous folk

traditions. Major studies have been done by Stein, Lalou, Tucci, Hoffman, Eliade, Heissig, Snellgrove, and other historians of religion. Recently, studies by young anthropologists and musicologists such as Geoffrey Samuel, Martin Brauen, Samten Karmay, Robert Paul, Ricardo Canzio, and others promise to help expand our understanding of these traditions even further. A long article on "Tibetan Archaic Religious Traditions" written by me can be found in Vol. I of *World Spirituality: An Encyclopedic History of the Religious Quest* (New York: Crossroad Publishing Co.). For specific and fuller references, see the present "Bibliography."

8. Eva Dargyay's study, *The Rise of Esoteric Buddhism in Tibet*, goes a long way toward filling out the actual historical circumstances surrounding the early establishment of Buddhism in Tibet. In particular, she argues convincingly that Padmasambhava was not the only early siddha responsible for advancing the cause of Buddhism there. Rather, such figures as the Vairotsana and Vimalamitra played roles of equal importance in the founding of the earliest order there.

9. This topic is much too large to adequately address here, and I am currently working on a separate monograph that fully discusses the history of Buddhist sacred biography in India and Tibet. Here, however, a few brief and general comments may be posited. Our main source for Buddhist siddha biographies in India is Abhayadatta's late eleventh or early twelfth-century work on the Eighty-Four Siddhas [see English translations by James Robinson and Keith Dowman]. Regarding these biographies, we may note that they are all much briefer than their later Tibetan counterparts; that they invariably recount the lives of lay [as opposed to monastic] practitioners; and that they fall into two distinct types—the majority of them [four-fifths of the eighty-four] focusing in stylized ways upon the importance of the Mahāmudrā guru himself rather than upon the training of the siddha-to-be or upon the latter's subsequent enlightened activity, while a fifth of them are longer and more individuated in style and focus upon the accomplished siddha—usually publicly accompanied by a tantric consort—who performs often bizarre examples of wonder-working enlightened activity and power.

Generally speaking, all Tibetan namtar rely upon Abhayadatta's work and include compositions of both types: those that emphasize the future siddha's training and those that emphasize the accomplished siddha's powers. However, in Tibet over time we see the interesting reunification of yogic practice and monasticism, and as a consequence we witness shifts of emphasis in the Tibetan examples.

10. Again generally speaking, because Tantric Buddhism had to prove its veracity and effectiveness over Tibet's older indigenous beliefs, the namtar produced in connection with the founding of the earliest orders [the Nyingmapa and the Kagyüpa] are those that most greatly emphasize the siddha's wonder-working powers, giving scant attention to that siddha's background, education, training, or gurus. Again, one notes that such namtar focus upon the lay tantric practitioner in the company of his or her tantric consort. One has only to consider the famed namtar of Padmasambhava as an example of this type of composition. The later Tibetan namtar, on the other hand, such as those produced in connection with the Sakyapa and Gelukpa orders, demonstrate that tantric practice and monastic life have been reunited; and the whole career of the siddha, from early training through post-enlightenment activity, is recounted while the displays of wonder-working power are downplayed.

11. The early hagiographies of the Christian "confessor saints" portray rugged and heroic individuals whose utter commitment to their faith was meant to uplift and inspire others. They chronicle the lives of men and women who, having felt the "call to Christ," entered his service. Usually after having publicly advanced the faith by founding monasteries or stewarding large numbers of disciples, they bravely and willingly chose the hard, solitary life of the contemplative, and to a few devoted followers they revealed their holiness through the performance of miracles.

    The Western scholarly tradition has generally taken a dim view of hagiography. Indeed, in the West "hagiography" has come to be defined as any idealizing or worshipful biography, the implication being that such texts are naively exaggerated accounts written to edify a devoted, though gullible, popular audience and, as a consequence, are of little historical worth. One need only peruse the writings of H. Delehaye on this subject to see with what condescension such texts are regarded. The two most common accusations leveled against hagiography are that (1) there are in them numerous duplications of descriptions of holiness and (2) they describe a preponderance of miracles.

12. Many scholars working with this material have tended to confine it to the province of popular literature, viewing siddha lives as the products of and for popular spirituality and as being folkloric. For example,

Mircea Eliade wrote, in his *Yoga, Immortality and Freedom*, p. 305: "...a number of the Nāthas and Siddhas put more emphasis than their predecessors had done upon the value of magic and Yoga as inestimable means for the conquest of freedom and immortality. It was especially this aspect of their message that struck the popular imagination; we still find it echoed today in folklore and the vernacular literatures." It must be noted that Eliade found this feature of namtar valuable, however, and he followed the above remark with the statement: "It is for this reason that the latter seem to us of great value for our inquiry."

David Snellgrove, too, agrees with this assessment of namtar. In *Buddhist Himalāya*, p. 86, he calls namtar "popular accounts (in which) the goal of perfection seems to be immortality." Snellgrove voiced this assessment with specific reference to the lives of the Eighty-Four Siddhas of the Śaivitic and Buddhist traditions. He considers that such namtar have value for depicting the general religious climate of the times. The full relevant passage here (p. 85) reads: "Both Buddhist and Shaivitic tradition preserve the memory of eighty-four great yogins or perfected ones (siddhas). Their biographies are to be found in the Tibetan canon, and although the tales related of them are of no direct historical worth, they portray well enough the general religious setting, in which the actual tantric texts originated." Giuseppe Tucci, in *Tibetan Painted Scrolls*, Vol. I, p. 151, admits that "an historian cannot ignore the *rnam-t'ar*," and indeed Tucci himself makes good use of them. However, his own general definition of namtar [see text of "Introduction,"] appears to me to be more obscuring of their true nature than clarifying. Albert Grünwedel, in *Die Geschichten der vier und achtzig Zauberers aus dem Tibetischen uberstez,* published in 1916, refers to namtar as both "phantastic" and "obscure." It seems to me that a negative and elitist bias shines through all of the above assessments, for all of them overlook the fact that these texts may be simultaneously both popular and profound.

13. This terminology was aptly applied by Reginald Ray in an unpublished paper, "The Vajrayāna Mahāsiddhas; Some Principles of Interpretation," read at the American Academy of Religion's meeting in San Francisco in December of 1977.

14. Tantric literature is often described as "esoteric" or "hidden." The meanings of tantric texts are said to be "veiled" from the ordinary, or uninitiated, reader owing to their being written in symbolic or so-called "twilight" language [*sandhyābhāṣā*]. This is especially the case

when practice instructions are to be communicated, since these are not intended to be readily grasped or to be practiced by persons not properly prepared to undertake such practice. Thus, the meanings of these texts are "hidden" or "veiled" until, being properly prepared, one can read their symbolic language with understanding. Again, what is instructional to advanced practitioners is "hidden" to unskilled ordinary beings. An interesting discussion of the language of the tantras can be found in Agehananda Bharati's *The Tantric Tradition*, pp. 164–184. Bharati argues throughout that such language should properly be understood as "intentional language" [*sandhābhāṣā*].

15. This point was duly noted by Reginald Ray's paper, cited above. On page 4 of that paper, Ray wrote: "... when one compares the contents of the Siddha biographies with those of the classical Tantras and their commentaries, one finds that they are basically the same, if presented in very different styles."

16. This fact is well noted by those within the Tibetan tradition. Other Western scholars working with namtar have also recognized this tripartite pattern. Tucci's work, for example, is cognizant of it. David Ruegg, in his translation of *The Life of Bu-ston Rinpoche*, pp. 44–45, notes the three-fold structure of namtar; and Luciano Petech's "Introduction" to Alfonsa Ferrari's translation of *mK'yen brtse's Guide to the Holy Places of Central Tibet*, p. XIX, takes note of this traditional three-fold pattern.

17. Most namtar contain all three "levels" of life story, though one or the other is most emphasized. Tucci, *Tibetan Painted Scrolls*, Vol. I, pp. 159–161, notes that Kedrub Je (mKhas-grub-rje) authored a "secret biography" of his guru, Tsongkapa, in addition to one treating primarily of the first two levels only. Another disciple of Tsongkapa, Jamyang Chöje Tashi Pelden [1379–1449], who helped to found Drepung monastery, is also remembered as the author of a famous "secret biography" of his teacher, called *Je Rin po che gsaṅ ba'i rnam thar*, and translated in several English versions as *Song of the Mystic Experiences of Lama Je Rinpoche.*

18. By this suggestion I do not mean to become embroiled here in the hair-splitting philosophical debates that have continued throughout the history of Buddhist literature over the issue of *nītartha* ["direct" or "definitive meaning"] versus *neyārtha* ["indirect" or "interpretable meaning"] teaching and scripture. There are already a number of excellent discussions of this important question. For example, see the fine essay,

"Buddhist Hermeneutics" by Robert Thurman, in *JAAR*, Vol. XLVI, 1978, and his translation of Tsongkapa's analysis of this issue in *Tsong Khapa's Speech of Gold in the Essence of True Eloquence*, Princeton University Press, 1984. I mean only to assert quite simply that the authors of tantric literature used skillful means and that they employed language in such a way that its "literal" meaning is not always its "final" meaning.

19. "Insider" is a literal translation of the Tibetan term, *nangpa* (naṅ pa). In Buddhist contexts it is used to refer to those who stand "inside" the Buddha's Dharma, as opposed to *chipa* (phyid pa), or "those standing outside" of it. Further, among the nangpa two divisions are recognized: (1) lay followers of the Dharma and (2) ordained monastic practitioners.

20. See Tucci's *Tibetan Painted Scrolls*, Vol. I, pp. 150–151.

21. The new order founded by Tsongkapa was known by various names: Riwo Gandenpa, Kadam Sarmapa (gsar ma pa), Gendenpa, and Gelukpa. Presumably, the order also came to be referred to as the Yellow Hats because of Tsongkapa's innovation of having the monks of his order wear yellow or saffron apparel, as did the original Buddhist monks of India. This signaled the great reform that he instituted in Tibet and that is set forth doctrinally in his mammoth work *The Great Stages of the Path to Enlightenment* [titled in Tibetan the *Lam rim chen mo*]. Snellgrove suggests, in *A Cultural History of Tibet*, p. 181, that "Westerners have borrowed from the Chinese the term "Yellow Hat" for the Gelukpa...." Whatever the actual origin of the epithet, it has come to be an unambiguous and readily identifiable feature of the order. The six life stories translated here cover the three-hundred year period during which the Gelukpas successfully appropriated more and more power and firmly established themselves in Tibet.

22. Snellgrove, *A Cultural History of Tibet*, p. 181.

23. For studies devoted primarily to the relationships between religion and politics in Tibet, see the works of Shakabpa, M. Goldstein, Bina-Roy, Theodore Woodcock, L. Petech, W. Rockhill, Pedro Carrasco, and Franz Michael listed in the present "Bibliography."

24. This is the same Jamchen Chöje Shakya Yeshe whom Tsongkapa had sent in his stead to the Ming court during the reign of the Chinese Emperor Yung-lo [reigned 1403–1424]. Tsongkapa received two

invitations from the Emperor to visit China. He declined the first, but after receiving the second, he sent Shakya Yeshe as his representative. Following his return from China, Jamchen Chöje founded Sera monastery in 1419. For further information, see Shakabpa, *Tibet: A Political History*, pp. 84–85.

25. Descriptive information on these famed Gelukpa institutions can be found in Waddell's *Tibetan Buddhism*, Tucci's *To Lhasa and Beyond*, Wylie's *The Geography of Tibet According to the 'Dzam-gling-rgyas-bshad*, and Ferrari's *mK'yen brtse's Guide to the Holy Places of Central Tibet.*

26. Some 125 years after his death, Gendündrub [1391–1475] was retroactively recognized as being the First Dalai Lama. An excellent English version of the life of Gendündrub can be found in Glenn Mullin's *Selected Works of the Dalai Lama I: Bridging the Sūtras and Tantras* (1985 edition, pp. 203–250). A very brief summary of Gendündrub's life is also provided by Sarat Chandra Das in his *Contributions on the Religion and History of Tibet* (published in 1881 and reprinted in 1970, pp. 110–111). Snellgrove, in *A Cultural History of Tibet*, p. 182, rightly notes that it was Gendündrub's "energy and ability which was mainly responsible for building up Tsong-kha-pa's school into an active expansive order ready and anxious to compete with the others on an equal footing."

27. According to Gendündrub's namtar, he was instructed by a vision of the Goddess Pelden Hlamo to construct Tashilünpo. Shakabpa, *op. cit.*, p. 91, says that Gendündrub was able to build the monastery because of the generous financial help he received from one "Dargyas Pon Palzang." The monastic facilities housed about three thousand monks.

28. The site chosen by Gendündrub for Tashilünpo is important because, as Snellgrove, *op. cit.*, p. 182, points out, this location was "on the very edge of the territory dominated by the powerful princes of Rin-spungs who had the militant support of the Karma-pa Red Hat hierarchy." Over the course of its history, Tashilünpo monastery in particular came under violent attack from the rival Karma Kagyü order and—as Gendündrub's own remarks show—he was aware of this potential threat from the very outset.

29. The Tibetan of this passage reads as follows: "*De'i tshe bkra śis lhun por thams cad mkhyen pa dGe-'dun-grub-dpal-bzaṅ-po 'phrin las dbyar mtsho ltar rgyas par bźugs pas khri rin po ches gtsos dGa'-ldan pa'i bla chen phal*

mo ches rje dGe-'dun-grub la rgyal ba gñis pa'i rgyal tshab tu 'byon dgos par gsol ba btap pas rje dGe-'dun-grub kyis kho bo dgra yul du dgra mkhar brtsig dgos pa yod pas 'di kha raṅ du rje'i bstan pa 'dzin pa yin/."

30. The title Panchen, or "greatly learned one" [a contracted form of the Sanskrit noun *paṇḍita* plus the Tibetan term "chen"] was not a new one and had been used prior to the time of Losang Chökyi Gyeltsen. However, the great prestige of the title First Panchen in connection with him results from the fact that it was conferred upon him by his famed disciple, the Great Fifth Dalai Lama, who at the same time officially recognized him as also being the incarnation of Amitābha Buddha. [The Great Fifth claimed for himself the honor of being the incarnation of Avalokiteśvara.] The line of Panchens thus created by the Fifth Dalai Lama thereafter became primarily associated with the Tashilünpo monastery. For more on the enumerations of the Panchens, see Tucci's *Tibetan Painted Scrolls*, Vol. II, pp. 413–414; G. Schulemann's *Geschichte Der Dalai-Lamas*; and S. Das's "The Lives of the Panchen Rinpoches or Tashi Lamas," in *JRASB*, 1882 and in *Contributions, op. cit.*, pp. 81–144.

31. The accounts of the First Panchen's activities presented both by Das, in *Contributions*, pp. 111–117, and by Fa-tsun, in *Encyclopaedia of Buddhism*, Vol. III, Fascicle 1, pp. 163–169, stress this aspect of his life.

32. According to Longdöl Lama's (kLoṅ-rdol-bla-ma's) famed catalog, the *Tsento* (*mTshan-tho*), the First Panchen was author of some 108 separate works. [The Tibetan listing of these compositions can be found in Lokesh Chandra's *Materials for the Study of Tibetan History*, Vol. 3., pp. 645–647.] Among the First Panchen's works are to be found his own autobiography of 450 folia, completed in 1720 by his successor, the Second Panchen, Losang Yeshe; several namtar [of Sanggye Yeshe, Ensapa, six of the First Panchen's predecessors from the extended enumeration beginning with Subhūti, and others], numerous sādhanas, especially devoted to Vajrabhairava, Guhyasamāja, Cakrasaṃvara, and Kālacakra; numerous texts on guru yoga, and some on Chöd. But perhaps most noteworthy, and certainly of vital importance to the present study, were his *bLa ma mchod pa* [*Guru-puja* or *Offering to the Spiritual Master*], *dGe ldan bKa' brgyud rin po che'i phyag chen rtsa ba rgyal ba'i gźun lam* [*Root Text for the Ganden Oral Tradition of Mahāmudrā, called the Main Path of the Conquerors*], and *Yaṅ gsal sgron me* [an autocommentary on the latter text, called *The Lamp of Re-illumination.*] These

latter two texts succinctly elucidate the Ganden Oral Tradition regarding Mahāmudrā. The first has come to set the standard for performance of all subsequent Gelukpa monastic liturgy and public ritual.

33. Tucci's *The Religions of Tibet*, pp. 134–135, gives a succinct description of the development of this religio-political phenomenon in Tibet. Also see the discussion on reincarnation in Franz Michaels's *Rule By Incarnation*, pp. 37-40.

34. See Gene Smith's "Foreword" to L. Chandra's Tibetan edition of the *Tibetan Chronicle of Padma-dkar-po*, p. 1.

35. The Fifth Dalai Lama conferred upon his guru, Losang Chökyi Gyeltsen, the title First Panchen; but soon, to increase the prestige of the position, retroactive validity was conferred upon the theory of his being an incarnation of Amitābha Buddha by extending those incarnations in a backwards series, said to begin with Tsongkapa's famed disciple, Kedrub Je. Thus, in the enumerations given by Tucci and Schulemann, we find the early list of Panchens to include Kedrub Je, Sönam Choklang, Gyelwa Ensapa, and Panchen Losang Chökyi Gyeltsen. Over time, the list of such incarnations was extended back even to India, with the first member of the series being declared to be Subhūti, the famed contemporary disciple of Śākyamuni Buddha himself. The most extensive enumeration of the Panchen incarnations of Tashilünpo therefore lists four Indian incarnations [Subhūti, Mañjuśrīkīrti, Lekden Je (Legs-ldan-'byed), and Abhayakāra-gupta] and six Tibetan incarnations [Gö Lotsawa Kukpa Hletse ('Gos lo-tsā-ba Khugpa Lhas-btsas), Sakya Pandita Künga Gyeltsen (Sa-skya Paṇḍita Kun-dga'-rgyal-mtshan), Yungtön Dorje Pel (Yuṅ-ston rDo-rje-dpal), Kedrub Je, Sönam Choklang, and Ensapa] prior to Losang Chökyi Gyeltsen. Thus, though Losang Chökyi Gyeltsen is actually the eleventh member of the extensive enumeration, he was the first incarnation in the series to be named with an ordinal number.

36. It would appear that at least by the beginning of the nineteenth century, this monastery was no longer a teaching college. We note, for example, Wylie's translation of the 1820 composition, the *'Dzam-gling-rgyas-bshad*, pp. 76–77, where Sangpu is described as follows: "In former times (Gsang-phu) had students of Dbu-ma and Tshad-ma and a large assemblage of monks; however, since the increase of such (monasteries) as Se-ra and 'Bras-spungs, this one has gradually declined, and now there is nothing there but a few married monks

who have chosen to follow the Sa-skya-pa...."

37. Chökyi Dorje's main retreat site was Garmo Chö Dzong. This hermitage is listed in the *'Dzam-gling-rgyas-bshad* [see Wylie's translation, p. 71]. It is described as being "not far to the south" of the Ensa monastery. Again, while all of these six siddhas became affiliated at some point in their lives with one of the three chief Gelukpa monasteries in Central Tibet, for the most part their chief spiritual activities were concentrated in the area of Tsang.

38. Ensa monastery was located northeast of Tashilünpo, on the eastern bank of the Sangchu (Saṅs-chu) river. Until the Chinese takeover of Tibet in 1959, Ensa monastery was regarded as one of the purest and most strict, in terms of monastic discipline, of all Gelukpa establishments. In 1980, Lama Thubten Zopa Rinpoche related to me the following anecdote regarding the monastery: "At devotionals, after each round of tea was finished, the monks of Ensa Gönpa would immediately turn their cups face-down. This was done to constantly remind each of them of the uncertainty of the time of death. Nothing was ever done casually, or without alertness, at Ensa."

39. *Lamdre* literally means "Path and Fruit." *Taknyi* literally means "the Two Examinations." Both terms have reference to the tantric oral traditions transmitted from the Indian siddha tradition to early members of the Sakya order. Moreover, both these terms have particular reference to the *Hevajra Tantra* [or the *Hevajra-mūla-tantra-rāja*]. For example, the great siddha Virūpa's treatise, *The Path and Its Fruits,* is said to have been written on the basis of all of the sūtras and tantras in general and on the Hevajra Tantra in particular. Likewise, Taknyi refers to an important commentary on the Hevajra Tantra, the latter itself being divided into two sections.

40. In Dargyay's *The Rise of Esoteric Buddhism in Tibet,* p. 222, the practice of *chulen* (*bcud len*) is described as follows: "'Taking only essences' (*bcud-len*) is a dietetic method; while practicing it the Yogi is not allowed to take any other food except the allowed essence of flowers or stones for example...." In recent years "pill retreats," as they are called, have been performed by increasing numbers of Western practitioners, and a number of instruction manuals on the subject have been published. Such manuals usually describe the proper retreat conditions and prospective retreatants, as well as the pill ingredients, something of their method of production, and their proper use. In 1983, Wisdom

Publications published a most informative pamphlet on this subject authored and guided by the Venerable Lama Thubten Yeshe. It is called, simply, *Taking the Essence.*

41. Information on Nāropa's Six Yogas can be found in a number of English language sources. For example, see Garma C.C. Chang's *Teachings of Tibetan Yoga*; Lobsang Lhalungpa's *The Life of Milarepa*; Tucci's *The Religions of Tibet* (especially pp. 98–109); Muses' *Esoteric Teachings of the Tibetan Tantra* (pp. 123–282); and Geshe Gyatso's *Clear Light of Bliss.*

42. The Sanskrit term vidyādhara literally means "possessor of knowledge." When used in relation to siddhas, however, that knowledge is always of the "magical" sort. Thus, vidyādharas are thought to be able to take birth at will, to transform themselves into any desired form or manifestation, to travel unimpededly to any destination, to assume the "rainbow body," etc.

43. The full title of the prayer is *dGa' ldan bka' srol phyag rgya chen po'i 'khrid kyi bla brgyud gsol 'debs/ kha skoṅ bcas bźugs//* (*Prayer, with Supplement, to the Lineage Lamas of the Ganden Oral Tradition of Mahāmudrā*). The prayer's colophon declares that it was composed by the eighteenth century Yongdzin Yeshe Gyeltsen [1713–1793] and that additions were made by the first Pabongka Rinpoche, Dechen Nyingpo [1878–1941].

44. The Tibetan rendered here as "total integration" is *zungjuk* (zuṅ 'jug). The term is of central importance in advanced tantric contexts generally and in discussions of Mahāmudrā practice in particular, for it is used to suggest the ultimate culmination of practice, the experience of the final and complete union, convergence, fusion, and inseparability of any number of technically defined "pairs," which results in their becoming "no longer two." Sometimes zungjuk is rendered simply as "enlightenment" or as "Buddhahood" itself. The "pairs" are described variously [for example, as subject and object, wisdom and method, śūnyatā and bodhicitta, or perception and experience], but in tantric contexts they usually refer to bliss and voidness, or again to the illusory body and the clear light. For more on this important term, see note 153, below, and Tucci's *The Religions of Tibet,* pp. 55–67. The specific English rendering of "total integration" for this term was suggested by Lama Thubten Yeshe.

45. That is, enlightenment itself.

46. This verse describes in concise form the entire process of the training in and the completion of the Path of Guru Yoga. In each case, the "three doors" of body, speech, and mind [which comprise the psychophysical totality of ordinary beings and which are subject to defilement and impurities] are juxtaposed with the three of the guru's purified form. The wish is then posited to realize the inseparability of the Buddha's holy body, speech, and mind and one's own. When such union or total integration is experienced, one becomes a Buddha, an enlightened being, in actuality.

47. There are also specific times during the monastic calendar when the reading of certain namtar is enjoined upon the community. For example, it is customary for Gelukpa clerics to read aloud the *Secret Biography of Tsongkapa* on the day commemorating his death and to read the namtar of other figures important to the order's development on dates commemorating their deaths.

48. From a conversation with Geshe Tardö in Charlottesville, Virginia, in early 1985.

49. The Venerable Chögyam Trungpa Rinpoche was once asked about the importance of "lineage" for one who was practicing. Though his remarks refer to the Kagyü tradition, the answer he gave [which is found in Judith Hanson's translation of *The Torch of Certainty*, p. 17] is appropriate in our context as well: "The lineage is very important for the practitioner. Each teacher in the lineage had his particular skillful way of teaching. Each has contributed a great deal to the wealth of the Kagyud tradition. Each one's life is a perfect example for us to study. Each one has left behind and passed on his experiences to us.

The lineage shows us that 'it can be done'—even by us! It makes us aware that the teachings represent not one but many lifetimes of work. Each teacher sacrificed a lot, went through a great deal of personal hardship and finally attained enlightenment. Belonging to this lineage makes us very rich and full of enlightenment-wealth. Being part of this family gives us immense encouragement and also a sense of validity [regarding that which we are trying to practice]. We realize that the teachings we now receive have come down from all of them."

50. For example, one common Refuge Formula goes:

The Guru is Buddha, the Guru is Dharma,
The Guru is Sangha also.

The Guru is the source of all [three].
To all the Gurus, I go for Refuge.

Another version says:

To the feet of the Venerable Lama,
Embodiment of the Three Jewels,
Profoundly I turn for refuge;
[Please] Bestow upon me your transforming powers.

51. See *Selected Works of the Dalai Lama III: Essence of Refined Gold*, translated by Glenn Mullin, Second Edition, 1985, p. 59.

52. See *The Life of Marpa the Translator*, Boulder, Prajna Press, 1982, p. xxxvi.

53. Gö Lotsawa, the author of the famed *Blue Annals,* explained in his discussion of the Mahāmudrā that the knowledge of Mahāmudrā, which is equivalent to knowledge of śūnyatā, cannot be realized in truth as long as it remains on the level of discursive reasoning. Yet one cannot use reasoning to get beyond a reason-grasped knowledge of it. Rather, in order to get beyond this reasoning state, one must use a means that is direct, nondiscursive, and intuitive, and only a guru's blessing provides such a means. Thus, Gö Lotsawa wrote [see *Blue Annals*, p. 839]: "Thus the antidote (of this inference, i.e. understanding of Relativity [here, śūnyatā]) which is not a mere theory, represents the knowledge of Mahāmudrā. This (knowledge) can be gained only through the blessing of a holy teacher (i.e. through initiation, and not through reasoning)."

54. Indeed, for all tantric study and practice, guru devotion is deemed indispensable. Tantric practice is complicated and difficult. If performed properly, it can usher in enlightenment in this very life, but if done improperly, it can produce dangerous consequences. The direct, personal guidance of a guru is therefore essential. From the student's side, proper understanding and performance of guru devotion is essential. A key textual reference outlining the latter is Aśvaghoṣa's *Fifty Stanzas of Guru Devotion.* This text is often taught before the giving of tantric empowerments.

55. In my opinion, one of the best discussions of this issue appears in Mullin's *Selected Works of the Dalai Lama III: Essence of Refined Gold* where, on pp. 59–80, His Holiness the (present) Fourteenth Dalai

Lama speaks about some of the dangers inherent in the notion of "seeing every action of the Guru as Perfect." His Holiness's remarks are eloquent, judicious, and especially appropriate in these times.

56. The Tibetan is *mÑes pa gsum.*

57. It is an often repeated counsel, especially in Mahāmudrā practice contexts, that "It was Buddha Vajradhara himself who said that one's Guru is to be seen as the Buddha." One of the textual loci for this assertion is the *Mukhagama of Mañjuśrī*, composed by the Indian Buddhist, Buddhajñānapada. In this text, Buddha Vajradhara says:

> It is I who dwell in the guru's body,
> I who receive offerings from aspirants.

Therefore, to please one's guru is to please all the Buddhas and to please Vajradhara, who embodies them all. The guru thus provides us with a precious opportunity. As Geshe Ngawang Dargyey states in his supplement to Aśvaghoṣa's *Fifty Stanzas of Guru Devotion* in *The Mahāmudrā Eliminating the Darkness of Ignorance*, p. 161: "Through devotion to your Guru, showing him respect, serving him and making offerings, you build up the merit that will allow you to become liberated from all your suffering. Such service is done not to benefit your Guru, but for your own sake. When you plant seeds in a field, it is not to benefit the earth. It is you yourself who will harvest the crops. Therefore with the proper devotional attitude towards your Guru—seeing him as a Buddha—the more positive energy you exert in his direction, the closer you come towards Buddhahood yourself."

58. The Tibetan for what I translate here as the "eight mundane concerns" is *'jig rten gyi chos brgyad.* This compound is often rendered "eight worldly dharmas," but I seek to avoid this translation because it leaves one of the terms [dharma] untranslated. The eight "concerns" are: gain, loss, reputation, disgrace, praise, blame, pleasure, and pain. According to Buddhist doctrine, as long as one's activities are bound up with such worldly and mundane concerns, one is not practicing the Dharma purely.

59. In this first paragraph, Ensapa alludes first to the three approaches to gaining insight about and mastery of the Dharma: insight gained from hearing the doctrine, that gained by pondering and reflecting upon it, and that gained by cultivating meditation upon it. He then tells us directly that any attempt to engage in these three approaches

that mixes them with any of the eight mundane concerns will result only in the continuance of saṃsāra. Rather than curing ourselves, we further poison ourselves. In short, Ensapa says: "Don't mix Dharmic activity with worldly activity! If it is mixed with worldly activity, it is not true Dharmic activity!" [Lama Zopa Rinpoche and others are famous today for their similar admonitions.]

60. These three "perfect virtues" of a lama are mentioned by Tucci in *Tibetan Painted Scrolls*, pp. 94–96, and by Lokesh Chandra in *Materials for a History of Tibetan Literature (Part I)*, p. 11. For additional "services" expected from a lama, see Franz Michael's *Rule by Incarnation*, pp. 132–136.

61. See for example, *A Short Biography of Je Tzong-k'a-pa* [based on lectures by Geshe Ngawang Dhargyey and edited by India Stevens], Dharamsala, Library of Tibetan Works and Archives, 1975, p. 23. A slightly revised version of this same *Biography* appears in *The Life and Teachings of Tsong Khapa*, edited by Robert Thurman, published by the Library of Tibetan Works and Archives in 1982. See there, p. 21.

62. Avalokiteśvara is the Buddhist deity of "Infinite Compassion."

63. This comment is actually a summation, done by C.F. Moule, of a paper by Mary Hesse entitled "Miracles and the Law of Nature." See *Miracles: Cambridge Studies in Their Philosophy and History*, edited by Moule; London: 1965. Moule himself notes, p. 238 ff., that the Greek word most commonly used throughout the New Testament was not *thaumasion* ("marvel") but *dunamis* ("power").

64. This is one of the most well-known enumerations of the various types of ṛddhi. For alternate translations of this particular passage, see R. Kloppenborg, *The Paccekabuddha*, pp. 52–53; Robinson's *Buddha's Lions*, p. 8; H. van Zeyst in *Encyclopaedia of Buddhism*, Vol. I, part I, p. 99; and Rhys-Davids' *Dialogues of the Buddha (Sacred Books of the Buddhists)* Vol. II, pp. 57–59.

65. A recent English version of this sūtra was published in two volumes, titled *The Voice of the Buddha: the Beauty of Compassion*. Berkeley: Dharma Publishing, 1983.

66. The *Mahāvastu*, in three volumes, was translated into English by J.J. Jones and published in the *Sacred Books of the Buddhists* series. London: The Pāli Text Society. See Vols. XVI, XVIII, and XIX.

67. Har Dayal, *The Bodhisattva Doctrine in Buddhist Sanskrit Literature*, p. 106.

68. Lobsang Jampa, a Geshe of the Gelukpa tradition, was the resident lama at the Kurukulla Center in Boston, Massachusetts. In April and July of 1989, I met with Geshe Jampa to discuss Tibetan sacred biography. The quoted materials above were recorded at the Milarepa Center in Barnet, Vermont, on July 3, 1989. I wish here to gratefully acknowledge his kind assistance. He passed away in May, 1991 of cancer.

69. The full Tibetan text of this life can be found in the Gelukpa liturgical manual, CP (162–173). Tucci (1949, I: 161) mentions another "secret biography" of Tsongkapa, written by Kedrub Je.

70. These excerpts are taken from Glenn Mullin's translation of Tashi Pelden's text (13–22). Mullin translates the text's title as *Song of the Mystic Experiences of Lama Je Rinpoche.* Describing the text, on p. 10 Mullin writes: "The word *Mystic* (*gSang ba*) in the title indicates that the song is essentially tantric in nature and imagery. *gSang-ba* also means *secret*, but in this case it is the oral explanations of the underlying meanings of the text that are secret, rather than the text itself. *Song of the Mystic Experiences* is memorized by almost all monks of the Geluk Tradition and is chanted in assemblies on all occasions especially related to Lama Tzong Khapa."

71. The Tibetan of this passage reads as follows: *de nas paṇ chen chos kyi rgyal mtshan gyi bka' bźin/ gaṅs/ ri sul/ nags khrod sogs du ma 'grims/ de'i tshe padma can gyi sgrub chu'i ñe 'khor gyi sa rnams skad cig de la sin dhu rar 'gyur ba źig yod pas yul ñer bźi dṅos daṅ mtshuṅs pa źig yod ces grags pa der rdzogs rim daṅ 'brel ba'i bla ma lha'i rnal 'byor bsgoms par mdzad pas chos kyi rgyal po tsoṅ kha pa chen pos źal gzigs/ de'i tshe rje rin po ches dam pa 'di la thun moṅ daṅ thun moṅ ma yin pa'i sñan brgyud kyi gdams ṅag yoṅs su rdzogs par gnaṅ/ lhag par rje rin po che'i phyi paṇḍi ta'i cha lugs naṅ gi phuṅ khams skye mched rnams 'dus pa'i lha tshogs su gsal ba'i thugs kar rgyal ba śākya thub pa de'i thugs kar rdo rje 'chaṅ bźugs pa'i bla ma'i rnal 'byor thun moṅ ma yin pa sems dpa gsum rtseg can de gnaṅ ṅo//.* The passage immediately following this one tells us that, "Thereafter, for a time the great siddha Chökyi Dorje chose not to completely abandon his coarse karmic body, but rather to remain in a sort of mystic support body which was nevertheless of the nature of a fully accomplished Total Integration Buddha Body...."

72. Sarat Chandra Das, in his *Contributions on the Religion and History of Tibet, op. cit.*, devotes a page [pp. 109–110 in the reprinted edition] to summarizing the life of "Gyal-wa Ton-Dub." Towards the end of his summary he writes, "At the age of seventeen he became a pupil of the sage Chhokyi Dorje and fully mastered the volume of precepts called Gahdan-Nen-gyud. Afterwards returning to Tsan he resided at the temple of Pamachen near the Panam-Chomolha-ri. Here his teacher the sage showed him the volumes of illusive mysticism." Of course, what is of interest here is Das's treatment of Pema Chan [which he writes as "Pamachen"]. He locates it geographically. In fact, in a note directly connected with his mention of "Pamachen," Das attempts to give even more precise details of the location of this "temple," though his note speaks only of the Chomolhari mountain range. Das's reading may be derived from his assumption that this location is associated with one of the "hidden countries" of Tibetan lore.

73. A. Bharati, *op. cit.*, p. 175, for example cites M. Shahidullah's *Les Chants Mystiques de Kāṇha et de Sarāhā*, as the locus for a list of "intentional" or "*sandhā*-words" in which *padma* as "lotus" is symbolically equivalent to the Sanskrit *bhaga*, or "vulva." Dasgupta's *An Introduction to Tantric Buddhism*, p. 105 notes that, according to the *Hevajra Tantra*, "Prajñā [i.e. highest insight] is called the female organ [*bhaga*] because it is the abode of all pleasure which is great bliss (*mahāsukha*)."

74. On the "twenty-four places" according to the body maṇḍala of Heruka Cakrasaṃvara, see *Clear Light of Bliss; Mahāmudrā in Vajrayāna Buddhism* by Geshe Kelsang Gyatso, p. 23.

75. See Shin 'ichi Tsuda's *A Critical Tantricism (Memoirs of the Research Department of the Toyo Bunko, No. 36)*. Tokyo: The Toyo Bunko, 1978. Tsuda devotes a section of his Chapter V (pp. 215–221) to "The Theory of Pilgrimage Places."

76. *Ibid.*, p. 221.

77. This was told to me by Lama Thubten Zopa Rinpoche.

78. For example, see Alex Wayman's discussion of this idea in his *Yoga of the Guhyasamājatantra*, pp. 234–235. Using Tsongkapa's *Pañcakrama* commentary, Wayman suggests [p. 238] that "rivers as external water agree with menses and blood as personal [or internal] water."

79. That is, by marking the disciple's forehead, throat and heart, thereby

symbolically blessing the "doors" of that one's body, speech, and mind, respectively.

80. This characterization of the *Miraculous Volume* is given by Geshe Lobsang Tarchin in his translation of Pabongka Rinpoche's *Liberation in Our Hands*, p. 172. Geshe Tarchin translates the Tibetan, *dGa' ldan sprul pa'i glegs bam*, as *Ganden Emanation Scripture*. In Michael Richards' translation of Pabongka Rinpoche's teachings, called *Liberation in the Palm of Your Hand* [Boston: Wisdom Publications, 1991], the Tibetan is rendered *The Miraculous Book of the Gelugpas*. It should be noted that on p. 244 of Richards' translation, it appears as though Pabongka Rinpoche is directly quoting from the *Volume*. The pertinent passage reads: "The following verses are taken from *The Miraculous Book of the Gelugpas*, so they are especially blessed...."

Notes to the Translations

81. The *Candrapradīpa-sūtra* is an alternate name for the *Samādhirāja-sūtra*. Buton's *History of Buddhism* uses both titles when referring to it. For example, see Obermiller's translation, part I, pp. 73, 85, 86, and 126, and part II, pp. 133 and 169. The sūtra is mentioned under the name "Candrapradīpa" in Kamalśīla's *Bhāvanākrama* and in Candrakīrti's *Prasannapadā*. In part II, p. 133 of Buton's *History*, we learn that the teacher Candragomin wrote a commentary on the Candrapradīpa called, in Tibetan, the *zla ba sgron ma'i 'grel pa*.

82. The Tibetan rendered here as "fierce revulsion" is *ngejung* (ṅes-'byuṅ). The term may also be rendered as "aversion to worldly concerns" or, simply, as "renunciation." Such turning away from worldly concerns is of primary importance for one seeking to enter the religious life. It is counted as the first of the "three essential principles of the path," *lam-gyi tsowo namsum*, summarized so succinctly by Tsongkapa in a verse text of the same name. The verses on renunciation, as translated by Geshe Wangyal [see his *The Door of Liberation*, p. 142], are as follows:

> Listen with clear mind, you fortunate ones
> Who direct your minds to the path pleasing to Buddha,
> Who strive to make good use of leisure and opportunity
> And are not attached to the joys of saṃsāra.
> Those with bodies are bound by the craving for existence.
> Without pure Renunciation, there is no way to still

Attraction to the pleasures of saṃsāra.
Thus, from the outset seek Renunciation.

The remaining two "principles" are the generation of bodhicitta [here, a mind of compassion] and the realization of the profound view regarding śūnyatā, or voidness of inherent self-existence.

83. The Tibetan reads *gyengdok* (gyeṅ dogs). *Gyeṅ* means "to wander," "to be agitated/disturbed," and "to be inattentive." *Dogs* adds the sense of being "doubtful," "fearful," and "apprehensive" regarding how one's time might be spent.

84. The full Tibetan passage reads: *dal 'byor rñed dka' daṅ nam 'chi cha med dran pas.* The rendering "precious human rebirth" is used for *deljor* (dal 'byor). *Dal 'byor* is itself an abbreviation for two compound terms: *dal ba brgyad*, meaning the "eight states of leisure" or the "eight freedoms," and *'byor ba bcu*, the so-called "ten endowments." The "eight freedoms" are described as the freedoms from being born (1) in one of the hells, (2) as a hungry ghost, (3) as an animal, or (4) as a long-life god, (5) in a barbarian or irreligious country, (6) with imperfect sense organs, (7) as a heretic, or (8) in a time or place where no enlightened being has manifested to show the path.

The "ten endowments" are made up of five personal endowments and five environmental ones, respectively: being born (1) with a human body and mind, (2) in a land where the Buddhist Dharma is flourishing, (3) with good bodily and mental faculties, (4) free of having committed any of the five "heinous" crimes [killing one's mother, father, or an arhat, wounding a Tathāgata, or causing disunity amongst the Buddhist saṅgha], and (5) having faith and confidence in the Dharma, (6) during a period in which a Buddha has appeared and (7) has taught the Dharma, (8) when the when the Dharma still flourishes, (9) when there are realized followers of the Dharma, and (10) receiving the compassionate assistance of others to aid one's Dharma development. When these eighteen conditions are satisfied and complete in a being, that is called a "precious human rebirth." Having fully contemplated these eighteen great blessings that constitute precious human rebirth, one is then encouraged to contemplate the uncertainty of the time of one's death. These two contemplations coupled together serve as forceful spurs to one's Dharma practice.

85. The Tibetan for the Sanskrit *kalyāṇamitra* is *gewai sheynyen* (dge ba'i bśes gñen). Both terms may be rendered as "virtuous friend" and

connote one's spiritual benefactor. Additionally, a contracted form of the Tibetan compound, *geshe* (dge bśes), is used especially by adherents of the Gelukpa school to refer to its revered teachers who have earned the highest monastic degrees.

86. *rGyud bla ma* is the Tibetan title for the late fourth-century Sanskrit work called the *Uttaratantra* and attributed to Maitreya. In fact, the *Uttaratantra* is one of the so-called Five Books of Maitreya, the other four being the (1) *Mahāyānasūtralaṃkāra* (Tib. *mDo sde rgyan*), (2) *Madhyānta-vibhaṅga* (Tib. *dbUs mtha' rnam 'byed*), (3) *Dharma-dharmatā-vibhaṅga* (*Tib. Chos daṅ chos ñid rnam 'byed*), and (4) *Abhisamayālaṃkāra* (Tib. *nṄon rtogs rgyan*). For an English translation of the *Uttaratantra*, see. E. Obermiller's "The Sublime Science of the Great Vehicle to Salvation, being a Manual of Buddhist Monism" in *Acta Orientalia*, IX, pp. 81–306. The text is not actually a tantra, but a Mahāyāna verse exposition, setting forth [according to Tsongkapa and others] a view in keeping with the Mādhyamika-Prasaṅgika view; this, in spite of the fact that the text's main subject deals with the "Tathāgata-garbha" theory. See Obermiller, p. 83.

87. The *Blue Annals* cites this monastic institution several times. On p. 341, Gö Lotsawa notes: "The disciple of gÑal-źig rGya-chin Ru-ba founded bDe-ba-can [in] (dbUs). After him, his nephew Saṅs-rgyas-dpal and others taught there." For other details, see Roerich's translation, pp. 308, 341, 542, 670, 737, and 1015. Dewachen (dDe-ba-can) is considered a "branch" (*lag*) monastery of Sangpu (gSaṅ-phu). *The Geography of Tibet* [Wiley's translation, p. 150] makes the following comment regarding Dewachen: "This monastery was founded by Zhig-po Shes-rab-pa and the Tsong-Kha-pa and Bla-ma Dbu-ma-pa, these two, lived there for some time."

88. The Tibetan is *lekpar gowa* (legs par go ba), "good understanding." Additionally, *go ba* connotes "clear perception." *Gowachen* (Go-ba-can) is an equivalent term for *Kepa* (mKhas-pa), ["learned" or "wise one"].

89. That is, the Mādhyamika, as expounded by Nāgārjuna, and the Yogācāra, as explicated by Asaṅga.

90. In the days of Tsongkapa and Jampel Gyatso, Sangpu was considered the most illustrious of Kadam monastic institutions, especially noted for its instruction in *U-ma* (dbU ma) [Mādhyamika], *tsema* (tshad ma) [logic], and *tsen-nyi* (mtshan ñid) [philosophy in general].

Describing this institution, the early nineteenth-century *The Geography of Tibet,* [Wiley, trans. pp. 76–77] declares:

> In former times, (Gsang-pu) had students of Dbu-ma and Tshad-ma and a large assemblage of monks; however, since the increase of such (monasteries) as Se-ra and 'Bras-spungs, this one has gradually declined, and now there is nothing there but a few married monks (khyim-btsun), who have chosen to follow the Sa-skya-pa. At the time of the summer-seminars (dbyar-chos), ten grwa-tshang of the Sa-skya-pa and the Dge-lugs-pa, such as Dga'-ldan Shar-rtse-pa, assemble there, and there are many (monks) who have obtained the rank of the difficult degree.

91. In former times, Kyormolung (sKyor-mo-luṅ) was likewise a famed monastic institution specializing in philosophy. *The Geography of Tibet* characterizes it thus and gives further details on its location, saying, on p. 77, that it was located "on the side of a mountain not very far from the north bank of the Dbus-chu." The *Blue Annals* [Roerich's translation, p. 79] gives the founder of Kyormolung as one Belti Jo-se (sBal-ti Jo-sras), a disciple of Takma Dorshong (Thag-ma rDor-gźoṅ). The *Annals* states: "sBal-ti became the abbot of Bran Ra-mo-che, and founded the monastery of sKyor-mo-luṅ." The *Annals* also reports, p. 83, that "rJe-btsun dam-pa bLo-bzaṅ grags-pa'i dpal (Tsoṅ-kha-pa, 1357–1419) thoroughly studied the Vinaya under the great abbot (mkhan-chen) bLo-gsal-ba at the monastery of sKyor- mo-luṅ." For other *Blue Annals* references to this institution, see pp. 190, 278, 302, 410, and 673.

    Also see Wayman's *Calming the Mind and Discerning the Real,* p. 18. Wayman notes that it was at Kyormolung that Tsongkapa "memorized in seventeen days the great commentary on Guṇaprabha's *Vinayasūtra.*"

92. Riwo Tse Nga (Ri-bo-rtse-lṅa) refers to the famed "five mountain peaks" of China's Shan-hsi province, known as *Wu ta'i shan.* According to Buddhist tradition, this area is especially connected with Lord Mañjuśrī. Thus, it is in perfect keeping with Jampel Gyatso's special devotion to Mañjuśrī that he should "in his dreams" visit this particular sacred spot. Numerous other illustrious Tibetan teachers and siddhas are said to have visited this same spot. For examples, see *Blue Annals,* pp. 220, 336, 492, 669, 679, 783, 846, 898, and 911.

93. Unidentified.

94. *Gan-do-la* is the Tibetan rendering for the Sanskrit, *gandhālaya*, literally "the abode [here, sanctuary] of fragrance." It usually is used to refer to the main hall of worship of a great monastery and is the place where its main image of the deity is kept.

95. *Se-mo-do* appears several times in the *Blue Annals*. [See pp. 461, 499, 522, and 675]. It is the name of a lake and of the hermitage situated near it. It seems to have been a favorite place for retreat and especially for the practice of yogic austerities. Many of Gampopa's (sGam-po-pa) immediate disciples and other Kagyüpa siddhas are said to have meditated there. An alternate spelling, as "Sen-mo-do," is given in the namtar of Baso Je, following.

96. Prior to achieving direct communication with Lord Mañjuśrī, Tsongkapa himself relied upon his "psychic" and trusted friend and teacher, Lama Umapa, also known as Pawo Dorje (dPa'-bo-rdo-rje), for "speaking" with Mañjuśrī. [According to Robert Thurman's *Tsong Khapa's Speech of Gold in the Essence of True Eloquence*, p 77: "Umapa was originally an illiterate cowherd who was suddenly smitten with a vision of Mañjuśrī, which he subsequently cultivated and eventually experienced all the time."] At this early stage in his career, when Tsongkapa wished to put a question to Lord Mañjuśrī, Lama Umapa served as his mystic-medium interpreter. Therefore, after hearing Jampel Gyatso's idea about doing an extended retreat, our text tells us that Tsongkapa together with Jampel Gyatso traveled to Tsang, there to "jointly counsel" [Tsongkapa and Lama Umapa] with Mañjuśrī regarding it. Later, Tsongkapa won the ability to communicate directly with Mañjuśrī, subsequently becoming famed as an incarnation of that very Lord.

97. That is, to abide by Jampel Gyatso's idea of doing a lengthy and strict retreat. This passage is especially interesting since it depicts Jampel Gyatso as having been the primary instigator for what later become famous in the annals chronicling the life of Tsongkapa.

98. Here *lamdre* (lam 'bras) [the "Path and its Fruits"] refers to that tantric system of theory and practice as set forth especially by the Sakya school of Tibetan Buddhism. According to Sakya tradition, the system was mastered and later propagated by Drokmi ('Brog-mi) [lit. the "nomad," 992–1074]. Drokmi studied in Nepal and India. Back in Tibet, he met the learned Indian paṇḍita Gayādhara, who, on the spot, passed on to him the teachings of lamdre. Drokmi later became

the guru of both Marpa [who later founded the Kagyü school] and Könchok Gyelpo (dKon-mchog-rgyal-po) [1034–1102]. The latter, in 1073, founded the great monastery of Sakya. The esoteric teachings of lamdre, together with the set of teachings called *taknyi* (brTags-gñis), form the basis of the Sakya view. Both sets of teachings rely heavily on the *Hevajra-tantra* and trace their origins back to the Indian siddha, Virūpa. The Gelukpa sometime describe the teachings of lamdre like this: *lam* means "common" or "shared" teachings [the sūtra, or non-tantric path]. By *'bras* is meant the Sakyas' "uncommon" or tantric teachings. The two thus are like Tsongkapa's *Lam-rim-chen-mo* and *sṄags-rim-chen-mo*, respectively. For more on the historical transmission of lamdre, see *Blue Annals*, Ch. IV. pp. 204–240; and Sherab Amipa's *A Waterdrop from the Glorious Sea*, pp. 16–20.

99. All the various namtar chronicling the life of Tsongkapa, when referring to the Wölka retreat, are in agreement with regard to the fact that Lord Mañjuśrī advised him to take into retreat with him eight carefully selected disciples. The namtar of Jampel Gyatso identifies the eight as being those recorded in this list. A slightly different enumeration is given by Wayman in his *Calming the Mind and Discerning the Real*, p. 22. There Wayman writes: "At the end of the Ape year, along with eight followers as prophesied by the Venerable Mañjugosha 'Jam-dkar-ba, he went to Bya-bral. (Of the eight, four were from Dbus: (1) Grags-pa dpal-ldan-bzaṅ-pa, (2) Rtogs-ldan byaṅ-seṅ-ba, (3) Gnas-brtan Rinchen rgyal-mtshan-pa, (4) Gnas-brtan bzaṅ-skyoṅ-ba; and four were from Mdo-smad: (1) Bla-ma Rtogs-ldan 'Jam-dpal Rgya-mtsho-ba, (2) Dge-bśes Śes-rab-grags, (3)Dge-bśes 'Jam-dpal Bkra-śis, (4) Dge-bśes Dpal-skyoṅ.)" Seemingly, in place of "Grags-pa-dpal-ldan-bzaṅ-pa," our text of the namtar of Jampel Gyatso offers "bLa-ma 'Jam-dkar-ba." The discrepancy is cleared up by Sumpa Kenpo's (Sum-pa mKhan-po) *History*, for there [p. 145] we find as part of the description of the eight, the passage: *skyor luṅ gi dge bśes 'jam-dkar-pa dpal-ldan-bzaṅ-po* ("the dge-bśes from sKyor-luṅ, 'Jam-dkar-pa dpal-ldan-bzaṅ-po"). Thus, "Grags-pa-dpal-ldan-bzaṅ-pa" and "bLa-ma 'Jam-dkar-ba" are one and the same. [Wayman's identification of "'Jam-dkar-ba" with Lord Mañjugoṣa appears to be in error here.] We know also that Lama "'Jam-dkar-ba" appears later in the namtar as an actual retreatant.

100. The Wölka retreat forms one of the most important and oft-mentioned episodes in the life of the great Je Rinpoche, Tsongkapa. Kedrub Je's namtar of Tsongkapa reports that Tsongkapa made his request to Lord

Mañjuśrī regarding the number of disciples to accompany him when he [Tsongkapa] and Lama Umapa, on a visit to Lhasa, shared a small room on the upper floor of the Jokang (Jo-Khaṅ) cathedral. All accounts of Tsongkapa's life agree that he was advised to take eight disciples with him: four from Central Tibet and four from the eastern provinces.

Wayman [*Calming the Mind and Discerning the Real*, p. 22] makes the Wölka retreat of signal importance to the establishment of the Geluk order.

As to Tsongkapa's own practices and meditative experiences during this famed retreat, much has been recorded. Wayman, for example, p. 22, writes:

> At that time he saw the faces of the thirty-five Buddhas of Confession, and often saw Maitreya in the shape of the Sambhogakāya, Bhaiṣajya-guru (the healing Buddha) in yellow garb, Maitreya as a seated Nirmāṇa-kāya, and the Buddha Amitāyus. He reviewed in his mind the glorious practice of the Bodhisattva recorded in the *Buddha-Avataṃsaka-sūtra* and modeled his conduct accordingly.

And the *Life* of Tsongkapa edited by R. Thurman and published by the Library of Tibetan Works and Archives, p. 17, records:

> During the first phase, both master and disciples undertook intensive generation of spiritual energy and purifcation of the obscurations in order to demonstrate the indispensibility of such practices from the outset. Je Rinpoche personally performed three and a half million full-length prostrations and one million eight hundred thousand mandala offerings. Indeed, his prostrating form wore an impression in the floor of the temple; and at the conclusion of the mandala offerings his forearm was raw and bleeding.

Wölka district lies east of the city of Lhasa and slightly to the south, but still on the northern bank of the Tsangpo river. In the *Blue Annals*, Wölka is mentioned most often in connection with Kagyü masters such as Marpa, Milarepa, and Gampopa. For specific references, see *BA* pp. 187, 465, 468, 477, 888, 892, 918, 1040, and 1076.

101. Describing the Chölung hermitage, *The Geography of Tibet*, pp. 91–92 records:

> Southeast of there is the mountain 'O-de-gung-rgyal, behind which is the mountain retreat (ri khrod) called 'Ol-kha Chos-lung. There were the sleeping-quarters of the Master Bla-ma, which were constructed according to the instructions from the 'Dul-ba (Skt. Vinaya), and also the prints of the Master's hands, feet, and knees, which were made while he was practicing ascetic rites. There appear distinctly there, such things as many letters on the surface of a stone mandala, which were self-originated when *Rje rin po che* (the Precious Master: ie., Tsong-kha-pa) had visions of the *Thirty five buddhas*, a ma-ni on the surface of a rock, which was written by the Master himself with his finger, and the prints of the Master's back and the designs of his girdle and gown.

102. The full Tibetan passage reads: *de dus bka'gdams pa rnams kyi phyag len ltar lam thun moṅ ba la gtso bor blo sbyoṅs pa.* I have translated *lam thun moṅ ba* as "ordinary path." It may also be rendered as "common-" or "shared-path" and refers to those nontantric ascetic practices that can be performed by all. The more "specialized," tantric, practices are referred to as "extraordinary," "uncommon," or "unshared" practices: in Tibetan, *thun moṅ ma yin ba.*

103. *Nyime Sengge* (gÑis med seṅ ge) is an old idiom of colloquial Tibetan. It was used derogatorily of one who merely used the paraphernalia of the tantras to appear mighty but who, in truth, lacked the requisite preparation and inward realization to be counted a truly accomplished one. Thus, on the outside, such a one might appear a veritable Buddha "lion" but inwardly remain worthless, for himself as well as for others. In modern usage, the phrase is used especially of a monk who confuses or attempts to mix power and politics with true religious practice.

104. The Tibetan reads: *phyis mgar phug tu* ["Later, at mGar-phug…] In fact, this cave in Wölka was already famous prior to the days of Tsongkapa. Wylie, *GOT*, p. 172, comments:

> According to the *VSP*, Padma-Sambhava, at the time he held the name Mkha-'gro-gar-byed-pa, lived there for a time and concealed a Yum gter-ma. Then during the intermediate period, the Bka-brgyud-pas built a temple there. Then later on, two Dge-lugs-pa Lamas, Dbu-stod-pa Chos-dpal bzang-po and Gru-skya-ba BLo-bzaṅg rgya-mtsho lived there for some time (*VSP*, folio 158–b).

According to the *Blue Annals*, pp. 463–65, one of the nephews of Gampopa, the ācārya Gompa (sGom-pa) [1116–1169], after being converted by his uncle and given the monastic name Tsültrim Nyingpo ('Tshul-khrims-sñiṅ-po), "preached extensively the Doctrine for one year at mGar-phug of 'Ol-kha. Then in the autumn he proceeded towards sGam-po, and told the monks of his intention of residing in seclusion without seeing anyone."

However, the cave's sacredness was enhanced by the presence of Tsongkapa, for the *Geography of Tibet* notes, p. 91, that it was "the *sgrub-khang* of the master [the "meditation place"] of Tsongkapa (which is called) 'Ol-kha Mgar-phug."

105. The Tibetan clearly indicates that the retreatants showed special deference to both Tsongkapa and Lama Jamkarwa. That the latter was a geshe is attested to by Sumpa Kenpo's account. Perhaps he was also much older or physically more frail than the others. The exact reason is unclear.

106. The Tibetan reads: *śug pa'i dka' thub byas (pa). dKa' thub* is equivalent to the Sanskrit term, *tapas*, here "penance" or "austerities." *Śug-pa* means "juniper," and *Śug-'bru-pa*, "juniper berry."

107. The Tibetan form used for *chang* (chaṅ) [a Tibetan beer] here has, in both editions of this namtar, been misspelled as siṅ-po. The correct spelling would be *bsiṅ-bo* or even *bsiṅ-gu*. The term is an archaic form still in use in some dialects of Western Tibet and is used colloquially to refer to chang.

It is often customary when performing certain tantric rituals to imbibe prescribed amounts of beer or other forms of liquor. Because of the diffculties of obtaining this, the Wölka retreatants substituted plain water.

108. *Śug-'bru-ba.*

109. The Tibetan is *Daknyi Chenpo* (bdag ñid chen po). It is equivalent to the Sanskrit *mahāsattva*, literally "Great Person." Often one finds the combined epithets "bodhisattva-mahāsattva" in Mahāyāna Buddhist texts such as the *Prajñāpāramitā* literature.

110. What I have rendered throughout as "oral advice, explanatory commentaries, and detailed practice instructions" translates the ubiquitous Tibetan compound found throughout these namtar, *khrid man ṅag źal śes*. The three Tibetan elements are close in meaning, all referring to

instructions to a disciple that help to clarify the meaning of a given text or practice. *Tri* (Khrid) and *shelshe* (źal śes) may refer to commentaries that are written or oral, but *men-ngak* (man ṅag) is used solely for key oral instructions imparted by a guru directly to his or her disciple.

111. *Kyerim* (bsKyed rim) (Skt. *utpatti-krama*) and *Dzokrim* (rDzogs rim) (Skt. *saṃpanna-krama*), meaning, respectively, "Generation Stage" and "Completion Stage," are terms used exclusively in connection with the practices of the highest tantras, those of the anuttara yoga class. With regard to the three lower classes of tantra, other terminology is employed: *tsenche* (mtshan bcas), yoga performed "with [reliance upon] images" of a deity, and *tsenme* (mtshan med), yoga performed "without [reliance upon] images" of a deity.

The "two stages" in reference to the highest, anuttara yoga, tantric class refer respectively to (1) that stage wherein one practices visualizing oneself as a given deity and one's ordinary world as that deity's maṇḍala, thinking of all sounds heard as the deity's mantra, etc., and (2) that stage wherein, having attained identity with the deity, one performs the yogic techniques of controling the vital energies [prāṇa] and the mystic drop [bindu] until one is successful in uniting the illusory body and the clear light yogas, thus ushering in the experience of total integration [zungjuk] and enlightenment itself.

For more detailed information on the Four Classes of Tantra, see Lessing and Wayman's translation, *mKhas-grub-rje's Fundamentals of the Buddhist Tantras.*

112. The Tibetan is Sang De Jik (gSaṅ-bDe-'Jigs), referring respectively to Sangdü (gSaṅ-'dus) [Guhyasamāja], Demchok (bDe-mchog) [Cakrasaṃvara-Heruka], and Jikje (Jigs-byed) [Bhairava]. In a number of places, Ketsün Sangpo's edition of these namtar erroneously gives *sde* for *bde.*

113. The school and general practice known as *Chöd* (gCod) [literally, "cutting off," with reference to the ego] goes back to the South Indian ascetic Padampa Sanggye (Pha-dam-pa Saṅs-rgyas) [died 1117], who visited Tibet on a number of occasions. It is sometimes divided into two wings: "male Chöd" [*pho gcod*] and "female Chöd" [*mo gcod*] referring to the doctrines of Padampa Sanggye and Machik Labdrönma (Ma-gcig Lab-sgron-ma) respectively, the latter having been Padampa Sanggye's consort and a realized master in her own right. The chief monastic center for the Chöd school is Dingri on the modern-day

northern border of Nepal. On the practice side, Chöd aims at completely cutting asunder the whole process of discursive thought *nampar tokpa* (rnam par rtog pa). Various of the Tibetan schools adopted this tantric method and adapted it to their own respective philosophical view.

In the present context, then, the "profound path of Chöd" as taught by Tsongkapa to the eight retreatants would be specific to the Gelukpas' tantric view. As part of its method, much outer paraphernalia is employed: special clothing, the use of drums and other musical instruments, and so on. Chöd is usually practiced in cemeteries or other remote places, and instructions for its practice are kept quite secret. Thus, for the Gelukpa, teachings on Chöd comprise one of the school's two special *nyengyü* (sñan brgyuds) or "oral traditions," the one focusing on *Mahāmudrā*, the other on Chöd.

For information of Chöd of a general sort, see Tucci, *The Religions of Tibet*, pp. 39, 87–92, 122, 207, and 260; and Evan-Wentz's *Tibetan Yoga and Secret Doctrines*, pp. 277–334.

114. The Tibetan given throughout these namtar for *Great Miraculous Volume* is *sprul pa'i glegs bam chen mo*. The giving over of the *Miraculous Volume* marks the "seal" of transmission and attests to the perfected realization of a disciple. As might be expected, the *Miraculous Volume* is not an ordinary book. According to Gelukpa tradition, it is quite invisible and of the nature of light. There is a humorous story told about how the First Panchen, Losang Chökyi Gyeltsen, kept an "empty" space on his bookshelves. When it was asked why he did this, one of the Panchen's disciples replied, "That is where the *Miraculous Volume* is kept!"

Some Geluk masters assert that parts of the *bLa-ma mchod-pa* [the Gelukpas' most comprehensive liturgical text, composed by the First Panchen] are taken directly from the *Great Miraculous Volume.* Others maintain that the *Volume* is synonymous with the King Tantra itself, the *Guhyasamāja Tantra*, especially as explicated by Tsongkapa. Whatever the actual content of the *Volume*, it is viewed as most precious and as encompassing the whole of the pith tantric teachings given directly by Lord Mañjuśrī to Tsongkapa. These make up the Ganden Oral Tradition of Mahāmudrā practice.

The Gelukpa history of the respective human recipients of the *Miraculous Volume* is shrouded in mystery. The standard Geluk Mahāmudrā lineage as we now have it comes down to the present.

However, there are at least two differing traditions regarding who was the last Geluk siddha to actually receive and hold the *Miraculous Volume*. One tradition asserts that Kachen Yeshe Gyeltsen [given as no. 16 of the present lineage and compiler of the namtar anthology from which the present translations are derived] was the last recipient. He is said to have returned the *Volume*, for safekeeping, to the Ganden gods. This tradition asserts that Pabongka Rinpoche, Trinley Gyatso [no. 33 of the lineage], using his powers of insight, then set forth the extended lineage, composing the prayer that gives the lineage up to His Holiness Trijang Rinpoche.

An alternate tradition maintains that the First Panchen himself was the last human to hold the *Miraculous Volume* and that he returned it to the gods for safekeeping. As to which particular Ganden god the *Volume* was entrusted to at that time, there are again varying opinions. The most common speculation says that the *Volume* was returned to the wrathful protector Kālarūpa. Another view asserts that the *Volume* was bound over to the protection of Dorje Shukden (rDo-rje Śugs-ldan).

Of the six namtar presented here, the *Great Miraculous Volume* is explicitly mentioned only in the first four: the lives of Jampel Gyatso, Baso Chökyi Gyeltsen, Chökyi Dorje, and Gyelwa Ensapa.

115. The idiomatic phrase in Tibetan reads: *sa 'ur rdo 'ur du rdol ba na*, "(it was as if his) very foundation had been completely shaken and rearranged, as if by an earthquake or explosion."

116. Meldro Gyelteng (Mal-gro rGyal-steṅ). This refers to the monastery called Gyelpo Teng (rGyal-po-steṅs) located at Meldro northeast of Lhasa. According to the *Blue Annals*, p. 305, "Gul-pi-pa, the Great, founded (the monastery) of rGyal-po-steṅs at Mal-gro (dbUs)." Meldro itself is a valley in Penyül ('Phan-yul). For the Gelukpa, the region of Meldro is especially associated with the early Kadampa teachings, owing to its being a main center of Geshe Chekawa's (dGe-bśes 'Chad-kha-ba) [1101–1175] activities. It was this Chekawa who set into print the essential *lojong* (blo-sbyoṅ) teachings of Lord Atīśa through his famed text, *bLo-sbyoṅ-don-bdun-ma* [*Spiritual Transformation, in Seven Parts*].

117. The *Blue Annals*, p. 276, records that one of Chekawa's disciples by the name of Se Chilbupa (Se sPyil-bu-pa) [1121–1189] had four yogin disciples. One of these, Gyapang Tangpa (rGya-span-thaṅ-pa) founded the monastery at Pangsa (sPaṅ-sa).

118. The Tibetan is *dben gnas se ba roṅ.*

119. I have rendered the Tibetan, *chos brgyad*, as "eight mundane concerns." The term is commonly rendered as the "eight worldly dharmas," but this leaves a part of the phrase untranslated. The eight are: concern with pleasure and pain, gain and loss, praise and blame, and reputation and obscurity.

120. This passage indicates that Jampel Gyatso, in much the same way as Lama Umapa, had developed such mastery of the meditative cycles associated with Lord Mañjuśrī and, as a result, had attained to such "intimacy" with that Lord that he too was able to serve as a medium and interpreter for him.

121. The Tibetan is *drag po'i las*, an abbreviation for *drag po'i 'phrin' las. Drag* may also be rendered "powerful" in this context. Sometimes a fourfold set of activitites [*las*] are delineated: (1) *zi ba'i 'phrin' las* ("peaceful activity") (2) *rgyas pa'i 'phrin las* ("expanding or enriching activity"), (3)*dbaṅ gi 'phrin' las* ("overpowering activity"), and (4) *drag po'i 'phrin las* ("terrific, fierce, or powerful activity"). Eva Dargyay translates *'phrin las* [trinley] as "charismatic activities" in her *The Rise of Esoteric Buddhism in Tibet*, p. 229. Das' entry for *'phrin-las*, in his *A Tibetan-English Dictionary*, p. 854, obscures its true sense.

122. Perhaps this Chöje Dülwa (Chos-rje 'Dul-ba) is the same as Chöje Dülwadzin Drakpa Gyeltsen (Chos-rje 'Dul-ba-'dzin Grags-pa-rgyal-mtshan), who, together with Darma Rinchen (Dar-ma-rin-chen), helped to begin the actual construction of Ganden monastery. However, from this abbreviated reference, it is impossible to say with certainty.

123. The hagiographer's intention here is to indicate the unbiased and non-sectarian character of Jampel Gyatso's enlightened activities. This seems to be the meaning behind the phrase that says that Jampel Gyatso "discussed the Dharma with teachers of every sort..." [i.e., even lamas of different sects].

124. That is, the "three sets of vows," *dompa sum* (sdom pa gsum) assumed at each successive stage of practice or at each successive *yāna*, namely: (1) the monastic, or *vinaya* vows aimed at "personal liberation" (*so so thar kyi sdom pa*), (2) the bodhisattva vows (*byaṅ chub sems dpa'i sdom pa*), and (3) the tantric vows (*rigs 'dzin sṅags kyi sdom pa*).

125. The "three doors" (*sgo gsum*) are the three "passageways" of activity: the body, speech, and mind of an individual. By these three, various kinds of karmic activity are created.

126. *Poṣadha* (*gso sbyoṅ*). By means of observing various *poṣadha* vows, one aims at the reparation of faults through abstinence and penance. *Poṣadha* usually involves fasting but may also include other forms of abstinence for a prescribed period of time.

127. *Kleśa* is the Sanskrit for the Tibetan *nyönmong* (ñon moṅs) literally, "afflictive, defiling emotions." The term is applied especially to the three primary forces of greed [or lust], hatred, and ignorance, these three being further described as the very source of saṃsāra, the world of suffering, itself.

128. The Tibetan is *Kha na ma tho ba'i dri ma.* It means literally that Jampel Gyatso was completely freed of "any fault which, if committed, might be painful or difficult to confess." The phrase is applicable to all nonvirtuous activity, however slight. Thus, one committing no nonvirtuous deeds at all is "completely pure, having nothing to hide."

129. Describing Wölka Samten Ling ('Ol-kha bSam-gtan-gliṅ), *The Geography of Tibet* [Wylie, trans., p. 91] states: "Southeastward from there is the mountain-retreat (*ri-khrod*) called 'Ol-kha Bsam-gtan-gling, where there are three (receptacles) known as being great in bestowing blessings, such as a likeness of *Rje rgyal ba gnyis pa* (The Master, Second Buddha—i.e., Tsong kha-pa), and such places as the *sgom-khang*, where the Master himself practiced meditation on the Dus-kyi-'khor-lo (Skt. Kālacakra), and near that is the *sgrub-khang* of the Master (which is called) 'Ol-kha Mgar-phug."

130. Skt.; Tib. *tshogs 'khor.* A *gaṇacakra* is commonly described as a "tantric feast." Here, it is a communal ritual performed amongst tantric adepts usually involving elaborate sensual offerings.

131. *Bodhicitta* (Tib. *byaṅ sems*) [jangsem]. In nontantric contexts this refers to the mind of enlightenment in both its relative [compassion] and absolute [the view correctly comprehending voidness] senses. In the present context, however, it has a tantric meaning and connotes the pure essence of the white seminal fluid. Tantric Mahāmudrā makes use of the two so-called "drops" (Skt. *bindu*; Tib. *thig-le*). There are two types of "drops" in the body: the white and the red. The white corresponds to seminal fluid and the red to blood. There are both gross and

subtle forms of these white and red drops, the sublest ones abiding in the central channel of the heart, while the gross forms flow through the other channels (*nāḍīs*). A tantric adept works at manipulating these drops, causing them to melt and flow in such a way as to engender the experience of great bliss (*mahāsukha*). For a more detailed description of the specific yogic technique alluded to by this section of Jampel Gyatso's Life, see Chang's *Teachings of Tibetan Yoga*, pp. 64–68, and Geshe Kelsang Gyatso's *Clear Light of Bliss: Mahāmudrā in Vajrayāna Buddhism*, pp. 17–66.

132. *bDe stoṅ gi tiṅ ne 'dzin.* That is, the samādhi (*tiṅ ne 'dzin*) or meditative absorption, wherein bliss (*bDe*) and voidness (*stoṅ*, for *stoṅ pa ñid*) are experienced as inseparable.

133. The Tibetan is *Tokden* (rTogs-ldan). This is the most common epithet associated with Jampel Gyatso. Thus, there is a slight play on words here. Another common epithet for Jampel Gyatso is *Drubpai Wangchuk* (Grub-pa'i-dbaṅ-phyug) [Lord of (Meditative) Accomplishment].

134. Here again, Jampel Gyatso's biographer depicts that one's great intimacy with Lord Mañjuśrī, so that even the great Tsongkapa himself relied upon Jampel Gyatso's powers of communication with that Lord in order to interpret matters of great importance to him. This passage is interesting precisely because it seems clearly to indicate that Tsongkapa regarded Jampel Gyatso's close connection with Mañjuśrī as being on a par with that of Lama Umapa.

135. On Luyipa [alternately called Luipa], see Robinson's *Buddha's Lions*, pp. 22–24, and the *Blue Annals*, pp. 234, 385, 389, 804, 852, and 869.

The text known under the title *'Dod 'jo* refers to the commentarial treatise composed by Tsongkapa on Luyipa's method. Its longer title is *Lu-yi-pa'i mNon rtogs kyi bsad pa.* The text focuses on the proper method of practicing the *Cakrasaṃvara Tantra.* The shorter title, *'Dod-'jo*, here suggests that this commentary presents the "easy to follow" or "easy method" (*'jo*) to attain "bliss" [here, *'dod*, the "desired"]. The *Blue Annals*, p. 389, comments that by composing this treatise, Tsongkapa "revived the practice of the Cakrasaṃvara... which had deteriorated (in Tibet)."

136. Dorje Neljorma (rDo-rje-rnal-'byor-ma) (Skt. Vajrayoginī, "Diamond Yogic Practitioner") is the female deity who is the chief consort of Lord Cakrasaṃvara. She is alternately called Dorje Pakmo (rDo-rje-'phag-

mo) (Skt. Vajravārāhī, "Diamond Sow"). It is said that the latter name is used to emphasize her function, while the former name indicates her essence. Her essence is the wisdom that congizes the inseparability of bliss and voidness. This wisdom in action functions to destroy confusion and ignorance, symbolized by the pig. On this explication of the "goddess," see Geshe Gyatso's *Clear Light of Bliss*, p. 243.

137. A *tsuklakang* (gtsug lag khaṅ) is, according to Das's *Dictionary*, p. 1002, "the chief hall of worship and assembly in any large monastery." Tucci describes this area at Ganden monastery in his *To Lhasa and Beyond*, pp. 111 and following.

138. The offering song *Tiṅ-'dzin-spir-legs-ma* is chanted by monks and yogic practitioners in connection with offering the "eight auspicious emblems" to a given deity as part of the performance of a meditative *sādhana*, as well as on certain occasions of general offering ceremonies. While other Tibetan sects employ this song in their rites, adherents of the Gelukpa school perform the chant with a unique tune and use a special pace. They trace the origin of this particular method of chanting the song to this particular event, which occurred during the construction of Ganden's tsuklakang.

139. The context of this mention of ḍākinīs betrays perhaps a bit of overzealous apologetic on the part of Jampel Gyatso's biographer. The latter wishes to shore up his case that ordinary beings can be mistaken about the actual nature of these beings. For though these ḍākinīs were seen by ordinary beings chanting offering songs during the construction of Ganden's main chapel and were assumed to be ordinary women, they were *not* ordinary women but ḍākinīs. Just so, our biographer means for us to conclude, the woman in the red hat seen visiting Tsongkapa's chambers was *not* an ordinary woman, but Vajrayoginī herself, the chief goddess-consort to the Lord Cakrasaṃvara.

140. The Tibetan passage reads: *dṅos stobs rig pas gźi lam 'bras gsum thams cad thugs su chud pa 'di yin/*. In this context, though *lam 'bras* occurs, the fuller phrase, *gźi lam 'bras gsum* refers to the "three bases of the path and its fruits." Here the "three" would seem to mean the "three essentials" of the path as set forth by Tsongkapa. For more on these "three," see *supra*, note 82.

141. For more on the description of the "super-knowledges" (*abhijñās*) and the specific "powers of magical transformation," see Har Dayal's *The*

Bodhisattva Doctrine in Buddhist Sanskrit Literature, pp. 106–116.

142. Buddha Sengge Ngaro (Seṅ-ge-ṅa-ro) refers to a form of Lord Mañjuśrī. Gelukpa tradition holds that, in the future, Tsongkapa will reincarnate in this world in this form [as Buddha Sengge Ngaro]. Iconographically, the form is peaceful, two-armed, rides upon a lion, and—on lotuses stemming from each shoulder—bears aloft the *Prajñāpāramitā* text and the sword of wisdom.

143. Baso Chökyi Gyeltsen is here described—and thereby distinguished from Jampel Gyatso's other disciples—by the special term, *bKa'-babs*. *bKa'-babs* is used exclusively in reference to that singular disciple in whom the guru has complete confidence, knowing that such a one will successfully fulfill the high duty entrusted to him or her. Thus from among all his numerous disciples, Jampel Gyatso especially commissioned Baso Je to become the next holder of the Geluk Mahāmudrā Oral Tradition teachings.

144. The Tibetan is *thugs kyi sras*.

145. This Chennga Lodrö Gyeltsen (sPyan-sṅa bLo-gros-rgyal-mtshan) was also a disciple of Kedrub Je. In *Materials for a History of Tibetan Literature*, Part 3, p. 12, Lokesh Chandra describes "Spyan-sṅa Blo-gros-rgyal-mtshan" as being "the actual disciple (*dṅos-slob*) of Mkhas-grub Dge-legs." Chandra also gives a list of Chennga Lodrö's writings, according to Longdöl Lama's *mTshan tho*, on pp. 639–640.

In the "Introduction" to his own *Collected Works*, we read that "Spyan-snga Blo-gros-rgyal-mtshan was born into the famed lineage of Dgyer which had produced a series of Bka'-gdams-pa masters beginning with Dgyer-sgom Chen-po Gzhon-nu-grags-pa (1090–1171).... The title Spyan-snga refers to an honor bestowed upon the lineage by the Phag-mo-gru-pa overlords."

The dates for Lodrö Gyeltsen are generally accepted to be 1402–1471, though other sources give varying ones: Tucci's *Tibetan Painted Scrolls*, p. 123, gives 1392–1470, and Gö Lotsawa's *Blue Annals*, p. 317 gives 1390–1448. Sumpa Kenpo's *Re'u mig*, however, on p. 42, lists his birthdate as 1402. Again, his "Introduction" records that "Among his masters were his paternal uncle, Spyan-snga Rin-chen-kun-dga'-blo-gros who bestowed upon him in his seventh year his first monastic ordination., Mkhas-grub Rje, Chos-rje Blo-gros, Tshogs-chen Mkhan-po Yon-tan-rin-chen and Slob-dpon Nor-bzang-pa (from whom he received his final monastic vows). His chief guru, however, was Grub-chen 'Jam-dpal-rgya-mtsho (1356–1428), who represented the ascetic tradition of the early Gelukpa masters." Moreover, the "Introduction" records: "Among his most important works on the *lo-sbyoṅg* practice is the famed *Blo-sbyoṅg Chos kyi sgo 'byed* which is still admired today. Most of his writings are directly in the Bka'-gdams-pa tradition. He also wrote a number of *lta khrid* showing that various academic studies can be used in meditative practice. He authored *bsdus-don* to [Śantideva's] loved *Bodhicaryāvatāra* and [to Nāgārjuna's] *Suhṛllekha* and a biography of his master 'Jam-dpal-rgya-mtsho."

146. The Tibetan reads: *dal ba'i rten la sñiṅ po no blangs*, literally, "he grasped, or realized, the essence of human birth." An alternate way of saying this is that he "made his life meaningful." In short, Jampel Gyatso successfully accomplished the goal, in truth, of all religious practice: to make this life truly meaningful.

147. The Tibetan is *dal ba'i rten*. See above, note 84, for the full implications of this phrase, where "support of leisure" refers to a "precious human rebirth."

148. The Tibetan reads: *dga' ldan chos kyi pho braṅ du gśegs par dgoṅs tel*. Here *dgs' ldan pho braṅ* really does mean the main chapel at Ganden monastery founded by Tsongkapa, where the latter's relics are enshrined. Jampel Gyatso wished to end his life in nearness to his root lama, Tsongkapa.

However, as Wylie has rightly noted in *The Geography of Tibet*, 152, the name is often used to refer to the central chapel at Drepung ('Bras-spuṅs) monastery as well. Wylie writes:

> Dga-ldan-pho-brang is the name of the palace at 'Bras-spungs in which [the] "Abbot of 'Bras-spungs" lived. In 1578, Bsod-sams rgya-mtsho was given the tile of Ta-la'i Bla-ma... but he was still the "Abbot of 'Bras-spungs." When the Fifth Dalai Lama was given temporal rulership of Tibet... he eventually vacated this "palace" at 'Bras-spungs and moved into the newly built Potala. According to Das, the Dga-ldan-pho-brang was built by Dge-'dun-rgya-mtsho (*JLCT*, p. 171), i.e., the man credited as being the Second Dalai Lama.

149. Here, the Tibetan reads simply: *bDe bar gśegs*, literally, "passed into happiness."

150. The Tibetan is *dad pa'i rten*, literally, a "support (*rten*) for (their) faith

and devotion (*dad*)." The more common Tibetan rendering is *mchod rten*, a "support or receptacle for worship (*mchod*)." Both terms are Tibetan equivalents for the Sanskrit caitya or stūpa. Such a structure is usually a solid masonry reliquary mound having a small innermost cavity where the ashes or other relics of a saint are enshrined.

151. We are not told at what age Baso Je became ordained. However, given that he was born in 1402, it is quite possible that he took teachings and perhaps even ordination directly from Tsongkapa himself, since the latter died in 1419.

152. A literal translation of the Sanskrit term *tripiṭaka* and the Tibetan *sde snod gsum*, the term refers to the two collections or "baskets" of the Buddha's discourses [the sūtra collection and the Vinaya collection] plus a third collection of later commentarial materials referred to as the Abhidharma.

153. The Buddhist tantras were first given a fourfold classification by the great redactor of the Tibetan Canon, Butön (Bu-ston) Rinpoche [1290–1364]. Butön's system of classification was later accepted and followed by Tsongkapa. The four classes of tantra are: (1) *krīya-tantra*, (2) *cārya-tantra*, (3) *yoga-tantra*, and (4) *mahānuttara-yoga-tantra*.

154. That is, his primary teacher, prior to his meeting with his Mahāmudrā guru, was his own brother, Kedrub Je. It is a fairly well-established fact that the two—Baso Je and Kedrub Je—were brothers. Lokesh Chandra, for example, in his *Materials for a History of Tibetan Literature*, Part 3, p. 11, states that Baso Chökyi Gyeltsen was "the brother (*sku-mched*) of Mkhas-grub Dge-legs, one of the two chief disciples of Tsoṅ-kha-pa." Any remaining doubts concerning the actual kinship of the two men can be put to rest by comparing the opening paragraphs of the respective namtars of each. The passages, in the Tibetan, when describing place of birth and parents are identical, veering only with regard to birth dates.

155. "All-knowing" translates the Tibetan phrase *thams cad mkhyen pa*. It is a title of great respect usually reserved for the highest ranking lamas, such as the Dalai Lamas. It is, however, also used, as can be seen throughout these six namtar, as a reverential form applied to other learned masters.

156. In these accounts, in addition to hearing of prophesies being made by the wisdom ḍākinī, Vajrayoginī, we also see them being given directly

by Lord Mañjuśrī. In this particular case, we also know of Jampel Gyatso's relation of special intimacy with this particular deity.

157. The Tibetan is *grub chen*. The Sanskrit equivalent is *mahāsiddha*.

158. *Nyengyü* (sÑan-rgyud) is, in Tibetan, a synonym for *Kagyü* (bKa'-rgyud). Both terms may be rendered "oral tradition" [the tradition that is passed on through direct speech and hearing], and both have special reference to the esoteric traditions that are passed on through an unbroken succession of "ear-whispered" or verbal instructions given directly from guru to disciple. The Gelukpas recognize two unique oral tradition lineages: that associated with the practice of Mahāmudrā and that associated with the practice of *Chöd* (*gCod*).

159. That is, the three chief meditative deities whose propitiation and cultivation comprise the main core of the Geluk Mahāmudrā practice.

160. On the Chöd tradition see *supra,* notes to the translation of Jampel Gyatso's namtar, note 113. In addition to the sources mentioned there, there is also a more recent and extremely interesting article on this subject by Janet Gyatso. The essay is entitled "The Development of the Gcod Tradition" and appears in *Soundings in Tibetan Civilization*, Delhi: Manohar Publications, 1985, pp. 320–341. Though focused primarily upon issues of the historical transmission of this particular practice lineage, Gyatso's study also neatly summarizes the philosophical underpinnings of the tradition. For example, on p. 320, she writes: "Conforming to the ideology of Buddhist praxis as a whole, Gcod is performed by the Tibetan yogin primarily to facilitate clarification of mind and the understanding of reality. The teaching is based on the notion that the ignorance and attachment that are the roots of human suffering can be eradicated simultaneously with the destruction of our subjugation to the obstructive but illusory situations of life, as personified by the various demons. In the central sādhana of Gcod the practitioner meditatively imagines that he is offering the parts of his physical body as food (phuṅ po gzan bsgyur) to devils, ghouls and gods, leaving behind a purified state of consciousness in which all phenomena are understood in their true sense."

161. There are, of course, many different forms of Jampelyang ('Jam-dpal-dbyaṅs) [Mañjuśrī], the deity who embodies the Buddha's wisdom. This particular reference, which links the title "mGon-po" with the deity's name, would seem to indicate that we here have reference to a Mañjuśrī

in his wrathful aspect, perhaps even to his form as Shinje She (gŚin-rje-gśed) [Yamāntaka].

162. The Tibetan reads: *gsaṅ ba las kyaṅ ches gsaṅ ba rnams yoṅs su rdzogs par gsan źiṅ/.*

163. Throughout my translations, the Tibetan compound term zungjuk is rendered "total integration." The term's Sanskrit equivalent is *yuganaddha.* A general meaning for both terms is "union" or "fusion," by which is intended "the complete and inseparable union of two members of a pair." Within tantric contexts, that "pair" is composed of the illusory body and the clear light, once these have been successfully realized by an accomplished yogic practitioner. Specifcally within Mahāmudrā contexts, the terms refer to that state of consummate inseparability ushered in by virtue of accomplishing the yogic method of forcing the subtle mind/consciousness-bearing winds down and then up into the central channel [*avadhūti*] of the "illusory" or arcane body.

164. Guru Yoga (*bla ma lha'i rnal 'byor*) is the very heart of all the practice lineages. It refers to the yogic methods and consequent realization of seeing one's own teacher, or guru, as the deity. Such a view is integral not only to one's progress on the path but to one's ultimate understanding of the final goal of practice. For more on the importance and functioning of guru yoga in Tibetan practice, see the present "Introduction."

165. That is, just as was the case with his Mahāmudrā guru, Jampel Gyatso [and as with all the practice-lineage siddhas to be discussed here], after contemplating the essential meaning of life according to the seven key points of lojong, or "spiritual transformation" [the rarity and preciousness of human rebirth, the certainty of death, and the uncertainty of the hour of death, etc.], Baso Je decided to forgo teaching in order to devote himself fully to meditation.

166. The passage in Tibetan is a difficult and ambigious one. It reads in part: *Ba so lhun grub bde chen bzuṅ nas/.* I have translated the passage as if it speaks of a particular meditative attainment by Baso Je. However, it might also be the case that "Ba-so Lhun-grub-bde-chen" is the actual name of a monastery where Ba-so-rje became abbot [he "took hold of the reins of the Lhun-grub-bde-chen monastery located at (the place) Ba-so."]. Apparently, prior to 1959 there was a monastery located at Baso, but the date of its founding remains obscure. If it already existed

prior to 1400, then Baso Je could conceivably have been asked to become its abbot. If, on the other hand, the place itself only became known because of Baso Je's meditative retreats and accomplishments there [that is, if it became a monastic seat only after, or due to, Baso Je's presence], it would seem better to leave the translation as given herein. I have questioned numerous Gelukpa lamas about this passage and the particular problems it raises, and all have so far shared my own puzzlement regarding it.

167. The Tibetan term, *Chöje* (Chos-rje) has the Sanskrit equivalent *Dharmasvāmin.* I have translated the term throughout as "Dharma Master."

168. This Riwo Dechen (Ri-bo-bde-chen) ["Great Bliss Mountain"] is not the famed Gelukpa monastic compound situated in Chonggye ('Phyoṅ-rgyas). Baso Je's tiny hermitage was established in Shab (Śab), a district lying between Sakya and Shigatse in Tsang. It would appear that until he was called to become abbot of Ganden, Baso Je made this hermitage in Tsang the seat of his main teaching activities.

169. Out of compassion, having once again become involved with teaching activities, Baso Je again feels drawn to return to completely isolated retreats. Again we see him contemplating, according to lojong teachings, and now firmly determining to abandon all forms of worldly activity in order solely to meditate. But, as we shall see, such solitary retreat was not to be his fate, for soon he was summoned to assume the reins of Ganden.

170. Pelgyi Ri (dPal-gyi-ri) refers to the mountain in southern India where the great scholar-siddha Nāgārjuna is said to have spent his last days absorbed in deep meditation.

171. This appears to be an alternate spelling for the "Se-mo-do" that is mentioned in the namtar of Jampel Gyatso.

172. Śawari here refers to Śavaripa, one of the famed eighty-four Buddhist siddhas of India. He too is said to have lived in the mountains of southern India on the mountain called Vikrama. A brief translation of his life story is found in James Robinson's *Buddha's Lions: The Lives of the Eighty-Four Siddhas*, pp. 37–40. Śavaripa was a hunter who was converted to the Dharma by Lord Avalokiteśvara himself. Though Robinson's translation does not mention the meditational deity upon which Śavaripa based his tantric practices, according to Tibetan

tradition that deity was Mahākāla, the wrathful manifestation of the Buddha's compassion. Throughout these six namtar we see the Geluk siddhas contemplating modeling their lives upon those of earlier siddhas in the Mahāmudrā tradition.

173. Here the great wisdom ḍākinī herself, in the form of Vajrayoginī, appears in her role as prophetess and adviser.

174. The explicitness of Vajrayoginī's prediction and advice is interesting here, for, unlike any of the other siddhas considered in this study, the great teacher Baso Je, it is predicted, will come to master the Oral Tradition even while he is engaged with the countless duties of running a major monastic establishment. Moreover, he not only masters it while so engaged, he manages to produce three disciples who, under his guidance, also come to full realization of it.

175. The Dharma Master Lodrö Chökyong (bLo-gros-chos-skyoṅ) is called "Yang-sde-ba bLo-gros-chos-skyong" in Longdöl Lama's *Collected Works* and "Drung bLo-gros-pa" in Gö Lotsawa's *Blue Annals*. He was the fifth throneholder of Ganden. Baso Je became the sixth throneholder. A list of the first seven abbots of Ganden is given in the *Blue Annals*. George Roerich's translation of that text, on pp. 1079–1080, after noting that Tsongkapa was Ganden's first abbot, records the following: "His Regent (rGyal-tshab)... acted as abbot for 13 years till the year Iron-Female-Hog (1431 A.D.). In this year he handed over the abbotship to mKhas-grub dGe-legs-dpal, and himself embraced a solitary life, and departed to Potala (i.e. died) in the year Water-Male-Mouse (1432 A.D.) at the age of 69. mKhas-grub dGe-legs-dpal occupied the abbot's chair for eight years till the year Earth-Male-Horse (1438 A.D.), and then passed away. The Dharmasvāmin Legs-pa Gyeltsen... was born in the year Wood-Hare (1375 A.D.), and became abbot... in the year Earth-Female-Sheep (1439 A.D.), at the age of 65. He died at the age of 76 in the year Iron-Male-Horse (1450 A.D.). Druṅ bLo-gros-pa was born in the year Earth-Female-Serpent (1389 A.D.), and became abbot in the year Iron-Male-Horse (1450 A.D.), at the age of 62. He remained abbot till the year Water-Female-Sheep (1463 A.D.), during which he appointed to the chair Ba-so-ba, aged 62, and himself became an ascetic. After that they asked the Dharmasvāmin bLo-gros brtan-pa to occupy the chair."

176. The great Gendündrub [1391–1474] was retroactively named the First Dalai Lama just over a century following his death. However, during

his lifetime he was already famed as being one of Tsongkapa's brightest young disciples and later for founding the great Gelukpa monastic institution Tashilünpo [Mound of Auspiciousness], the first of its kind outside the environs of Lhasa. Born in a cowshed, the son of nomadic tribespeople, Gendündrub was raised as a shepherd until, at age seven, he was placed in Nartang monastery. He was only twenty-five when, in 1415, he first met the Venerable Tsongkapa, who passed away some four years later. However, this auspicious confluence between guru and disciple greatly affected the young monk, and already in this young disciple Tsongkapa could see the signs of future greatness. Indeed, Tsongkapa recognized Gendündrub as being one of his most uniquely talented students. In short, he viewed this young disciple of his as being a true *bka' babs,* one specially qualified to carry out his guru's charge and to accomplish that charge with complete success. According to Tsongkapa's namtar, in 1417, perhaps seeing the signs of his own approaching death, Tsongkapa gave to the young Gendündrub a special cloak and vestment and predicted that the latter would perform glorious activities in the Tsang region of Tibet. The prediction was certainly to prove true since, owing to Gendündrub's great missionary efforts, Tashilünpo was subsequently established on the outskirts of Shigatse, the chief city of Tsang. For more on the life of Gendündrub, see Glenn Mullin's *Selected Works of the Dalai Lama I: Bridging the Sūtras and Tantras.* Ithaca, New York: Snow Lion Publications, Second Ed., 1985.

177. "Like a lake in summer" translates the Tibetan, *dbyar mtsho.* It is meant to imply that Gendündrub carried out his numerous virtuous activities effortlessly, just as a lake in summer benefits numerous beings without effort. Many such poetic images and idioms adorn these namtar.

178. The Tibetan is *gyeltsab* (rGyal-tshab). The term bears the sense of royal power and sovereignty. It may also be rendered as "heir" or, in this context, simply as "abbot."

179. The Tibetan is *Gyelwa Nyipa* (rGyal-ba-gñis-pa) and literally means "Second Buddha." In Gelukpa contexts, it is often used as an epithet for Tsongkapa. Among the Nyingmapa, this epithet is used solely with reference to the founder of that order, the siddha Padmasambhava.

180. This remark by Gendündrub is most important and significant since it gives us, in that one's own words, an inside view of the historical development of the Gelukpa order. As mentioned previously, Gendündrub was one of Tsongkapa's most intelligent and energetic disciples. Indeed,

in David Snellgrove's opinion [see his *A Cultural History of Tibet*, p. 182], it was Gendündrub's "energy and activity which was mainly responsible for building up Tsongkapa's school into an active expansive order ready and anxious to compete with the others on an equal footing." Such expansion was not, however, by Gendündrub's time, viewed with the acceptance and warmth that Tsongkapa had himself experienced in Lhasa. Tsang was then primarily a stronghold of the Kagyüpa order, and Gendündrub's ambitious undertaking there in the name of the Gelukpas would not have been viewed as warmly. Consequently, as his words here make clear, Gendündrub felt it necessary that he remain at the newly founded Tashilünpo in order to safeguard it from potentially hostile forces. [I translate *dgra mkhar* simply as "fortified mansion," though "a strong foundation against enemies" could be substituted here. The phrase translated as "enemy camp" is *dgra yul*. It could also be rendered "hostile territory."] Thus, it was because Gendündrub saw it as necessary that he remain at Tashilünpo that he advised those at Ganden to invite Baso Je to become their next abbot.

181. The Tibetan system of dating is somewhat cumbersome. *Rabjung* (rab byuṅ) refers to the cycle of sixty years by which Tibetan dating has been calculated since 1027. Prior to the eleventh century, the Tibetan calendar was based on a twelve-year cycle with each year named after a given animal: Mouse, Ox, Tiger, Hare, Dragon, Serpent, Horse, Sheep, Monkey, Bird, Dog, and Hog. In 1027, the sixty-year cycle was introduced which combined the names of these animals with the five elements: Wood, Fire, Earth, Iron, and Water. Each element is repeated twice and combined with two different animals and, to distinguish between the two successive element years, "Male" is added to the first and "Female" to the second. For cross-checking Tibetan dates with Western ones I have relied chiefly upon the excellent dating tables provided as appendices in Ketsün Sangpo's *Biographical Dictionary of Tibet and Tibetan Buddhism*. There is also, of course, P. Pelliot's study, in *JA*, 1913, pp. 633–667 and the interesting essay on "The Tibetan Sexagenary Cycle" which forms "Appendix D" in Chattopadhyaya's *Atīśa and Tibet*, pp. 563–573.

182. This is the fuller title of the Ganden monastery, founded by Tsongkapa in 1409. It is certainly the most famous of all Gelukpa institutions. The Sanskrit equivalent of Ganden is Tuṣita, the joyous heavenly abode of the future Buddha, Maitreya.

183. Another epithet for Tsongkapa, by which he is likened to the Great Protector [*mGon*], Mañjuśrī ['Jam-dpal-dbyaṅgs]. Sarat Chandra Das's *Dictionary* also notes, p. 453, that "'Jam-mgon-bla-ma" is "an address of politeness to the hierarchs of the S'akya school." However, throughout this series of stories, the reference is always intended to apply only to Tsongkapa.

184. The Tibetan is *thugs kyi bcud phyuṅ ba. bCud* is a common synonym for *nyingpo* (sñiṅ-po) ["essence" or "heart"], and literally means "sap," "juice," or "nectar." *Phyuṅ ba* here means "excess" or "overflow," as of a liquid from a vessel. A slight variant on the translation could be that Baso gave the teachings "in a manner which overflowed, as if directly, from the very heart of the Jamgön Lama, Tsongkapa."

185. That is the two main branches, wings, or doctrinal systems of the Mahāyāna, or "Great Vehicle," especially as articulated in the writings of Nāgārjuna [the Madhyamaka] and of Ārya Asaṅga [the Yogācāra].

186. Panchen is the abbreviated Tibetan equivalent for the Sanskrit term *mahāpaṇḍita*, which literally means a "greatly learned one."

187. The phrase, "blessed—unlike others..." here translates the Tibetan *byin rlabs kyi bka' bab gźan las che ba.* Here again, the key term is *bka' babs.* It is used to denote that singular disciple who, in the eyes of his or her guru, is judged to be capable of successfully fulfilling the guru's charge. This is an extremely important but often overlooked notion.

188. *Shabdrung* (Źabs-druṅ) nowadays is a title borne by certain political officials and government servants. We know from the First Panchen, Losang Chökyi Gyeltsen's, autobiography that this particular title and others underwent changes in the sixteenth and seventeenth centuries. Its exact meaning in earlier times is unclear.

189. Neynying (gNas-rñiṅ) [literally, "ancient abode, or dwelling"] was the name not only of a particular monastic complex but also of a lesser school of Tibetan Buddhism, the Neynyingpas. Gene Smith tells us in his introductory remarks to *The Autobiography of the First Panchen Lama*, p. 4, that this school later merged with the Gelukpa and that "the merging of the Gnas-rnying-pa with the Gelukpa was complete [by the time of the First Panchen]. Tashilunpo became the heir to the religious interests held by the Gnas-rnying lineage in both Gtsang and Bhutan.... This pattern of growth through the incorporation of the moribund lesser sects was especially common in Gtsang."

190. It appears that this lama may be the same "gNas-rñiṅ, Kun-dga'-bde-legs (Rin-chen-rgyal-mtshan)" who would later serve as abbot during the novice ordination of the Second Dalai Lama, Gendün Gyatso.

191. This characterization of Baso is a literal rendering of the Tibetan, which reads: *byin rlabs kyi gter chen po*/.

192. Throughout these namtar we see these yogi-saints taking an active part in "patronizing the arts." Here, Baso Je commissions great improvements for the chapel at Ganden during his tenure as its sixth abbot. Sanggye Yeshe (Saṅs-rgyas-ye-śes) will later do likewise for the monastery founded by his Mahāmudrā teacher, Ensapa; and the First Panchen, Losang Chökyi Gyeltsen, was a most prodigious patron. Tsongkapa himself, it may be recalled, is famed in part for the many important renovations of buildings and refurbishments of statues that he commissioned.

193. The Tibetan reads: *rdo rje mched gsum po* and later *slob ma rdo rje mched gsum*, [literally, "three brothers, vajra disciples"]. They are referred to as the "Dorje Brothers" because each one had "Dorje" as an element of his name and because each was said to have ultimately won the "vajra [rainbow] body" of an enlightened being.

194. The Tibetan for "rainbow body" is *jalü* ('ja' lus). The term is generally used to refer to the manner in which a siddha's body is said to vanish, at that one's death, like a rainbow or like the colors of a rainbow. This apparition "seals" or verifies that siddha's mastery of the highest tantric techniques. However, *'ja' lus* has a long history. It is connected, almost certainly, with the pre-Buddhist tradition of divine kingship in Tibet where, it was said, each day the king descended to earth via a *dmu* [a type of rainbow-like rope which joined heaven and earth] and each evening he vanished, or journeyed back to heaven, by dissolving back into that *dmu*. See A. Stein's *Tibetan Civilization*, pp. 48, and 224–225, for intriguing comparisons between this latter phenomenon and certain advanced Buddhist yogic techniques.

195. That is, at Riwo Gepel, the mountain behind Drepung on the slopes of which a special hermitage is situated.

196. *Ḍāka* is the Sanskrit equivalent of the Tibetan *pawo kandro* (dpa' bo mkha' 'gro). Like its feminine counterparts, *ḍākinī* and *kandroma* (mkha' 'gro ma), the term's literal meaning is "one who goes in the sky"; but *dpa' bo* and its feminine counterpart, *dpa' mo*, carry the

additional sense of "powerful" and "warrior-like." It is sometimes translated as "hero" on this account. *Ḍāka* alone refers to the masculine semiwrathful yidam or tutelary deity. The *ḍāka* functions both as messenger and as protector.

197. In an abbreviated life story of the Third Dalai Lama, we find a most interesting allusion to our "dPal-ldan-rdo-rje of sTod-luṅ." As translated by Glenn Mullin [see the latter's *Selected Works of the Dalai Lama III: Essence of Refined Gold*, p. 226], the Third Dalai Lama, "So-nam Gyatso… returned to Dre-pung in order to meet with and study under To-lung-pa Pal-den Dor-je, one of the three chief disciples of Gyal-wa Wen-sa-pa. Each of these three had allegedly attained full enlightenment in one lifetime and had manifested the esoteric rainbow body as a sign of their accomplishment. Under To-lung-pa, So-nam Gya-tso received all the ear-whispered traditions coming from Lama Tsong-khapa." To begin with, Pelden Dorje (dPal-ldan-rdo-rje), as our text indicates, was a disciple of Baso Je, not Ensapa. The latter had many esteemed disciples, but the "three Dorje Brothers" are not listed among them. That the three came to be associated with Ensapa in Yeshe Gyeltsen's account of the Third Dalai Lama's life gives clear indication of their importance and uniqueness within the tradition. It also shows that sometimes errors were made in the larger biographical anthologies.

198. Here the Tibetan is simply *dpa' bo.*

199. That is, he exchanged teachings with the Gendün Gyatso [1475–1542] who was retroactively named the Second Dalai Lama. Thus, it would seem clear that part of 's fame arises out of the fact that he gave instruction in the Gelukpa Mahāmudrā Oral Tradition to one of the early Dalai Lamas. Here, with the actual name supplied, we know that it was the Second Dalai Lama whom he instructed.

200. The Tibetan reads: *grub chen 'di'i ṅo mtshar rmad du byuṅ ba'i rnam par thar pa ni da lta ñid du 'chad par 'gyur rol.*

201. As previously mentioned, the Dharma Master Lodrö Tenpa became the seventh abbot of Ganden. When Gö Lotsawa [1392–1481] completed his famed *Blue Annals* in 1478, this Lodrö Tenpa was still alive and still serving as abbot of Ganden. [See above, note 175.]

202. In order, the Tibetan titles of these works are: (1) *Dus 'khor gyi bskyed rdzogs kyi khrid,* (2) *dbU ma'i lta khrid chen mo,* (3) *rDo rje 'jigs byed kyi bskyed rdzogs kyi khrid,* and (4) *sÑiṅ po don gsum gyi khrid,* respectively.

The *Vaiḍūrya-ser-po* [see Lokesh Chandra, editor, Delhi: International Academy of Indian Culture, 1960, p. 68] lists only three titles for Baso Je, omitting the "Instructions on... Vajrabhairava." Longdöl Lama's famed catalog, the *mTshan-tho*, lists four works by Baso, arrived at by separating the "Generation" and "Completion" instructions on Kālacakra [treating these as two separate texts], counting the text on Vajrabhairava, and combining the titles of (2) and (4) above as follows: *dbU ma'i lta khrid rgyas 'brin bsdus gsum sñiṅ po don gsum.* Of the four commentaries mentioned in Baso Je's namtar, it would seem that the *dbU ma'i lta khrid* is the most highly regarded. Describing the latter text, Hlakar Tenpa Gyeltsen (Lha-mkhar Yoṅs-dzin bsTan-pa-rgyal-mtshan) in his brief "Preface" to Volume 7 of the *Mādhyamika Text Series* [New Delhi, 1973] states: "This magnificent presentation of the essential import of the Madhyamika doctrine is one of the most esteemed lta khrid [commentaries upon a given philosophical view] for the Dge-lugs-pa. Indeed it is the only work of Ba-so that circulated widely in Tibet." A. Wayman thinks [see his *Calming the Mind and Discerning the Real*, p. 70] that this same Baso Je wrote one of the "added four *Mchan bu* (*ṭippaṇī*), a type of commentary somewhat like our annotations, but which runs along with the actual text in smaller type" [to Tsongkapa's *Lam rim chen mo*]. However, it would appear, given the various lists of Baso Je's writings [none of which mentions such a *mchan bu*] and the relative prominence such an annotation would have commanded had he composed it, that our Baso Chökyi Gyeltsen did not author such a *mchan bu.*

203. That is, *dGa'-ldan chos kyi pho braṅl*. As Wylie notes, in his translation of *The Geography of Tibet*, p. 152, note 350: "Dga'-ldan-pho-brang is [also] the name of the palace at 'Bras-spungs in which [the] 'Abbot of 'Bras-spungs' lived." However, here the reference is clearly to the Ganden monastery and to its *chos kyi pho braṅ*, since Baso had been abbot of that institution prior to his death.

204. The Tibetan, *Mi-pham-'jam-dpal-sñiṅ-po*, is a bit unclear here. It seems to be a compound [and I have translated it as such] made up of *Mi-pham* [the Future Buddha, Maitreya] and *'Jam-dpal-sñiṅ-po* [the Bodhisattva, Mañjuśrīgarbha]. In the *Blue Annals*, p. 1079, we are told [about Tsongkapa] that following his death, "he will become the Bodhisattva Mañjuśrīgarbha ('Jam-dpal-sñiṅ-po) in the Heaven of Tuṣita.... (and)... in [the] future he will become the Tathāgata Siṃhāsvara (Seṅ-ge'i ṅa-ro)." Given the emphasis on guru devotion

throughout all these six namtar, it is probably the case that both deities are intended and that, further, both are embodied in none other than Tsongkapa himself.

205. That is, we are told that both of Chökyi Dorje's parents were " wandering ascetics." The Tibetan is the compound term *bya bral. Bya* means "work" or "that which is to be done." *Bral* means "to be free of that." Thus, a *jadrelpa* (bya bral pa) is someone who has abandoned the domestic sphere and worldly concerns in order to devote more time to religious practice. As Barbara Aziz's excellent study of Ding ri [see her *Tibetan Frontier Families*] has shown, there were and are many ways available to practicing Buddhists, only one of which is the way of the cloistered monk or nun. In her study, Aziz discusses a number of itinerant practitioners: wandering ascetics who spend a great deal of time traveling on religious pilgrimages. Chökyi Dorje's parents were such practitioners.

206. Here the author of the namtar adds additional esteem to the familial lineage of Chökyi Dorje by having his parents hail from the same region of Tibet that produced the great Tsongkapa himself. That region is Amdo, a province north of Kham and far to the northeast of Ü-Tsang, the central province wherein the capital city Lhasa is located.

207. Ü-Tsang is actually composed of four divisions, or *ru*, two belonging to Ü proper and two to Tsang.

208. Tanak [literally "black horse"] refers to "the valley of a river of the same name which flows from the north into the Tsang po (river)" according to *Mk'yen brtse's Guide to the Holy Places of Central Tibet* [Ferrari, trans., p. 157]. Tucci's *LAB*, pp. 118–119, and Wylie's *GOT*, p. 89, both mention a Nyingmapa monastery in this region by the name of "rDo-rje-brag," but no information seems available about this particular monastery, rTa-nag rDo-rje-gdan.

209. In the Gelukpa tradition it is common to assert that the great siddha Chökyi Dorje attained the siddhi of immortality, so no one especially worries about supplying dates for him. Even so, Zuiho Yamaguchi [editor, *Catalogue of the Toyo Bunko Collection of Tibetan Works on History*, 1970, p. 129] suggests the dates "1457–1541 (?)" for him. It is hard to know upon what Yamaguchi bases his speculation. However, since Chökyi Dorje's Mahāmudrā guru was Baso Je [1402–1473] and his chief disciple was Gyelwa Ensapa [1505–1566], we at least have some

limiting factors for historical speculation. It is of interest that a year of birth is suggested in Chökyi Dorje's namtar. We are told that he was born "in the year of the Ox." Still, between 1414 and 1505 there were no fewer than seven "Ox" years from which to choose. Because no element-marker [see note 181 on Tibetan system of dating, above] is designated, arriving at an exact date of birth remains impossible.

210. In short, we are told how Chökyi Dorje's wandering ascetic parents mapped out their pilgrimages. They visited the places where the holy ones toward whom they felt devotion had been born, had practiced meditation, had gained realizations, and had later taught. A type of "outer," or lay, guru devotion activity is portrayed here.

211. The Tibetan here reads: *Dam can chos kyi rgyal po.* He is the chief *Dharmarāja* of all the class of *damchen* (dam can) [literally, "having oathed"] deities. A form of Yama, he is usually depicted in quite fearsome aspect. For more on this particular deity and on this specific class of wrathful protecting deities, see R. Nebesky-Wojkowitz's *Oracles and Demons of Tibet.*

212. The goddess Vajrayoginī again appears here, in her form as prophetess, to alert Baso Chökyi Gyeltsen about the imminent arrival of his chief Mahāmudrā disciple.

213. A similar story is told regarding Tsongkapa himself. As Wayman summarizes it in his *Calming the Mind and Discerning the Real,* p. 16: "In his third year, the chos-rje (*dharmasvāmin*) Don-grub Rin-chen brought horses, sheep, and many valuable gifts to the father [of Tsoṅ-kha-pa] and commanded, "You must present me this boy of yours!" The father agreed and enthusiastically entrusted the boy to the monk's care.

214. The Tibetan is *rab tu 'byuṅ.* See below, note 24, on the three "grades of monastic ordination."

215. The Sanskrit equivalent by which Tibetans often refer to this great siddha is *Dharmavajra.* Both names may be rendered "Indestructible Dharma" or "Indestructible Truth."

216. The Tibetan reads: *brda sprod kyi gtsug lag slob pa sogs.*

217. The Tibetan reads: *rgyal sras bdag ñid chen po. rGyal sras* is literally a "son (*sras*) of the Buddha (*rGyal ba*), or a bodhisattva. *bDag ñid chen po* is the Tibetan equivalent of the Sanskrit *mahāsattva.* The compound

term, bodhisattva-mahāsattva, is often found as a characterization of a particular type of holy personage, especially in the Mahāyāna's *Prajñāpāramitā* literature.

218. *Shi-ne* (źi gnas) Skt. *śamatha.*

219. Hlaktong (lhag mthoṅ) Skt. *vipaśyanā.* The two meditative elements, *źi gnas* and *lhag mthoṅ*, are essential to any further progress. The meditator first trains in developing still, clear concentration [having the mind settled or "abiding in peace," a literal translation of *źi gnas.*] Then that one focuses such clear concentration upon a Dharmic object of meditation. With a calm and clear state of mind, one is then capable of the type of "higher seeing" [*lhag mthoṅ*] that leads to insight. The passage tells us that first Chökyi Dorje mastered these two essential elements of meditation. Thereafter, he effortlessly mastered whatever Dharma he practiced.

220. *Kyebu Sum* (skye bu gsum), the so-called "three scopes," "three types," or "three levels" of beings. The lowest-level person sees his or her own misery and wishes release from suffering and a happy rebirth for him or herself. The middle-level person sees that the nature of saṃsāra is suffering, and so desires Nirvāṇa. But the person of highest scope sees that all beings suffer and so seeks to attain enlightenment in order to benefit all beings. The way in which one practices, or treads the Buddhist path, is thus directly related to one's own attitude and motivation.

221. *Jangchub Kyi Sem* (byaṅg chub kyi sems). Skt. *bodhicitta.*

222. *Nyelam Dorje Tekpa* (nye lam rdo rje theg pa). *rDo rje theg pa* is the Tibetan equivalent of the Sanskrit, Vajrayāna. It is called the "short-cut path" or the "speedy path" [*nye lam*] because, by successfully treading it, one may attain complete enlightenment in just a single lifetime.

223. Dükyi Korlo (Dus-kyi-'khor-lo.) The tantric corpus of texts dealing with the "Wheel of Time" Buddha. This elaborate system of tantra has in recent times been given publicly in the West by both His Holiness the Dalai Lama and by the Venerable Kalu Rinpoche. For fairly comprehensive treatments of this particular tantric corpus, see *The Kalachakra Tantra: Rite of Initiation for the Stage of Generation* by Tenzin Gyatso, the Fourteenth Dalai Lama [translated and edited by Jeffrey Hopkins], Boston: Wisdom Publications, 1985 and *The Wheel of Time: The Kalachakra in Context* by Geshe Lhundub Sopa [with Roger Jackson and John Newman], Madison, Wisc.: Deer Park Books, 1985.

224. That is, by the wisdom ḍākinīs as we have seen, who usually predict the arrival of the appropriate candidate to receive the Oral Tradition teachings and, subsequently, the *Miraculous Volume.*

225. Tib. *Ye śes mka' 'gro.*

226. Tib. *sras kyi thu bo.*

227. One of four of the most renowned Gelukpa monasteries [the others being Ganden, Sera, and Tashilünpo], the fuller name of Drepung is Pelden Drekar Pungpa (dPal-ldan-'bras-dkar-spuṅs-pa) ["Resplendent Mound of White Rice"]. This monastery, famed for having had more than 7,000 resident monks, was situated roughly four miles west of Lhasa on the north bank of the Kyichu and on the side of the mountain known as Riwo Gepel. It was founded in 1416 by Jamyang Chöje Tashi Pelden [1379–1449], a personal disciple of Tsongkapa. [As notes in *GOT*, p. 79: "In former times, it had seven grwa-tshang, but now it has only four, namely: Sgo-mang, Blo-gsal-gling, Bde-yangs, and Sngags-pa."]

228. There are, generally speaking, three levels of ordination: (1) *rabtujungwa* (rab tu 'byuṅ ba) (Skt. *pravrajyā*), or the rank of "novice," wherein some ten vows are enjoined, (2) *getsül* (dge tshul) (Skt. *śrāmaṇera*) ordination, which enjoins the taking of some thirty-six vows, and (3) *gelong* (dge sloṅ) (Skt. *bhikṣu*), full ordination which enjoins the observance of some 253 vows.

229. Hlamo Maksorma is a form of the Great Protectress of Tibet and the chief Protectress of the Gelukpa order, Pelden Hlamo. In her form as Maksorma she is also called "dMag-zor-gyi-rgyal-mo Remati." A chief feature of this wrathful guardian is the *zor*, a sickle-like weapon. For more on this goddess and the various forms of Hlamo, see R. Nebesky-Wojkowitz's *ODT*, pp. 24-31, and Tucci's *TPS*, II, pp. 590–594.

230. The Tibetan reads *mGon-po-źal.* A common alternate name for this deity is *Nag po chen po*, or *Mahākāla.* According to some Tibetan iconographic texts, there are as many as seventy-five different forms of Gönpo (mGon-po), though his appearances as the black, "four-armed," "six-armed," "one-faced,"or "four-faced" wrathful deity are the most common. Unusual in the Tibetan Buddhist pantheon, Mahākāla is both a Great Protecting Deity [a *sungma* (sruṅ ma) or *dharmapāla*] and a tutelary deity, or yidam, representing wrathful compassion. For more on the Gönpos, see Nebesky-Wojkowitz's *ODT*, pp. 38–67.

231. The Tibetan reads only *rim lṅa'i khrid.* It is probably the case however, given the proximate mention of his *Stages of the Path to Enlightenment,* that the reference is to Tsongkapa's commentary, *Lamp Thoroughly Illuminating the Five Stages* [*Rim pa lṅa rab tu gsal ba'i sgron me*], which itself discusses Nāgārjuna's *Five Stages* [the famed *Pañcakrama*].

232. The Tibetan reads *'dus pa'i khrid* ["a commentary on Guhyasamāja," reading *'dus* as short for *gSaṅ-'dus*] and *lag rjes yig chuṅ thor bu ba.*

233. He thereby demonstrates for future disciples how one may come to gain the three kinds of wisdom or insight enumerated since early Buddhism in India. These three are: (1) *śrūtamayī-prajñā,* or the "insight gained from hearing," (2) *cintamayī-prajñā,* or "insight gained from reflecting upon what is heard," and (3) *bhāvanāmayī-prajñā,* or the "insight gained from concentrated meditation upon that."

234. The "four *kāyas*" are the (1) *Nirmāṇakāya,* (2) *Saṃbhogakāya,* (3) *Dharmakāya,* and (4) *Svabhāvikakāya,* the latter representing the combined essence of the first three.

235. That is, Buddha Vajradhara, said to head all tantric practice lineages.

236. "The sacred water of Pema Chan..." translates the Tibetan, *pad ma can gyi sgrub chu.* The use here of "Pema Chan" as a supposed place-name is of particular interest since the tantric context also suggests at least the possibility of an alternate [symbolic, intentional, "twilight," or veiled] meaning at work. I have discussed the hermeneutical concerns in working with tantric biographies in two articles that focus on just this particular episode in Chökyi Dorje's namtar. Those articles are "The Search for Padma-can; A Study in the Interpretation of Tibetan Sacred Biography" in *The Journal of Religious Studies.* Vol. XIII, No. 1, Spring 1985. Patiala, India: Punjabi University, pp. 56–73; and "On the Nature of Namtar: Early Gelukpa Siddha Biographies" in *Soundings in Tibetan Civilization,* Aziz and Kapstein, eds. Delhi: Manohar Publications, 1985, pp. 304–319.

237. The Tibetan is *sems dpa' gsum rtseg can.*

238. The Tibetan is *za ma tog.* Literally rendered "basket" or "receptacle," here the term is used in its tantric or mystic sense. That is, to ordinary beings, Chökyi Dorje's *za ma tog* is his physical body. However, since he has long ago perfected the goal of Mahāmudrā practice and consequently attained the "rainbow-body," which is invisible to ordinary

beings, this great being chooses to appear as if he has an ordinary, physical body. He does so only so that others may be able to see, communicate, and take teachings from him. Hence, Chökyi Dorje's *za ma tog* is actually not a conventional or ordinary physical body. It is rather a "mystic support body."

239. The Tibetan is *gtso bor gnas gsum.* The three are the "desire" realm, the "form" realm, and the "formless" realm.

240. The Tibetan here for "smallpox" is *'brum bu.* What is of special interest here, however, is that later we see that Enapa's reincarnation [the First Panchen, Losang Chökyi Gyeltsen] is also stricken with this disease, and at about the same age.

241. We hear this account, from Ensapa's point of view, in the next namtar translated herein.

242. The hermitage of Garmo Chö Dzong is mentioned in *The Geography of Tibet,* p. 71. There it is written: "Not far to the south is the place called Mgar-mo-chos-rdzong, where Grub-chen (Skt. Mahāsiddha) Chos-kyi-rdo-rje achieved realization of the truth." But Wylie's notes to this section indicate that he knew nothing further about either the hermitage or its most famous hermit. On p. 140 of *GOT* we find: "Mgar-mo chos-rdzong: unidentified" and "Chos-kyi-rdo-rje: unidentified."

243. That is, the lamdre teachings.

244. Tib. *'Ja' lus rdo rje'i sku.*

245. The Tibetan reads *rnam rtogs mi mṅa' źiṅ.* The compound *rnam rtogs* is short for *rnam par rtogs pa,* the Tibetan equivalent for the Sanskrit *vikalpa,* "discursive thought." To say that Chökyi Dorje accomplishes all his aims for humankind "without the least trace of discursive thought" is to say that his mind is completely purified, unruffled, and resting in the realization of voidness. Thus his virtuous activities flow out from him effortlessly and with true, unadulterated compassion.

246. The Tibetan reads *yid bźin gyi nor bu daṅ dpag bsam gyi śiṅ bźin du.*

247. The term used for "Buddha" throughout this namtar is the Tibetan Gyelwa (rgyal-ba) (Skt. *Jina,* "Conqueror" or "Victor"). A more common Tibetan compound for "Buddha" is Sanggye (Saṅs-rgyas), but Gyelwa is used here, I believe, because it echoes "Gyelwa Ensapa." As perceived by the Gelukpa tradition and by our present biographer, the

two are nothing short of identical. This namtar, with all its legendary embellishments, is not only cast in the mold of "a Buddha's life," it *is* a Buddha's life, the life of an enlightened being, a Gyelwa.

248. Hlakü. I am unsure about the precise location of this place. Neither Wylie's *GOT* nor Ferrari's *Guide* mentions it. Within the brief summary of the life of Ensapa found in Sarat Chandra Das's *Contributions*, p. 109, Das wrote the following: "This great scholar was born in the year 1505 A.D. at Lha-khu-phu-pen-sa situated on the north bank of the great river Tsanpo, near the famous monastery of Chamalin, in the district of Da-gya in west Tsan." Since Das does not employ precise transliterations for the Tibetan names, one is still left guessing. I assume, for example, that the orthographically correct spelling for the "famous monastery" of his passage is [dGe-rgyal] Bye-ma-gling, as our text tells us. But for what does Das's "Da-gya" stand? I think the only safe assumption about all this is that Hlakü is somewhere in the region of Tsang that is known, generally, as "Lha-tse."

249. The Tibetan reads *dGe-rgyal-bye-ma-gliṅ.* Again, I have been unable to locate a monastery by this name in either Wylie's or Ferrari's geographies. We know that Ensapa, as his name suggests, hailed from the environs of Ensa (dbEn-sa), a region far to the west of Lhasa and just slightly northeast of Shigatse. This monastery must have been highly regarded by members of the Gelukpa Order, but it does not loom large on Tibetan maps.

250. Sönam Choklang or Chokyi Langpo (Phyogs-kyi-glaṅ-po), whose dates are 1438–1505, was retroactively reckoned to have been one of the early Panchen or "Tashi" Lamas before these were given ordinal numbers: First, Second, etc. The so-called Panchen incarnations of Tashilünpo are regarded as having extended back, in place and time, to India and to the monk Subhūti, one of the Buddha's disciples. Counting from Subhūti, Sönam Choklang is listed as ninth on the list of incarnations, just prior to Gyelwa Ensapa himself, and just after Kedrub Je. It was Ensapa's reincarnation, Losang Chökyi Gyeltsen, who was honored with the title of "First Panchen Lama." Thereafter, tradition extended the lineage backwards in time. Lists of the Panchen incarnations can be found in Waddell's *Tibetan Buddhism*, p. 236, and in Gene Smith's introductory remarks to *The Autobiography of the First Panchen Lama*, p. 11. In *Contributions*, pp. 81–110, Das gives brief summaries of the lives of the Panchens up to and including the First

Panchen, Losang Chökyi Gyeltsen.

Based upon Das's rendering, the life of Sönam Choklang may be summarized as follows: He too was born in Tsang. Apparently his parents were poor. Because the baby had a pale complexion, his parents nicknamed him "Be'u" ["calf"]. Eventually, the boy was taken before the Ganden throneholder. When the latter asked the boy his name, he answered, "Be'u." The throneholder [who would probably have been at this time the Dharma Master Lodrö Chökyong, the abbot just before Baso Je] then renamed the boy, declaring that henceforth he would be called Sönam Chökyi Langpo (bSod-nams-phyogs-kyi-glaṅ-po) ["Bull on the Side of Virtue"]. He then admitted him to the monastery of Ganden. There Sönam completely mastered the Buddhist scriptures before returning to Tsang, where he drew a large following of disciples. He is said to have commissioned a large metal statue of the Buddha and to have founded a small monastery named Üding [Chos-'khor-dbus-sdiṅs (?)], also called the Lower Ensa monastery. Towards the end of his life, after sending numerous students to higher studies at Tashilünpo and Drepung, he retired into solitude where he not only enjoyed a rich inner, spiritual life but also wrote a number of commentaries.

251. Here again, we see that the life of Ensapa is modeled clearly upon that of the Buddha himself, for only such a one is said to "determine" his parents in just this way prior to taking birth. It may be recalled that before the future Buddha, Siddhārtha Gautama, took birth, he first made what are called the "Five Great Observations" [translated by Warren in *BIT*, p. 40]: "He observed, namely, the time, the continent, the country, the family, and the mother and her span of life." At this point in the namtar we have seen Ensapa complete all these "determinations."

252. That is, he uttered the sacred mantra of Avalokiteśvara, the Buddha of Infinite Compassion.

253. The Tibetan reads: *dkar phyogs skyoṅ ba'i lha daṅ sruṅ ma.*

254. Tib. Okmin ('Og-min); (Skt. *Akaniṣṭha.*) The highest heaven of the "form realm," said to be presided over by the Buddha Akṣobya and the Bodhisattva Vajrasattva.

255. I have been unable to find this lama listed in the various chronicles. We know from this account that he was an abbot of Drepung [Riwo Gepel]. Having discerned the birth of Ensapa as being like the birth of

a second Buddha, this abbot journeyed to Ensa to "baptize" the baby. It was apparently this abbot who named the babe Gönpo Kyab.

256. Mahāmāyā was, of course, the Buddha's mother.

257. The Tibetan reads: *mig gyi bdud rtsi.*

258. This teacher becomes Ensapa's primary, or root, guru. It is this Je Kyabchok Pelsangpo who leads him through all his studies, sūtra and tantra alike. He is not, however, Ensapa's chief Mahāmudrā instructor, that teacher being Chökyi Dorje. The importance of Je Kyabchok Pelsangpo cannot and should not be underestimated, however. One of the most salient ideas demonstrated by the Ensapa namtar is that which forms the very heart of guru devotion practice. Both Je Kyabchok Pelsangpo and Chökyi Dorje are Ensapa's gurus and are revered as such. Indeed, whereas Chökyi Dorje gave over to Ensapa the Geluk Mahāmudrā teachings, Je Kyabchok Pelsangpo was revered not only for having accomplished total integration himself but also for having completely cast away any notion of the "eight mundane concerns," which is perhaps the hallmark of all truly Dharmic accomplishment and activity. Ensapa himself composed a long namtar about his teacher, Je Kyabchok Pelsangpo. Later, the First Panchen Lama would also compose a namtar and prayer devoted to him.

259. The Tibetan for what I translate as the "eight mundane concerns" is *jikten gyi chö gye* ('jig rten gyi chos brgyad). This compound is usually rendered in English as the "eight worldly dharmas," but this leaves one of the terms in the Sanskrit. I base my translation upon the kinds of activities enumerated in the list of eight. These are: gain, loss, fame, disgrace, praise, blame, pleasure, and pain. Buddhist teachings say simply that any actions performed with these ideas as goals [gain, praise, pleasure] or shunned because of possible negative consequences [loss, dishonor, blame] are not purely performed activities. An enlightened being performs activities completely divorced from such mundane concerns.

260. Precociousness and a general aloofness during childhood are features that characterize much of Western, and especially Christian, hagiography. That Ensapa would often, as a very young child, run away from home to perform prayers and meditation exercises is a key feature of his namtar.

261. *Hlakpai hla* (lhag pa'i lha).

262. That is, in 1515. According to the Tibetan system, a child is one year old at birth and, hence, two years old on his or her first birthday.

263. It seems probable that this is the monastery founded by Sönam Chokyi Langpo.

264. The Tibetan is *khyim nas khyim med par.* This is the traditional way of saying that someone becomes ordained. Such a one abandons the "domestic sphere" [*khyim*] and enters upon the life of a "homeless" [*khyim med pa*] practitioner.

265. The Sanskrit is "Siddhārtha."

266. Skt. "*Śuddhodana*," meaning "Pure Food."

267. This is, of course, the great Tsongkapa. Tsongkapa is referred to in this way in order to indicate that he is really "three beings in one." That is, outwardly, he is the enrobed monk Losang (bLo-bzaṅ) ['grags-pa]; inwardly, he is Śākyamuni Buddha, Tubwang (Thub-dbaṅ) and, secretly, he is none other than the great lord of tantric practice, Dorje Chang (rDo-rje-'chaṅ). To think of one's guru as embodying these three is the heart and goal of guru devotion. We have seen Chökyi Dorje achieving his consummate Mahāmudrā experience while performing this very practice. Here, the Ensapa passage continually plays upon this idea. Just as the Buddha was named "accomplisher of all his goals"[Don-grub], the same is so for Ensapa. Additionally, he is also named Losang to show his spiritual kinship with Tsongkapa, since that was the first part of the monastic ordination name of Tsongkapa. Because it is recognized that Ensapa will become an enlightened being, a Buddha, he is given the names of two Buddhas.

268. See note 179, above. Again, within the Gelukpa tradition, this title is generally reserved only for Tsongkapa. Here it is applied to another "Second Buddha," Gyelwa Ensapa.

269. Ketsün Sangpo's Tibetan reads: *phag lo rta zla'i rtshes bcu la.* Earlier, the same text reads, *phag lo zla ba daṅ po'i rtshes bcu'i.* This would seem to make the "first month" [*zla ba daṅ po*] and the "horse-month" synonyms.

270. Tib. *so so tarpai dompa* (so so thar pa'i sdom pa). Literally, the "vows of individual liberation." The Sanskrit equivalent would be the vows of *pratimokṣa.*

271. I take this to be a reference to the "great guardian kings" of the four quarters of the world, according to Buddhist cosmology. The four guardians are: (1) Dhṛtarāṣṭra, the white guardian of the east and king of the Gandharvas, (2) Virūḍhaka, green guardian of the south and king of the Kumbhāndas, (3) Virūpākṣa, red guardian of the west and king of the Nāgās, and (4) Vaiṣravana, yellow guardian of the north and king of the Yakṣas.

272. The Tibetan reads: *pha rjes bus zin pa źig bya ba'i phyir.*

273. That is, Riwo Gepel, or Drepung monastery. Das's summary of Ensapa's life [in *Contributions*, p. 109] says that he entered "Tasi-lhunpo."

274. That is, from the "Lha-ri-rtse mkhan-po," Drakpa Döndrub.

275. Tib. *dPe chos rin spuṅs.* The title of a book written by the famous Kadampa geshe, Potowa Rinchen Sel (Po-to-ba Rin-chen-gsal) [1031–1105]. In this work, Potowa teaches the Dharma solely by means of analogy and example. The title is sometimes rendered as *Potowa's Dharma Similes.*

276. A *lung* (luṅ) is a blessing given by a teacher to a student that enables the latter to read a text with comprehension. Such a blessing is conferred when the teacher reads aloud a section of the text with the student. I translate the term as "oral recitation blessing." A *jenang* (rjes gnaṅ) is a rite performed in order to grant the disciple permission either to practice a given meditation or to attend the fuller empowerment necessary for entering into that meditative practice. I translate *rjes gnaṅ* as "practice permission."

277. Tib. *sNar thaṅ brgya rtsa. The Hundred [Rites] of Nartang* is the famous anthology of meditative practices [Skt. *sādhana*] said to have issued originally from Atīśa, and which were later compiled by the seventh abbot of Nartang (sNar-thaṅ) monastery, Chim Namka Drak (mChims Nam-mkha'-grags) [abbot from 1254–1290].

278. Tib. Menla (sMan-bla), the "Medicine Buddha." For more on his history and practice, see Raoul Birnbaum's *The Healing Buddha,* Boulder: Shambhala, 1979.

279. Tösam Ling, which literally means "the place for hearing and reflecting," is one of the three colleges [*dratsang/grva tshaṅ*] of Tashilünpo. The other two colleges are Kyilkang Dratsang (dKyil-khaṅ grva tshaṅ) and Shartse Dratsang (Śar-rtse grva tshaṅ).

280. Düdra, which I have translated literally as "precise definitions," is really a comprehensive course in logic and logical thinking which can be geared effectively even for younger students. Vostrikov in his *Tibetan Historical Literature* [trans. by Gupta, 1970, pp. 60–61], provides a wonderful summary of its contents: "*Bsdus grva* is the name of a course of eristics taught during the first three years to novices in the monastic philosophic school (*mtsha-ñid grva-tshaṅ* or *chos-grva*). It is divided in three degrees according to the degree of difficulty. Its aim is to train a novice in the art of right and fluent argumentation by teaching him how to put every argument or even every idea into the form of a regular syllogism; and also to teach him quickly and rightly to react on every counter-argument set out by the opponent. The opponent questions, the disputant answers. He answers briefly in one of four ways. (1) If he agrees he says simply: "Yes!" (*ḥdod*). (2) If he doubts, he asks: "For what reason?" (*ciḥi phyir*), if the reason is not given. If he disagrees he must at once detect where the fallacy lies, and two possibilities are open: the mistake lies either in the minor (*phyogs-chos*) or in the major premise (*khyab-pa*). (3) If the fault lies in the minor premise he says: "The logical reason unreal" (*rtags ma grub*), i.e. not contained in the subject, or minor term. (4) If it lies in the major premise he must at once answer: "No invariable connection" (*khyab-pa ma byuṅ*) between the middle term (or reason) and the major term.... Having this aim in view the course of *bsdus-grva* begins by some examples of discussions on the connotation of the simplest notions, e.g. colour in general and particular colours, form in general and particular forms, etc. A double result is achieved, the novice gets quite precise logical definitions of current notions with which logic or philosophy are dealing, and he acquires a proficiency in applying the syllogistic formulation with its three terms to every argument and thought. The founder of this system of teaching *bsdus-grva* and at the same time the author of the first school book on it, according to Tibetan tradition, is the Tibetan lama Phyva-ba Chos-kyi-seṅge, who lived in the twelfth century (1109–1169)."

281. I have been unable to identify this scholar and the specific text alluded to here.

282. I take it that the "Dzam-la dmar-po" here is a reference to the deity better known as "Jambhala" [god of wealth]. For more information on this particular deity, see Nebesky-Wojkowitz's *ODT*, pp. 68–81 and especially pp. 75–76.

283. Tib. *mGon po'i bka' chen bcu gsum.*

284. Again, these are the outer, inner, and secret forms of Chögyel, chief guardian deity of the Gelukpa Mahāmudrā tradition. See note 211, above. Also, see the illustration of this figure herein.

285. Tib. *gTum po khyuṅ lṅa.*

286. Tib. *Tshe riṅ mched lṅa.* Nebesky-Wojkowitz devotes an entire chapter in *ODT* [pp. 177–202] to these "five long-lived sisters" and related goddesses.

287. Tib. *Nā ro chos drug gyi khrid.*

288. Tib. *Paṇ chen chos rgyan gyi bsre 'pho.* I am unable to further clarify either the specific author or subject matter of the text alluded to here.

289. Both these texts are unknown to me. There is, however, among the *Collected Works* of Ensapa, a text called *Phyag rgya srog rtsol du 'gro ba'i man ṅag daṅ rdzogs rim la le tshan gñis.*

290. Tib. *Ne gu chos drug gyi khrid.* That is, the "Six Yogas of Niguma," female consort of the great Indian siddha Nāropa and tantric adept in her own right. Niguma established her own tradition of practice which she passed on to one Tibetan yogi, Kyungpo Neljor (Khyuṅ-po-rnal-'byor). This lineage of practice is preserved by the Shangpa Kagyüpa (Shangs-pa bKa'-brgyud-pa). For more on this tradition, see the "Tantric Yogas of Sister Niguma" in *Selected Works of the Dalai Lama II,* Glenn Mullin, trans. New York: Snow Lion Publications, 1985, pp. 92–151.

291. For detailed accounts concerning these various protector deities, see Nebesky-Wojkowitz's *Oracles and Demons of Tibet.*

292. I have corrected the orthographic error that reads *chos rgyas* here to read, properly, *Chos-rgyal.*

293. According to Das's *Dictionary,* p. 645, Don-źags "seems to be a Tantrik manifestation of Avalokiteśvara."

294. Tib. *Ye śes kyi dkyil 'khor dṅos su gjigs.*

295. Tib. *bLa ma daṅ yi dam dbyer mi phyed pa.* Of course, experiencing the inseparability of one's lama and one's personal tutelary deity is the hallmark of accomplished guru yoga practice.

296. Tib. *dGra nag daṅ gśed dmar lha lṅa.*

297. Questions of dating present genuine problems, especially in the Ensapa namtar. The "monkey year" following Ensapa's birth would have come in 1512; the next would have come in 1524. In 1512, Ensapa would have been only eight years old by Tibetan reckoning, while in 1524 he would have been twenty. Since the account has already told us about episodes and events that occurred when Ensapa was eight and eleven, it is more likely here that when these "maṇḍala-viewing" experiences take place he is around twenty. Two problems remain: (1) Ensapa is said to have met his Mahāmudrā guru, Chökyi Dorje, when he [Ensapa] was seventeen and (2) he is said to have connected with Chökyi Dorje only after Je Kyabchok had passed away. Not all the "facts" in a namtar can be said to jibe at all times.

298. Tib. *lus dben daṅ ṅag dben.* These are in fact the first two of some five [or six, depending upon the specific system of tabulating] successive experiences of the Completion Stage of tantric practice, especially as explained according to the *Guhyasamāja Tantra.* Called "isolations" (*dben*), these two denote the "isolation of body" (*lus dben*) and the "isolation of speech" (*ṅag dben*). The progression of attainments is enumerated as follows: (1) isolation of body, (2) isolation of speech, (3) isolation of mind, (4) illusory body, (5) clear light, and (6) union. As Tucci [see his *ROT*, p. 263] summarizes it: "The Sa skya pa and the dGe lugs pa recognize a fivefold division of the 'method of achievement'.... after the preliminary isolation of the body (*lus dben*) follows (1) isolation of the word (*ṅag dben*); (2) isolation of the mind (*sems dben*) through concentration of the mind on three points or drops (*thig le*) in the nose, the heart and the genitals; (3) isolation of the *māya*-body (divided into pure and impure); (4) isolation of the light, which is also divided into two kinds (*dpe,* exemplary, reflected in the moment of experience in which it is received, and later real, *don,* in the moment of actualization); (5) coincidence (*zung 'jug*) of the moment of experience with that which is beyond experience (Buddhahood)." As Tucci also notes here, further explanations concerning these Completion Stage experiences are given by D. Ruegg, in his *The Life of Bu-ston Rin po che,* pp. 101 ff, note 1. These six are also briefly discussed in Lati Rinbochay and J. Hopkins' *Death, Intermediate State and Rebirth,* pp. 70–71; and in *The Blue Annals,* p. 415.

299. The text records here that Je Kyabchok Pelwa had reached the age of "seventy-eight," (*dguṅ lo bdun cu don brgyad*). However, another problem with dating surfaces, since, earlier, the text mentioned that Je

Kyabchok Pelsangpo was sixty-three. If he is now seventy-eight and just now finishing up his stewardship of Ensapa, it means that the latter took instruction from him for at least fifteen years. It would be hard to imagine that Ensapa began his tantric studies with this master at age two! Either the earlier age of "sixty-three" should be revised to read "seventy-three" or the latter date of "seventy-eight" should be revised to read "sixty-eight." Either way of revising would make the duration of Ensapa's tantric studies with this master amount to approximately five years, a more likely time frame since Ensapa has yet to meet with Chökyi Dorje, and that meeting is said to have occurred when he reached seventeen years of age.

300. Tib. *Zuṅ 'jug dbaṅ gi rgyal po'i sku (thob).*

301. Tib. *'Ja' ltar phra źiṅ rgyun chad pa med.*

302. Tib. *sma ra dkar po'i 'ag tshom can.*

303. Tib. *rten 'brel 'grig pa.* Das's *Dictionary*, pp. 297–8, defines the compound term as "good or auspicious coincidence."

304. Tib. *nyepa Sum* (mñes pa gsum). These "three types of delight" refer to the three behaviors one ought properly to show toward one's teacher and which consequently "please" that one. Stated simply, a disciple should: (1) bring to the teacher offerings, (2) show respect in both body and speech, and most importantly, (3) do as the teacher instructs.

305. Tib. *bum pa gaṅ byo'i tshul du*, literally "in the manner of" (*tshul du*) "transferring" (*byo pa*) from one "vessel" (*bum pa*) into another.

306. Again, there is mention of the "eight mundane concerns." One of the hallmarks of Gyelwa Ensapa is that he accomplished this feat and hence practiced the Dharma purely. Like his teacher before him, though he perfectly accomplishes the tantric instructions having to do with the Ganden Oral Tradition of Mahāmudrā, he does so planted firmly upon the essential basis of having completely cast away the "eight mundane concerns."

307. Tib. *sku sa rus pa la lci ba'i thal ba.*

308. *Nyönmong* (ñoṅ moṅs); (Skt. *kleśa*). I translate this term as "afflictive emotion" because such emotions actually inflict pain and harm upon oneself as well as upon others, but it is often translated simply as "defilement" or even as "poison." The kleśas are generally enumerated

as three: hatred, greed [or passion], and delusion, but sometimes two others are added: arrogance and envy.

309. Tib. *rgyal ba gyuṅ gi sgrub gnas 'brag rgya bo rdo rje'i pho braṅ.* I am unable to identify this specific location.

310. Tib. *A tsaryī 'phral skad.* The text has, just previously, distinguished between colloquial (*'phal skad*) and classical (*legs sbyar gyi skad*) languages. It here mentions the colloquial language, *A tsaryī.* But the latter is more than just a spoken dialect. It is said to be a language specially used in the Indian tantras and by Indian ascetics. Commenting upon the latter, Roerich writes in *The Blue Annals*, p. 43: "the text has a-tsa-ra <Skrt. ācārya, used in Tibetan to denote an Indian ascetic, a sādhu."

311. Here, for the first time in any of these namtar, "Padma-can" is said to have an alternate name: "Padma-'od." As I have stated in a number of places, the place name "Padma-can" is conspicuously absent from any map of Tibet I have ever seen. This fact, along with certain descriptions of the supposed place I have been given by certain lamas, allows me to speculate that this particular place name may be a veiled or secret way of referring to, in this case, a female sexual partner (Skt. *karmamudrā*). ["Padma" which means "lotus" also means, in the veiled language of the tantras, "vagina."] But the place name "Padma- 'od," or more specifically "Padma-k'od," does appear on some maps and is described in some sources. For example, on Bell's map [see his *The People of Tibet*] one finds "Pemakochen." Waddell [in *Tibetan Buddhism*, p. 278] cites it as a district in southern Tibet where certain monasteries are located. Edwin Bernbaum [*The Way to Shambhala*, pp. 69–70] calls it a "hidden country" but describes it as being "along with Sikkim... one of the two hidden countries best known to Tibetans." It is said to be a country of jungles where countless wild animals roam. Ensapa is said not only to have meditated in this place but to have delivered his first teachings at a hermitage located there. Here, I believe, there is room for the imagination.

312. I have been unable to identify either the siddha, *, or his "paṇḍita" incarnation, Künkyen Lekpa Döndrub.

313. The Tibetan reads only *mDzod.* Contrary to what is said immediately following its mention in the text, I was unable to find a single text bearing this word as part of its title among those listed in Ensapa's *Collected Works.*

314. Two different editions of the *Collected Works* are printed. One, based upon the Tashilünpo redaction, was published in 1976 by Döndrub Dorje (Don-'grub-rdo-rje). The other [and the one available to me during this project] is the *Blo bzaṅ bKa' 'bum: the Collected works (Gsum 'bum) of Dben-sa-pa BLo-bzaṅ-don-grub*, Vol. I [of a two volume set] reproduced from a manuscript from Sang-ngak Chöling (gSan-snags-chos-gliṅ) in Kinnaur, Sumra, H.P., 1977.

315. Tib. *Luṅ bstan gsaṅ ba'i me loṅ.*

316. Dromtönpa ('Brom-ston-pa) was the devoted Tibetan disciple and heir to Ārya Atīśa. According to religious annals, he was born in Tölung (sTod-luṅ) in 1005. He met Atīśa in Ngari (mṄa'-ris) and together they traveled to Kyirong (sKyid-roṅ) and Central Tibet. Following Atīśa's death, Dromtön went to Radreng (Rva-sgreṅ) and there, in 1056, built a main temple. The Radreng monastery thereafter became the chief center for the Kadampa. Dromtön died in 1064. For more on his life, see *BA*, pp. 251–265.

317. That is, Ensapa received full ordination from the Second Dalai Lama, Gendün Gyatso [1475–1542]. A biographical account of this renowned lama is found in Glenn Mullin's translation, *Selected Works of the Dalai Lama II*, pp. 199–211.

318. One of two statues of the Buddha to reach Tibet very early on. This particular image of Śākyamuni, known as the Jowo (Jo bo), was brought by the Chinese wife of Tibetan King Songtsen Gampo (Sroṅ-bstan-sgam-po) [d. 649]. It was originally placed in the temple of Ramoche, which the Queen founded. A second statue of the Buddha, said to have been brought by the king's Nepalese wife, was housed in the Jokang (Jo-khaṅ).

319. This text is reputed to be the "last will and testament" (*bKa' chems*) of King Songtsen Gampo. According to Shakabpa's *TPH*, p. 335, the work is "a gter-ma (cached-treasure book) discovered by Jo-bo Rje Atisha." In the same book by Shakabpa, p. 5, it is stated that "The Indian pandit, Atisha, who visited Tibet in the eleventh century, discovered a document in a pillar of the Jokhang, or central temple, in Lhasa, that was written according to tradition during the reign of Songtsen Gampo in the seventh century. This document provided evidence in favor of the second tradition for the origin of the Tibetan people." This "second tradition" says that the Tibetans are descended

from the union of a male monkey who was an incarnation of the deity Avalokiteśvara and a local mountain ogress.

320. The full title of Sera, one of the most esteemed of Gelukpa monasteries, is Sera Tekpa Chenpö Ling (Se-ra-theg-pa-chen-po'i-gliṅ). The monastery was founded in 1419 by one of Tsongkapa's closest disciples, Jamchen Chöje Shakya Yeshe.

321. Tib. *So thar gyi mdo.*

322. Tib. *Chos sgrags kyi mdo.* It is unclear whether the title as given in the Tibetan ought to be rendered something like "The Sūtra on Various Doctrines, Brought Together" (*sgrags*) or whether it contains a spelling error (*sgrags* for *grags*). Of course, if the latter is the case, it may be that the *chos grags* stands for the Sanskrit "Dharmakīrti."

323. On the practice of "fasting," see note 40, above.

324. Here the Tibetan reads only *sGron gsal*, so it is not possible to say with certainty which particular commentary is intended.

325. Tib. *bDe mchog gdan bźi.*

326. The verse in Tibetan reads *Ñi śu rtsa bźi'i mkha' 'gro'i gtso/ dPa' bo chen po 'dir bźugs la/ Chu skes khoṅ pa'i pad dkar bźin/ sBas pa'i tshul gyis byin gyis rlobs//.* So it was that, according to Ensapa himself, his chief protector-deity, Mahākāla, instructed him to build his monastery upon that very site.

327. Tib. *gTer duṅ gi lo rgyus.* The meaning of *gter duṅ* is certainly unclear here. A work bearing this exact title is nevertheless present among those collected in Ensapa's *Collected Works* (*bKa' 'bum*).

328. According to Longdöl Lama's *mTshan tho*, the Ensapa *bKa' 'bum* contains some ninety-eight separate works. The great majority of these are devoted to meditative and ritual practices and [to quote from the "Preface" of the Kinnaur edition of the *bKa' 'bum*] "to the esoteric practices of the guru yoga in which the Bkra-shis-lhun-po tradition specializes." There can be little doubt that one of Ensapa's most enduring contributions to the vitality of the Gelukpa practice tradition consists—apart from his own pure practice—in the works he composed on meditational, devotional, and liturgical subjects.

329. That is, during the great "first month" of the monastic calendar. This

period commemorates the miracle contests that took place in Śrāvastī as a result of which the Śākyamuni successfully defeated the "heretics." [The date of Ensapa's passing away was 1566].

330. Here the Tibetan reads *Tsaṅ roṅ gyi yul lhan drug brgyar.* It is interesting that Sanggye Yeshe's most famous disciple, the First Panchen, also was born in this town. At the beginning of the First Panchen's namtar we read *Tsaṅ roṅ gyi yul lhan źes bya ba drug brgya.* I take it then that "drug-brgya" [six hundred] refers to the number of families who lived there. This is clearly how Das, in *Contributions*, p. 111, reads it as well. In his brief summary of the First Panchen's life, Das writes: "The important town of Lhen, containing six-hundred families, is situated on the confines of Tsaṅ-roṅ." Nevertheless, it remains true that the namtar of the First Panchen treats both "Lhan" and "Drug-bryga" as actual names and as synonymous ways of referring to the town wherein both Sanggye Yeshe and, later, the First Panchen took birth. I have been unable precisely to locate this town either in the *Geographies* translated by Wylie and Ferrari or on any of the standard maps.

331. Again, as in the namtar of Gyelwa Ensapa, the Buddhist tradition is referred to in this way. The Tibetan reads *dkar phyogs kyi lha.*

332. Why? We must assume, I believe, that Ensapa's monastery was nearby to Lhan or that he took an active interest in the births of children that "were accompanied by wondrous signs." Clearly, through some type of clairvoyance or foreknowledge, Ensapa knew when his chief spiritual heir had taken birth.

333. Apart from the details given here regarding Yönten Sangpo, I have been unable to identify him further.

334. Tib. *dge bsñen gyi sdom pa.* That is, he received the five vows of a layman: not to kill, steal, commit sexual faults, take intoxicants, or lie.

335. Clearly, by Sanggye Yeshe's time, this place was an active monastery. It is here called by its full name, Baso Hlündrub Dechen. It is probably safe to assume that this monastery is not too far from the Ensa monastery of Chökor Üding. Sanggye Yeshe took his novice vows at the Baso monastic complex.

336. Tib. *dge tshul gyi sdom pa.*

337. Here the Tibetan for "Second Buddha" is *Dam pa thub pa'i dbaṅ po gñis pa.*

338. For more on the so-called "armed deities" (*mTshon lha*), see Nebesky-Wojkowitz's *Oracles and Demons of Tibet.*

339. That is, the philosophical treatises attributed to Ārya Maitreya [and said to have been brought back from the Tuṣita heaven by the fourth century Indian philosopher, Ārya Asaṅga], which are said to number five: the *Mahāyānasūtrālaṃkāra* (*mDo-sde-rgyan*), the *Mahāyānottaratantraśāstra* (*Theg-pa-chen-po-rgyud-bla-ma'i-bstan-bcos*), the *Madhyāntavibhaṅga* (*dbUs-daṅ-mtha'-rnam-'byed*), the *Dharmadharmatāvibhaṅgakārikā* (*Chos-daṅ-chos-ñid-rnam-par-'byed-pa'i-tshig-le-ur-byas-pa*), and the *Abhisamayālaṃkāra* (*mṄon-par-rtogs-pa'i-rgyan*).

340. That is, the six great pandits of Buddhist India: Nāgārjuna, Asaṅga, Dignāga, Dharmakīrti, Āryadeva, and Vasubandhu.

341. The "Two Most Excellent Ones" is here a reference to the two Indian Vinaya masters, Gunaprabha and Śīlaprabha.

342. We learn that this particular teacher becomes Sanggye Yeshe's main or primary guru apart from Ensapa. He seems to have been a quite renowned teacher during Sanggye Yeshe's time, with affiliations at the Tanak, Tashilünpo, and Gyüme (rGyud-smad) monastic institutions. We are informed later that Sanggye Yeshe composed a prayer to, and the namtar of, this teacher.

343. It would appear that this dratsang (*grva tshaṅ*) is connected to the Tanak monastery. Perhaps this is the same rTa-nag rDo-rje monastery mentioned in the namtar of Chökyi Dorje.

344. The "three religious activities" of a Dharma Master are said to be: (1) *'chad*, (2) *rtsod*, and (3) *brtsom*. According to Lokesh Chandra [in *Materials*, p. 11] these are defined as the abilities "to explain the sacred doctrines, to discuss them refuting the antagonist's thesis, [and] to put one's own system in writing" respectively.

345. Nyangtö (Myaṅ-stod) [also written as Nyaṅ-stod] is a district of Tsang. Wylie's translation of *GOT* mentions it on pp. 54, 70, 73, and 115. On page 115, Wylie writes: "Myang-stod is the name for the upper reaches of the Myang, or Nyang-chu, which rises in the eastern part of Gtsang called Nyang-stod, and flows westwardly, entering the Tsang-po (Brahmaputra) near Shigatse."

346. That is, after he had prostrated himself before this master by way of

showing respect and requesting instruction.

347. This is the famed treatise on logic composed by the great Indian sage, Dharmakīrti.

348. The Tibetan reads *'Jam-dbyaṅs-dge-'dun-blo-bzaṅ gi rnam 'grel gyi yig cha.*

349. Tib. *yid 'phrog par gyur to.*

350. The Tibetan used here for "debate" is *dam bca'.* Normally this term is rendered as "a promise, or a vow." However, in contexts such as these, [when the various namtar are discussing or describing the features of monastic education], the term means "sitting for debate" or simply, "taking oral exams."

351. Shartse is one of Ganden's two famed "colleges," or dratsang (*grva tshaṅ*). The other is Jangtse (Byaṅ-rtse).

352. Tib. *phyogs las rnam par rgyal ba'i grags pa' 'an thob po.*

353. This is an extremely important pair of terms in Buddhist scriptural and philosophical theory. According to both Butön and Tsongkapa, Buddhist scriptures may be divided into those whose meaning is revealed "directly" (Tib. *ṅes pa'i don*; Skt. *nītartha*) and those whose meaning is revealed "indirectly" following additional interpretation (Tib. *draṅ ba'i don*; Skt. *neyārtha*). For a brief but helpful treatment of this, see Thurman's "Buddhist Hermeneutics" in *JAAR.* A much fuller treatment can be found in Thurman's translation of Tsongkapa's famed treatise on this subject, *Distinguishing the Interpretable and the Definitive Meanings of All the Scriptures of the Victor* (*gSung rab kyi drang ba dang nges pai don rnam par phye ba gsal bar byed pa legs par bshad pai snying po*) in *Tsong Khapa's Speech of Gold*, 1984.

354. Wylie's *GOT* mentions this monastery. On p. 139, it is noted: "This monastery is called Dpal 'khor sde in the Gyantse Chronicles (*TPS*, p. 666) and Dpal-'khor-bde-chen of Nyang-stod in *VSP*, where it says that it was founded by Rab-brtan-kun-bzang-'phags, the ruler of Rgyal-mkhar-rtse, and Mkhas-grub Chos-rje Dge-ldan-legs-dpal-bzang-po, who acted as patron and chaplain (respectively) (*VSP*, folio 197–b). For descriptions, see *JLCT* (pp. 90–1), *LAB* (p. 41), Waddell (p. 278)."

355. The Tibetan for "school rounds" is *grva skor.* The "Four Difficulties" (*dka' bźi*) refers to the four difficult subjects that had to be mastered in

order to earn the religious degree of the institution. Prior to the time of the Fifth Dalai Lama, these subjects were four in number. Since his time, the traditional number of studies is five and includes: Vinaya, Abhidharma, Pramāṇa, Madhyamaka, and Prajñāpāramitā.

356. The Tibetan *dbyar skyes* is translated here literally.

357. The Tibetan reads: *zaṅ ziṅ gi bsñen bkur*. The term *bsñen bkur* means "to offer services, or pay respect"; but *zaṅ ziṅ*, as Das's *Dictionary*, p. 1090 notes, is used to denote concrete, material offerings.

358. Describing the monastery of Gangchen Chöpel, Wylie [in *GOT*, pp. 70 and 138] tells us that it was located in "the fief of Bsam-'grub-rtse (Shigatse)" and that it "was founded by Pan-chen Bzang-po bkra-shis-pa, the second abbot (khri-thog) of Tashilunpo (Bkra-shis-lhun-po)."

359. The *bLo-sbyoṅ-don-bdun-ma* is one of the primary texts of the Kadampa and Gelukpa orders on the practice of mental or spiritual transformation. Aimed at carefully delineating the practice in "seven essential steps" (*don bdun ma*), this particular text was authored by the Kadampa master Geshe Chekawa from the oral transmission passed down from the famed Indian master, Atīśa, who had received the teachings from his guru, Dharmakīrti of Sumātra. For a wonderfully clear explanation of this text by the First Dalai Lama, see Glenn Mullin's translation in *Selected Works of the Dalai Lama I; Bridging the Sūtras and Tantras*, [1985 edition], pp. 57–105.

360. Here the Tibetan is *smad rgyud grva tshaṅ*.

361. The Tibetan simply records *rgyud kyi rgyal po* or, literally, the "King of the Tantras" for what I further specify as the *Guhyasamāja*. That the epithet refers to this particular tantra can be verified by the fact that Tsongkapa refers to it thus in the title of his famed commentary *Lamp Thoroughly Illuminating [Nāgārjuna's] "The Five Stages," Quintessential Instructions of the King of Tantras, the Glorious Guhyasamāja* [*rGyud kyi rgyal po dpal gsaṅ ba 'dus pa'i man ṅag rim pa lṅa rab tu gsal ba'i sgron me*]. What I have translated as "the true essence (hidden beneath) the literal meaning" is given in Tibetan as *tshig don gyi de kho na ñid*, literally the "thatness of the meaning of the words."

362. These three "arts" make up a large part of the curriculum of the tantra colleges. They are *gar* (ritual dancing), *thig* (maṇḍala drawing), and *dbyaṅs* (ritual singing and music).

363. "Fire offerings" and "maṇḍala preparation" are, in Tibetan, *sbyin sreg* and *dkyil chog*, respectively.

364. Here, Gyelwa Ensapa refers to his disciple Sanggye Yeshe by the title of the religious degree that the latter has attained. Das [*Dictionary*, p. 1169] describes *rabjampa* (rab 'byams pa) as "a diploma resembling in a manner the degree of Doctor of Divinity which the Buddhist priesthood confers on monk students of sacred literature." The title clearly refers to one who is very learned in the scriptures. According to *The Structure of the Ge-lug Monastic Order* [see the present "Bibliography," p. 69]: "There are two other Ge-lug monasteries besides those at Gadan, Se-ra and Dra-pung that award degrees similar to the Geshe degree based on mastery of the same five subjects listed above. Tra-shi lhun-po monastery (bKra-shis lhun-po dGon-pa), the seat of the Panchen Lama, awards the Ka-ch'en (bKa'-chen) degree and Sha-drub-ling monastery (bShad-bsgrub-gling dGon-pa) awards the Rab-jam-pa (Rab-'byams-pa) degree."

365. Again, on Pelden Hlamo, Chief Protectress of the Dharma and especially sacred to the Gelukpa, see Nebesky-Wojkowitz's *ODT*, Chapter 1, pp. 22–37.

366. Deyang (bDe-yaṅs) is one of the four monastic colleges of Drepung. The other three are Gomang (sGo-maṅ), Losel Ling (bLo-gsal-gliṅ), and Ngakpa (sṄags-pa).

367. Tib. *bka' gdams lha bźi.*

368. The term translated as "winter meditation robe" is *kubem* (sku bem). It is fairly common paraphernalia, especially for monks engaged in study in one of the tantra colleges. However, in my early translation efforts, this term caused me no end of worries and led me down a number of false "mystical" tracks. See the "Preface."

369. This passage and scene may be seen, I think, as re-enacting the Buddha's conquest of Māra and the latter's frightening hordes. It is at least intended to "seal" Sanggye Yeshe's conquest over fear, a requisite for more advanced tantric practices.

370. It would appear from this passage that Sherab Pelsang had been an abbot at Drepung and that Sanggye Yeshe took the seat after him.

371. Sanggye Yeshe, like Baso Je before him and the First Panchen after him, was a great patron of the arts in Tibet. His renovations and additions to

the Ensa monastery and his commissioning of numerous holy statues are universally praised.

372. That is, the Third Dalai Lama, Sönam Gyatso [1543–1588]. For an account of his life, see Glenn Mullin's translation in *Selected Works of the Dalai Lama III: Essence of Refined Gold* [1985 edition], pp. 221–240. Sanggye Yeshe appears twice in this account of the Third Dalai Lama's namtar. A section of it [Mullin's translation, p. 227] records the following: "After his ordination, a letter of invitation came from Ta-shi Lhun-po Monastery of Southern Tibet, asking him to come to Tsang to teach the holy Dharma. Subsequently he left for Tsang.... On the way he stopped at Wen Monastery [Ensa monastery] in order to offer prayers and to meditate before the image of the mighty yogi Gyal-wa Wen-sa-pa. At the request of Khe-dub Sanggye Ye-she he stayed here for some time and gave several discourses to the assembly of monks."

373. For further details on the "Twenty-One Forms of Tārā" and on the entire cult of Tārā, see Stephen Beyer's *The Cult of Tara: Magic and Ritual in Tibet.* A wonderful commentary by the First Dalai Lama on the "Twenty-One Verses in Praise of Tārā" and two Tārā *sādhanas* can be found in Mullin's translation, *Selected Works of the Dalai Lama I: Bridging the Sūtras and Tantras* [1985 edition, pp. 122–148].

374. Langmikpa was one of Sanggye Yeshe's teachers and one of the most renowned lamas of his day. The Tibetan gives his title more fully as "rJe Rin-po-che gLaṅ-mig-pa." This lama appears again early in the namtar of Sanggye Yeshe's chief disciple, the First Panchen. It was this same Langmikpa whose powers of clairvoyance confirmed that Gyelwa Ensapa had indeed reincarnated in the young Losang Chökyi Gyeltsen.

375. This lama is mentioned, along with Sanggye Yeshe and others, as being an important teacher during the time of the Third Dalai Lama. The latter's biography [see *Selected Works of the Dalai Lama III*] records, for example [in Mullin's translation, p. 230], the following : "The news of Gyal-wa So-nam Gya-tso's prospective visit to Mongolia caused considerable consternation amongst the Tibetans, who feared for his safety and well-being on a precarious journey of this nature. When eventually he left from Dre-pung, a large assembly of high monks, officials and devotees set out on the first step of the journey with him for auspicious purposes. Both the former and present Ganden Throne Holders were

there, as well as the chief monks from Gan-den, Se-ra and Dre-pung. Included in the group were a large number of renowned masters, such as Rin-chen Po-kar, Tsang-pa Pan-chen Rik-pa Seng-ge [i.e., the Rigpa'i Sengge of our text], Sanggye Ye-she of Wen Monastery, Pon-lob Ta-shi Rik-pa, and Kar-pa Pon-lob Nam-kha Jam-pa of Gyal Monastery.... "

376. Samdrub Tse (bSam-'grub-rtse) is both a way of referring to a town [Shigatse] and to the fief held under the Tsangpa rulers. During the time of Sanggye Yeshe, the ruling family was the Rinchen Pungpa (Rin-chen-spuṅs-pa). Wylie, in *GOT*, p. 142, states that: "(Sde-pa Nor-bu-bzaṅg-po) of Rin-spungs took control of Bsam-'grub-rtse (Shigatse) in Nyang-smad in 1435, and from then on, most of the government of Gtsang was held by those of Rin-spungs until 1565, when control was taken over by Gtsang-pa Zhing-gshag Tshe-brtan rdo-rje." Our text would seem to indicate that while he was staying at Tashilünpo [in Shigatse] either the monk officials there or some lay officials of the Rinpungpa pleaded with him to return to the abbot's throne at Drepung. He did so.

377. The Tibetan reads *'phags pa 'jig rten dbaṅ phyug*. This is also a name for Avalokiteśvara. It is possible, therefore, that we may read here "heirs to the holy lineage of Ārya Avalokiteśvara."

378. The Tibetan reads *gñug mar gnas pa*. The term *gñug* may also be rendered "ordinary" state, indicating ordinary beings in their unawakened state, living within the realms of saṃsāric suffering.

379. We learn from the namtar of the First Panchen how it was that Sanggye Yeshe verified the identity of the former. See the following translation of the life story of the First Panchen.

380. Tib. *sku tshe 'di'i tha ma'i źal chems.*

381. For the full titles of these and other works by Sanggye Yeshe, see Longdöl Lama's *mTshan-tho*. By my count, there are some forty-three separate works.

382. Again here a problem of dating surfaces. Though the Tibetan of our text reads that Sanggye Yeshe traveled to the Rong Jamchen monastery on the "twenty-fifth day of the twelfth month," it later declares that he died there on the "fourteenth day of the eleventh month" of the same year. I have accordingly changed the first date to read "twenty-fifth day of the *tenth* month."

383. Under the heading "Roṅ-byams-pa," Das's *Dictionary* records: "Of a district in the mountainous country situated in the north of Tsang where in a monastery a huge image of Maitreya Buddha was constructed by Lama Sems-dpah chen-po Gshon-nu-rgyal-mchog." Wylie's translation of the *GOT*, p. 72, adds the name of the statue's commissioner, saying: "East of that [i.e., of the Rin-chen-spungs-pa rdzong] half a day's journey is the huge statue of Byams (Skt. Maitreya), which was constructed by Rin-spungs Sde-pa Nor-bu-bzaṅg-po, and which is known as the [Gtsang] Rong-Byams-chen." For more on this monastery's history and development, see also the *Blue Annals*, p. 340.

384. According to Buddhist theory regarding "death, the intermediate state, and rebirth," for forty-nine days directly following what we normally term "death," a person's subtle mind (*yid kyi lus*) exists in an "intermediate" space (*bar do*). According to His Holiness the present Dalai Lama [in the foreword to Hopkins and Lati Rinbochay's *Death, Intermediate State and Rebirth*, p. 10]: "Those born within the realms of desire and form must pass through an intermediate state, during which a being has the form of the person as whom he or she is to be reborn. The intermediate being has all five senses, but also clairvoyance, unobstructiveness and an ability to arrive immediately wherever he or she wants.... If a place of birth appropriate to one's predispositions is not found, a small death occurs after seven days, and one is reborn into another intermediate state. This can occur at most six times, with the result that the longest period spent in the intermediate state is forty-nine days." When in this intermediate state, the mind is very subtle and most powerful. If one has not attained enlightenment in one's lifetime, the bardo state offers another chance to win complete liberation by unifying one's subtle consciousness with the Enlightened "mind-body complex" of a Buddha. Thus the monks held special ceremonies involving the maṇḍala of Sanggye Yeshe's main *yidam*, Vajrabhairava, throughout the course of the forty-nine days immediately following his death.

385. Sanggye Yeshe's chief disciple, the Venerable First Panchen himself, composed one of the most revered texts on such "offering to the lama" practices. Indeed, his *bLa ma mchod pa* has become the standard liturgical text for this particular rite among all Gelukpa adherents.

386. The Tibetan reads: *chaṅ mas dad pa chen pos thugs dgoṅs yoṅs su rdzogs*

pa mdzad do. Is the line added solely to strengthen the claim that the patrons (*sbyin bdag*) were of "various sorts?" Is there a "veiled" tantric allusion here?

387. *Ringsel* (Skt. *śarīram*) are the jewel or crystal-like "remains" left behind after an accomplished yogi or other holy person's body has been cremated. Das's *Dictionary*, p. 1182, describes them as being "small very hard glittering particles." In Trungpa and Fremantle's translation of *The Tibetan Book of the Dead*, p. 58, they are said to be "like shining round stones, white or greenish in colour, and are kept as relics and often eaten just before death." I have seen the *ringsel* left behind after Lama Yeshes's corpse was cremated. Clumped in tiny mounds, they were like miniature pearls, dusky white and jewel-like. The different clumps did seem to distinctly form the shapes of certain organs. Such *ringsel* are said to attest to the accomplished practice of the yogi and are treated as holy relics.

388. The last section of this sentence, in Tibetan, reads: *rtsa dbu ma byaṅ sems dkar dmar gyis gaṅ ba.* Here, *tsa uma* (rtsa dbu ma) refers to the "central channel" (Skt. *avadhūti*) of the arcane body visualized by the advanced yogi. It is filled up with the white and red *jangsem* (byaṅs sems) (Skt. *bodhicitta*). The latter is a specialized, tantric use of the term *bodhicitta.* Here it stands for the subtle "drops" [also called *bindu* in Sanskrit and *thig le* in Tibetan]. The white "drop" is defined as the pure essence of the white seminal fluid, the red "drop" as the pure essence of the blood. In advanced yogic practices, when the "drops" are made to melt and flow through the channels, their action gives rise to the experience of bliss.

That the *ringsel* remains of Sanggye Yeshe's body formed the shape of the central channel attests in dramatic fashion to his accomplishments in this area.

389. The mention of so important a figure as Ba Yeshe Wangpo is not accidental here. All of the foregoing siddhas were declared by their respective namtars to have hailed from "distinguished lineages." However, the man mentioned first in the First Panchen's account is none other than the chief of the so-called "select seven," the first seven Tibetans to be ordained by Śāntirakṣita in the eighth century, thereby becoming the first Tibetan Buddhist monks. The 'Ba' family [variously spelled sBa, rBa, dBa', sBas, or dBas] was thus intimately connected with the very introduction of Buddhism into Tibet. Indeed, tradition says that it was

Yeshe Wangpo, also known as "gSal-snaṅ of sBa," who journeyed to India and Nepal and arranged that an invitation be extended to Śānti-rakṣita to visit Tibet in order that the Doctrine of the Buddha might be established there. The First Panchen's family claimed descent from this distinguished sBa' clan.

390. According to the *Blue Annals* [see pp. 517, 518, 532–536, 722, and 781], Yakde Panchen (gYag-sde Pan-chen) [1299–1378] was a Sakya scholar who became one of the most famous disciples of the great Kagyüpa master, Karmapa Rangjung Dorje (Raṅ-byuṅ-rdo-rje) [1284–1339]. Yakde Panchen is renowned as having had 108 teachers, as having been a great ascetic, and as having founded the Evam monastery. A brief account of his life can be found in the *Annals*, pp. 532–536.

391. The various sources disagree about the dates for Chökyi Gyeltsen. His own *Autobiography* gives the year as "me-yos" [Fire Hare, 1567]. Ferrari's *Guide* [p. 145] follows this date. Both Das's *Contributions* [p. 111] and Lokesh Chandra's *Materials* [p. 21] give "1569" as his date of birth. Our hagiographer, Yeshe Gyeltsen, however, writes "lcags-pho-rta" [Iron Male Horse, 1570] and Tucci in *ROT* [p. 42] and Fa-tsun [*EOB*, p. 163] follow the 1570–1662 dates. For the sake of consistency I have kept to the dates given in the text I have translated herein.

392. Similarly, there are some discrepancies concerning the name of the First Panchen's father. Fa-tsun [p. 164] gives "Tshe-riṅ dpal-'byor" as the father's name, and Sumpa's *History* gives "Kun-dga' dpal-'byor." Once again, I follow Yeshe Gyeltsen's text, which reads: "to a father called Kun-dga'-'od-zer… he was born…" Gene Smith's "Introduction" to the First Panchen's *Autobiography* [p. 7] adds: "His father was a pious man and seems to have been a nephew of Ensapa Sangs-rgyas-ye-shes (1525–1590)."

393. Here the Tibetan reads simply *Śes rab sñiṅ po.*

394. Again, the abbreviated title is given as *'Jam dpal mtshan brjod.* Fa-tsun's composite summary of the life of the First Panchen [in *EOB*, p. 164] states the following regarding the latter's precociousness with respect to this particular text: "During his childhood he was accustomed to the recitations of the *Ḥjam-dpal gyi mtshan yaṅ-dag-par brjod-pa* by the members of his family, and so he began to recite this sūtra himself five times each day when he was five years old." A recent

translation of this work, with annotations, is provided by A. Wayman's *The Mañjuśrī-nāma-samgiti, Chanting the Names of Mañjuśrī,* Boston: Shambhala, 1984.

395. As mentioned above in the notes to Sanggye Yeshe's namtar, Lang-mik-pa was one of Sanggye Yeshe's teachers and a renowned lama in his own right. He was apparently noted for having attained the siddhi of clairvoyance, and so, for both reasons, it was natural that Sang-gye Yeshe would have asked him to verify the authenticity of the reincarnation.

396. Tib. Tamdrin (rTa-mgrin). One of the most important of the Protectors of the Dharma (Skt. *dharmapāla*), Tamdrin is also a deity of the yidam type. He is described as having the body of a man and a horse's head, which, according to Das's *Dictionary* [p. 530], "neighs fearfully to frighten beings who are mischievous to Buddhism."

397. Tib. Riksum Gönpo (rigs gsum mgon po). These three "Guardians of Tibet" are Avalokiteśvara, Mañjuśrī, and Vajrapāṇi.

398. Tib. Drölma (sGrol-ma).

399. Tib. Namgyelma (rNam-rgyal-ma).

400. Here only the abbreviated title is given: *rGyas stoṅ pa.*

401. Here "Rahula" refers to the wrathful deity who rules the great and minor planetary gods. He is described in Nebesky-Wojkowitz's *ODT* [pp. 259–263] as having nine heads—the top one being that of a raven—and a body "covered by a thousand eyes." It is said that when he bares his teeth a mist of illnesses issues from his mouth. His right hand holds a makara-banner, and his left clutches a bow and an arrow that is shot into the heart of those who break their religious vows. The lower part of his body is the coiled tail of a snake.

402. Shanglön (Źaṅ-blon) is also a wrathful guardian deity having the head of a bird. Nebesky-Wojkowitz's *ODT* mentions him on pp. 21, 140, 293, and 327.

403. Tib. *rGyud bźi'i luṅ sogs sman dpyed.* That is, the *Four Tantras of Medical Science*, namely the Root Tantra, the Explanatory Tantra, the Oral Tradition Tantra, and the Subsequent Tantra. The fuller title of the *rGyud bźi* is *bDud rtsi sñiṅ po yan lag brgyud pa gsaṅ ba man ṅag gi rgyud.* The Root and the Explanatory Tantras of this text are translated

with annotations by Dr. Yeshi Donden in *The Ambrosia Heart Tantra*, Dharamsala: Library of Tibetan Works and Archives, 1977.

404. Tib. *mGram so.*

405. The Tibetan reads *mi rtag pa* [impermanence] *rgyud la 'khruṅs* [took birth in his stream of consciousness] or, as I have rendered it, in his "mental continuum" (*rgyud*).

406. It is significant that this month was chosen for the young Losang Chökyi Gyeltsen's first ordination. It is perhaps the most important month of the Buddhist monastic calendar. It is the first month, so the New Year's celebrations are held during it, and Tsongkapa chose to make it the time of the Great Prayer Festival as well. The first month is called the "Month of Miracles" (*'phrul zla ba*) because it commemorates the great "miracles at Śrāvastī" during which the Buddha successfully competed with six non-Buddhist masters in a contest of miracles. The contest took place from the first to the fifteenth of the month. Just as the Buddha conquered the forces hostile to his doctrine during this time, so this young one went forth in his time to assume his place as one of the Doctrine's greatest defenders.

407. The Tibetan reads: *rGyas sras bka' 'bum.* I am unable to identify the specific text.

408. This "Śa-ra-ba" appears to refer to one of the early Kadampa geshes.

409. The Tibetan reads: *Jo bo'i lam yig rgyas 'dus.* It is unclear whether this *lam yig* was written by Atīśa or is a commentary upon a work by him.

410. That is, the *bKa' gdams glegs bam.* Wylie, in *GOT* [pp. xx and 164] tells us: "The full title of this work is *Jo-bo rje-lha-gcig dpal-ldan a-ti-sha'i rnam-thar bla-ma'i yon-tan chos-kyi 'byung-gnas sogs bka-gdams rin-po-che'i glegs-bam.* It is in two volumes, the first dealing with the life of Atīśa and the second with that of 'Brom-ston."

411. Yangchenma (dByaṅs-can-ma). This is the goddess of learning and eloquence, famed among Hindus and Buddhists alike. She embodies beauty as well as clarity of speech. Fa-tsun's account states: "In the spring of [his fourteenth year] he practiced the 'Sādhana of Sarasvatī-devī' for seven days, during which period he had (it is said) the privilege of being spiritually supported by the goddess in person." In the account translated herein, we get a detailed description of the event as told from the First Panchen's own point of view. Because of

his success with this meditation, his intelligence is said to have become "vast as the sky."

412. Butön Rinpoche (Bu-ston Rin-po-che), also known as Butön Lotsawa (Lo-tsa-ba) and as Rinchen Drub (Rin-chen-grub) [1290–1364], was one of the most renowned monk-scholars that Tibet has produced. His fame stems from his mammoth efforts in translating, in codifying the Tibetan Buddhist canon, and in producing one of the earliest authoritative histories of Buddhism in Tibetan [his *Chos 'byuṅ*]. More on the life of this exemplary saint may be found in (1) D. Ruegg's translation, *The Life of Bu ston Rin po che.* [Serie Orientale Roma, Vol. XXXIV], Rome: Is. M.E.O., 1966; (2) Kuo Yuan-hsing's "Bu-ston, Lo-tsa-ba" in *Encyclopaedia of Buddhism*, Vol. III Fascicle 4, pp. 545–548; and (3) Janice D. Willis's "Bu-ston" in *The Encyclopedia of Religion*, New York: The Free Press [Macmillan], 1987.

413. Tib. *bLo sbyoṅ gi rim.*

414. That is, on the *dPe chos rin spuṅs.*

415. That is the *Be'u bum sňoṅ po.* Das's *Dictionary* [p. 876] says of this work that it is "the ancient book on religion and religious history of the Kadampa school compiled by Dge-ses Dol Rinpoche." *The Blue Annals*, p. 830, attributes the text to Potowa (Po-to-ba), the famous Kadampa Geshe.

416. Tib. *'Dus pa'i 'grel pa bźi sbrags su.*

417. Tib. *bKa' gdams lha bźi.*

418. Tib. *rDo rje phreṅ ba.* The *Vajramālā* is one of the chief so-called "Explanatory Tantras" that comments upon the *Guhyasamāja Tantra.* The author of the *Vajramālā* is one Abhayakāragupta[pada]. *The Blue Annals*, p. 1046, gives the following interesting summary of this siddha's life: "The ācārya Abhaya who was endowed with a mind free of illusions in regard to any of the systems of the Prajñāpāramitā or Tantra, from the Lesser sciences... to the Anuttara-yoga-Tantra. Because he had recited the mantra of Vajra-yoginī in his former life, in this life Vajra-yoginī in the form of an ordinary woman appeared before the ācārya Abhaya. Because of his steadfast attitude of a strict monk, he did not admit this woman. (His) great teachers, such as Kā-so-ri-pa and others, told him that he had acted wrongly by not availing himself of the method through which one could realize the sahaja-

jñāna. On many occasions he prayed to Vajra-yoginī. The goddess appeared to him in a dream, and said: 'Now, in this life you will not be united with me. But, if you were to compose many commentaries on profound Tantras and many rites of Maṇḍalas, you would soon become a fortunate one.' Following her instructions, he composed... [four "Explanatory Tantras" including the *Vajramālā*]." The fuller title of this work is, in the Sanskrit, *Vajrāvalināma-maṇḍalasādhana* and, in the Tibetan, *dKyil 'khor gyi chö ga rdo rje phreṅ ba.* [Tg. rGyud, No. 3140]. For an illustration of how the *Vajramālā* functions as an explanatory work, see A. Wayman's use of it in his *Yoga of the Guhyasamājatantra.*

419. The *Mi tra brgya rtsa* refers to the voluminous compilation of meditative, ritual, and liturgical texts composed by the Indian siddha Mitra, also called Mitrayogin and Ajitamitragupta. A most marvelous life of this siddha is given in the *Blue Annals* [pp. 1030–1039]. Briefly, he was born in Orissa in Eastern India. He became a student of Lalitavajra, who had been a direct disciple of the great Tilopa. Thence, his life is narrated in terms of twenty "miracles," e.g.: "For 12 years he meditated at Kha-sar-paṇa. Avalokiteśvara surrounded by his retinue manifested himself to him, and expounded the Doctrine to him, and he attained spiritual realization... (this is his first miracle).... There were 12,000 monks at Odantapurī, and there was discord among them. One of the parties was supported by the Buṅ-śiṅ king who led his troops against the monastery. (Mitra) threw his mace, and the troops terror stricken decamped. No harm resulted to the monks and the vihāras. This was (his) third (miracle).... Again, the King ordered wood to be piled up, and placed the Teacher on top of it. For three days he set fire to it, but the Teacher remained unburnt. This was (his) seventh miracle.... Mitrayogin then showed himself sitting amidst clouds in the Sky. This was (his) ninth miracle.... Then in the... South, there were two yakṣas who used to devour an old and a young man of the town each day. He subdued them and built a temple. This was (his) twelfth miracle.... In order to kindle the faith of the monks, he cast a magic glance (upwards), and all the birds of the sky came down on his hand and obeyed his words... The king of Vārāṇasī thinking in himself: 'I shall not let this Teacher go to another place,' made him stay in a vihāra, and sealed its gate. Thereupon the Teacher was seen playing on top of a large boulder, lying outside the vihāra, and simultaneously sitting inside the vihāra. This was (his) seventeenth

miracle. Then when he was living inside the house of an ascetic, two monks drove away two figures resembling him which appeared outside and inside the house, and when they peeped through a hole inside the house, they saw him preaching the Doctrine to the eight classes of gods and demons. This was (his eighteenth miracle.... He met Avalokiteśvara who told him: 'Son of good family! You should bestow for the sake of the living beings of future times the initiations of the four classes of Tantras at one time.' This was (his) nineteenth miracle." This he apparently did, for the text tells us that after the king of Vārāṇasī had worshipped him for seven days, he was given "initiations of all the classes of Tantras in a single maṇḍala at one time." The system worked out by Mitra for administering such all-encompassing initiations is what comprises the contents of the text, or collection of texts, known as the *Mi tra brgya rtsa.*

420. Tib. *Ma brgyud.* The tantras of the highest class (Skt. *mahānuttara-yoga*) are classified as "father," "mother," or "mixed" tantras depending upon whether their central focus and practice stresses the goal of developing the "illusory body" [in the father tantras], the "clear light" [in the mother tantras], or a blend of both of these at once. On this division of tantras, Tucci in *The Religions of Tibet* [p. 73], states: "The basic distinction between 'Father'-Tantra and 'Mother'-Tantra relates to differences in doctrinal and ritual content. These can be summarized as follows...: the two approaches place the stress differently with respect to the central principles of the entire fourth Tantra group (bla na med rgyud), the *maya*-body and light. In the 'Father'-Tantras the *maya*-body, which corresponds to the 'means' (*thabs*), to action, has the upper hand, while the role assigned to light (*'od gsal = shes rab*, higher cognition) is secondary. Examples of Tantras of this sub-class are *gSang ba 'dus pa, rDo rje 'jigs byed,* and so on. With the 'Mother'-Tantras the balance is reversed. Examples of this sub-class would be *'Khor lo bde mchog* and *Dus kyi 'khor lo.*"

421. That is, suddenly his inner eye of visionary experiences reverted to his ordinary "outer" eye, and as a consequence he began to "think," using discursive reasoning. Under these circumstances, of course, the "vision" disappeared.

422. Barawa ('Ba-ra-ba) [1310–1391] was an accomplished Mahāmudrā practitioner, famed for the intense diligence of his meditative practice. He is said to have founded the monastery of Bari ('Ba'-ri). Also, as the

First Panchen would later do, he was one of few lamas to have visited Bhutan prior to the seventeenth century. On the life of Barawa, see the *Blue Annals*, pp. 692–3, 748, 752, and 896.

423. Tib. *rJe mi la'i rnam mgur.* Milarepa, of course, is Tibet's most famous yogi, and this text is renowned throughout the Tibetan religious world as the *Hundred Thousand Songs of Milarepa.* For an excellent translation of the *Songs*, see the two-volume work of the same name by Garma C. C. Chang.

424. The "Utpala" flower refers to the blossom of a species of lotus that is blue in color.

425. After the first month, the fourth month is next in importance on Buddhist monastic calendars. Two ceremonial days occur during this month. The seventh day of the fourth month celebrates the birth of the Buddha; the fifteenth day, both the festival of the Buddha's enlightenment and his entry into Nirvāṇa.

426. Tib. *rig rluṅ.* Literally the "science of breath," the term also refers to the manipulation of the so-called wind-humour. It is not uncommon to practice breathing exercises as part of a medicinal treatment.

427. Tib. *Chos-kyi-grags-pa.*

428. A *chöten* (mchod brten) [Skt. *stūpa*] is a reliquary mound, a tomb encasing the relics of a saint.

429. Tib. *Zla-ba-grags-pa.*

430. Kedrub Sanggye Yeshe had died prior to Losang Chökyi Gyeltsen's final ordination. That ordination was thus performed in 1591 by his next closest teacher, Panchen Damchö Yarpelwa. The latter was the fourteenth in the succession of abbots of Tashilünpo since its founding by Gendündrub. Of course, Losang Chökyi Gyeltsen had many other teachers as well. In addition to those mentioned by our text, his autobiography names a veritable army of teachers, among them: Kachupa Pelgön (bKa'-bcu-pa dPal-mgon), Kyetsel Geshe Drangchenpa (sKyed-tshal dGe-bśes Graṅs-can-pa), Drungtso Tandrin Sangpo (Druṅ-'tsho rTa-mgrin-bzaṅ-po), Shi-ne Kachupa Tsültrimpa (Źi-gnas dKa'-bcu-pa Tshul-khrims-pa), Neynying Shabdrung Ralo Tulku (gNas-rñiṅ Źab-druṅ Rwa-lo sPrul-sku), Chöje Ayupa Drepa Ngawang Drakpa (Chos-rje A-yu-pa bGres-pa Ṅag-dbaṅ-grags-pa), Ganden Tripa Damchö Pelbar (dGa'-ldan Khri-pa Dam-chos-dpal-'bar), Segyü Gyüchen

Sanggye Gyatso (Srad-rgyud rGyud-chen Saṅs-rgyas-rgya-mtsho), and many others.

431. Here the Tibetan for "Lord Buddha" reads *sTon pa thub pa'i dbaṅ po.*

432. Tib. *Jo źal rnam gñis.* That is, before the two statues of the Buddha brought to Tibet by the Nepalese and Chinese wives of King Songtsen Gampo. The Chinese wife is said to have brought the image known as the Jowo, which is installed in the temple of Ramoche, which she built. The second statue is said to have been brought in the dowry of the Nepalese wife. It is an image of Mikyö Dorje (Mi-bskyod-rdo-rje) and is housed in the temple of Trülnang ('Phrul snaṅ).

433. Riwo Genden is an alternate name for the great monastery of Ganden.

434. *'Grel chen* literally means "The Great Commentary" (Skt. *Mahāṭīka*). Here, the text referred to is probably the *'Grel chen dri med 'od,* [*The Great Commentary Called The Stainless Light* (Skt. *Vimalaprabhā*)]. This work is an extensive commentary on the *Kālacakra Tantra.*

435. Gendün Gyeltsen (dGe-'dun-rgyal-mtshan) is the lama listed immediately after the First Panchen in the Geluk Mahāmudrā Lineage Prayer. There he is referred to as "the Mahāsiddha (gNas-bcu Rab-'byams-pa) Gendün Gyeltsen." Our text tells us that he is the "vajra-holding ācārya" who gives teachings to the First Panchen regarding the "Collected Works of the Second Dalai Lama, Gendün Gyatso" and who instructs him on some of the tantric texts associated with the cycle of Guhyasamāja. Though here he is mentioned only once and amidst numerous other teachers, it would seem that he was one of the most influential teachers of the tantras that the First Panchen had. Fa-tsun's composite "life" of the First Panchen [in *EOB,* p. 165] mentions him twice, as follows: "[The First Panchen] studied the *Ḥdus-pahi ḥgrel-pa bshi sbrag* and the works of Dge-ḥdun-rgya-mtsho (Second Dalai), and various kinds of *anujñā-vidhi* from Dge-ḥdun rgyal-mtshan"; and "In 1603 he went secretly to Lhasa and prayed for the elimination of disasters, and he also secretly visted Dge-hdun rgyal-mtshan, from whom he learned several kinds of profound teachings." What is of particular interest here has to do with the reversing and sharing of the teacher-disciple roles. That is, Gendün Gyeltsen was clearly an important teacher of Chökyi Gyeltsen's; but it was the latter who instructed the former in the methods of the Ganden Oral Tradition of Mahāmudrā. As a result of practicing this method, the First Panchen's teacher

becomes his successful disciple and wins a place in the Ganden Oral Tradition Lineage immediately following him.

436. Damchö Pelbar [1523–1599] was the twenty-sixth throneholder of Ganden.

437. *Khros-nag* literally means the "Black Wrathful One." I am unable to more precisely identify this particular deity.

438. Tib. *gCod gźun skal ldan 'jug ṅogs.*

439. Tib. *mjal yaṅ źib tu.*

440. About Yerpa, Tucci in *LAB* [p. 106] says: "Going to Ganden gave me the opportunity to see Yerpa, one of the most ancient stations of Tibetan Buddhism. It is another monastic town carved out in the live rock overhanging a fertile valley bounded by mountain ridges some eight miles E. of Lhasa. Padmasambhava, Atīśa and other great Buddhist missionaries from India spent some time there in meditation." Bell, pp. 56–7, gives a photo of the place where Atīśa lived.

Tsel Gungtang was the birthplace of many sages, among them Tsongkapa's disciple, Jamchen Chöje Shakya Yeshe, who built the famed Sera monastery. At Tsel Gungtang there also stood a monastery founded by Zang Tsöndrak (Zang Brtson-grags) in 1187. The *Blue Annals* [pp. 711–717] gives an account of the disciples of its founder and the successive abbots of the monastery.

441. The title "dKa' bcu" according to Das's *Dictionary*, p. 50, is given to a Buddhist monk-scholar "who has acquired such great proficiency in sacred literature as to be able to interpret the meanings of a term in ten (*bcu*) different ways." The passage indicates that the First Panchen's students were among the very best of Gelukpa scholars.

442. Here the Tibetan is *Lam rim chuṅ ba.*

443. The Tibetan term *rten* ["bases" or "supports"] may refer to any object of religious faith, including statues, stūpas, paintings, ritual paraphernalia, even the small clay "tsa-tsas." As previously mentioned, Losang Chökyi Gyeltsen was a prodigious patron of such religious art.

444. That is, to equal in accomplishment the great tantric siddhas such as Milarepa and Śa-ba-ri-pa, previously mentioned.

445. Tib. *sa gsum.*

446. The description here is not of the ordinary dream state. Rather, it implies that the First Panchen had attained to such a meditative plane that he could employ his so-called "subtle body" (*yid kyi lus*) to perform actions that would be impossible to accomplish under ordinary circumstances in waking life. Numerous stories are told about advanced tantric adepts making use of their "subtle bodies" in similar ways. Lama Zopa once said of Lama Yeshe that "owing to Lama Yeshe's having attained the subtle, illusory body, he read—so many books—at night!"

447. A very similar list of texts is given by Fa-tsun's source. See *EOB*, p. 165.

448. I have been unable to further identify this particular teacher.

449. The practice of "taking only essences" (*bcud len*) refers to the yogic method of fasting that consists of taking no other food than specially prepared pills with water. The "pill retreat" at Wölka is described in the namtar of Jampel Gyatso. In 1983 a pamphlet for use in such retreats was prepared by Lama Yeshe and published by Wisdom Publications (London). The pamphlet devotes four and a half pages to the sacred pills' ingredients.

450. That is, he became a *repa* (ras-pa), one "clothed only in cotton." The great yogi Milarepa is so named because he followed this tradition. His name was only "Mila"; "repa" was added owing to his practice of wearing only cotton even in the frigid climes of Tibet. No doubt his accomplished practice of *tummo* (gTum-mo) heat helped to keep him warm enough! For a time, we are told, the First Panchen practiced in this way.

451. This is the Gangchen Chöpel monastery mentioned in the namtar of Sanggye Yeshe [See note 358]. Its founder, Panchen Sangpo Tashi (bZaṅ-po-bkra-śis) [1410–1478], according to Ferrari's *Guide*, p. 157, "was a great dGe lugs pa Lama... After the death of dGe 'dun grub in 1474, he was for four years abbot of bKra śis lhun po." Again, according to Gene Smith's "Introduction" to the First Panchen's *Autobiography*, [p. 7], Gangchen Chöpel was one of the leading teaching establishments of Tsang during the sixteenth and seventeenth centuries. At a relatively young age, Losang Chökyi Gyeltsen was asked to assume the duties of abbot of this monastery. Fa-tsun's account [*EOB*, p. 165] reads: "... in 1598, he was invited by the monks and donors of the Gaṅs-can-chos-ḥphel monastery to be its abbot. This monastery... was at first a centre of Tantric Buddhism, but later exoteric Buddhism

was also taught there; it was divided into the southern and northern courts. He lectured on the *Lam-rim che-ba* for the monks in the monastery and taught them the ways of practice. Since then he often lived in the Gaṅs-can chos-ḥphel monastery and propagated the Dharma as well as repaired the shrine-halls of the monastery."

452. Becoming abbot of Tashilünpo [and at the age of only thirty-one] was undoubtedly one of the great moments of Losang Chökyi Gyeltsen's career. By this time [i.e., by 1600] he was already abbot of three institutions: Ensa monastery, Gangchen Chöpel, and Tashilünpo; but as we shall see, the list does not stop there.

453. The Great Prayer Festival, or *Mönlam* (sMon lam), had been conceived and inaugurated in Lhasa by the great Tsongkapa at the very beginning of the fifteenth century. It continued to be centered there and is observed even today. Losang Chökyi Gyeltsen instituted the observance, as the text tells us, for the first time in Tsang.

454. That is, the Fourth Dalai Lama, Yönten Gyatso [1589–1617]. Yönten Gyatso was the only one of the Dalai Lamas to be born outside of Tibet proper. He took birth in Mongolia. Briefly summarizing his life, Glenn Mullin writes [See "Appendix Two" to his *Selected Works of the Dalai Lama I*, pp. 253–4]: "A direct descendant of Altan Khan, he fulfilled Sonam Gyatso's [i.e., the Third Dalai Lama's] promise to the Mongolians to return to them in his future life. Because he was born outside of Tibet, his official recognition and enthronement took longer than usual, and he was not brought to Tibet until he was twelve years old... The fourth Dalai Lama did not write any significant works, but instead dedicated his time and energy to study, practice and teaching. He passed away in early 1617." According to what we know of his birthdate, he would have arrived in Lhasa sometime in 1600.

455. The Tibetan reads: *phyi naṅ gi rkyen du mas bskul te bkra śis lhun po'i mkhan slob thams cad kyis mjal bar byon.* Fa-tsun's account says: "In the autumn of [1603]... the officiating monks of Bkra-śis lhun-po monastery all went to Dbus to pay homage to [Yon-tan-rgya-mtsho], and after that the Master remained in Dbus to transmit the various teachings to Yon-tan rgya-mtsho. The position of Buddhism was elevated day by day." The point of these passages seems to have to do with the importance attributed to Losang Chökyi Gyeltsen's "confirmation" of Yönten Gyatso as the true incarnation of the former Dalai Lama. We

see the weight that Chökyi Gyeltsen's voice had in such matters and the respect and reverence he was shown as a teacher in his day.

456. That is, such were Chökyi Gyeltsen's teaching abilities that the Fourth Dalai Lama requested that he come to stay at his own residence at Drepung. The official residence of the Dalai Lamas was changed to the Potala only following its construction during the time of the Great Fifth Dalai Lama.

457. Radreng (Rva-sgreṅ) monastery [most often written phonetically as "Re-ting"] was chief among Kadampa institutions. This great monastery was founded by Dromtön Gyelwai Jungne ('Brom-ston rGyal-ba'i-'byuṅ-gnas), who had been Atīśa's main Tibetan disciple, in 1057. For a list of its abbots, see the *Blue Annals*, pp. 265–267.

458. About "rGyal Me-tog-thaṅ," Ferrari's *Guide*, p. 48, states: "At the border between 'Ol k'a and Dwags po lies rGyal me tog t'aṅ, a residence of rGyal ba dGe 'dun rgya mts'o...." The two men were likely going to visit the monastery built by the Second Dalai Lama in that valley. Ferrari's *Guide* again says [on p. 122]: "In the Rgyal me tog t'aṅ valley lies the C'os 'k'or rgyal monastery... , founded in 1509 by the Second Dalai Lama dGe 'dun rgya mts'o." [Ferrari adds: "It was destroyed by the Dsungars in 1718 and was rebuilt shortly after by the great regent K'an c'en nas."]

459. It is of special significance that the First Panchen's namtar mentions just these particular sites. They are the sites specially venerated in connection with the Gelukpa ascetic practice traditions and are, as we have seen, especially connected with the Ganden Oral Tradition of Mahāmudrā and with the early practitioners of that tradition.

460. *Nyungney* (smyuṅ gnas). The practice of fasting as part of a religious observance, usually performed for a specific number of days and often combined with observing silence, in keeping with rules of the Buddhist *Vinaya.*

461. Saraha is perhaps the best known of the Eighty-Four Mahāsiddhas of India. A brief account of his life is translated in James Robinson's *Buddha's Lions*, pp. 41–43. More on his life, together with a translation of Saraha's "King Dohās," is to be found in Herbert Guenther's *The Royal Song of Sahara.*

462. The Tibetan reads *gZim khaṅ Goṅ sprul pa'i sku.* The term *gzim khaṅ*

(pa) here refers not to the more common definition as "dwelling" or "house" but to one of the ranks of the monastic hierarchy. The *gzims khaṅ pa* is, in the words of Tucci [in *ROT*, p. 138]: "a kind of representative of the government chosen by turns from among the monks." It would appear from this passage that "Goṅ sprul sku" was a Sera monk holding this position.

463. The First Panchen actually made several trips south to spread Buddhism to the Monpas of Bhutan. Gene Smith notes in his "Introduction" to the First Panchen's *Autobiography*, p. 4, that "With the biographies of few other Tibetan teachers who visited Bhutan before 1616, the Panchen's autobiography gives us our only observations on the historical and ethnological aspects of Bhutan from the viewpoint of the outsider."

464. This same Sönam Gelek Pelsangpo [1594–1615] is listed as being the third [ordinally numbered] in the lineage of the "Pan-chen bSod-grags Incarnations ('Bras-spuṅs gzims-khaṅ Goṅ-ma)." For others in this particular lineage, see Gene Smith's "Introduction" to the First Panchen's *Autobiography*, pp. 11–12.

465. This is, of course, a spiritual and euphemistic way of saying that he died. He would have been, by Tibetan reckoning, twenty-nine years old.

466. Thus, following the Fourth Dalai Lama's death, Losang Chökyi Gyeltsen was asked to assume the reins of abbot at both Drepung and Sera monasteries. Thus, in 1617, he was serving as abbot of five monasteries, three of them being the most powerful Gelukpa institutions of his day. In 1626 he was also asked to become abbot of Ganden's Jangtse college, and in 1642 he accepted as well the abbot's chair at Shalu (Źa-lu), Bu-stön's former monastery in Tsang.

467. In order to keep the translation of the First Panchen's namtar roughly the same length as the others appearing here, I have taken the liberty here of skipping over a number of pages of the text. [In the edition by Ketsün Sangpo, in *BDOT*, I have not translated pages 483–492.] Briefly summarizing, these pages deal with the Panchen's unabated zeal and energy expended to further the Dharma. He traveled in 1618 to Gu-ge, in Ngari (mṄa'-ris), and taught there for over four months. In 1622 he traveled to Drepung and ordained the Fifth Dalai Lama. In 1623 a dispute arose between the Drikungpa ('Bri-guṅ-pa) sect and the Pakdrupa (Phag-gru-pa), and the First Panchen brought them to

reconciliation. In 1626 he became abbot of Ganden's Jangtse and refurbished the gilded roof of Tsongkapa's stūpa. He commissioned two complete sets of the Buddhist Canon. He gave profound teachings and advanced secret initiations to the Fifth Dalai Lama, Sechen Chöje (Se-chen Chos-rje), and others. Later, in 1643, he commissioned silver statues of the great masters of India, and in 1645 he constructed the main shrine hall at Ensa monastery. He received the Fifth Dalai Lama for a stay at Tashilünpo, etc. All these virtuous activities were carried on amidst the religious and political tensions that were rampant throughout the country. Thus, the First Panchen was indeed a tireless worker, an enlightened being.

468. During most of the lifetime of the First Panchen, a bitter rivalry had been going on that pitted the Tsangpa lords against those of Central Tibet and in consequence the Karma Kagyüpas, with Tsangpa backing, against the Gelukpas, with Mongol backing. The Tsangpa ruling family had, however, maintained friendly relations with one branch of the Mongols, the Chogthu, and in the words of Tsepon Shakabpa [*Tibet: A Political History*, p. 103]: "... in 1635 the Chogthu Chief sent his son, Arsalang, with ten thousand troops into Tibet to wipe out the Ge-lug-pa sect." No doubt this is why the First Panchen's namtar singles out this particular date. As it turned out, however, Arsalang and Gushri Khan, the Geluk champion, met and managed a truce. Arsalang later entered Lhasa with only his personal bodyguards and showed respect towards and took teachings from the Dalai Lama. However, he was later assassinated; and the tensions, uncertainties, and intermittent bloodshed continued for some years. During many of the most tense situations, the First Panchen himself was the one responsible for bringing about a truce.

469. For more on the internal and external strife that threatened to thoroughly consume any political stability for Tibet during this time, see Shakabpa's *Tibet: A Political History*, especially pp. 100–124; Tucci's *ROT*, pp. 39–42; and Stein's *Tibetan Civilization*, pp. 75–85.

470. The Tibetan reads *gŚin-rje'i 'jig rten mi yul du 'phos pa ltar*. Of course, Shinje (gŚin-rje) (Skt. *Yama*) is the "Lord of the Dead" and the ruler of the "lower regions."

471. The "evil forces of the five forms of degeneracy" here translates the Tibetan *sñigs ma lṅa'i gdon*. The term *gdon* may also be rendered "evil spirit" or "disease-causing demon." The *sÑigs ma* (Skt. *kaṣāya*) are

counted as five. In the Sanskrit, they are: *āyuḥ-kaṣāya, dṛṣṭi-k., kleśa-k., sattva-k.,* and *kalpa-k.*; namely, the life-span of beings is decreasing, beings have distorted views, there is an increase of afflictive emotions, beings themselves are degenerate, and the great eon itself is nearing its end. Such are the five signs of consuming degeneracy. A Buddha, it is said, is born to counteract them.

472. In fact, the First Panchen on numerous occasions used his soothing songs (*ñams mgur*) to sue for reconciliation between the different factions that threatened Tibet's overall stability.

473. Indeed, Fa-tsun's account [*EOB*, p. 168] devotes a separate section to the First Panchen's "Activities to Stop Wars." I quote portions of it here: "In the seventh month of 1621, when the troops of Gtsaṅ were stationed at Bkyaṅ-thaṅ sgaṅ, the Mongolian army made a surprise attack on them and killed several hundred men. On hearing this news the Master came out in a hurry to make peace, and consequently both the Tibetan and Mongolian armies agreed to offer Lhasa to him as their common gift, and vowed never to fight with each other again within an area under the gleam of the golden roof of the Jo-khaṅ monastery.... In 1614 the outlaws of Mongolia plundered the cattle of Mtsho-phu and invaded the region of Ḥbri-guṅ. Another war broke out. The Master again went to the spot to make peace and saved many lives at the risk of his own... In 1657 [i.e., when he was eighty-eight years old, five years before his death] he succeeded in ending the dispute between the Mongolian army and Khams-po dwags-koṅ, and in prevailing upon both parties to release more than two hundred well-learned monks under their custody. Peace was thus restored in the country."

474. For more on the Great Fifth Dalai Lama [1617–1682], see Shakabpa's *Tibet: A Political History*; Tucci's *Tibetan Painted Scrolls*, I, pp. 57–76; Snellgrove and Richardson's *A Cultural History of Tibet*, especially pp. 195–203; and *EOB*, pp. 169–174. It was, of course, the Fifth Dalai Lama who created the line of the grand Panchen Lamas precisely by bestowing this title own his own guru, Losang Chökyi Gyeltsen. Commenting on this rather daring innovation in Tibet's religious and political history, Tucci, in *ROT*, pp. 41–42, writes the following: "The prestige of the *dGe lugs pa* school (also called *dGa' ldan pa*) received a new impulse in the time of the Fifth Dalai Lama through the appearance of a second supreme spiritual dignitary alongside the Dalai

Lama. This was the *Pan chen* (from the Sanskrit term *Mahā-paṇḍita*, 'great scholar'); his monastery was *bKra shis lhun po*. The *Pan chen* are re-incarnations too, in that the divine presence of *'Od dpag med* (Skt. *Amitabha*, the god of Infinite Light) takes up his earthly dwelling in them. The theory of the *Pan chen* incarnations was introduced by the Fifth Dalai Lama in order to raise the rank of *Blo bzaṅg Chos kyi rgyal mtshan* (1570–1662). In this case too, retrospective validity was conferred upon the theory, and the series was held to begin with *mKhas grub rje*, so that *Blo bzaṅg Chos kyi rgyal mtshan* became the fourth incarnation. As already indicated, this evolution indicated a noticeable growth of the prestige of the *dGe lugs pa* school, who now claimed as their own three supreme religious dignitaries: the Dalai Lama, the *Pan chen* and the *Khri rin po che* (*dGa' ldan khri pa*) or grand abbot of *dGa' ldan*." Details regarding the actual date of the Dalai Lama's conferral of the title on Chökyi Gyeltsen are not clear, though most sources place it prior to Gushri Khan's campaign of 1642. In any case, we can be fairly certain that Chökyi Gyeltsen was in his late sixties or early seventies when he became the First Panchen.

475. As can be imagined, the First Panchen's disciples are too numerous to list. To begin, he was chief tutor to both the Fourth and Fifth Dalai Lamas. He also taught and ordained many of the most eminent monks of his day, whether Tibetan or of neighboring countries. Smith's "Introduction," p. 7, says of him: "He would remain the most prominent teacher of the great incarnations of Tibet and Mongolia for almost fifty years." Moreover, it is said, he gave the *bhikṣu* ordination to upwards of 50,000 beings. If one includes lay people as well as monk disciples, it seems that his followers numbered at least 100,000.

At the end of the First Panchen's *Autobiography*, after stating that the number of his disciples was indeed countless, several students are enumerated. According to my translation of the pertinent passage [from folio 237], the first ten of the Panchen's chief disciples were: (1) Gyelwa Tamche Kyenpa Ngawang Losang Gyatso (rGyal-ba Thams-cad-mkhyen-pa [the Fifth Dalai Lama], Ṅag-dbaṅ bLo-bzaṅ-rgya-mtsho); (2) Wangchuk Tsöndrö Gyeltsen (dBaṅ-phyug brTson-'gros-rgyal-mtshan); (3) Guge Chöje Nyingtob Gyatso (Gu-ge Chos-rje sÑiṅ-stobs-rgya-mtsho); (4) Dorje Dzinpa Könchok Gyeltsen (rDo-rje-'dzin-pa dKon-mchog-rgyal-mtshan); (5) Neychu Rabjampa Gendün Gyeltsen (gNas-bcu Rab-'byams-pa dGe-'dun-rgyal-mtshan); (6) Tapukpa Damchö Gyeltsen (rTa-phug-pa Dam-chos-rgyal-mtshan); (7) Shabdrung Hlapa Losang Tenpa Dargye (Źabs-druṅ Lha-pa bLo-bzaṅ-bstan-pa-dar-rgyas); (8) Kyishö Shabdrung Ngawang Tendzin Trinley (sKyid-śod Źabs-druṅ Ṅag-dbaṅ-bstan-'dzin-'phrin-las); (9) Kachen Namka Dorje (dKa'-chen Nam-mkha'-rdo-rje); and (10) Sechen Chöje (Se-chen Chos-rje) [the King of Mongolia].

476. The First Panchen was an incredibly prodigious author and was responsible for some of the most important and enduring liturgical, devotional, and tantric practice treatises to issue from the Gelukpa. His *bLa ma mchod pa* [*Guru Puja* or *Offering to the Spiritual Master*] serves as the standard work detailing essential daily practice. His *dGe ldan bka' brgyud rin po che'i phyag chen rtsa ba rgyal ba'i gźun lam* (*The Main Path of the Buddhas; the Root Text for the Ganden Oral Tradition of Mahāmudrā*) is a succinct and classic exposition on Mahāmudrā.

According to Longdöl Lama's *mTshan-tho* catalog, some 108 individual works were composed by the First Panchen. They cover a wide range of subjects, though works on the tantras and meditative exercises account for the vast majority [65 works]. He kept excellent records and composed his own impressive *Autobiography* [completed in 1720 by the Second Panchen Lama, Losang Yeshe (bLo-bzaṅ-ye-śes) using notes made by the First Panchen's attendants] consisting of some 450 folios, or roughly 1000 pages! He seems to have had a special penchant for sacred biography and was author of a number of namtar. For example, he wrote the namtar of "the three Ensapa Oral Tradition lamas" [Je Kyabchok Pelsangpo, Ensapa, and Sanggye Yeshe] as well as of the lineage-holders stretching back to India. For fuller details see Longdöl Lama's *mTshan-tho*; and Fa-tsun's account in *EOB*, p. 169, where a cursory listing is given.

477. All accounts of the First Panchen's life agree that he died in 1662. According to our text's date of birth, he would have been ninety-three at the time. Ketsün Sangpo's Tibetan edition of the life [see his *BDOT*, pp. 465-494] errs on p. 494 when it gives for the year, *śiṅ pho stag* ["Wood Male Tiger"], because the latter description would correspond to the date 1664. In my translation, I have amended the text to read correctly "Water Male Tiger," [i.e., 1662].

Glossary

Two glossaries are provided here. The first contains most of the technical terms and the names of the deities and persons that appear in this study, whether in Sanskrit (*S.*), Tibetan (*Tib.*), or English. [Tibetan terms are listed according to their first pronounced letter.] The second glossary provides a list of Sanskrit and Tibetan equivalents.

abhijñā (Skt.; Tib. mṅon śes)

The so-called "super-knowledges" or miraculous powers mentioned in the early Pāli literature and carried over into the Mahāyāna. A bodhisattva is said to acquire these five (or six) powers, defined as: (1) supernal vision, (2) supernal hearing, (3) the ability to read others' thoughts, (4) the ability to see the arising and passing away of others, (5) the ability to work wonders (*ṛddhi*) of transformation and creation, and (6) the ability to see the destruction of all the negative "outflows" (*āsravas*).

abhiṣeka (Skt.; Tib. dbaṅ skur)

Tantric initiation. Literally, "a sprinkling of water from above." The term originally referred to the coronation ceremony of an Indian monarch. Later, it came to name the ritual marking entrance into the esoteric doctrine of Buddhism.

ācārya (Skt.; Tib. slob dpon)

An accomplished master of the traditional subjects of study and meditation. Also, an official position in a given monastery.

Akṣobhya (Skt.; Tib. Mi-bskyod-pa)

Literally, "the Immovable." Name of the Saṃbhogakāya form of Buddha-nature, and a central deity in the *Guhyasamāja Tantra.*

amṛta (Skt.; Tib. bdud rtsi)

Literally, "Deathless." The sacred nectar, or ambrosia, used in Vajrayāna initiations and practice.

anitya (Skt.; Tib. mi rtag pa)

Impermanence. One of the quintessential doctrines of Buddhist theory.

arhat (Skt.; Tib. gnas brtan; also, dgra bcom pa)
One who has destroyed (*hata*) the three great enemies (*ari*) of greed, hatred, and ignorance. The ideal saint of Theravādin Buddhism.

ārya (Skt.; Tib. 'phags pa)
A title of great respect meaning "noble."

Asaṅga (Skt.; Tib. Thogs-med)
The fourth-century Buddhist philosopher who founded the famed *Yogācāra* school.

Atīśa (Skt.; Tib. Jo-bo-rje)
The eleventh-century Indian Buddhist sage who journeyed to Tibet in order to rejuvenate the Buddhist doctrine there. His teachings led to the creation of the Kadampa order of Buddhism in Tibet.

auspicious confluence (Skt. pratītya-samutpāda; Tib. rten 'brel)
Here, the coming together of factors or conditions to form a given situation. Also, the coincidence giving rise to fitting or auspicious circumstance.

avadhūti (Skt.; Tib. rtsa dbu ma)
The central channel, or vein, of the arcane body generated by the tantric adept.

Avalokiteśvara (Skt.; Tib. sPyan-ras-gzigs)
Literally, the "Lord who looks [lovingly] down [upon suffering beings]." The name of the deity who embodies the compassion of the Buddha.

Bhaiṣajyaguru (Skt.; Tib. sMan bla)
The Buddha as "Healer," also called the "Medicine Buddha."

bodhi (Skt.; Tib. byaṅ chub)
Enlightenment. The term used to characterize the *summum bonum* of Mahāyāna Buddhist practice.

Bön (Tib.)
A general name for the indigenous, pre-Buddhist religion of Tibet.

dben sa (Tib.)
Literally, any "isolated place." A term used in reference to an isolated spot suitable for meditative retreat.

sbas yul (Tib.)
A so-called "hidden" country. One of the legendary hidden paradises of Inner Asia.

'Bras-spuṅs (Tib.)
One of the three great Gelukpa monastic institutions near Lhasa. The monastery was founded in 1416 by Jamyang Chöje Tashi Pelden.

Buddha (Skt.; Tib. Saṅs-rgyas)
Literally, an "Awakened One." The title given to one who has attained complete enlightenment. Used especially with reference to Siddhārtha Gautama, the sixth-century Indian founder of the Buddhist Doctrine.

bya bral (Tib.)
Literally, "one who is freed (*bral*) from householding obligations or work (*bya*)." Used to characterize a "wandering ascetic."

byaṅ chub sems (Tib.; Skt. bodhicitta)
The term is generally used to mean "the thought of enlightenment." Here, it is also employed in its tantric sense to refer to the "white drops" (*Tib. thig le; Skt. bindu*) generated and manipulated in the arcane body by a tantric adept.

byaṅ chub sems dpa' (Tib.; Skt. bodhisattva)
Literally, "one whose very mind and being (*sattva*) are intent on enlightenment (*bodhi*)." The ideal saint of Mahāyāna practice.

sbyin bdag (Tib.; Skt. dānapati)
A patron or sponsor, especially of religious persons or undertakings.

Cakrasaṃvara (Skt.; Tib. bDe-mchog)
A semiwrathful [heruka] deity of the wisdom, or mother tantra, class of tantric practice. One of the three chief deities meditated upon in association with the Ganden Oral Tradition of Mahāmudrā.

gCod (Tib.)
The tantric meditative system chiefly attributed to Padampa Sanggye [d. 1117], which is based upon the *Prajñāpāramitā* and which, from the practical side, aims at cutting off the ego and cutting through (*gcod*) discursive thought. The Gelukpa order has incorporated its own oral tradition of *gcod* practice.

bcud len (Tib.)

The yogic practice of "taking only the essences" of various vegetable and mineral substances.

chos (Tib.; Skt. dharma)

The term used, especially in Buddhist philosophical contexts, to refer to any existent reality or phenomenon, however fleeting in terms of temporal duration.

Chos (Tib.; Skt. Dharma)

The Holy Teaching of the Buddha. Buddhist Doctrine, generally.

chos kyi brgyad (Tib.; Skt. aṣṭau lokadharmāḥ)

The eight mundane concerns that occupy the minds of beings in *saṃsāra,* namely: gain, loss, fame, disgrace, praise, blame, pleasure, and pain.

Chos kyi dbyiṅs (Tib.; Skt. Dharmadhātu)

Literally, the "realm of [all] *dharmas,*" this term is used to characterize the totality of existents. It is also used as an epithet for ultimate existence.

Chos-kyi-rdo-rje

The Gelukpa Mahāmudrā siddha who is revered for having attained the highest siddhi [enlightenment in one lifetime], for winning the siddhi of immortality, and for instructing the famed Ensapa in the methods of Mahāmudrā.

chos rje (Tib.; Skt. Dharmasvāmin)

A title of respect given to one who is viewed as being a "master of the Dharma."

chos 'byuṅ (Tib.)

Literally, the "arising" (*'byuṅ*) and development of the Buddhist Dharma (*Chos*). Generally used for texts that present a history of Buddhism.

mchod brten (Tib.; Skt. stūpa)

Literally, a support (*rten*) for worship (*mchod*). Originally, a memorial mound containing the relics of Śākyamuni Buddha and symbolizing the Dharmakāya, or "Truth Body," of the Buddha. Later, the relics of other enlightened beings were deposited in similar structures and also venerated.

'chad (Tib.)

The ability to explain the doctrines of Buddhism. One of the three skills, or "virtues," of the perfect *lama*, the other two being *rtsod* and *brtsom*—the abilities to debate effectively and to compose, respectively.

ḍāka (Skt.; Tib. dpa' bo mkha' 'gro)

Literally, a "warrior sky-goer." Specifically, a masculine semiwrathful or wrathful *yidam*, who may also function as a messenger or as a protector.

ḍākinī (Skt.; Tib. mkha' 'gro ma)

Literally, "she who goes in the sky." A wrathful or semiwrathful feminine *yidam* symbolizing voidness and insight. She is the tricky and playful inspirer who instigates or occasions consummate insight.

Dam-can Chos-rgyal (Tib.)

One of the chief "oath-bound" protecting deities of the Tibetan pantheon. This is the deity who protects the *Miraculous Volume* of the Ganden Oral Tradition teachings on Mahāmudrā.

gdams ṅag (Tib.; Skt. upadeśa)

Oral instruction communicated directly from guru to disciple. An alternate Tibetan term is *man ṅag.*

gdan sa (Tib.; Skt. vihāra)

A main monastic see. The chief monastery of an order.

bde (Tib.; Skt. sukha)

The bliss simultaneously accompanying insight of the highest order. In tantric contexts, the bliss that accompanies the insight into voidness.

delights, three

The three behaviors on the part of a disciple that delight a guru, namely: respectful behavior in body and mind, material and mental offerings, and doing what the guru instructs.

rDo-rje-'chaṅ (Tib.; Skt. Vajradhara)

Literally, "Holder of the Vajra," Vajradhara is the name used for the Dharmakāya, or "Truth Body," of Buddha and for the deity who heads the tantric practice lineages. According to the various traditions of Tibetan tantrism, he is the source from which the tantric teachings originated and from which all such lineages issue. Thus, according to the Kagyüpas, the Mahāmudrā teachings were passed directly from Vajradhara to Tilopa and, through the latter, to Nāropa, Milarepa, etc. According to the Gelukpas, the Mahāmudrā lineage descended from the Buddha Vajradhara to Lord Mañjuśrī. Tsongkapa then received the teachings directly from Lord Mañjuśrī himself.

rDo-rje-phag-mo (Tib.; Skt. Vajravārāhī)

Known as the "Diamond Sow," Vajravārāhī is the female deity who, as insight incarnate, functions to destroy ignorance, symbolized by the pig's head. She is alternately referred to as "Vajrayoginī."

rDo-rje-phreṅ-ba (Tib.; Skt. Vajramālā)

The *Vajramālā* is an important explanatory tantra on the view and methods associated with the *Guhyasamāja* tantric cycle.

rDo-rje-rnal-'byor-ma (Tib.; Skt. Vajrayoginī)

Literally, "Diamond Yogic Practitioner," Vajrayoginī is the female deity who is the chief consort of Lord Cakrasaṃvara. The name "Vajravārāhī" is used to emphasize her *function*, which is to destroy the ignorance of holding the view of an inherently existent "I," while the name "Vajrayoginī" is used to indicate her *essence*, which is the insight that cognizes the inseparability of bliss and voidness.

sdom pa (Tib.; Skt. saṃvara)

Vows, especially the three "sets" of vows: monastic discipline [*pratimokṣa* vows], the Mahāyāna's "Thought of Enlightenment" [*bodhicitta* vows], and tantric practice [*vajrayāna* vows].

'dul ba'i 'dzin (Tib.; Skt. Vinaya-dhara)

A "vinaya-holder" is a keeper of the monastic discipline. Here, the epithet is used in reference to Jampel Gyatso in particular.

rdzogs chen (Tib.)

Literally, the "Great Encompassment" or "Great Completion," the term is used to characterize the experience of the ultimate state of realization. The name for the *summum bonum* of tantric practice, especially in the Nyingmapa order.

rdzogs rim (Tib.; Skt. sampanna-krama)

The second of the "two stages" of highest yoga tantric practice, called the "Completion Stage." That stage wherein, having attained identity with the deity, the tantric adept performs the yogic techniques of controlling the vital energies (*Skt. prāṇa*) and the mystic "drops" (*Skt.*

bindu) until he or she is successful in uniting the "illusory body" and the "clear light" yogas so as to usher in the experience of "total integration" (*Tib. zuṅ 'jug*), enlightenment itself.

gaṇacakra (Skt.; Tib. tshogs 'khor)
Generally described as a "tantric feast," the term refers to a communal ritual performed by tantric adepts.

Ganden (Tib.; Skt. Tuṣita)
The Sanskrit name refers to the "heaven" of Tuṣita, whence all Buddhas issue, and which is now presided over by Lord Maitreya, the future Buddha. Here, *dGa'-ldan* [Ganden] refers to the great monastic institution near Lhasa founded by Tsongkapa himself in the year 1409.

dge 'dun (Tib.; Skt. saṅgha)
The Sanskrit term *saṅgha* literally means "an assemblage" [here, of religious practitioners]. It refers primarily to the monks and nuns forming the Buddhist clergy. In Tibetan the term *dge 'dun* is composed of two elements: *'dun*, meaning "having the desire for" and *dge*, or "virtue." Thus, the Tibetan compound term designates "an assemblage of beings who seek virtue and emancipation."

dGe lugs pa (Tib.)
The order founded by Je Rinpoche, Tsongkapa. The name literally means the "Tradition of the Virtuous Ones." The order is also known under various other names, such as Kadampa Sarpa (bKa' gdams pa gsar pa) [the "new Kadampa"], the Gandenpa (dGa' ldan pa), and the "Yellow Hat" school.

dge tshul (Tib.; Skt. śramaṇera)
A Buddhist monk of the intermediate rank, who has taken the thirty-six vows.

dge sloṅ (Tib.; Skt. bhikṣu)
A fully ordained Buddhist monk, who has taken the 253 vows of full ordination.

dgon pa (Tib.; Skt. vihāra)
Literally, a "place of meditation." The term is used to refer to a monastery.

dgon thag (Tib.)
Meditation strap. The strap, or rope, worn by advanced yogic

practitioners to hold their bodies in meditative posture.

mgon khaṅ (Tib.)
The special chapel in a monastery where images of the wrathful protector deities are kept.

grva tshaṅ (Tib.)
A monastic college.

Guhyasamāja (Skt.; Tib. gSaṅ 'dus)
The central deity of the *tantra* of the same name. This tantra, which is also known as the "King of all Tantras," is one of the so-called "father tantras" (*pha rgyud*) of the highest (*bla na med rgyud*) class of tantras, wherein generation of the "illusory body" is given preference over the development of the "clear light" yogas.

guru (Skt.; Tib. bla ma)
A superior teacher. A master of the Dharma, capable of imparting both instruction (*luṅ*) and empowerment (*dbaṅ*).

guru puja (Skt.; Tib. bla ma mchod pa)
A ritual ceremony dedicated to the lineage lamas of a given order.

rGyal ba gñis pa (Tib.)
Literally, a "Second Buddha." Used herein to refer to Tsongkapa. Among the Nyingmapas, the term is used in reference to Padmasambhava.

rGyal ba Seṅ-ge'i-ṅa-ro (Tib.; Skt. Buddha Siṃhāsvara)
According to the Gelukpa, this is the form that Tsongkapa will assume in the future. Iconographically, the deity is a form of Lord Mañjuśrī.

rGyud bla ma (Tib.; Skt. Uttaratantra)
An important late fourth-century text attributed to Maitreya.

brgyud (Tib.)
Lineage. The unbroken, pure, and continuous transmission of the teachings.

sgrub chen (Tib.; Skt. mahāsiddha)
Literally, "great accomplished one." The term is used most frequently to refer to the famed group of eighty-four Indian Buddhist siddhas. Here, any greatly accomplished Buddhist tantric adept.

isolations, three

This terminology refers to the first three [of the five, or six] stages of yogic accomplishment as articulated by the *Guhyasamāja Tantra.* The three are: "isolation of body" (*lus dben*), "isolation of speech" (*ṅag dben*), and "isolation of mind" (*sems dben*), respectively. Thereafter follows the achievement of the experience of the "clear light" and the "illusory body," finally culminating in the experience of the unification of these latter two, which is the consummate experience of Buddhahood itself.

Jina (Skt.; Tib. rgyal ba)

Literally, "Conqueror." A common epithet for a Buddha.

Je btsun (Tib.)

A title meaning "Reverend" or "Venerable." An honorific form addressed to revered teachers.

rjes gnaṅ (Tib.)

A ceremony of oral recitation and blessings that empowers a student to study a given text or to practice a prescribed *sādhana.*

bka' babs pa (Tib.)

Literally, "a specially commissioned one." A disciple who is deemed specially qualified to carry out a teacher's charge with complete success.

bka' chems (Tib.)

A great person's last will and testament. Here, a teacher's final words of advice to his disciple.

bKa' gdams pa (Tib.)

The order of Tibetan Buddhism founded in the late eleventh century by the Indian master Atīśa and his closest Tibetan disciple, Dromtönpa. This order was later absorbed into the Gelukpa.

dKra-śis-lhun-po (Tib.)

The great Gelukpa monastic institution established in 1447 in Tsang by Gendündrub.

dka' bźi (Tib.)

Literally, the "Four Difficulties." A way of referring to the four areas of monastic study to be mastered, namely: Vinaya, Pramāṇa, Prajñāpāramitā, and Madhyamaka. Here, one who successfully does this earns the title of "*bKa' chen.*"

dkon mchog gsum (Tib.; Skt. triratna)

In Buddhism, the "three most precious jewels," namely: the Buddha, the Dharma, and the Saṅgha.

sku bem (Tib.)

A heavy woolen monastic robe, allowed as special apparel for monks of the various Tantra Colleges.

Kha che (Tib.)

The Tibetan name for Kashmir.

kha na ma tho ba (Tib.; Skt. avadya)

Literally, "not praiseworthy." Anything shameful, disgraceful, or subject to blame. The term is used here with particular reference to Jampel Gyatso, who kept his monastic vows so well that he was completely above blame, having not even the slightest fault or transgression to conceal.

mkhan po (Tib.)

An abbot. Also, as "instructor," one of the chief officers required at any ordination ceremony. According to the Buddhist Vinaya, five monks are necessary for ordination: the instructor (*mkhan po*), the teacher (*slob dpon*), the master of esoteric secrets (*gsaṅ ston*), and two assistants.

mkhar (Tib.)

A mansion, citadel, or fortress.

'khar gsil (Tib.)

A mendicant's staff. The staff carried by the early Buddhist monks of India. Also sometimes called a "warning staff" since the brass rings attached to its top were jingled by the monk in order to signal small animals of his approach.

kleśa (Skt.; Tib. ñon moṅs)

The "afflictive, defiling emotions," especially those forces primarily active in the production of *saṃsāric* states: greed, hatred, and ignorance.

bskyed rim (Tib.; Skt. utpatti-krama)

The first of the "two stages" associated with the practices of highest yoga tantra. Called the "Generation Stage," it is preliminary and preparatory to the practices taken up during the "Completion Stage."

lam (Tib.; Skt. mārga)

Literally, "path," here the term refers to the Buddhist path.

Lam rim (Tib.)

An abbreviated title for the *Lam rim chen mo,* [*The Great Stages of the Path (to* Enlightenment*)*], composed by Tsongkapa, and which serves as the fundamental source for the followers of the Gelukpa order with regard to both philosophical view and practical applications.

lo tsa ba (Tib.)

The term used to refer to a great translator.

bla ma (Tib.; Skt. guru)

A superior teacher. See entry for "guru."

blo sbyoṅ (Tib.)

The contemplative and meditative exercises elaborated by Atīśa and his subsequent Tibetan disciples of the Kadampa order for aiding mental development and spiritual transformation.

lha (Tib.; Skt. deva)

Here, any deity of the Buddhist pantheon.

lhag mthoṅ (Tib.; Skt. vipaśyanā)

Literally, "higher seeing" or "higher vision." The term refers to that stage of meditative achievement wherein clear discriminative attention is brought to bear on a given object of meditation. The stage of "higher seeing" follows that of "calm abiding" and so represents a type of "discerning" that is of a higher order.

Lho mon (Tib.)

The Tibetan name for Bhutan.

luṅ (Tib.)

An oral recitation blessing. A reading transmission. Also, instruction.

Mādhyamika (Skt.; Tib. dbU ma)

The philosophical school of thought founded by the great sage Nāgārjuna, which offers pristine analyses concerning the proper understanding of voidness (*śūnyatā*) and which is accorded great esteem by all the major orders of Tibetan Buddhism.

Mahākāla (Skt.; Tib. Nag-po-chen-po)

A major "protective deity" (*mgon po*), Mahākāla is black in color and wrathful in form. He is thought of as the wrathful aspect of compassion and appears in numerous iconographic forms. While he is mentioned in all of the accounts herein, he was especially important to Gyelwa Ensapa.

Mahāmudrā (Skt.; Tib. Phyag rgya chen po)
Literally, the "Great Gesture," or "Great Seal." Mahāmudrā refers both to the ground of reality and to those advanced tantric meditative methods relied upon by the *siddhas* of India and Tibet to lead them to the supreme attainment of enlightenment in one lifetime. Interpreting the term's philosophical position poetically and aesthetically, a contemporary author translates the term as the "Magnificent Stance."

mahāsiddha (Skt.; Tib. grub chen)
See entry under "grub chen."

Mahāyāna (Skt.; Tib. theg pa chen po)
Literally, the term means the "Great Vehicle." Philosophically, the various schools of the Mahāyāna expand the earlier teachings on voidness (*śūnyatā*) so that the latter has reference to both the "selflessness of the so-called 'self'" (*atmannairātmya*) and the "selflessness of all *dharmas*" (*dharma-nairātmya*). From the practice side, the Mahāyāna schools stress compassionate activity, aimed at the universal liberation from *saṃsāra* of all beings without exception.

maṇḍala (Skt.; Tib. dkyil 'khor)
The Tibetan compound term literally means "center and periphery." Maṇḍalas are diagrams or models, of the universe and of reality itself, that are used as aids to meditative/spiritual transformation. They are usually represented as a diagram with a central deity surrounded by other symbolic components. Though they are often painted, they may be made of colored sand as well. They are always conceived of as being three-dimensional, and the constructed form has the basic structure of a palace having a center with four doors, or gates, in the cardinal directions.

maṇi (Skt.; Tib. nor bu)
Literally, a jewel. "Maṇi" is also a way of referring to the famed six-syllable mantra of Avalokiteśvara: *OṂ MA ṆI PAD ME HŪṂ.*

Mañjuśrī (Skt.; Tib. 'Jam-dpal-dbyaṅs)
One of the chief deities of the Buddhist pantheon, Mañjuśrī

represents the wisdom aspect of the Buddha. He was Tsongkapa's primary tutelary deity.

mundane concerns, eight.

See entry under *chos kyi brgyad.*

nāḍī (Skt.; Tib. rtsa)

The channels or pathways in the arcane body generated by a tantric adept. The mind-bearing "winds" (*prāṇa*) are said to course through the *nāḍī.*

naṅ pa (Tib.)

Literally, an "insider." Here, the term refers to any follower of the Buddhist path.

ṅes 'byuṅ (Tib.)

Renunciation. This term is defined in Tibetan as "what protects the mind, following disgust at *saṃsāra.*" It is not a slight feeling or emotion, but a strong revulsion from the ills of *saṃsāra.* Further, such fierce revulsion, coupled with clearly seeing the faults of *saṃsāric* existence, combine to lead one to true renunciation, said to be the first essential requisite for following the Buddhist path.

sñan rgyud (Tib.)

Oral tradition. This term is a synonym for *bka' brgyud,* or orally transmitted lineage. The term *sñan* carries the additional connotation of being "pleasing to the ear." Again, the Gelukpa recognize two *sñan rgyuds*: an oral tradition of *gcod* practice and an oral tradition of Mahāmudrā.

sñigs ma (Tib.; Skt. kaṣāya)

The so-called five "degeneracies" or "signs of the *Kāli-yuga,*" namely: beings have decreased life spans, they have wrong views, they are overcome by passion and the afflictive emotions, are themselves degenerate, and the age, itself, is coming to an end. A Buddha is said to appear in order to counteract these five.

Nāgārjuna (Skt.; Tib. kLu-sgrub)

The renowned Indian Buddhist sage who founded the Madhyamaka school based upon his explication of the doctrine of *śūnyatā,* especially as presented in his work the *Mūlamadhyamakakārikā.*

rnam thar (Tib.)

The term used to refer to a genre of religious literature that records the "complete liberation life stories" of accomplished tantric practitioners. *Siddha* biographies.

neyārtha (Skt.; Tib. draṅ don)

The indirect or "interpretable" meaning. An important term in Buddhist hermeneutics employed to characterize primarily the *sūtras*, which reveal their true meaning only after further elaboration and explication.

nītartha (Skt.; Tib. ṅes pa'i don)

The direct, final, or "definitive" meaning. Used of texts that directly reveal their true meaning as stated.

Padmasambhava (Skt.; Tib. Pad-ma-'byuṅ-gnas)

The eighth-century Indian *siddha* usually credited with having established Buddhism in Tibet. Together with the Indian monk-scholar Śāntirakṣita, he founded the earliest order of Buddhism in Tibet, the Nyingmapa.

Pan chen (Tib.; Skt. mahāpaṇḍita)

Literally, a "greatly learned one." Used as an honorific.

dpal (Tib.; Skt. śrī)

An honorific form meaning "glorious" and "resplendent."

Poṣadha (Skt.; Tib. gso sbyoṅ)

The Buddhist vow and ritual of fasting and other forms of abstinence for a prescribed period of time.

prajñā (Skt.; Tib. śes rab)

Insight of the highest order, especially that which cognizes the true meaning of voidness (*śūnyatā*). It is defined as being of three types: that insight gained by "hearing" the Doctrine (Skt. *śrūta-mayī-prajñā*), that gained by "pondering and reflecting" upon it (*cinta-mayī-prajñā*), and that gained through "cultivating meditation" upon it (*bhāvanā-mayī-prajñā*). The last practice engenders the culminating achievement, since it leads to direct realization of the teachings and, thereby, to complete liberation.

pratimokṣa (Skt.; Tib. so so thar pa)

Literally, "toward individual liberation." The term is used to designate that set of vows enjoined by the *Vinaya* upon Buddhist monks and nuns seeking liberation from *saṃsāra*.

pravrajyā (Skt.; Tib. rab tu 'byuṅ ba)

Literally, the "going forth" from home into homelessness. The initial level of Buddhist monastic ordination.

sprul pa'i glegs bam chen mo (Tib.)

The *Great Miraculous Volume* said to contain the various methods of the Ganden Oral Tradition of Mahāmudrā. The *Miraculous Volume* is an important *leit motif* in these namtar.

sprul sku (Tib.; Skt. nirmāṇakāya)

Literally, a "magically created body." The form assumed by enlightened beings in order to teach other sentient beings. Also, a title given to the recognized reincarnations of high *lamas* in Tibet.

Rab 'byams pa (Tib.)

One of the highest monastic degrees awarded by Gelukpa institutions upon successful completion of rigorous studies of the sacred scriptures. It is roughly equivalent to the *dGe bśes* and *dKa' chen* degrees. In these accounts, it is the way Gyelwa Ensapa refers to Sanggye Yeshe, owing to the latter's having earned the degree from Tashilünpo.

rab 'byuṅ (Tib.)

A term referring to the sixty-year cycle of the Tibetan system of dating. The term is also the name of the first year of the cycle.

rab tu 'byuṅ ba (Tib.; Skt. pravrajyā)

A newly ordained Buddhist monk. See the entry under *pravrajyā*.

rainbow body (Tib. 'ja' lus)

Here, the result of accomplished Mahāmudrā practice, wherein the *siddha* is able to dissolve his coarse physical body into a radiant "rainbow body."

ri khrod (Tib.)

A mountain retreat site. A hermitage isolated in the mountains.

riṅ bsrel (Tib.; Skt. śarīra)

The relics or bodily remains left after the cremation of an advanced tantric adept. They are usually described as small, hard, pearl-like particles of various colors and, as in the case of Sanggye Yeshe here, they sometimes form themselves into clumps or shapes of various organs, said to remain from the "arcane body" of the saint.

rinpoche (Tib. rin-po-che)
Literally, a "precious one." An honorific term used for a Tibetan *guru.*

sādhana (Skt.; Tib. sgrub thabs)
A descriptive ritual and meditation text. Also the meditation practice it outlines.

samādhi (Skt.; Tib. tiṅ ṅe 'dzin)
The term used in meditation theory to denote the state of complete and total absorption, wherein consciousness and the object of meditation are unified.

samaya (Skt.; Tib. dam tshig)
The special vows of commitment, especially those in tantric practice between a guru and disciple. The most important *samaya* is maintaining a proper attitude towards one's root guru.

saṃsāra (Skt.; Tib. 'khor ba)
Literally, "continuous going," *saṃsāra* refers to the round of transmigratory experience, which arises chiefly out of ignorance and is characterized by suffering, uneasiness, pain, and discomfort. One who attains enlightenment is completely freed from this cycle.

Śāntirakṣita (Skt.; Tib. Źi-ba-'tsho)
The eighth-century Indian monk-scholar who journeyed to Tibet, taught the Buddhist Hīnayāna and Mahāyāna doctrines there, and ordained the first seven Tibetan monks.

Sarasvatī (Skt.; Tib. dByaṅs-can-ma)
The "Goddess of Learning and Eloquence" in both the Hindu and Buddhist pantheons. She appears several times in these namtar and was the special tutelary deity of the First Panchen, Losang Chökyi Gyeltsen.

Se ra (Tib.)
One of the three great Gelukpa monasteries near Lhasa. Sera was founded in 1419 by Jamchen Chöje Shakya Yeshe, a direct disciple of Tsongkapa.

siddha (Skt.; Tib. grub thob)
One who succeeds in attaining enlightenment in one lifetime using tantric means. The subjects of the namtar translated herein.

siddhi (Skt.; Tib. dṅos grub)
The "magical" powers that accrue to a *siddha.*

sindhura (Skt.)
A bright scarlet powdery substance consisting of red lead, or vermilion. The powder is used, especially in tantric initiations involving the female *yidam* Vajrayoginī, to mark the "three doors" [of body, speech, and mind] of the disciple.

Sog yul (Tib.)
The Tibetan name for Mongolia.

stages, two.
The two stages of highest yoga tantric practice, namely the "Generation Stage" (Skt. *utpatti-krama*) and the "Completion Stage" (Skt. *sampanna-krama*).

stoṅ pa ñid (Tib.; Skt. śūnyatā)
The quintessential teaching of Mahāyāna Buddhism. The theory of voidness. The characterization of the ultimate state of things as being devoid of an abiding "self" or essential nature.

śug 'bru ba (Tib.)
The kernel, or berry, of the juniper tree. The epithet won by Jampel Gyatso by virtue of his having encouraged the "juniper berry" pill retreat at Wölka and by virtue of his having subsisted throughout the retreat on the fewest of such pills, made from ground juniper berries.

sūtra (Skt.; Tib. mdo)
A discourse given by the Buddha that elaborates some point of Buddhist doctrine. A sacred scripture of the Buddhists.

gsuṅ 'bum (Tib.)
Literally, the "collected sayings" of a teacher. The term is used to refer to the collected writings or collected works of such a one. *bKa' 'bum* is a synonym for the term.

lta ba (Tib.; Skt. dṛṣṭi)
View. Used especially of a philosophical position.

tantra (Skt.; Tib. rgyud)
Literally, "continuity," the term is used to refer both to the texts that elaborate the views and practices of Vajrayāna Buddhism and to those practices themselves.

Tathāgata (Skt.; Tib. De bźin gśegs pa)
Literally, the "Thus Gone (or "Thus Come") One." The term is an epithet for the Buddha.

thar pa (Tib.; Skt. mokṣa)
Liberation.

thugs kyi sras (Tib.)
Literally, "heart-disciple." This term is used with reference to a teacher's closest disciples. Heart-disciples are usually the ones who later author the teacher's biography. However, they need not necessarily be the students who are chosen to advance a particular lineage or transmission, these being more properly called *bka' babs pas*. For example, Chennga Lodrö Gyeltsen wrote the biography of his teacher, Jampel Gyatso; but the latter chose Baso Je as the singular *bka' babs* to whom he entrusted the Oral Tradition teachings on Mahāmudrā.

Trikāya (Skt.; Tib. sku gsum)
Literally, "three bodies." This term refers to the Three Bodies of Buddhahood: the Dharmakāya (Tib. *chos kyi sku*) or "Body of Truth," which is enlightenment itself; the Saṃbhogakāya (Tib. *loṅs spyod rdzogs sku*) or "Enjoyment Body"; and the Nirmāṇakāya (Tib. *sprul pa'i sku*), that body magically created in order to instruct beings, which is called the "Emanation Body."

Tripiṭaka (Skt.; Tib. sde snod gsum)
Literally, the "three baskets" or "collections" of scripture setting forth the Buddhist teachings. These include the collections of *Sūtra* [Buddha's discourses], *Vinaya* [stories and axioms related to monastic discipline], and *Abhidharma* [later commentarial works].

Tsoṅ-kha-pa (Tib.)
The renowned fourteenth-century Tibetan Buddhist teacher who founded the Gelukpa order and authored voluminous works on Buddhist doctrine and practice.

gtsug lag khaṅ (Tib.)
The main assembly hall and place of worship in a monastery.

rtsa ba'i bla ma (Tib.)
One's primary, or "root," teacher.

upāya (*Skt.; Tib. thabs*)

Skillful means. Insight (*prajñā*) in action. In tantric iconography, *upāya* is represented by the male deity. He is active compassion. His partner, the female deity consort, represents highest insight. Thus, the symbol of complete and perfected enlightenment is shown to be the perfect "union" of these two.

Vajrabhairava (Skt.; Tib. rDo-rje-'jigs-byed)

The wrathful aspect of the Buddha's wisdom and insight. He was Sanggye Yeshe's main tutelary deity.

Vajrayāna (Skt.; Tib. rdo rje theg pa)

Literally, the "Diamond (or, Indestructible) Vehicle." That form of Mahāyāna Buddhism which, while based firmly upon the vow to liberate all beings, offers the "speedy path" (*nye lam*) set forth in the *tantras* as a way of attaining complete Buddhahood in one's very lifetime.

vidyādhara (Skt.; Tib. rig 'dzin)

Literally, a "holder of knowledge," *vidyādharas* are said to possess arcane and magical knowledge. Because such beings are able to assume different manifestations at their will, they are also said to be "deathless" or indestructible. Chökyi Dorje, of these namtar, is famed as one who, owing to his successful Mahāmudrā practice, attained to the state of "a deathless *vidyādhara*."

Vinaya (Skt.; Tib. 'dul ba)

That portion of the Buddhist *Tripiṭaka* that deals with monastic discipline and Buddhist ethics in general.

vows, three.

See entry under *sdom pa gsum.*

yab sras (Tib.)

Literally, "Father and Son," by which is meant, in these contexts, the pair of the guru and his disciple.

ye śes (Tib.; Skt. jñāna)

That type of transcendent or supramundane knowledge possessed by the Buddhas.

Ye śes mkha' 'gro ma (Tib.; Skt. Jñānaḍākinī)

The feminine principle of ultimate insight. Often rendered "wisdom ḍākinī," the term is also a common epithet for Vajrayoginī.

Ye-śes-rgyal-mtshan (Tib.)

The eighteenth-century monk-scholar and *siddha* who compiled the great anthology of Kadampa and Gelukpa namtar, selections from which are translated here. He is revered by Tibetan folk tradition for having risen from lowly beginnings to the esteemed office of *yoṅs 'dzin* (tutor) to the Eighth Dalai Lama. He is also counted among the lineage-holders of the Geluk Mahāmudrā tradition.

yi dam (Tib.; Skt. iṣṭadevatā)

The Vajrayāna practitioner's personal or guardian deity. That special deity to whom one's mind is bound.

yoga (Skt.; Tib. rnal 'byor)

The term *yoga* is derived from the Sanskrit root, *yuj*, "to join together." Thus, it generally refers to practices—both physical and mental—aimed at bringing about a state of holistic integration.

yuganaddha (Skt.; Tib. zuṅ 'jug)

Throughout these translations, this term is rendered "total integration." A common rendering is "union," as between any number of standard technical pairs, such as the "illusory body and the clear light"; but the sense is that the two no longer remain two separate entities. "Total integration" is the fifth and final division of "Completion Stage" practice. Yogically, its practice involves continued mastery in forcing the consciousness-bearing "energy winds" (*prāṇa*) into the central channel (*avadhūti*) of the arcane body generated by the practicing adept. Its accomplishment is the simultaneous experience of bliss and voidness.

za ma tog (Tib.; Skt. karaṇḍa)

In ordinary speech, this term means "basket," "carrier," or "receptacle." It sometimes also refers to the human body. In the namtar of Chökyi Dorje, however, the term is used in a mystic sense. Here it is but a prop, a form taken on by the *siddha* so that he might teach others. Having achieved the "rainbow body" through his practice of Mahāmudrā, he merely assumes the appearance of having a physical body so that he can communicate the teachings.

zaṅ ziṅ (Tib.)

Material offerings.

źi gnas (Tib.; Skt. śamatha)

Literally, the Tibetan means "to dwell in peace." The term has reference to the fundamental meditative practice aimed at developing calm, unwavering clarity and peace of mind. The development of *źi gnas* is essential for the arising of "higher vision" (*lhag mthoṅ*).

Sanskrit-Tibetan Glossary

Here, Sanskrit terms are arranged according to the English alphabetical order.

Sanskrit	*Tibetan*
abhijñā	mṅon śes
abhiṣeka	dbaṅ bskur
ācārya	slob dpon
Akaniṣṭha	'Og-min
Akṣobhya	Mi-bskyod-pa
Amitābha	'Od-dpag-med
amṛta	bdud rtsi
anitya	mi rtag pa
antarābhava	bar do
arhat	gnas brtan; dgra bcom pa
artha	don
ārya	'phags pa
Asaṅga	Thogs-med
Atīśa	Jo-bo-rje
avadhūti	rtsa dbu ma
avadya	kha na ma tho ba
Avalokiteśvara	sPyan-ras-gzigs
avidyā	ma rig pa
Bhaiṣajyaguru	sMan-bla
bhikṣu	dge-sloṅ
bhūmi	sa; rim
bindu	thig le
bodhi	byaṅ chub
bodhisattva	byaṅ chub sems dpa'
Buddha	Saṅs-rgyas
Cakrasaṃvara	dDe-mchog
Candrapradīpa-sūtra	*Zla-ba-sgron-ma'i-mdo*
ḍāka	dpa' bo; mkha' 'gro
ḍākinī	dpa' mo; mkha' 'gro ma

Sanskrit	*Tibetan*
dānapati	sbyin bdag
deva	lha
dharma	chos
Dharmadhātu	chos dbyiṅs
Dharmakāya	chos sku
dharmapāla	chos skyoṅ
Dharma-rāja	chos kyi rgyal po
Dharmavajra	Chos-kyi-rdo-rje
dṛṣṭi	lta ba
duḥkha	sdug bsṅal
dveṣa	źe sdaṅ
gaṇacakra	tshogs 'khor
Guhyasamāja	gSaṅ-'dus
guru	bla ma
guru puja	bla ma mchod pa
guru yoga	bla ma lha'i rnal 'byor
heruka	khrag 'thuṅ
Hīnayāna	theg pa dman; theg chuṅ
homa	sbyin sreg
jina	rgyal ba
jina-putra	rgyal sras
jñāna	ye śes
Kālacakra	'Dus-kyi-'khor'lo
Kālarūpa	Dam-can Chos-rgyal
kalyāṇamitra	dge ba'i bśes gñen
karma	las
karmamudrā	las kyi phyag rgya
kaṣāya	sñigs ma
kleśa	ñon moṅs
kośa	mdzod
Madhyamaka	dbU-ma
Mahākāla	Nag-po-chen-po
mahāmudrā	phyag rgya chen po
mahānuttara-tantra	bla na med rgyud
mahāpaṇḍita	pan chen
mahārāja	rgyal chen
mahāsattva	bdag ñid chen po
mahāsiddha	grub chen

Sanskrit	*Tibetan*
Mahāyāna	theg pa chen po
manas	yid
maṇi	nor bu
maṇḍala	dkyil 'khor
Mañjuśrī	'Jam-dpal-dbyaṅs
mantra	sṅags
mārga	lam
moha	gti mug
mokṣa	thar pa
mūla-guru	rtsa ba'i bla ma
nāḍī	rtsa
Nāgārjuna	kLu-sgrub
neyārtha	draṅ don
nirdeśana	'chad
Nirmāṇakāya	sprul pa'i sku
Nirvāna	mya ṅan las 'das pa
nītartha	ṅes pa'i don
Padmasambhava	Pad-ma-'byuṅ-gnas
Poṣadha	gso sbyoṅ
prajñā	śes rab
prāṇa	rluṅ
Pratimokṣa	so so thar pa
pratītya-samutpāda	rten 'brel; rten ciṅ 'brel par 'byuṅ
ba	
pravrajyā	rab tu 'byuṅ ba
rāga	'dod chags
rasāyana	bcud len
sādhana	sgrub thabs
Śākyamuni	Jo-bo
samādhi	tiṅ ṅe 'dzin
śamatha	źi gnas
samaya	dam tshig
Saṃbhogakāya	loṅs spyod rdzogs sku
sampanna-krama	rdzogs rim
saṃsāra	'khor ba
saṃtana	brgyud
saṃvara	sdom pa
saṅgha	dge 'dun

Sanskrit	*Tibetan*
Śāntirakṣita	Źi-ba-'tsho
śaraṇa	skyabs
Sarasvati	dByaṅs-can-ma
śarīram	riṅ bsrel
sarvajñānata	thams cad mkhyen pa
śāstra	bstan bcos
siddhi	dṅos grub
śramaṇera	dge tshul
śrī	dpal
Subhūti	gÑas-brtan Rab-'byor
Śuddhodana	Zas-gtsaṅ-ma
Sūgata	bDe bar gśegs pa
sukha	bde
śūnyatā	stoṅ pa ñid
sūtra	mdo
tantra	rgyud
tapayā	dka' thub
Tathāgata	De-bźin-gśegs-pa
ṭippaṇi	mchan bu
trikāya	sku gsum
Tripiṭaka	sde snod gsum
triratna	dkon mchog gsum
Tuṣita	dGa'-ldan
upadeśa	gdams ṅag; man ṅag
upāya	thabs
utpatti-krama	bskyed rim
Uttaratantra	*rGyud-bla-ma*
Vaiṣravana	rNam-thos-sras
vajra	rdo rje
Vajrabhairava	rDo-rje-'jigs-byed
Vajradhara	rDo-rje-'chaṅ
Vajramālā	*rDo-rje-phreṅ-ba*
Vajravārāhī	rDo-rje-phag-mo
Vajrayāna	rdo rje theg pa
Vajrayoginī	rDor-rje-rnal-'byor-ma
vidyādhara	rig 'dzin
vihāra	dgon pa
vikalpa	rnam par rtog pa

Sanskrit	*Tibetan*
vimokṣa	rnam par thar pa
vipaśyanā	lhag mthoṅ
yāna	theg pa
yoga	rnal 'byor
yogi	rnal 'byor pa
yoginī	rnal 'byor ma
yuganaddha	zuṅ 'jug

Bibliography

Primary Sources in Tibetan

Byaṅ chub lam gyi rim pa'i bla ma brgyud pa'i rnam par thar pa rgyal bstan mdzes pa'i rgyan mchog phul byuṅ nor bu'i phreṅ ba (*Biographies of the Eminent Gurus in the Transmission Lineages of the Graded Path Teachings, Called The Jewelled Rosary*) by Tshe-mchog-gliṅ Yoṅs-'dzin Ye-śes-rgyal-mtshan: (a) a wood-block printed copy from the Nepalese Mahāyāna Gönpa at Kopan, Nepal; (b) the above work in an edition reproduced by Ngawang Gelek Demo, New Delhi: Gedan Sungrab Minyam Gyunphel Series, Vols. 18 and 19, 1970 and 1972; and (c) selected namtar from Vol. 5 of Ketsün Sangpo's *Biographical Dictionary of Tibet and Tibetan Buddhism*, Dharamsala: Library of Tibetan Works and Archives, 1973, pp. 195–208, 224–229, 230–241, 242–265, 266–282, and 465–494.

dGa' ldan bka' srol phyag rgya chen po'i 'khrid kyi bla brgyud gsol 'debs [kha skoṅ bcas bźugs] (*Prayer, with Supplement, to the Lineage Lamas of the Ganden Oral Tradition of Mahāmudrā*) by Tshe-mchog-gliṅ Yoṅs-'dzin Ye-śes-rgyal-mtshan, (with additions by Pha-boṅ-kha Rinpoche: (a) a handwritten copy of nine folio sides, without colophon; (b) a printed Tibetan edition set into print by Dam-pa-blo-gros of Tsha-pa-roṅ, and published by the Hidden Treasury of Good Explanations Press [undated]; (c) a printed Tibetan edition published by the Mongolian Lama, Guru Deva, Sarnath: Pleasure of Elegant Sayings Printing Press, 1965; and (d) a handwritten copy printed in 1982 on the occasion of the first FPMT "Enlightened Experience Celebration" that took place in Bodhgaya, India.

dPal ldan bla ma dam pa rigs daṅ dkyil khor rgya mtsho'i mṅa' bdag bka' drin gsum ldan yoṅs 'dzin pandi ta chen po rje btsun ye śes rgyal mtshan dpal bzaṅ po'i sku gsuṅ thugs kyi rtogs pa brjod pa thub bstan padmo 'byed pa'i ñin byed (*Narration of the Life of the Greatly Learned Esteemed Tutor, Ye-śes-rgyal-mtshan*) by the Eighth Dalai Lama, 'Jam-dpal-rgya-mtsho. The 1795 edition, edited and reproduced by Ngawang Gelek Demo. New Delhi: Gedan Sungrab Minyam Gyunphel Series, Vol. 11, 1969.

Dus gsum rgyal ba'i spyi gzugs rje bla ma bka' drin zla med yoṅs 'dzin chos kyi rgyal po rje btsun ye śes rgyal mtshan dpal bzaṅ po'i 'khruṅs rabs gsol 'debs byin rlabs baṅ mdzod 'dren pa'i śiṅ rta ces bya ba bźugs so (a seven-folio metrical biography of Ye-śes-rgyal-mtshan, together with a prayer for his protection, composed by bLo-bzaṅ-chos-kyi-dbaṅ-phyug).

Chos smra ba'i dge sloṅ blo bzaṅ chos kyi rgyal mtshan gyi spyod tshul gsal bar ston pa nor bu'i phreṅ ba źes bya ba bźugs so (*The Autobiography of* [*the First Panchen*] *bLo-bzaṅ-chos-kyi-rgyal-mtshan*). Edited and reproduced by Ngawang Gelek Demo, with an English Introduction by Gene Smith. New Delhi: Gedan Sungrab Minyam Gyunphel Series, Vol. 12, 1969.

SECONDARY SOURCES IN TIBETAN

Individual Works, by author:

('Dul-nag-pa) dPal-ldan-bzaṅ-po. *dGa' ldan lha brgya ma*: (a) a handwritten Tibetan edition, without colophon; (b) English translation by Alexander Berzin. *The Hundreds of Deities of the Land of Joy*. Dharamsala: Library of Tibetan Works and Archives, 1979.

(Dwags-po) bLo-bzaṅ-'jam-dpal-lhun-grub. *Lam rim 'byor spyod*. English translation by Geshe Ngawang Dhargyey, *et. al. A Lam-rim Puja to Adorn the Throats of Those of Good Fortune*. Dharamsala: Library of Tibetan Works and Archives, 1974.

(First Panchen) bLo-bzaṅ-chos-kyi-rgyal-mtshan. *dGe ldan bka' brgyud rin po che'i phyag chen rtsa ba rgyal ba'i gźun lam*. (a) Tibetan edition found in *Je Tsoṅ kha pa gsuṅ dbu ma'i lta ba'i skor*. Sarnath: "The Pleasure of Elegant Sayings" Press, 1975, pp. 752–760. (b) English trans., Geshe Ngawang Dhargyey. *The Great Seal of Voidness*. Dharamsala: LTWA, 1975.

(First Panchen) bLo-bzaṅ-cho-kyi-rgyal-mtshan. *bLa ma mchod pa*. (Facing Tibetan and English). English trans., Alexander Berzin. *The Guru Puja*. Dharamsala: LTWA, 1979.

(kLoṅ-rdol-bla-ma) Ṅag-dbaṅ-blo-bzaṅ. *bKa' gdams pa daṅ dge lugs bla ma rags rim gyi gsuṅ 'bum mtshan tho*. Tibetan edition reprinted in Lokesh Chandra's *Materials for a History of Tibetan Literature*, Part 3. New Delhi: Śata-Piṭaka Series, Vol. 30, 1963.

(sDe-srid) Saṅs-rgyas-rgya-mtsho. *Vaiḍūrya ser po (A History of the Gelukpa Monasteries of Tibet)*. New Delhi: International Academy of Indian Culture, 1960.

(Sum-pa mkhan-po) Ye-śes-dpal-'byor. *dPag bsam ljon bzaṅ*. Edited by S.C. Das. Calcutta, 1908.

COLLECTED WORKS (GSUṄ 'BUM):

The Collected Works of dEn-sa-pa bLo-bzaṅ-don-grub (bLo-bzaṅ bka' 'bum). Sumra, H.P., 1977.

The Collected Works of Pha-boṅ-kha-pa Byams-pa-bstan-'dzin-phrin-las-rgya-mtsho. New Delhi, 1973.

The Collected Works of mKhas-grub Saṅs-rgyas-ye-śes. New Delhi, 1973.

The Collected Works of sPyan-sṅa bLo-gros-rgyal-mtshan of rGya-ma rin-chen sgaṅ. New Delhi, 1983.

The Collected Works of Tshe-mchog-gliṅ Yoṅs-'dzin Ye-śes-rgyal-mtshan. New Delhi: Tibet House Library, 1974.

SECONDARY SOURCES IN WESTERN LANGUAGES

Albertson, Clinton. *Anglo-Saxon Saints and Heroes.* New York: Fordham University Press, 1967.

Allione, Tsultrim. *Women of Wisdom.* London: Routledge & Kegan Paul, 1984.

Amipa, Sherab Gyaltsen. *A Waterdrop From the Glorious Sea: A concise account of the advent of Buddhism in general and the teachings of the Sakyapa tradition in particular.* Rikon, Switzerland: Tibetan Institute, 1976.

An, Li. "Buddhacarita-samgraha-sutra," in *Encyclopaedia of Buddhism.* Vol. III, Fascicle 3, 1973. (390–393).

Aris, Michael. "Some Considerations on the Early History of Bhutan," in *Tibetan Studies* (Martin Brauen and Per Kvaerne, editors). Zurich, 1978.

Attwater, Donald. *The Penguin Dictionary of Saints.* Middlesex, England: Penguin Books, Ltd., 1965.

Avedon, John F. *An Interview with the Dalai Lama.* New York: Littlebird Publications, 1980.

Aziz, Barbara N. *Tibetan Frontier Families: Reflections of Three Generations from D'ing-ri.* New Delhi: Vikas Publishing House Pvt. Ltd., 1978.

Bacot, Jacques. *La vie de Marpa le 'traducteur'.* Paris: Paul Geuthner, 1937.

Bapat, P. V. (ed.) *2500 Years of Buddhism.* New Delhi: Publications Division, Ministry of Information, 1965.

Bareau, André. "La légende de la jeuness du Bouddha dans les Sūtrapitaka et les Vinayapitaka anciens." *Bulletin de l'Ecole Francaise d'Extreme-Orient,* LXI, 1974, (199–274).

__________. "Le Parinirvana du Bouddha et la naissance de la religion bouddhique." *Bulletin de l'Ecole Francaise d'Extreme-Orient,* LXI, 1974, (275–300).

__________. *Recherches sur la Biographie du Bouddha dans les Sutrapitaka et les Vinayapitaka anciens: de la Quête de l'éveil a la conversion de Sariputra et de Maudgalyayana.* Paris: Ecole Francaise d'Extreme-Orient, 1963.

__________. *Les Sectes Bouddhiques du Petit Véhicule.* Saigon: 1955.

__________. "The Superhuman Personality of Buddha..." in Kitagawa and Long (eds.), *Myths and Symbols: Essays in Honor of Mircea Eliade.* Chicago: University of Chicago Press, 1969.

__________. "Un Personage Bien Mysterieux: L'Epouse du Buddha." in *Indological and Buddhist Studies* (Volume in Honour of Professor J. W. De Jong on his Sixtieth Birthday), Canberra: Faculty of Asian Studies, 1982, (31–59).

Basham, A. L. *The Wonder That Was India.* New York: Grove Press, Inc., 1954.

Baynes, Norman H. "The Thought-World of East Rome" (24–46) and "The Pratum Spirituale" (261–270), in *Byzantine Studies and Other Essays.* London, University of London: The Athlone Press, 1960.

Beal, Samuel. *The Romantic Legend of Sakya Buddha.* London, 1875.

Bell, Charles. *The People of Tibet.* Oxford: Clarendon Press, 1928.

__________. *Portrait of the Dalai Lama.* 1946. Boston: Wisdom Publication, 1987.

Berglie, Per-Arne. "On the Question of Tibetan Shamanism," in *Tibetan Studies.* Zurich: Volkerkundemuseum der Universitat Zurich, 1978, (39–51).

Bernbaum, Edwin. *The Way to Shambhala.* New York: Anchor Books, 1980.

Berzin, Alexander (trans.) *The Mahāmudrā Eliminating the Darkness of Ignorance.* Dharamsala: Library of Tibetan Works & Archives, 1978.

Beyer, Stephan. *The Buddhist Experience.* Encino, California: Dickenson Publications, Inc., 1974.

__________. *The Cult of Tārā: Magic and Ritual in Tibet.* Berkeley: University of California Press, 1973.

Bharati, Agehananda. *The Tantric Tradition.* London: Rider, 1965.

Bhardwaj, Surinder Mohan. *Hindu Places of Pilgrimage in India: A Study in Cultural Geography.* Berkeley: University of California Press, 1973, 1983.

Bhattacharyya, Benoytosh. *An Introduction to Buddhist Esotericism.* Mysore: (Humphrey Milford) Oxford University Press, 1932.

Boyer, Regis. "An Attempt to define the typology of medieval hagiography", in *Hagiography and Medieval Literature: A Symposium.* Denmark: Odense University, 1981 (27–36).

Brown, Peter. "The Rise and Function of the Holy Man in Late Antiquity," in *The Journal of Roman Studies*, Vol. LXI. London: Society for the Promotion of Roman Studies, 1971, (80–101).

__________. *The Cult of the Saints: Its Rise and Function in Latin Christianity.* Chicago: University of Chicago Press, 1981.

Budge, E. A. W. (trans.) *The Paradise of the Holy Father.* (2 vols.) (1907). Rpt., New York: Burt Franklin, 1972.

Burman, Bina Roy. *Religion and Politics in Tibet.* New Delhi: Vikas Publishing House Pvt. Ltd., 1976.

Bu-ston. *History of Buddhism.* E. Obermiller (trans.) Heidelberg: University of Heidelberg, 1931.

Campbell, Joseph. *The Masks of God: Oriental Mythology.* 1962. New York: Penguin Books, 1977.

Carrasco, Pedro. *Land and Polity in Tibet.* Seattle: University of Washington Press, 1959.

Carrithers, Michael. *The Forest Monks of Sri Lanka.* Delhi: Oxford University Press, 1983.

Chadwick, N. *The Age of the Saints in the Early Celtic Church*. London: Oxford University Press. 1961.

Chakravarti, Chintaharan. *Tantras: Studies on Their Religion and Literature*. Calcutta: Punthi Pustak, 1972.

Chandra, Lokesh, (ed.) *Materials for a History of Tibetan Literature* (Parts 1 and 3) (*_ata-Pitaka Series*, vols. 28 and 30). New Delhi, 1963.

__________. (ed.) *Tibetan Chronicle of Padma-dKar-po* (*_ata-Pitaka Series*, Vol. 75). New Delhi, 1968.

__________. "The Authors of Sumbums," in *Indo-Iranian Journal* (Vol. II), 1958, (110–127).

Chang, Garma C. C. *Teachings of Tibetan Yoga*. New Hyde Park: University Books, 1963.

__________. *The Hundred Thousand Songs of Milarepa* (2 vols.) Boulder: Shambhala, 1977.

Chattopadhyaya, Alaka. *Atīśa and Tibet*. Calcutta, R. D. Press, 1967.

__________ and Lama Chimpa (trans.) *Tāranātha's History of Buddhism in India*. Simla: Indian Institute of Advanced Study, 1970.

Clebsch, William A. *Christianity in European History*. New York: Oxford University Press, 1979.

Colgrave, B. "The Earliest Saints' Lives Written in England," in *Proceedings of the British Academy*, No. 44, 1958, (35–60).

__________, (ed. and trans.) *The Life of Bishop Wilfred by Eddius Stephanus*. Cambridge, 1927.

__________, (ed. and trans.) *Two Lives of Saint Cuthbert*. Cambridge, 1940.

Collingwood, R. G. *The Idea of History*. Oxford University Press, 1946.

Conze, Edward. *Buddhist Wisdom Books*. London: Allen and Unwin, 1958.

__________. *The Prajñāpāramitā Literature*. The Hague: Mouton & Co., 1960.

__________, ed. *Buddhist Texts Through the Ages*. New York: Harper Torchbook edition, 1964.

Cowell, E. B. *The Jātaka or Stories of the Buddha's Former Births* (6 vols.)

Cambridge, 1895–1907.

Crapanzano, Vincent. *Tuhami: Portrait of a Moroccan.* Chicago: The University of Chicago Press, 1980.

Dargyay, Eva. *The Rise of Esoteric Buddhism in Tibet.* Delhi: Motilal Banarsidass, 1977.

__________. "A gTer-ston Belonging to the dGe-lugs-pa School," in *The Tibet Journal.* Vol. VI, No. 1, Spring, 1981, (24–30).

Das, Sarat Chandra. *Contributions on the Religion and History of Tibet,* (1881 and 1882). Rpt., New Delhi: Manjusri Publishing House, 1970.

__________. *A Tibetan-English Dictionary.* Rpt., Delhi: Motilal Banarsidass, 1970.

__________. *Indian Pandits in the Land of Snow,* (1893). Rpt., Calcutta: F. K. L. Mukhopadhyay, 1965.

__________. "The Monasteries of Tibet," in *JASB.* New Series, I., April 1905.

Dasgupta, S. B. *An Introduction to Tantric Buddhism.* University of Calcutta, 1958. Rpt., Berkeley: Shambala, 1974.

__________. *Obscure Religious Cults.* Calcutta: F. K. L. Mukhopadhyay, 1962.

Datta, Bhupendranath. *Mystic Tales of Lama Tāranātha,* (1944). Rpt., Calcutta: Ramakrishna Vedanta Math, 1957.

David-Neel, Alexandra. *Initiations and Initiates in Tibet.* London, 1931.

__________ and Lama Yonden. *The Superhuman Life of Gesar Ling.* 1933. London: Rider, 1959.

Dawes, Elizabeth and Baynes, N. H. *Three Byzantine Saints.* 1948. Crestwood, N.Y.: St. Vladimir's Seminary Press, 1977.

Dayal, Har. *The Bodhisattva Doctrine in Buddhist Sanskrit Literature.* 1932. Delhi: Motilal Banarsidass, 1970 and 1975.

Decleer, Hubert. "The Working of Sādhana: Vajrabhairava," in *Tibetan Studies.* Zurich, 1978, (113–123).

Delehaye, Hippolyte. *The Legend of the Saints.* 1907. University of Notre

Dame Press, 1961.

Demiéville, Paul. *Le Concile de Lhasa.* Paris: Impr. nationale de France, 1952.

Donden, Yeshi. *The Ambrosia Heart Tantra.* Dharamsala: Library of Tibetan Works and Archives, 1977.

Douglas, K. and Bays, G. (trans.) *The Life and Liberation of Padmasambhava* (2 vols.) Emeryville, CA: Dharma Publications, 1978.

Douglas, Mary. *Natural Symbols: Exploration in Cosmology.* 1970. New York: Pantheon Books, 1982.

Douglas, Nik and White, Meryl. *Karmapa: The Black Hat Lama of Tibet.* London: Luzac and Co., Ltd., 1976.

Dowman, Keith (trans.) *Masters of Mahamudra: Songs and Histories of the Eighty-Four Buddhist Siddhas.* Albany, N.Y.: State University of New York Press, 1985.

__________. *Sky Dancer: The Secret Life and Songs of the Lady Yeshe Tsogyel.* London: Routledge & Kegan Paul, 1984.

__________. *The Legend of the Great Stupa and the Life Story of the Lotus Born Guru.* Emeryville, CA: Dharma Press, 1973.

__________. *Tilopa's Advice to Naropa,* (limited edition). Kathmandu, 1979.

Dundes, Alan (ed.) *Sacred Narrative.* Berkeley: University of California Press, 1984.

Dutt, Nalinaksha. *Buddhist Sects in India.* Calcutta: F. K. L. Mukhopadhyay, 1970.

__________. *Early Monastic Buddhism.* Calcutta: F. K. L. Mukhopadhyay, 1971.

Dutt, Sukumar. *Buddhist Monks and Monasteries of India.* London: George Allen & Unwin. 1962.

__________. *The Buddha and Five After Centuries.* London: Luzac, 1957.

Eck, Diana L. *Banaras: City of Light.* Princeton: Princeton University Press, 1983.

Eimer, Helmut. "Life and Activities of Atīśa (Dīpamkara Śrījñāna). A Survey of Investigations Undertaken," in *Tibetan Studies* (eds. Brauen and

Kvaerne), Zurich, 1978, (125–135).

Ekvall, Robert. *Religious Observances in Tibet: Patterns and Functions.* Chicago: University of Chicago Press, 1964.

Eliade, Mircea. *Shamanism: Archaic Techniques of Ecstasy,* (1964). (Bollingen Series LXXVI). Rpt., Princeton University Press, 1974.

__________. *Yoga: Immortality and Freedom.* New York: Bollingen Foundation Inc., 1958; and (Bollingen Series LVI) New York: Pantheon Books, 1958.

__________. *Images and Symbols.* New York: Sheed and Ward, 1969.

__________. *Myths, Dreams and Mysteries* (trans., Philip Moiret). New York: Harper, 1967.

Evans-Wentz, W. Y., ed. *The Tibetan Book of the Dead.* 1927. London: Oxford University Press, 1968.

__________. *The Tibetan Book of the Great Liberation.* 1928. London: Oxford University Press, 1968.

__________. *Tibet's Great Yogi Milarepa,* 1928. London: Oxford University Press, 1969.

__________. *Tibetan Yoga and Secret Doctrines.* London: Oxford University Press, 1958.

Farmer, William R. "Jesus and the Gospels: A Form-critical and Theological Essay," in *Perkins Journal.* Vol. 2, No. 2, (Winter 1975), (1–62).

Fa-tsun. "Blo-bzaṅ Chos-kyi rGyal-mtshan" in *Encyclopaedia of Buddhism.* Vol. III. Fascicle 1. Colombo: Government of Ceylon, 1971, (163–169).

Fenner, Peter. "Some Western Analogues to Madhyamaka Philosophy," in *Teachings from Tusita.* New Delhi: Mahayana Publications, 1981, (127–133).

Ferrari, Alfonsa. *mK'yen brtse's Guide to the Holy Places of Central Tibet.* (Serie Orientale, Roma, vol. XVI.) Rome: Is.M.E.O., 1958.

Foucaux, Phillippe E. *Le Lalita-Vistara.* Paris, 1884–1892.

Foucher, A. *La Vie du Bouddha, d'apres les textes et les monuments de l'Inde.* Paris, 1949.

Frauwallner, Erich. *The Earliest Vinaya and the Beginnings of Buddhist Literature.* (Serie Orientale Roma, vol. VIII). Rome: Is.M.E.O., 1956.

Getty, Alice. *The Gods of Northern Buddhism,* (1928). Rpt., Rutland, Vermont: Charles Tuttle, 1962.

Goldstein, Melvyn. "The Circulation of Estates in Tibet: Reincarnation, Land, and Politics," in *Journal of Asian Studies,* No. 32, (445–455).

__________. *Tibetan English Dictionary of Modern Tibetan.* Kathmandu: Ratna Pustak Bhandar, 1975.

Gordon, Antoinette. *The Iconography of Tibetan Lamaism.* Rutland, Vermont: Charles Tuttle, 1959.

'Gos-lo-tsa-ba. *The Blue Annals.* George Roerich (trans.) Calcutta: Royal Asiatic Society of Bengal, 1949.

Govinda, Anagarika. *Foundations of Tibetan Mysticism.* London: Rider and Co., 1960.

__________. *Psycho-cosmic Symbolism of the Buddhist Stupa.* Emeryville, CA: Dharma Publishing, 1976.

Grunwedel, A. *Die Geschichten der vier und achtzig Zauberers aus dem Tibetischen ubersetz.* Baessler Archiv. V. Leipzig, 1916.

Guenther, Herbert V. *The Jewel Ornament of Liberation.* Berkeley: Shambhala, 1971.

__________. *The Life and Teaching of Naropa.* Oxford: Clarendon Press. Rpt., London: Oxford University Press, 1971.

__________. *The Royal Song of Saraha: A Study in the History of Buddhist Thought* (1968). Rpt., Berkeley, CA: Shambhala, 1973.

__________. *Tibetan Buddhism in Western Perspective.* Emeryville, CA: Dharma Publications, 1977.

__________. "Mahāmudrā: The Method of Self-Actualization," in *The Tibet Journal,* July/September, Vol. I, No. 1, 1975, (5–23).

__________. *The Tantric View of Life.* Boulder: Shambhala, 1976.

__________. *Treasures on the Tibetan Middle Way.* Berkeley, CA: Shambhala, 1975.

Guenther, Herbert and Kawamura, Leslie (trans.) *Mind in Buddhist Psychology*. Emeryville, CA: Dharma Publishing, 1975.

Gyaltsen, Khenpo Konchog and Rogers, Katherine. *The Garland of Mahamudra Practices*. Ithaca, NY: Snow Lion Publications, 1986.

Gyatso, Geshe Kelsang. *Clear Light of Bliss: Mahamudra in Vajrayana Buddhism*. London: Wisdom Publications, 1982.

Gyatso, Janet. "The Development of the *Gcod* Tradition" in *Soundings in Tibetan Civilization*. (Aziz and Kapstein, eds.) New Delhi: Manohar, 1985, (320–341).

Gyatso, Tenzin, H. H. the XIVth Dalai Lama (trans. and ed., Jeffrey Hopkins). *Kalachakra Tantra: Rite of Initiation for the Stage of Generation*. London: Wisdom Publications, 1985.

Gyatso, Tenzin, H. H. the XIVth Dalai Lama. *My Land and My People*. 1962. New York: Potala Corp., 1977.

__________. *The Opening of the Wisdom-Eye*. Wheaton, Illinois: The Theosophical Publishing House, 1972.

__________. *Introduction to Tibetan Buddhism*. New York: Harper and Row, 1975.

Hanson, Judith (trans.) *The Torch of Certainty*. Boulder: Shambhala, 1977.

Hawley, John Stratton (ed.) *Saints and Virtues*. Berkeley: University of California Press, 1987.

Heissig, Walther. *The Religions of Mongolia*. 1970. (Translated from German by Geoffrey Samuel.) Berkeley: University of California Press, 1980.

Heruka, Tsang Nyon. *The Life of Marpa the Translator*, trans. by the Nalanda Translation Committee, Boulder: Prajna Press, 1982.

__________. *The Life of Milarepa*. Lobsang P. Lhalungpa, (trans.) Boulder, London: Shambhala Publications, Inc., 1984.

Hillman, James. "Anima I and II." Zurich: Spring Publications, 1973 & 1974.

Hoare, F. R. (ed. and trans.) *The Western Fathers*. New York, 1954.

Hoffmann, Helmut. *The Religions of Tibet*. New York: The Macmillan Company, 1961.

Hopkins, Jeffrey (ed. and trans.) *Tantra in Tibet: The Great Exposition of Secret Mantra by Tsong-ka-pa.* London: George Allen and Unwin, 1977.

Hopkins, Jeffrey and Lati Rinbochay. *Death, Intermediate State, and Rebirth in Tibetan Buddhism.* Valois, NY: Gabriel/Snow Lion, 1979.

Inada, Kenneth (ed. and trans.) *Nāgārjuna's Mūlamadhyamakakārikā.* Tokyo: Hokuseido Press, 1970.

Johnston, E. H. (trans.) *The Buddhacarita or Acts of the Buddha* (1936). Rpt., Delhi: Motilal Banarsidass, 1972.

__________. *The Saundarananda of Aśvaghosa* (1928). Rpt., Delhi: Motilal Banarsidass, 1975.

Jones, C. W. *Saints' Lives and Chronicles in Early England.* Ithaca: Cornell University Press, 1947.

Jones, J. J. (trans.) *The Mahāvastu* (Sacred Books of the Buddhists, Vols. XVI–XVII). London, 1949–57.

__________. *The Mahāvastu,* Vol. II, (1952). Rpt., London: Pali Text Society, 1976.

Joshi, Lalmani. *Studies in the Buddhistic Culture of India.* Delhi: Motilal Banarsidass, 1967.

Jung, Carl. G. *Psyche and Symbol.* Violet S. De Laszlo (ed.) New York: Anchor Press, 1958.

__________. *Psychology and Religion.* New Haven: Yale University Press, 1972.

__________. *Two Essays in Analytic Psychology.* Princeton: Princeton University Press, 1972.

Jung, Emma. *Anima and Animus.* Zurich: Spring Publications, 1974.

Kalff, Martin M. "Dākinīs in the Cakrasamvara Tradition," in *Tibetan Studies* (eds. Brauen and Kvaerne). Zurich, 1978, (149–162).

Karunaratna, Upali. "Buddhacarita," in *Encyclopaedia of Buddhism.* Vol. III. Fascicle 3. Colombo: Government of Sri Lanka, (389–390).

Katz, Nathan. "Anima and mKha'-'gro-ma: A Critical Comparative Study of Jung and Tibetan Buddhism," in *The Tibet Journal,* Vol. 2, No. 3, Autumn, 1977, (13–43).

__________. *Buddhist Images of Human Perfection.* Delhi: Motilal Banarsidass, 1982.

Katz, Steven T. *Mysticism and Philosophical Analysis.* London: Sheldon Press, 1978.

Kee, Howard Clark. *Miracle in the Early Christian World: A Study in Sociohistorical Method.* New Haven: Yale University Press, 1983.

Kieckhefer, Richard and Bond, George D. *Sainthood: Its Manifestations in World Religions.* Berkeley: University of California Press, 1988.

Klinger, Ross E. "The Tibetan Guru Refuge: A Historical Perspective," in *The Tibet Journal,* Vol. V., No. 4, Winter, 1980, (9–19).

Kloppenborg, Ria. *The Paccekabuddha: A Buddhist Ascetic.* Leiden: E. J. Brill, 1974.

__________ (trans.) *The Sutra on the Foundation of the Buddhist Order (Catusparisatsutra).* Leiden: E. J. Brill, 1973.

Kluckhohn, Clyde. *The Use of Personal Documents in Anthropology.* New York: Social Science Research Council, Bulletin 55, 1945.

Kris, Ernst. "A Psychological Study of the Role of Tradition in Ancient Biographies," in *Psychoanalytic Explorations in Art.* New York: Schocken Books, 1964, (64–84).

Kunga, Lama and Cutillo, Brian. *Drinking the Mountain Stream: New Stories and Songs by Milarepa.* New York: Lotsawa, 1978.

Kvaerne, Per. "Aspects of the Origin of the Buddhist Tradition in Tibet," in *Numen,* 19, 1972, (22–40).

Lalou, Marcelle. "Rituel Bon-po des funérailles Royales," in *Journal Asiatique,* Vol. 240, No. 3, 1952, (339–362).

Lamotte Étienne. *Histoire du Bouddhisme Indien.* Louvain: Museon, 1958.

__________. "La Légende du Bouddha," in *Revue de l'histoire des religions,* Vol. 1343, 1947, (37–71).

Langer, Susanne K. *Philosophy in a New Key: A Study in the Symbolism of Reason, Rite, and Art.* Cambridge: Harvard University Press, 1957.

Langness, Lewis L. *The Life History in Anthropological Science.* New York: Holt, Rinehart and Winston, 1965.

Lauf, Detlef Ingo. *Secret Doctrines of the Tibetan Books of the Dead.* Boulder: Shambhala, 1977.

Law, Bimala C. *The Lineage of the Buddha (Buddhavamsa).* London, 1938.

__________. *The Life and Work of Buddhaghosa* (1923). Rpt., Delhi: Nag Publishers, 1976.

Lawlor, Hugh Jackson and Oulton, J. E. L. (trans.) *Eusebius: The Ecclesiastical History and the Martyrs of Palestine.* (2 vols.) London: Society for Promoting Christian Knowledge, 1928.

Lessing, Ferdinand. *Yung-Ho-Kung, An Iconography of the Lamaist Cathedral in Peking, with Notes on Lamaist Mythology and Cult.* Stockholm: Report of the Sino-Swedish Expedition, 1942.

__________ and Wayman, Alex. *Mkhas grub rje's Fundamentals of the Buddhist Tantras.* The Hague: Mouton, 1968.

Lhalungpa, Lobsang. *The Life of Milarepa.* New York: E. P. Dutton, 1977. Rpt., Boulder: Shambhala, 1984.

__________ (trans.) *Mahamudra: the Quintessence of Mind and Meditation.* Boston: Shambhala, 1986.

Li An-che. "Lamasery in Outline," in *Journal of the West China Border Research Society,* 14, Series A, 1942, (36–68).

__________. "The Sakya Sect of Lamaism," in *Journal of the West China Border Research Society,* Vol. 16, 1945, (72–86).

__________. "Rñin-ma-pa: the Early Form of Lamaism," in *Journal of the Royal Asiatic Society,* 1948, (142–63).

__________. "Bon: the Magico-Religious Belief of the Tibetan-speaking peoples," in *Southwestern Journal of Anthropology,* Vol. 4, 1948, (31–42).

__________. "The Bkah-Brgyud Sect of Lamaism," in *Journal of the American Oriental Society,* Vol. 69, No. 2, 1949, (51–59).

Mahāthera, Paravahera Vajirañāna. *Buddhist Meditation in Theory and Practice.* Colombo: M. D. Gunasena, 1962.

Malalasekera, G. P. "Buddha" in *Encyclopaedia of Buddhism.* Vol. 3, Fascicle 3. Colombo: Government of Sri Lanka, 1973.

Mallmann, Marie-Therese de. *Iconographique sur Mañjuśrī.* Paris: Ecole

Francaise d'Extreme-Orient, 1964.

__________. *Introduction a l'Etude d'Avalokiteśvara.* Paris: Annales du Musee Guimet, 57, 1948.

Mango, Cyril. *Byzantium: The Empire of New Rome.* New York: Charles Scribner's Sons, 1980.

Masson, J. Moussaieff. "The Psychology of the Ascetic," in *Journal of Asian Studies,* Vol. 35, 1976, (611–25).

Michael, Franz. *Rule by Incarnation: Tibetan Buddhism and Its Role in Society and State.* Boulder: Westview Press, 1982.

Mol, Hans. *Identity and the Sacred: A sketch for a new social scientific theory of religion.* Oxford: Basil Blackwell and Mott Limited, 1976.

Moule, C. F. D. (ed.) *Miracles: Cambridge Studies on Their Philosophy and History.* London: A. R. Mawbray and Co. Ltd., 1965.

Mullin, Glenn (trans.) *Bridging the Sutras and Tantras* (works by the First Dalai Lama). Ithaca: Gabriel/Snow Lion, 1982. Rpt., 1985.

__________. *(The Seventh Dalai Lama's) Songs of Spiritual Change.* Ithaca: Gabriel/Snow Lion, 1982. Rpt., 1985.

__________. *Selected Works of the Dalai Lama III: Essence of Refined Gold.* Ithaca: Snow Lion Publications, 1983. Rpt., 1985.

Muses, C. A. (ed.) and Chang, C. C. (trans.) *Esoteric Teachings of the Tibetan Tantra,* (1961). Rpt., York Beach, Maine: Samuel Weiser, Inc., 1982.

Nanayakkara, S. K. "Avalokitesvara," in *Encyclopaedia of Buddhism,* Vol. 2, Colombo, 1966, (407–415).

Nariman, J. K. *Literary History of Sanskrit Buddhism (From Winternitz, Sylvain Levi, Huber),* 1919. Rpt., Delhi: Motilal Banarsidass, 1972.

Nebesky-Wojkowitz, René. *Tibetan Religious Dances.* The Hague: Mouton, 1976.

__________. *Oracles and Demons of Tibet: The Cult and Iconography of the Tibetan Protective Deities.* Graz/Austria: Akademische Druck-u. Verlag-sanstalt, 1975.

Nigg, Walter. *Warriors of God: The Great Religious Orders and their Founders.* New York: Alfred A. Knopf, 1959.

Norbu, Jigme and Turnbull, Colin. *Tibet.* New York: Simon and Schuster, 1968.

Ñyanamoli, Bhikkhu (trans.) *The Path of Purification (Visuddhimagga).* (2 vols.) Berkeley: Shambhala, 1976.

Obermiller, E. (trans.) *History of Buddhism by Bu-ston.* Heidelberg, 1931–32.

__________. "The Sublime Science of the Great Vehicle to Salvation: Being a Manual of Buddhist Monism," in *Acta Orientalia,* IX, (81–306).

Pal, Pratapaditya. *The Art of Tibet.* New York: The Asia Society, 1969.

__________ and Tseng, Hsien-Ch'i. *Lamaist Art: The Aesthetics of Harmony.* Boston: Museum of Fine Arts.

Pardue, Peter. *Buddhism.* New York: The Macmillan Company, 1968.

Paul, Robert A. *The Tibetan Symbolic World: Psychoanalytic Explorations.* Chicago: University of Chicago Press, 1982.

Petech, Luciano. "The Dalai-Lamas and Regents of Tibet: A Chronological Study," in *T'oung Pao,* Vol. XLVII, 1959, (368–394).

Prats, Ramon. "The Spiritual Lineage of the Dzogchen Tradition," in *Tibetan Studies,* Zurich, 1978, (199–207).

Rabten and Dhargyey (Geshes). *Advice From a Spiritual Friend.* Boston: Wisdom Publcations, 1984.

Rahula, Walpola. *What the Buddha Taught.* 1959. New York: Grove (Evergreen), 1962.

Ram, Rajendra. *A History of Buddhism in Nepal.* Delhi: Motilal Banarsidass, 1978.

Rao, S. K. Ramachandra. *Tibetan Meditation.* New Delhi: Arnold-Heinimann, 1979.

__________. *Tibetan Tantrik Tradition.* New Jersey: Humanities Press, 1978.

Ray, Reginald. "The Vajrayāna Mahāsiddhas: Some Principles of Interpretation." Unpublished paper, delivered at the December, 1977 AAR meetings in San Francisco, California.

Reynolds, Frank and Capps, Donald, (eds.) *The Biographical Process: Studies in the History and Psychology of Religion.* The Hague: Mouton, 1976.

Reynolds, Frank E. "The Many Lives of Buddha: A Study of Sacred Biography and the Theravāda Tradition," in Reynolds and Capps (eds.), *The Biographical Process.* The Hague: Mouton, 1976, (37–61).

Rhys-Davids, Caroline A. F. *Psalms of the Sisters,* (1909). Rpt., Pali Text Society, 1948 and 1989.

Rhys-Davids, T. W. (trans.) *Buddhist Birth-Stories (Jataka Tales) and the Nidana-katha,* 1880. London: George Routledge and Sons, Ltd., 1925.

Richardson, Hugh E. "The Karmapa Sect: A Historical Note," in *Journal of the Royal Asiatic Society,* 1958–59, (139–64 and 1–18).

Robinson, James B. (trans.) *Buddha's Lions: The Lives of the Eighty Four Siddhas by Abhayadatta.* Berkeley: Dharma Publishing, 1979.

Rockhill, W. W. "The Dalai Lamas of Lhasa and Their Relations with the Manchu Emperors of China 1644–1908," in *T'oung Pao,* Vol. XI, 1910, (1–104).

Roerich, George (trans.) *('Gos lo-tsā-ba's) The Blue Annals,* 1949 & 1953. New Delhi: Motilal Banarsidass, 1979.

Ryan, J. *Irish Monasticism: Origins and Early Development.* London and New York, 1931.

Ruegg, David Seyfort. *The Life of Bu-ston Rinpoche.* (*Serie Orientale Roma,* Vol. XXXIV). Rome: Is.M.E.O., 1966.

Samuel, Geoffrey. "Religion in Tibetan Society: A New Approach," in *Kailash,* Vol. 6, 1968, (45ff).

Sangharaksita, Bhiksu. *A Survey of Buddhism.* Bangalore: India Institute of World Culture, 1966.

Sankalia, H. D. *The University of Nalanda.* Delhi: Oriental Publishers, 1972.

Schmid, Toni. *The Eighty-Five Siddhas.* Stockholm: State Ethnographic Museum, 1958.

Schulemann, Gunther. *Die Geschichte der Dalai-Lamas.* 1911. Leipzig: Otto Harrassowitz, 1958.

Senart, E. *Essai sur la legende du Bouddha.* Paris, 1875.

Shakabpa, Tsepon W. D. *Tibet: A Political History.* New Haven: Yale University Press, 1967.

Shakya, Min Bahadur. *Icons of 108 Lokesvara*. Kathmandu: Young Men's Buddhist Association, 1979.

Sherpa Tulku (et. al.) "The Structure of the Ge-lug Monastic Order," in *The Tibet Journal*, Vol. 2, No. 3, Autumn, 1977, (67–71).

Sierksma, F. *Tibet's Terrifying Deities: Sex and Aggression in Religious Acculturation*. The Hague: Mouton, 1966.

Snellgrove, David L. *Buddhist Himālaya*. Oxford: Bruno Cassirer, 1957.

__________. *Four Lamas of Dolpo: Autobiographies of Four Tibetan Lamas (15th–18th C.)* 2 vols. Oxford: Bruno Cassirer, 1967.

__________. *The Hevajra Tantra*, (2 vols.) London: Oxford University Press, 1959.

__________ and Richardson, Hugh E. *A Cultural History of Tibet*. 1968. Boulder: Prajna Press, 1980.

Sopa, Geshe Lhundub. *The Wheel of Time: The Kalachakra in Context*. Madison, WI: Deer Park Books, 1985.

__________ and Hopkins, Jeffrey. *Practice and Theory of Tibetan Buddhism*. New York: Grove Press, Inc., 1976.

Spiro, Melford E. *Buddhism and Society*. 1970. Berkeley: University of California Press, 1982.

Stein, R. A. *Tibetan Civilization*. Stanford: Stanford University Press, 1972.

Stevens, India and Marshall, J. (eds.) *A Short Biography and Letter of Je Tzong-k'a-pa*. Dharamsala: Library of Tibetan Works and Archives, 1975.

Tambiah, Stanley. *The Buddhist Saints of the Forest and the Cult of the Amulets*. Cambridge: Cambridge University Press, 1984.

Taring, Rinchen Dolma. *Daughter of Tibet*. 1970. Boston: Wisdom Publications, 1986.

Tarthang Tulku. *Crystal Mirror*, Vol. 1, No. 1, Spring, 1971.

Tharchin, Geshe Lobsang (trans.) *The Essence of Nectar by Yeshe Tsöndru*. Dharamsala: Library of Tibetan Works & Archives, 1979.

Thinley, Karma. *The History of the Sixteen Karmapas of Tibet*. Boulder: Prajna Press, 1980.

Thomas, Edward J. *The Life of Buddha as Legend and History.* London: Routledge and Kegan Paul, 1949.

Thurman, Robert A. F. "Buddhist Hermeneutics," in *Journal of the American Academy of Religion,* 46, No. 1, 1978.

__________. *The Holy Teaching of Vimalakīrti: A Mahāyāna Scripture.* University Park: The Pennsylvania State University Press, 1976.

__________ (ed.) *Life and Teachings of Tsong Khapa.* Dharamsala: Library of Tibetan Works and Archives, 1982.

__________. *Tsong Khapa's Speech of Gold in the Essence of True Eloquence.* Princeton, NJ: Princeton University Press, 1984.

Toussaint, Gustave-Charles. *Le Dict de Padma (Padma Thang-yig).* Paris: E. Leroux, 1933.

Trungpa, Chogyam. *Born in Tibet.* Boulder: Shambhala, 1977.

__________ and Fremantle, F. *The Tibetan Book of the Dead.* Boulder: Shambhala, 1975.

__________ and Nalanda Translation Committee. *The Rain of Wisdom.* Boulder: Shambhala, 1980.

Tsering, Nawang. *Buddhism in Ladakh: A Study of the Life and Works of an Eighteenth-Century Ladakhi Saint Scholar.* New Delhi: Sterling Publishers Pvt. Ltd., 1970.

Tsuda, Shin'ichi. *A Critical Tantricism* (Memoirs of the Research Department of the Toyo_Bunko, No. 36). Tokyo: The Toyo Bunko, 1978.

Tucci, Giuseppe. *Tibetan Painted Scrolls* (3 vols.) Rome: La Libreria dello Stato, 1949.

__________. *To Lhasa and Beyond.* Rome: Libreria dello Stato, 1956.

__________. *The Religions of Tibet* (1970). Rpt., Berkeley: University of California Press, 1980.

__________. *The Theory and Practice of the Mandala.* London: Rider, 1961.

__________. *Tibetan Folk Songs from Gyantse and Western Tibet.* Ascona, Switzerland: Artibus Asiae Publishers, 1966.

__________. *The Tombs of the Tibetan Kings.* (*Serie Orientale* I.) Rome:

Is.M.E.O., 1950.

Turner, Victor and Turner, Edith. *Image and Pilgrimage in Christian Culture: Anthropological Perspectives.* New York: Columbia University Press, 1978.

Van der Leeuw, G. *Religion in Essence and Manifestation* (2 vols.) 1933. New York: Harper & Row, 1963.

van Zeyst, H. G. "Abhiñña," in *Encyclopaedia of Buddhism*, Vol. 1, Part 1. Colombo: The Government Press, 1961.

Vostrikov, A. K. *Indian Buddhism.* Delhi: Motilal Banarsidass, n.d.

Wach, Joachim. "Types of Religious Authority," in *Sociology of Religion.* Chicago: University of Chicago Press, 1944, (331–374).

Waddell L. Austine. *Tibetan Buddhism: With Its Mystic Cults, Symbolism and Mythology, and Its Relation to Indian Buddhism.* 1895. New York: Dover Publications, 1972.

Waddell, Helen (trans.) *The Desert Fathers.* 1936. Ann Arbor: University of Michigan Press, 1972.

Waldschmidt, Ernst. *Die Uberlieferung vom Lebensende des Buddha* (2 parts). (Philologisch Historische Klasse, 3rd series, nos. 29 and 30) Gottingen: Akademie der Wissenschaften 1944, 1948.

Wangyal, Geshe. *The Door of Liberation.* 1973. Boston: Wisdom Publications, 1995.

Ward, Benedicta. *Miracles and the Medieval Mind: Theory, Record and Event.* Philadelphia: University of Pennsylvania Press, 1982.

Warder, A. K. *An Introduction to Indian Historiography.* (Monographs of the Department of Sanskrit and Indian Studies, University of Toronto), Bombay: Popular Prakashan, 1972.

Warren, Henry Clarke. *Buddhism in Translations.* 1896. New York: Atheneum, 1968.

Watson, Craig E. "The Introduction of the Second Propagation of Buddhism in Tibet According to R. A. Stein's edition of the *sBa-bzhed*," in *The Tibet Journal*, Vol. V., No. 4, Winter, 1980, (20–27).

Wayman, Alex. *Calming the Mind and Discerning the Real: Buddhist Meditation and the Middle View from the Lam rim chen mo of Tson-kha-pa.*

New York: Columbia University Press, 1978.

__________. *The Buddhist Tantras: Light on Indo-Tibetan Esotericism.* New York: Samuel Weiser, 1973.

__________. *The Yoga of the Guhyasamājatantra.* Delhi: Motilal Banarsidass, 1977.

__________ (trans.) *Chanting the Names of Mañjuśrī: A Translation of the Mañjuśrī-nāma-saṃgīti.* Boulder: Shambhala, 1984.

Weeraratne, W. G. "Avadāna," "Avadāna-kalpalata," and "Avadāna-Sataka" in *Encyclopaedia of Buddhism.* (Vol. II, Fascicle 3.) Columbo: Government of Ceylon, 1967, (395–398, 398, and 398–400).

Weinstein, Donald and Bell, Rudolph. *Saints and Society: The Two Worlds of Western Christendom, 1000–1700.* Chicago: The University of Chicago Press, 1982.

Williams, Michael W. "Charisma and Sacred Biography," in *Journal of the American Academy of Religion,* 1982.

Willis, Janice D. *On Knowing Reality: The Tattvārtha Chapter of Asaṅga's Bodhisattvabhūmi.* New York: Columbia University Press, 1979.

__________. *The Diamond Light of the Eastern Dawn: An Introduction to Tibetan Buddhist Meditations.* New York: Simon and Schuster, 1972.

__________. "Archaic Tibetan Religious Traditions," in *World Spirituality: An Encyclopedic History of the Religious Quest,* Vol. I., Crossroads, 1986.

__________. "Preliminary Remarks on the Nature of rNam-thar: Early dGe-lugs-pa Siddha Biographies," in *Soundings in Tibetan Civilization.* Aziz, Barbara and Kapstein, Matthew (eds.) New Delhi: Manohar, 1985.

__________. "The Life of sKyong-ru sprul-sku: An Example of Contemporary Tibetan Hagiography," in *The Tibet Journal,* Vol. VIII, No. 4, Winter, 1983.

__________. "Bu-ston," in *The Encyclopedia of Religion.* New York: Macmillan/Crossroads, 1987.

__________. "Kamalaśīla" in *The Encyclopedia of Religion.* New York: Macmillan/Crossroads, 1987.

__________. "Śāntiraksita" in *The Encyclopedia of Religion.* New York:

Macmillan/Crossroads, 1987.

Wittgenstein, Ludwig. *Culture and Value* (trans., Peter Winch). Chicago: University of Chicago Press, 1980.

__________. *Philosophical Investigations* (G. E. M. Anscombe, trans.) 1958. New York: Macmillan Publishing Co., 1968.

__________. *Tractatus Logico-Philosophicus.* 1921. (D. F. Pears and B. F. McGuinness, trans.) London: Routledge & Kegan Paul, 1961.

Wylie, Turrell V. *A Place Name Index to George N. Roerich's Translation of the Blue Annals.* Rome: Is.M.E.O., 1957.

__________. "A Standard System of Tibetan Transcription," in *Harvard Journal of Asiatic Studies,* 22. 1959, (261–67).

__________ (trans.) *The Geography of Tibet According to the 'Dzam-gling-rgyas-bshad.* (Serie Orientale Roma) Rome: Is.M.E.O., 1962.

__________. "Dating the Death of Nāropa." *Indological and Buddhist Studies* (Volume in Honour of Professor J. W. de Jong on his Sixtieth Birthday). Canberra: Faculty of Asian Studies, 1982, (687–692).

__________. "Reincarnation: A Political Innovation in Tibetan Buddhism," in *Proceedings of the Csoma De Korös Memorial Symposium.* Budapest: Akademéiai Kiadoó, 1978, 579–586.

Yamaguchi, Zuiho (ed.) *Catalogue of the Toyo Bunko Collection of Tibetan Works on History.* Tokyo: The Toyo Bunko, 1970.

Zimmer, Heinrich. *Myths and Symbols in Indian Art and Civilization.* 1946. New York: Harper & Row, 1962.

Zurcher. *The Buddhist Conquest of China.* 2 vols. Leiden, 1959.

Index